QUESTION AUTHORITY

MARK KINGWELL

Question Authority

A Polemic about Trust in Five Meditations

BIBLIOASIS
WINDSOR, ONTARIO

FIRST EDITION
10 9 8 7 6 5 4 3 2 1

Library and Archives Canada Cataloguing in Publication

Title: Question authority : a polemic about trust in five meditations / Mark Kingwell.
Names: Kingwell, Mark, 1963- author
Description: Includes bibliographical references.
Identifiers: Canadiana (print) 20240454553 | Canadiana (ebook) 20240457498
ISBN 9781771966412 (softcover) | ISBN 9781771966429 (EPUB)
Subjects: LCSH: Authority—Social aspects. | LCSH: Authority—Philosophy.
LCSH: Trust—Social aspects. | LCSH: Critical thinking. | LCSH: Skepticism.
Classification: LCC HM1251 .K56 2024 | DDC 303.3/6—dc23

Edited by Daniel Wells
Copyedited by Martin Ainsley
Typeset by Vanessa Stauffer
Cover designed by Michel Vrana

Published with the generous assistance of the Canada Council for the Arts, which last year invested $153 million to bring the arts to Canadians throughout the country, and the financial support of the Government of Canada. Biblioasis also acknowledges the support of the Ontario Arts Council (OAC), an agency of the Government of Ontario, which last year funded 1,709 individual artists and 1,078 organizations in 204 communities across Ontario, for a total of $52.1 million, and the contribution of the Government of Ontario through the Ontario Book Publishing Tax Credit and Ontario Creates.

PRINTED AND BOUND IN CANADA

The closer one is to a source of power, the quieter it gets. Authority and money surround themselves with silence, and one can measure the reach of someone's influence by the thickness of the hush enveloping them.

Hernan Diaz, Trust

To immerse himself further in the state of the inside of his head, to marvel anew at its august authority, he lit a cigarette.

Kingsley Amis, Take a Girl Like You

In those disaster movies, the hero always says, "Trust me," and the one who is about to die says, "Do I have a choice?"

"No."

That's what the hero says.

Jenny Offill, Weather

Contents

Introduction

THE TIMES OF ONE'S PHILOSOPHICAL reflection always seem full of portent. These pages are no different. I write at a time of large-scale democratic reckoning, coupled with crumbling trust in public institutions and their elite functionaries. This includes scientists, journalists, judges, academics, businesspeople, civil servants, and politicians. More people will cast electoral votes in 2024 and 2025 than at any other moment in human history: a so-called super-cycle election event that involves sixty-four sovereign nations around the planet—including India and the United States, most of Europe, and dozens of nations many people would struggle to locate on a map—accounting for 49 percent of the total global population. Together, these countries control most of the combined natural resources, financial power, and military hardware of the entire human project.[1]

The results of this great tallying of political desire are, naturally, beyond any single person's assessment. The many millions of votes being cast might also take years to show their genuine effect in public policy, cultural attitudes, and geopolitical shifting. But despite the obvious display of popular will, or maybe simply because of it, this is not a moment to feel much reassurance about the future of *liberal* democracy or transnational justice—what we might call the cosmopolitan dream. There are dark signs of rising right-wing authoritarianism everywhere, mobilization in rich nations against the flow of migrants, and entrenchment of economic disparity that seem to deepen with every passing month. Existential threats, meanwhile—from climate disaster, from artificial intelligence, from old bogeys like nuclear war and fundamentalist rage—are the background noise of news feeds, doomscrolls, and the incessant demands of everyday life.

But elections are only a necessary condition of democratic accountability, not yet sufficient to the goals of genuine legitimacy. The challenges of global life also demand responsible, transparent institutions with effective regulatory controls. Until we decide to off-load the work of such institutions to nonhuman agencies—a dangerous tendency, as the 2008 financial crisis reminds us—these systems will be staffed and controlled by imperfect humans. If the systems require expertise to function effectively, the granting of influence to such experts must be based on their reliable qualities or credentials. Trust works in large measure on assumptions about who people *are*, not just what they do before our eyes. We trust because we cannot observe and judge everything ourselves.

This becomes harder as the tasks of shared human aspiration and global survival become more decentralized, even as partisan differences show up more and more vividly. The presence of *affective polarization* in democratic nations has grown perceptibly since the turn of the millennium. This is the term political scientists use to describe negative feelings about political opponents. *Affective* because it is a matter of feeling: that the "other side" is not just divergent in views but beyond redemption, perhaps insane or evil. Actual policy differences may be less stark, but that does not matter when demonization of the other is the order of the day. People vote with their feelings. More drastically, they shape their worlds to fit those feelings. Division is as division does.[2]

What today's fraught circumstances urgently need, then, are the same countermeasures that societies have always required and, unfortunately, too often lack: trustworthy authority and leadership. When authority is absent, trust is impossible—and vice versa.

This felt lack of leadership is not just a complaint about elected representatives and their all-too-human failings. Nor is it a blanket objection to elites, based on their evident tendencies toward obstinacy, arrogance, and cowardice—the defects of character exposed when personal weakness meets power. These vices are drawbacks in private life, certainly, but in public life they are trust-destroying viruses. They spread and infect the body politic. And thus, all too often, elite capture means not only that a given power structure is compromised by self-interest, but also, worse, that it is extended past its valid jurisdiction. Expertise in one area does not de facto confer heft in another: a good scientist, for example, can be a bad public health official, not because of bad science but because of poor judgment.[3]

Elites are tolerable features of complex systems, but only if they resist the proximate dangers of self-replication, entrenchment, and expanding privilege. They must also, subject to rational scrutiny, stay in the appropriate lane and engage in vigorous internal criticism. Power corrupts across both sectors and generations: a self-regarding elite in turn corrupts new entrants to the elite's echelons.[4]

These are all points to explore at the nexus of trust and authority. Most of all, though, the trust question raises a challenge we must issue to ourselves. That challenge is to approach the duties of civic life with a sense of commitment. In this endless blame game, we must ultimately point the finger at ourselves. That means, as I shall argue, a combination of respect for the collective enterprise and a healthy measure of critical assessment of those engaged in it. We have seen a great deal of the latter lately, and not enough of the former. Distrust of authority is not a viable theory of civic identity; it must be balanced with a sense of responsiveness to the needs of others.

I will label the resulting quality, a virtue or ethical habit, *compassionate skepticism*. I mean by that the deployment of constructive disbelief governed by awareness of shared vulnerability. It counts as a virtue because it is, to use Aristotelian language, a habituated trait of character that is also a disposition to act. To possess such a quality is to act upon its urgings, and vice versa. Cultivating the disposition, fashioning roles and habits that make for its flourishing, is the work of all of us. We live in a time when many of the strongest habits we have are bad—bad for us, bad for others, bad for the environment, bad for politics, bad for everything we care about. But humans are creatures of habit, and breaking harmful ones is hard work.

I will lean heavily on the idea of habit in what follows, in part because trust itself is a matter of good habits, often exhibited against all odds. The remarkable thing about human societies is that they function at all, given all the primitive tendencies working against them. Even at the level of basic cognition, we are far more likely to incline to superstition and misinformation than to execute the hard work of tracking true knowledge and forging a stable rational subject. As the philosopher Dan Williams notes, "lies, conspiracy theories, misinformation, bias, pseudo-science, superstition and so on are not alien perversions of the public sphere." On the contrary, "[t]hey are the epistemic state of nature that society will revert to in the absence of fragile—and highly contingent—cultural and institutional achievements."[5]

That contingency is precisely what occupies me in these pages: the sheer unlikelihood and fragility of our social cooperation. Also, per the corollary point, I flag throughout these pages the urgency of avoiding any slide back into a state of nature that is at once epistemic and political. I mean that wasteland of alternative facts and competing rationalities, all fought on a razed battleground that might once have been a rational public sphere, called public life. Make no mistake about this paradox of human existence: there is every reason for people not to be rational. In terms of basic urges and instincts, we have to acknowledge that logical reasoning and truth-seeking do not come naturally to us. They are possibilities of our nature, but not, as it were, the resting state. And yet, our rational capacity has long been considered the best part of ourselves—especially when it is conjoined with the kind of "unselfing" that makes for connection with other people and with ideas beyond self-interest. Reason and emotion are not contraries but partners. Moreover, we sometimes find ourselves precisely in those moments when we seem most alien to ourselves. Only a reflective, textured account can make sense of that common feature of being a person.

Pursuing these lines of thought, gathering the threads, teasing out what we might call the ethico-cognitive potential of consciousness within all the daily dross and distraction, requires the telling of a good story. I mean a story about ourselves and the world, and about how the two fit together. Story is itself so basic to the human mind that we find ourselves unable to experience life without its shapes and tropes. Personal identity, with its attendant burdens of responsibility and choice, is unthinkable without the continuity of narrative. And just as repetition can aid us when we need guidance, so narrative can provide shape to our temporal thrownness. Habit and narrative are closely linked in the project of individual life, in short, as they are in politics understood as shared life. The conjunction both offers and demands good pattern recognition, but it also then demands the recognition of good patterns over bad.

I realize this is all quite abstract—an inevitable feature of doing philosophy even of the applied or practical variety. My hope is that the details of what follows will clarify everything contained in these introductory paragraphs. For now, the best way to answer all these complex (and never-ending) challenges will be to form new habits to replace old, harmful ones—or, more accurately in the present case, to revive and cultivate potential but endangered habits of trust and responsibility. These positive human habits have been comprehensively frayed, by technology's disconnection-through-connection, by the polarization of public discourse, and by the reduction of everything to a kind of abstracted video game where other people are no longer seen as entirely real. Habits are powerful, but they are not inevitable. The first step is recognizing how they come to take hold of us. The second step is then to challenge them. The third is to execute this program of recovery with better habits—habits of flourishing, including trust in each other and in the institutions we all need to meet the complexities of twenty-first-century life.

Authority must be questioned so that it becomes better, not in order to tear down all possible guidelines for living. We need good rules, good games governed by the rules, and better players to play the games—real people, actual citizens, not avatars or handles. Politics is, after all, a very serious game of justification, wherein participants must offer arguments, if sometimes only implicit ones, for why they have something that someone else does not. Unlike many other games, but in common with the best of them, this game allows for winners and losers but also embraces the wisdom that sometimes true achievement lies in the defeat of any need for victory. Thus do we transcend competition to create community and even glory.

Such high-toned sentiments invite immediate skepticism, I realize. Most of us are well versed in skepticism already. It is the dominant habit of the age. Indeed, the restless urge to question everything might be considered the keynote of both modern and postmodern realities: questioning things is what got us here, but it is also what now makes for confusion. Compassion is another story. Its etymology suggests an idea of fellow feeling, or empathy; but there is also a suggestion, with use, of a relevant command—that compassion entails not just recognition of another's suffering, but a positive duty to relieve it. In this manner, compassionate skepticism may take its place alongside other, more familiar political virtues like reasonableness and civility.[6]

Compassion is that rare thing, a strong feeling with an equally strong rational basis. Its arousal is, in part, a recognition of shared vulnerability. But that recognition also calls forth an ethical and political response, itself a conjunction of feeling and reason. I experience pain at the pain of others; their suffering causes me to suffer. Absent sociopathic deficit, this is the natural order. Kant and other rationalist philosophers remind us that our fellow-travellers on the moral plane are other rational agents—or, at least, we and they wish to be so. One of the things we have learned to accept since Kant's time is that the class of rational agents may not all be human.

Even more important than this extension of care and regard is a point that Kant tends to discount altogether. He focuses on our rational powers, and hence our responsibilities. But reason is also a burden, and sometimes a weakness in ourselves. Reason can mask the more fragile inwardness of consciousness, that part of ourselves that includes an awareness of both weakness and wonder in the world. Once we know it, we cannot unknow the fact of suffering.

Extending the thought, we might judge that the power of reason is valuable only insofar as it allows us to perceive the shared weakness of its own vessels. But we also know that compassion has limits, of both duration and distance. Like all powers, its effective range is limited, and fatigue afflicts its exercise. The call of reason—and the duty of responsibility to each other—is therefore endless. My guiding thought in what follows is that only a close examination of that responsibility will enable the program of compassionate skepticism we need as the basic algorithm of justice—meaning not some specific distribution of goods, or even an idealized vision of post-ideological harmony, but a perpetual negotiation of our shared vulnerability.

The matter is urgent and transcends the usual divisions of left and right—themselves unhelpful labels that invite blockages of thought. The background condition of this discussion is our current state of *permacrisis*: the collision of multiple critical problems whose conjunction renders effective response to any one of them impossible. Crisis demands a response, but too much of it strains our abilities.

I am going to accept, without much further notice, that this is an accurate description of our current condition. I will argue, instead, that the permacritical state can, and should, be analyzed in terms of the Enlightenment imperatives that descend directly from Immanuel Kant's landmark essay "What Is Enlightenment?" (1784), where he defends a popular version of the rational universalism that has grounded two centuries of human aspiration.

This focus might strike some readers as odd, or tendentious. Surely an eighteenth-century philosopher, white and male and stuffed with the prejudices of his time, is no guide for today? My underlying motivation in featuring Kant is not one of scholarly resuscitation, or of special pleading. I am not proposing to defend the universalist rationality of Kant or his project of transcendental idealism. My goals are more modest. I will focus on the injunction offered at the end of Kant's essay: the familiar Latin motto *sapere aude*. This is usually translated as *think for yourself* in English and is, more recently, joined with another imperative—*question authority*—as part of a popular slogan found on lapel buttons and bumper stickers. The two commands seem to fall naturally together, as do the basic notions of authority and trust.

As I discuss in part 1, the paradox of both imperatives is part of their appeal. They command us to do precisely what stands logically opposed to the act of obeying them. But that tangled logic is also a way of thinking about our current predicament, where the critics of authority have been so successful in some quarters that basic social trust no longer seems possible. Like Kant before us, we have a tall order in marshalling the forces of reason and fellow-feeling against the zero-sum imperatives of the dominant-force model.

For simplicity, I will understand *trust* as mutually beneficial but non-contractual and non-dominating relations between agents. Trust exists in the form of bonds and expectations: in effect, it is a linked chain of promises, mostly but not invariably implicit. I promise to act in a certain way even as I expect you to act in a coordinate way. Joint ventures thus become possible, sometimes in ways that do not require central control. Our outward display of trustingness is matched by trustworthiness in the relevant partner or institution. The alignment of parties is essential, since trust extended without corresponding uptake by trustworthy actors is no better than gullibility. That is why trust fields, where we seek to join our plans and desires to others, are so often the playground of confidence games, swindles, and free riders. Collective-action problems also loom, since any social coordination is dependent on everyone following good rules. Hence the need for regulation at the margins, where pure self-interest will not guarantee coordination. Tragedies of the commons and races to the bottom are familiar kinds of collective-action problems: each seeking a locally rational goal, we condemn everyone, including ourselves, to a worse outcome through destruction of shared goods. Collective-action problems are social-agent situations that require regulation because trust is insufficient to prevent the downward spiral of self-defeating individual action.

These trust agents may be individuals or representatives of structures, or the structures themselves, in the form of institutions and professions. Trust between friends is often thought the paradigm case, but that degree of shared obligations and reliance is in fact rare outside of very close associations of people, perhaps a handful of others for each of us, and in any case no viable basis for social organization and coordinated action. The "friends" of social media do not meet the case. We require larger frameworks of social cooperation and guidance to achieve our evolving goals, but these need not be held together with the strong glue of personal attachment. In fact, as we will see, they function better when they *do not* depend on the personal, but instead offer trust as a matter of form, between strangers. Trust is not personal. This may seem counterintuitive but is essential. (I go into this more in part 3.)

We trust a bank to be sound not because we like the teller with whom we interact (though that may help!), but because the teller's institution is transparent and solid—and backed by a deposit-insurance corporation. But such institutions, we should always remember, are ultimately composed of individuals and their desires. So, not only do we expect these structures to help coordinate our actions with those of others, but we also expect them to be accountable for their own functioning. Sometimes, this is effected by isolating individuals within the structure as the bearers of responsibility: impeaching elected officials, bringing to law the officers of a firm. But sometimes the structure itself is held responsible, as when corporations are considered legal entities open to litigation.

In line with this necessity of accountability, I will understand *authority* to be the ability of trust agents to vest themselves or others with *legitimate power*, not merely force. That power may be economic, political, or social in some broad sense. It may also become larger than the sum of relevant individuals, and so potentially "faceless" or "mute." This is the downside risk of impersonality. Authority is therefore in need of redemption or validation. The hidden genius of the trust-authority relationship as a social technology is that one valid relationship can act as a reliable keystone of an entire authoritative complex. I need only feel trust for the basic honesty and competence of my financial advisor, for example, not every employee of the investment firm: that person stands for the power of the financial system. The system may fail, but not because my advisor is a bad person. (He may be, but that's not the problem.)

Individuals exert authority through charisma, wit, knowledge, wisdom, and experience—the virtues and vices usually classed under "force of personality." Institutions extend their authority through such persons but can also function with lower levels of virtue and without exceptional individuals. Collective knowledge, proven procedure, and tested method can function with minimally virtuous agents of basic honesty, integrity, and devotion to duty. As we know too well, even that minimal standard of virtue is sometimes too much to expect. That is when trust wavers and authority crumbles. The members of an appeals court or a philosophy faculty do not have to be paragons of wisdom, though it is wonderful if they are; they *do* need to be scrupulous about their power and the trust placed in them because of it. (Yes, even philosophy professors have a certain species of power and a corresponding duty of trust.) This back-and-forth in the trust cultivation of those who generate discourse is the focus of parts 2 and 3.

The necessary third term working within the trust-authority nexus is, of course, *belief*. For any trust system to function, even the most basic and strongest ones between friends or lovers, there must be some pool of shared belief. In some cases, this will mean, in effect, a web of shared experience, sensibility, and obligation. I trust my friend because he and I have been through so much together; I know he has my back. I trust my lover because she has saved my life countless times; she sustains me. But trust in impersonal cases—and the authority it both creates and promotes—depends on beliefs that are less immediate. Moreover, trust institutions often rely for their authority on the possession and deployment of the special class of belief we call knowledge. A public health measure is valid if backed by good science. A policy decision demands public assent if its statistical analysis is solid. Authoritative media or social science is constructed through rigorous checking of facts.

These trust institutions are all importantly public. Sometimes they may achieve the status of public goods, as in goods that can be enjoyed by everyone without diminishing their ongoing value for all—in the jargon, *nonexclusive* and *nonrival* goods. Roads, parks, and state-funded schools are classic examples of these, all of them backed by government regulation. Many trust institutions, however, are either public-private hybrids (much shared city space falls into this category) or outright private—for instance, most media outlets and many of the most influential universities. These may be regulated in some respects—the presidents of Harvard and Penn can be called before Congress, since they enjoy government subsidies even as private concerns—but their devotion to public service and shared ends is always provisional.

That counts as one kind of problem or limitation on the public nature of institutional authority. Much of it must be driven by good intentions and voluntary compliance. Media outlets have to agree that there is a public interest governing their actions, and universities must reaffirm constantly their devotion to the goals of science and learning. Just as important is buy-in from the other side: the public must value the institutions and the functions they perform. When disdain for universities and the media—or politics, or even science—grows large in the public mind, the entire trust structure is threatened.

In liberal-democratic societies with market economics, we also allow for a certain measure of opting out. I mean the decision by some subset of the population to choose private rather than public forms of certain goods. A two-tier health system, for example, can allow the wealthy access to forms of care denied to the larger public. Elite education is not just elite in effects, it is often gated by opportunity costs that go well beyond academic ability or other ideals of the meritocracy. As of this writing, Ivy League tuition is running at approximately US$65,000 a year, plus about US$20,000 more in annual living costs. Those are not figures for the faint of heart or light of wallet. More on this in part 2.[7]

Even in aspects of authority that should be beyond private defection, there are reasons to be cynical. Equality before the law, for example, sounds like the most basic nonrival and nonexclusive rule there could be; and yet, we all know that access to justice—and, sometimes, avoidance of its consequences—is unevenly distributed across populations. One reason for insisting that individuals should not be allowed private options in some public domains is that such defections are unjust. Another reason is that they make the public version of the domain worse than it might be. Making it mandatory for the children of the wealthy to attend public schools has the net effect of making those schools better.

When we all have stake in the game, the game has a chance to prosper. When people can defect from the game at will, or enjoy its benefits without paying its penalties, we all suffer. Any game can tolerate a certain amount of marginal defection—cheating, sly moves, uncalled infractions, and the like—but we must not lose confidence in the game itself. Marginal bad actors cannot be allowed to dominate. When they do, the straight players start to feel like dupes—and so they begin to court perverse incentives to defect themselves. "One of the most direct ways to improve a flawed system is simply to end the ability of rich and powerful people to exclude themselves from it," the critic Hamilton Nolan writes.[8] Make the rich play! They will force government to fix a broken system that would otherwise remain broken.

The game is better when all of us have skin in it. Good games beget good players, and good players in turn bolster and maintain the game's health. The crisis of trust begins at home. What kind of player are you?

* * *

THE EXAMPLES GIVEN SO FAR suggest how difficult, and yet how essential, it is to establish true authority—the kind that deserves and rewards our trust. I will leave for part 4 the tricky task of deciding what kinds of belief count as knowledge. For now, it is enough to isolate the problem. As the ancient Greek philosophers knew, there is a constant slippage in the human mind between opinion and knowledge. Hence the legacy of *doxa* and *episteme*, the Greek terms for opinion and knowledge, respectively. We moderns inherit the ancient assumption that a chasm yawns between the two. But we have abandoned, in large measure, the metaphysical assumptions that made distinguishing between them tractable. We do not, for the most part, subscribe to Plato's theory of transcendental ideas, or even to any of its less-demanding descendants.

We want truth without the baggage, in other words. But in so wanting, truth seems to slip between our fingers. Everyday discourse tends to elide the differences between opinion and knowledge, between beliefs that I happen to hold and the truth. This has always been so—Socrates and his interlocutors complain about it repeatedly—but our own time has elevated a flaw into an ideology, making a bug into a feature. We come to the public table with foregrounded suspicion about everyone's authority but our own, almost always to our great detriment. We do this in the name of individualism, and as an exercise of freedom—or so it seems. And worse, even when we try to untangle opinion from knowledge, we tend to slide back into presuppositions and prejudices. This condition in turn invites its own tangle: what the philosopher Hans-Georg Gadamer calls "the prejudice against prejudice," a kind of hamstringing of reason under the stress of constant suspicion.[9]

I try in what follows to untangle some of these knots, and so to make the solid—and socially necessary—bond among trust, authority, and knowledge more robust. This is never easy. Not all trust agents can or will recognize all forms of authority, for one thing. Online influencers have authority, for example, even if some of us disdain its nature and effects. The police force of a sanctioned polity has a monopoly on the use of force, even if we individually object to a given police action. But, at the same time, all forms of authority must remain, in principle, subject to questions about their legitimacy, otherwise they self-defeat. A given authority claim or network need not be in question at every moment—that would make for chaos—but legitimacy must be considered always provisional. Trust and authority are closely entwined concepts and achievements: they stand and fall together. Undermine authority on its merits, and trust is lost; erode trust in day-to-day workings, and authority will crumble.

I may not touch on all the worries of every reader concerned about trust and authority. That is in the nature of things. Any individual view is limited, by definition. As the inclusion of autobiographical details is meant to indicate, a book is the product of a particular mind, not an exercise of pure disinterested thought. My wish is that the forms of critical reflection pursued here might be extended wherever trust agents find them most relevant and useful. We cannot live without trust, and society cannot function without authority. That does not mean accepting authority claims on their face; it means challenging them just when, how, and to the extent that the effort will serve to make us all stronger and less vulnerable. And that is, in its way, a theory of justice.

The book is structured in five parts, each combining polemic with meditation. These meditations touch on perceived crises of authority and trust in each of the following general subject areas: (1) political ideology, (2) academia, (3) media, (4) organized religion, and (5) science, especially public health and artificial intelligence.

Originally, I tried to maintain a strict division of labour among these critical sectors, but the topics of authority and trust are so entwined—and so system-wide—that this outwardly obvious partition scheme proved unhelpful. There is a great deal more skepticism about the claims of politicians, academics, and journalists than there is about, say, medical doctors and engineers. With the very striking—and fraught—exceptions of climate change and public health, science gets a relatively clean report card.

I won't quote a lot of statistics in what follows. Statistics are one of things that people do not trust, and with good reason. We all hear some echo of Mark Twain's line, attributed upstream to Benjamin Disraeli, that there are three kinds of lies: lies, damn lies, and statistics. More on that later. For now, here is a statistic (or two of them) worth considering: a 2019 Pew Research Center poll found that 75 percent of Americans perceived a shrinking of trust in government, while 64 percent saw the same shrinkage of trust between citizens. Those numbers got worse over the pandemic years and are no better now. Citizens "see fading trust as a sign of cultural sickness and national decline," the study's authors noted. "Some also tie it to what they perceive to be increased loneliness and excessive individualism. About half of Americans (49 percent) link the decline in interpersonal trust to a belief that people are not as reliable as they used to be. Many ascribe shrinking trust to a political culture they believe is broken and spawns suspicion, even cynicism, about the ability of others to distinguish fact from fiction."[10] Naturally, such polls can only ever measure perception. Trust is not actually quantifiable. On the contrary, trust levels *are a function of their own perceived presence*. This is a tangle that comes with the territory: the good in question is spectral but essential. The statistics are worrying, therefore, but not surprising. We have heard them before.

Rather than dwell on the details of the trust crisis sector by sector, then—something that is done early and often already—I have decided here to strike out in a different direction. I became convinced that the state of trust crisis was not entirely the fault of the failing institutions—though they have much to answer for—but also lay in our evolving desires as citizens. Those desires face important problems of distortion and dependency: what I have called the *addiction to conviction*. The topical interventions are now highlighted by meditation titles that mimic five wry responses to the original imperative to question authority. Throughout, a focus on contemporary issues leads to searching questions about belief, expertise, truth, argument, and identity.[11]

This is, I should emphasize, an exercise in philosophical reflection. This book is not offered as a set of policy recommendations, or even what are sometimes called "actionable insights"—the sort of bullet-point plans for life that dominate some areas of the infosphere. I outline some rather hopeful advice about the virtues of good citizenship, especially at the end, but I am not offering more than what philosophy can ever reasonably provide, which is some measure of critical analysis of who we are and what we are up to. I have not delved into the details of democratic reforms that might afford more rational electoral outcomes, and thereby (potentially) decrease ideological polarization; but there is a deep literature on this topic worth any citizen's attention.[12]

My aims are relatively modest. I maintain first, then, that the state of permacrisis does not lead to productive uncertainty; rather, it calls forth a circus of competing certainty claims, which confuse and confound us. In this sense, the work of the discussion is akin to what Maimonides saw as a "guide to the perplexed"—seeking reason concealed in the mysteries before us. Epistemic confusion has led to the deterioration of shared discourse, and hence to the disorder of the current public sphere. So, I then argue further that such dogmatic certainty is a form of addictive behaviour, and hence as hard to control as any other addiction. Indeed, it may be harder to manage, since the toxins involved are cognitive and emotional, not chemical. Its damage is system wide. And finally, in part 5, I offer some specific suggestions for a program of recovery that might alleviate some of the symptoms, and perhaps even a few of the causes, of our addiction to conviction. Like all recovery programs, this civic one must remain provisional and tentative—as well as ongoing.

This feature of perpetuity is more than just a standard convention of recovery narratives. We are familiar with the idea that the addict never fully overcomes addiction but rather stands in a position of perpetual recovery. More than this, though, the issue of trust is endlessly critical because it captures the fundamental relations of individuals to their shared world. Underneath the headline details of permacrisis, in other words, lie basic questions of social relations, communication, and trust. These are easy to sketch but very difficult to understand, much less dare to improve.

For example, one prominent philosopher, Robert Brandom, has noted that what is called *epistemic authority*—the reasons we have for believing things—is a complex function. Structures of belief can be sketched as a nested hierarchy of kinds, or sources, of belief: (1) sensual immediacy, (2) properties, (3) objects, (4) facts, and (5) laws. Each of these levels is distinct in its authority but builds on the earlier stages in a necessary progression. Together—if secured reliably—they offer a sound basis for trust. Without such fundamental trust, nothing in human affairs can ever make sense: the very ideas of *content* and *concept*, of necessary schemata for ordering understanding, fall to pieces. (Sketching the hierarchy is one thing; cashing it out is another.)[13]

But there are dangers greater than schema failure lurking here. A frequent error, in ordinary life as well as in philosophy, is mistaking one's own rational judgment for the truth of the matter. Thinking for yourself is good, in other words, but not *always* good.[14] Sometimes the smart thing is to *stop* thinking for yourself, as when a GPS system overrides your memories of the terrain, or when you must depend on medical advice that conflicts with Dr. Google and his hapless interns, your fingers. Expertise vested in other people is necessary for epistemic success, and so trust in those experts is likewise necessary. Systems, protocols, and standard operating procedures—also currencies, media, institutions, and professions—are developed precisely to pool human intelligence in ways that don't need to be repeatedly learned and can handle situations too complex for even one superlative person.

Epistemic autonomy is an intellectual virtue, yes—thinking for yourself is generally a good thing!—but its exercise is fraught with peril, a kind of inherent vice of looming arrogance. Perhaps courage comes closest among the specifically ethical virtues in plotting a course between risk and reward. Here, too, a positive trait is susceptible to an excess of self-belief, leading to a vicious imbalance in the failure we know as rashness. Idiomatically speaking, here "fortune favours the brave" and "who dares wins" run up against "look before you leap" and "discretion is the better part of valour." Epistemic autonomy likewise satisfies one aspect of human ambition (being self-governed) only at the cost of possible bad outcomes (failing for lack of appropriate know-how). We have a strong tendency to overestimate our own capacities in the name of autonomy. I may pride myself on not taking doctor's order at face value, but that does not make me a reliable authority on public health or vaccine protocols. Thinking I can fly the plane in an emergency may offer deep self-satisfaction, but only at the price of sending all of us to our doom. And no, despite all your detailed couchland ravings, you probably don't have a better game plan than that offensive coordinator you see on TV.

This kind of cost-benefit complexity in turn makes epistemic autonomy distinct from more obvious ethical virtues, such as generosity or temperance. These traits of character involve tracing a mean between too much and too little, but are not typically affected by gaps of knowledge. I can't really "get it wrong" in my attempts to be temperate, at least in the sense of overestimating my skill or knowledge of the matter at hand. But epistemic autonomy is also distinct from other epistemic virtues like consistency and truth tracking. Unlike those traits or habits of mind, we can easily pursue such autonomy past the point of good outcomes, and we can likewise overvalue its influence on what we should believe. Sometimes the best pathway to the truth is *not* thinking for ourselves, and sometimes (more often) our apparently autonomous thoughts are not really ones we have reached independently. (I leave aside here Emerson's much-quoted assertion that "a foolish consistency is the hobgoblin of little minds." The adjective *foolish* does all the heavy lifting in that casual condemnation of the "little statesmen, philosophers, and divines" who adore it.)[15]

Epistemic and ethical virtues are not so bright-line distinct that, in seeking a good life, we can pursue one class in the absence of the other. Habits of mind align with habits of character, and vice versa. Being a trusting person is sometimes *good*, as well as sometimes *smart*. The qualifiers I feel the need to insert there—the sometimes-fatal additional warning of *sometimes*—is really what this book is about. We rail at feckless journalists and overbearing civil servants, decry idiotic regulations and bankrupt faculties. But we all still need money, doctors, air traffic controllers, good information, science, rules of the road, and even tax collectors. More fundamentally, we all need *other people* who recognize our desires and weaknesses as worthy of consideration—even as we extend those same trusting presuppositions to them.

The problem of trust in this rubble-strewn post-Covid discursive landscape is thorny and divisive all by itself. Every authority is in doubt *even as* we rely more and more on stern conviction. One way of describing the basic problem is that autonomy has trumped authority in matters epistemic. That I *merely believe* something is lately considered more than enough sanction for my actions to be guided by it, and all standard authorities may go to hell. Such a condition, to put it mildly, cannot be sustained in coherent social existence.

* * *

MY GUIDING PRINCIPLE THROUGHOUT THESE pages is that polemic and meditation, though often thought incompatible, are in fact usefully conjoined forms of engagement. Indeed, they work to temper each other. The result is, you might say, something like meditation in times of emergency or civil war—to echo two extraordinary poets of the form, Yeats and O'Hara.[16]

Sometimes a polemic works best when it is thoughtful and not simply the expulsion of rhetorical hot air; but equally, a philosophical meditation may be leavened by urgency, topicality, even anger. The basic impetus of both styles is surely the same: *to understand the world* and so, perhaps, to change it. Marx was wrong when he suggested, in a much-quoted put-down, that philosophers have pursued the former to the detriment of the latter. Thought and action are not so clearly separated, and even pure theory offers its own kind of praxis. More simply still, we can say with confidence that the world changes first in the mind of the person who decides to change the world. That person can be you or me. If not us, then who?[17]

Pursuing these thoughts, I have tried to avoid over-reliance on what might be called *wonk widgets*: I mean the neat terms of art, clickbait examples, and quasi-technical labels that social scientists affix to tricky human phenomena to make them more pliable. We won't dispel the fug of jargon already swirling in current public discourse by countering it with even more inside-baseball terminology, especially if that metajargon comes with a dose of mansplaining smugness or tweedy self-satisfaction. Naming a phenomenon is not the same as explaining it, still less ameliorating its effects.

Language has become—ever was—the central battleground of sense making and power distribution across the public sphere. Like many of us, I am frustrated equally by blandly arrogant partisan catch-phrases and bafflegab as by wishfully precise counterlocutions from superior thinkers. I hope my efforts at accessibility pay dividends in what follows, but only readers can decide whether that is so.

What I want to offer here is a different *kind* of argument than those we usually see about crises of trust. I will address foundations, reasons, premises, and ideologies. The method is intended to be dialectical, finding its energy in the tension between positions. My hope is that this approach will generate less despair or alienation and more optimism about social trust and its ultimate proper aim, justice. We live in a shared world, whether we like it or not.

We are told that we live in an era of "bespoke realities," where people array themselves for public engagement with alternative facts and impregnable convictions that fit like a suit of tailored clothes.[18] But in fact the situation is even worse than that: the suits we don are mostly off the rack, not made to measure. We wear what already fits someone else and mimic the ways of wearing it by watching the swirls of novelty and conformity. The reality is "bespoke" only in the sense of being exclusive to the in-group wearers. This is teenage fashion, where every marker of "individuality" is already overdetermined by sales, marketing, and the cool kids in the yard.

The only counter to this disastrous self-negating fashion sense is epistemic vigilance. What might be a more helpful governing metaphor about public life, since fashion is so obviously a dead end? One critic has defined critical thinking as "a kind of immune system for our individual conceptions of reality, allowing us to parse truth and falsehood."[19] But, as with any immune system, epistemic defences are compromised when made insufficiently robust through malign viruses in the body politic, such as ignorance or deprivation. They may be fought with the usual disinfectants, truth and light and logic.

Are these sufficient to the disease, though? We have come to see that an epistemic immune system can also be overwhelmed through excessive stimulation. Or, like an addict's brain, it can offer damaging pleasure responses—forms of projection and acting out. For example: multiple conflicting accounts of a controversial subject, with arrays of duelling PhDs, can sap confidence in the immediate topic. More dangerously, it can erode our faith in the idea of expertise itself. *If the so-called experts disagree, who is to say what is right?* Into this epistemic power vacuum any toxic idea may creep and, worse, offer cascading pleasures of self-righteousness and justified anger.

Ideology is, by definition, bullet-proof and unfalsifiable. All objections or counterevidence are folded in as further proof of its original truth. When that impregnability is bolstered by authority, the effect is amplified, sometimes beyond any sort of rational cure.

Here the deciding factor is often a matter of alignment with other pre-existing beliefs, affiliations, or desires.[20] That is, I seek and therefore find "authoritative" claims to back up what I already believe. Such hybrid theories—half science and half unassailable conviction—are best characterized, in the words of Stanford University sociologist Jeremy Freese, as *vampirical*. In contrast to the way empirical theories function, vampirical conviction feeds on the otherwise healthy lifeblood of susceptible victims, their vital desire to believe, turning healthy cognitive agents into vassals of credulity through a kind of infectious transfusion. Vampirical enslavement cannot be killed by anything as basic as mere counterevidence because such evidence is always construed as further proof of external deception.[21]

To use a different but equally vivid metaphor, one suited to our cultural moment, the process of becoming ideologically committed may be considered a matter of getting "pilled," as in the famous red-pill/blue-pill scene of *The Matrix* (1999). In the original scene, the choice offered by Morpheus (Laurence Fishburne) to Neo (Keanu Reeves) is one between continued pleasant deception within the enslaving illusion of The Matrix, or difficult but courageous acceptance of the harsh reality of the world as it actually stands. "Red pill" was soon adopted by various groups, especially incel and white-supremacist communities, as a symbol for their tough adherence to seeing and speaking the truth. To be "pilled" is to see the world clearly—the opposite valence of the same revelatory intent that originally lay in being "woke."

Even worse—and yes, it gets worse—is that pilling can lead to forms of nihilism and aggressive anti-trust belief that comprehensively overwhelm the fragile structures of social cooperation. More recent analysis, as in the case of the would-be assassin of former president Donald Trump, thus speaks of black-pilling rather than red-pilling: that is, initiation, usually via online rabbit holes, into a condition of aggressive non-belief. If there is nobody left to trust, and nothing worth your moral allegiance, why not leap off the steep precipice of socially compliant behaviour? Such a deep derangement of otherwise well-ordered life is thankfully rare, and fringe in its influence; it is a species of social defection that should not really be considered ideological at all. But any general erosion of belief about shared social norms and expectations, including cognitive commitment to what counts as reality, is far more worrying. This routine decay of shared norms likewise creates numerous less violent but sometimes equally perverse incentives and side markets for grifting and cognitive con games. Here, where everything is fake because nothing is reliably real, free-floating identity claims, performative virtue, outrage surfing, and exclusive demands for bogus "moral clarity" carry the day. Issues of tangled complexity and nuance are reduced to questions that have only one right answer—and mobbing or cancelling awaits those who answer incorrectly.[22]

On the structural level, the possibility of general corruption in the highest echelons of government, law, business, and media is impossible to ignore. Convicted felon Donald Trump, for example, "failed spectacularly as an insurrectionist and as a disrupter of the civil service," political commentator Caroline Fredrickson wrote of the former grifter-in-chief, "and his clownish and chaotic style may well lead to failure again." Nevertheless, "he has succeeded time and time again in the art of the steal. If his long con continues into a second term, it will not only contribute to the fraying trust Americans have in their institutions, but also impair our ability to lead the world through a series of escalating crises."[23]

This lament assumes what many now doubt, namely that America has any residual reputation left to execute such leadership, even in theory. It is all too easy to grow cynical in such circumstances and to find in these claims and counterclaims just further evidence of the base urges of humankind. Now the tools of reason are no more than the finely honed torture implements of power. And yes, there are those who believe that there was no Enlightenment, and so the Kantian demands to *question authority* and *think for yourself*—the focus of this book—are misplaced and, worse, dangerous in their naïveté.[24]

I am not so cynical; nor am I inclined to the nihilism that may seem to yawn before the unrelieved cynic. The disrepair of public discourse and the erosion of trust are not free licence to misbehave. I think here of Christopher Hitchens, who properly defined the cynic as one who "hopes for the best but expects the worst" (a line which, not surprisingly, he almost certainly borrowed from someone else, as Google will authoritatively tell you). Moreover, accepting a free-for-all end-game of public trust takes no account of the dozens, even hundreds, of small acts of cooperation we execute every day. As noted, the remarkable thing about human society is not how many failures or defections it allows, but how often we voluntarily choose to cooperate even when it is against our bare self-interest. If nothing else, this shows that we are natural rule-followers—in large measure because we recognize that rules, when well articulated, offer net benefits to everyone.

Still, that optimism about our primate behaviour is not equal to the misalignments and defects in that same nature. We need some version of a *critical theory* of authority and trust. But what is a critical theory? In a time when one kind of such theory, critical race theory, has become—even just as a phrase—a red flag among raging bulls, it's worth exploring the issue before we go on.

* * *

CRITICAL THEORY, AT LEAST AS associated with Marxist-driven Frankfurt school social critique or more recent refinements such as critical race theory, is lately a suspect property. This project of "seeing through," or *Ideologiekritik*, is the dominant mode of theoretical engagement in (broadly) left-wing political theory. As I make clear in part 2, my own thinking about politics, culture, and justice is influenced by this school of thought, and I would class myself as continuing its range of applications.

The usual procedure is something like the following: (1) One encounters a certain feature of everyday life, perhaps a piece of "common sense" or "taken for granted" reality—this is just the way things are done. But then (2) contradictions or slippages are observed in the workings of the feature. Perhaps it is not a feature, but a bug? Perhaps there is something going on that we cannot see. And so (3) there is an effort at unmasking the aspects of the feature that make it seem "natural." If properly conducted, this effort leads in turn to (4) a realization that there is some underlying structure, system, or base that was concealed by the very naturalness of the natural feature—which is now dispelled! Typically, this act of revelation is accompanied by (5) the formation of political will about the underlying reality and its oppressive mechanisms.

In principle, this conceptual sequence is no different from—in fact proceeds directly out of—the standard appearance/reality metaphysics of both Western and Eastern philosophical traditions. (Plato and Laozi are, we might say, equally committed to tearing aside the veil of ordinariness to expose how things really work.) The distinctive critical-theoretical addition is the political consciousness involved at every moment: the basic assumption that ideological structures are present everywhere, maintaining their exclusive power even while erasing every trace of their origin.

But there are two distinct reasons to be wary of any runaway commitment to exposing the inner workings of social structures. These difficulties, or cautions, emerge not from the project's failure but, paradoxically, from its success. Skeptical thought has become too good at veil rending, or perhaps even addicted to it, just at the stage where its power of diagnosing addiction is strongest. These two limit-case worries are related and in fact might be considered different degrees of the same tendency.

The first caution comes from the philosopher Bruno Latour, famous for his own efforts at revealing social construction in knowledge. But two decades ago, well before the current crisis of authority, Latour offered a soul-searching account of his own doubts about where critical social theory had overextended its useful reach. In particular, he worried that the critical social project had become, largely as a victim of its own success, the very thing it set out to expose, a form of conspiracy theory.[25]

The worry seems misplaced, if not lunatic—until we exercise some self-scrutiny and identify the structural features of both cognitive modes. "In both cases," Latour writes, "you have to learn to become suspicious of everything people say because of course we all know that they live in the thralls of a complete *illusion* of their real motives. Then, after disbelief has struck and an explanation is requested for what is really going on, in both cases again it is the same appeal to powerful agents hidden in the dark acting always consistently, continuously, relentlessly."[26]

The chosen language and tone may differ, but that does not disguise the similarity of purpose in critical theory and some kinds of conspiracism. In fact, a sly academic might be even better at hiding their true commitments than the average QAnon or stolen-election doofus. "Of course, we in the academy like to use more elevated causes—society, discourse, knowledge-slash-power, fields of forces, empires, capitalism," Latour notes wryly, "while conspiracists like to portray a miserable bunch of greedy people with dark intents, but I find something troublingly similar in the structure of the explanation, in the first movement of disbelief and, then, in the wheeling of causal explanations coming out of the deep dark below."[27]

How different is that project, really, from the routine claims of MAGA goons that a new Trump presidency will expose "what's really going on"? Do these critical insights differ all that much from assertions about the extent of the Deep State collusion, which will be revealed by the only leader brave enough to do so? And, just as the proper response to a conspiracy claim is to question the plausibility of coordination and intent, we really ought to doubt that "power," or "capitalism," or "neoliberalism" are conscious, intentional forces, controlled by someone in particular.

The vast distrust people feel in global capitalism and its various "democratic" proxies opens up a dead ideological space into which any wacky idea might run. According to a 2023 Edelman Trust Barometer poll, only 20 percent of people in G7 countries think they will be better off in five years than they are now. Results from another Edelman poll in 2020 indicate serious trust deficits "driven by a growing sense of inequity and unfairness in the system"—no wonder, when the system is so obviously rigged to favour the few over the many and to compound inequality with pile-on benefits for winners. When people lose faith in the official state, especially when that state includes elected government, conspiracy and criticism both fit the system-busting populist bill. To true believers, it matters less whether the sacred text is *The Protocols of the Elders of Zion* or Herman and Chomsky's *Manufacturing Consent* than that each offers salvation through revelation. Both promise deliverance when the current arrangement and its apparatchiks are exposed and then swept from the scene.[28]

I exaggerate, of course, and I would sooner bet on the explanatory viability of spectacle-enabled settler colonialism as a master key to politics than I would plump for a global Zionist plot. The point is that both theories are heavily invested in the idea that only master keys will do, and that assumption is very dangerous indeed when it comes to the real world of democracy. We can compare this to the small blip of intense "exposure" that attended the failed assassination attempt on Donald Trump in the very eventful July of 2024. For MAGA true believers, this was another chapter in "the story of a fearless leader surrounded by shadowy forces and intrigue, of grand conspiracies to thwart the will of the people who elected him. A narrative in which Mr. Trump, even before a gunman tried to take his life, was already a martyr." For others, and based on exactly the same evidence, it was either a staged spectacle of fake violence to bolster that martyrological narrative, or else an inside job involving Secret Service members bent on some kind of internal coup.[29]

Conspiracy theory is thus, like critical theory, epistemically capacious. One way to describe the discursive similarity operating here is to highlight, as philosopher Joseph Heath has done, two main features of any conspiracy theory. They are: (1) apophenia and (2) intentionality bias. The first names the tendency of human perception to find patterns where there are none. This is a part of our evolutionary training, which is prone to unconscious displacement, as when we see faces in inanimate objects or mistake correlation for causality. The second is the related tendency to attribute conscious intention to acts and events that may lack these features. Our keen desire to *make sense* can become, in other words, an enemy to clear thinking. Sorting the wheat of reason from the chaff of distractions that surround us, now more than ever, is the first duty of compassionate skeptics.[30]

This kind of lurking self-negation—a failure of success, we might call it—is a genuine problem for any critical theory, but it remains a rather elaborate and academic one. Indeed, it is a theoretical problem for which theory's own tools may offer the best remedy. We cannot entirely avoid risks posed by reflexivity. Critical theorists may fall into the very traps they have set out to find: ideology-busting becomes an ideology of its own. With the creep of intolerant diversity, equity, and inclusion measures, the project of emancipation may devolve into a program of thought control, groupthink, curbed speech, tone policing, and knee-jerk censure of viewpoint diversity. Even worse, this creep is often executed by adding layers of crippling bureaucracy onto once-thriving institutions like banks, hospitals, and universities.[31]

This kind of ideological capture is a clear feature of our age. In this instance, the ideology in question is not typically, or not only, the unspoken assumptions of a given worldview—the sense of ideology that Marx identified as the proper target for attack by critical theory. Those assumptions may well be in play, but the more immediate danger in capture scenarios is that the biased and partial political aspirations of a slice of the political spectrum dominate a field in the form of unquestioned orthodoxy. These slices are what we used to call the Right and Left wings, and we still employ those terms even though the labels waver and grow hazy before our eyes. It's a pretty topsy-turvy world when down-the-middle lifetime pol Joe Biden is routinely denounced as "radical Left" by the actually fanatical Trump-shadowing right wing. This goalpost-shifting move is conceivable, of course, only within a political culture that has long considered the epithet "liberal"

to be an insult pure and simple, entirely detached from its associations with personal liberty and pluralism. The debased terms—and
the ensuing plays of jejune insult—shift along with the larger trends of
social change, such that a left-liberal of the recent past (I mean myself
now) might well run the risk of conservative appropriation when offering philosophical objection to runaway programs of social critique.

The conceptual link between these two distinct senses of ideology—hidden assumptions, on the one hand, and a specific partisan
commitment, on the other—is that they are both self-perpetuating
forms of thought. They offer attendant cognitive rewards for those
who indulge them. And they are habit-forming. It becomes almost
argumentative second nature to parse all objections as weaponization of ill will rather than rational counterpoints, and to defend one's
own proclivities as obvious, natural, and right. Such indulgence is a
danger to mental well-being but also, alas, to the larger body politic.
Conviction of this sort is not a drug that one can enjoy in isolation.
Admonitions against the pleasures of intoxication are unlikely to be
effective, just as they are with so-called social drinking. The problem
with ideological capture is precisely that its prisoners believe themselves to be free.

Trust becomes impossible when there is even a suspicion that an
institution or profession is beholden to a specific political agenda, or
when a particular viewpoint masquerades as impartial expertise. Such
masquerades are evident everywhere around us. Key stories go unre-
ported by the media, false claims ride unchecked. Academic activism
elbows aside dedicated devotion to historical fact. The legislatures
and even judiciaries serve the interests of those who appoint them
and pad their pockets with boondoggle monies to sweeten the deal.
These are the reasons why we feel our faith in authority of all kinds
slipping away. This process is much more insidious and spectral than
older and more familiar notions of authoritarian corruption—though
these remain always in play. An ideological quarry is harder to dis-

cern, its influence extended through discourse and habit, not by overt indoctrination or exercise of force. It can feel as though the object of critique is some kind of video-game zombie, operating by angle cheats and jump-scare attacks from behind. But we cannot give up the game, for the stakes are too high.

Given all that, there is no choice but eternal vigilance against the overreach of the mind's own tendencies toward righteousness. In other words, the project I am advocating here must extend, at the margin between first- and second-order thinking, to vigilance against vigilance and assessment of belief about belief. This is, if you like, a critical theory of critical theory. Articulating and extending that kind of thinking is what I attempt to do in the following pages. We should not give up on the project of critical theory; we should refine and refocus its power. There is no other way forward that does not involve retrenchment of one sort or another, a dismantling of pluralism and tolerance.

For one thing, it should be obvious that, however overweening or clunky, a shared belief system poised against all oppression and forever based on grievance is *not as bad* as convictions about alien organ harvesting, underground sex-trade cabals, and collusion between high officials and global-domination cartels. The second objection to academic critical theory is, in a way, a more searching version of the first. Variants hail from many sources, but my own preferred version comes from C. S. Lewis, writing in his public intellectual mode.

Writing about the dangers of critical thinking, especially of an easy "cynical" sort, Lewis notes that all social critique must have limits. "You cannot go on 'seeing through' things for ever," he says. "The whole point of seeing through something is to see something through it. It is good that the window should be transparent, because the street or garden beyond it is opaque. How if you saw through the garden too?" Lewis's point here isn't merely one of methodological drift, whereby critical thought becomes its own rigid ideology. He wants to argue, further, that we cannot evade some commitment, at some level, to a baseline conviction of some sort. "It is no use trying to 'see through' first principles. If you see through everything, then everything is transparent. But a wholly transparent world is an invisible world. To 'see through' all things is the same as not to see."[32]

Lewis's own first principles here, which involve an uneasy amalgam of Christian and Taoist belief, is not everyone's cup of tea, to say the least. This is so even for those of us, myself included, who found his cozy Narnia-era theology congenial. Who doesn't love Aslan? The kinship is deeper than one of adolescent fiction taste. Lewis's notion of a final end feels, in its domesticated Taoism, very much like the Force of George Lucas's imagined Star Wars universe.

Perhaps that is no bad thing: the Taoist injunction to find flow with the larger world is evergreen, and a proper rebuke to the frantic flexing of most workaday life. But let us be clear, without being invisible: such a fuzzy notion of what lies beneath conflict is no more suitable to the demands of angry pluralism, fractured public discourse, and deep cognitive divisions than, say, Plato's theory of the forms. All of them are "answers" only to those who already believe they know the truth, and that will not serve. The Mandalorians say, *This is the Way.* And it certainly is the way—for them.

* * *

ONE FEELS SOME SYMPATHY FOR the sentiment that critique must come to an end somewhere. We all want to stand on a good rock. That impulse to find firm foundation inclines some to establish a basic reality, often something to do with the "natural." Immanuel Kant succumbed to this thought after his own fashion. "Perhaps nothing more sublime has ever been said, or any thought more sublimely expressed," he said, "than in the inscription over the temple of Isis (Mother Nature): 'I am all that is, that was, and that will be, and my veil no mortal has removed.'"[33]

The problem is, we no longer quite believe that: neither Isis nor even Mother Nature reliably feature as deities in the modern pantheon. Rather, we find ourselves in a world where nothing is natural until we make it so—and then we argue that everything else is evil and beyond redemption. I imagine that we will forever argue about those limits: part of being human is forever wondering what it means to be human. Is maleness a matter of fundamental biology? Or is it a function of "sex assigned at birth," whatever we mean by that? Is personal identity inherited, assumed, performed, invented, imposed—or all of those? None? Is human nature a robust safeguard against the looming power of artificial intelligence, or just a passing fad of evolution?[34]

I think we can accept that all the critical thinking in the world gets unmoored if it is not in the service of some rational end or purpose, some vision of human flourishing. Even the most searching philosophical explanations come to an end somewhere. As Wittgenstein put it, at some point "my spade is turned." We hit a certain kind of bedrock and can dig no further. Knowing that, we do well to follow the advice of Epictetus, the Stoic philosopher who gathered his own wisdom from hard prison time. In his *Enchiridion* (ca. 125 BCE) he said, "You cannot learn what you think you already know."[35]

One baseline conviction in the meditative polemics I propose is a commitment to the virtues of civility, compassion, curiosity, and humility. Because we are in quest of truth, fuelled by doubt, many things we want to believe must fall away in our path. There is no truth without exposed falsehood; a high price must be paid for knowledge. The common saying suggests that we should trust people only as far as we can throw them. Suppose we take that as a sound basic principle of skepticism. It can only be enacted at a high psychic cost. Bodies will have to be forever tossed for testing, figuratively speaking. Very few will budge. Then, if things get out of hand, the mistrustful efforts will manifest more literally. The throws won't always appear in obvious forms like show trials and demands for performative loyalty. What is online mobbing, for instance, except a form of mistrust-motored trial by ordeal?[36]

Let us not be so quick to polarize our minds. Disagreement with others is inevitable in public life, as we all know, but so is *internal* struggle and confusion. Tearing away the veil becomes less an operation performed to liberate other people (who probably know better already anyway), and more a process of constant self-diagnosis and even, in its way, positive self-medication or inner therapy.[37]

This forever project of self-criticism can lead to intellectual melancholy: a perennial hazard of the hopeful. I mean the temptation to take on an identity of elegant Weltschmerz, like some nobly cynical paladin of cracked virtue in a fallen world. The philosopher as hard-boiled existential gumshoe: Jean-Paul Belmondo playing Philip Marlowe, with appropriate fashion choices, though maybe minus the smoking and drinking. The world is hell! Humankind is lost! These are the end times! Such posing offers its own peculiar satisfactions. But we cannot pause to indulge melancholy, histrionically or otherwise. We always have more work to do. And for this we require both critique and restoration of trust. To use once-popular academic language, a hermeneutics of suspicion must always be leavened by a hermeneutics of belief. Provisional authority, temporary conclusions, conjecture and refutation, falsifiability, the pursuit of the best explanation so far—these tenets of basic scientific method remain essential, in fact more necessary than ever.[38]

The task of critique is endless, then, not because there is no bottom to reach, but rather because what we seek at bottom are truth and justice. These are ideas, features of the human mind as it contemplates its world. And so, they will not submit easily, or without struggle, to the efforts of that same human mind. We are, to use a metaphor offered by the psychologist Julian Jaynes, like flashlights attempting to illuminate the source of our own light.[39]

In 1976, a bitter film satire of the television news industry, *Network*, made the deranged newsreader Howard Beale, played by

Peter Finch, into a cultural icon.[40] In the film's narrative, Beale's outbursts on the nightly news make his struggling broadcaster a national phenomenon. Encouraged by a cynical ratings-obsessed executive (Faye Dunaway), he goes viral, after the fashion of the day. His madman's wail over the airwaves—"I'm as mad as hell! And I'm not going to take this anymore!"—becomes a rallying cry of the fed up and pissed off. People begin shouting the mantra out of their apartment windows, joining together in a communal paroxysm of ineffectual rage.

You could draw several morals from this scenario. Perhaps it is a prescient view of our media-addled present, the anger and confusion all channelled into anonymous yelling. It might also be considered a sad commentary on the heedless pursuit of ratings that makes news of society's most offensive aspects and people. But I think it communicates, too, a strong basic frustration that only grows by the day. Why is there so much perfidy, corruption, and intolerance in a world capable of solving complex problems? Why are dishonesty and grifting so conspicuously rewarded when we all know it when we see it?

Perhaps this is simply the human condition? Yes, certainly. But we are also meant for higher and finer things, to use some old-fashioned language, and may be guided by what Abraham Lincoln called "the better angels of our nature." The first step along that path is taking some other lines of Howard Beale's and making them our new by-words. First: "I'm a human being, goddammit! My life has value!" And then, maybe even more important: "I'm all out of bullshit!"

We're used to calling bullshit on other people, other systems, the media, politicians, scientists—maybe even, like Howard, on life itself. There is great pleasure to be had here, of self-righteous justification. The pleasures can even become, as I suggest, addictive. But maybe we've become all too used to the reactive exercise of the call. I mean, the last thing I or anyone else could desire is *less* genuine scrutiny on the pools of power.

And yet, we must confront the possibility that performative distrust has extended too far and become its own reward. Such performances are quickly revealed as self-defeating, but along the way cast doubt on more genuine versions of the task. A good tool badly used blunts its own effect for jobs where it's needed most. The stakes are high. Our vulnerabilities get no better, our states of crisis no less obvious. We need the right tools, set to work in the right places.

Trust remains the most essential of all social technologies. It makes all other human—and posthuman—projects possible. Maybe the time has come for us to call bullshit on ourselves. Question authority? Yes, certainly. But that must include, in fact must begin with, looking in the mirror. We understand that the project of justice takes the form of large-scale conditional proposition, an overarching relation of *if* to *then*. If we want a stable and equitable world, then we will need the virtues of liberal democracy. If we want public discourse that contributes to these goals, we will have to accept reasonableness in argument and strive for rationality as well as feeling in our consciousness. There is no end to this work. The infinite task of justice starts with you and me, right here, right now. What good habits can we, against all inclination, form to edge out the toxic ones? How can we be more like real people, good players, trustworthy citizens? How far can we throw ourselves? Let's find out.

Before It Questions You

I

Says Who?

I BEGIN WITH A DELIBERATE provocation: *we are all addicted*. Everyone knows it; and yet we conspire to isolate this truth by pathologizing extreme versions of a basic human condition and seeing only those extremes as proper subjects for treatment. But addictive behaviour is far more widespread than our common ways of thinking and talking allow. Whether it's drugs, alcohol, work, weight-loss programs, shopping, online videos, gossip, gambling, apps, comic books, at-home delivery, or new phones—anything, really, that the heart desires—we can't seem to calm a relentless inner urge, a longing that will not be satisfied. It will only be renewed, with new levels of toxicity enabled by tolerance. That relentless death spiral may simply be the nature of desire, at least as it emerges in modern projects of individual identity. The absence of desire is death. But what if our desires themselves prove the death of us?

The least visible but perhaps most harmful addiction of all is *thinking ourselves right*. As I noted in the introduction, this particular form of cognitive dependency is something we may style *addiction to conviction*, what I call *doxaholism*. The simple definition of the condition is

47

this: harmful craving for and attachment to loud, divisive, and identity-conferring opinion. The *dox* prefix here comes from the Greek word for opinion, *doxa*, and is therefore a different derivation than *doxing*, the public internet shaming or vilification of individuals you dislike. As most readers will know, that usage comes from "dropping docs," shortened to indicate public display of any identifying or, sometimes but not necessarily, incriminating personal documents—these days often labelled "receipts."[1]

The two "dox" roots conjoin in practice by way of aggressive public campaigns of hatred, targeting, intimidation, deplatforming, and cancelling. Virulent opinion becomes the basis for a targeted cancelling campaign. Not all doxing carries this attendant energy of condemnation and shaming, and sometimes there are legitimate reasons for publicly identifying a bad actor, especially online. But the basic drive to expose is an unstable property: one person's self-righteous exposure is another person's public shaming. Doxing of any kind is relatively rare; doxaholism is, by contrast, more basic, widespread, and dangerous. It is grounded in forms of thinking that exhibit an aggressive combination of inclusion and exclusion. The inclusive part has to do with shared values and purposes: a kind of tribalism that by turns becomes aggressively exclusive, even punishing, of those who fall outside the enchanted circle of identity. The doubled movement—we are the in-crowd, therefore everyone else is the enemy—has no fixed ideological home. It is not a proprietary technology of left over right or believer over atheist. We can see such tribal acting out as, instead, an expression of Gemeinschaft—the sense of close-knit community that answers a deep human need for "kinship, blood relationship, feudal ties, social hierarchy, deference, honour, and friendship." Traditionally, this form of close social bond is contrasted with the ties of Gesellschaft—society in a larger, impersonal sense, held together by laws and transactions.[2]

Both kinds of association have their appeal. One way to sketch the polarities of the current moment is to note that *gemeinschaftlich* claims seem to dominate public discourse, underpinning both the overt gangsterism of the Trump-MAGA cabal and the sometimes-violent groupthink of leftist identity politics. Both factions see the looser ties of liberal society, with its abstract conventions for dealing with fellow citizens as strangers rather than friends, as leading to isolation, anomie, and widespread passive aggression—punctuated now and then by brutal outbursts of actual aggression. Both options in turn fail, I think, if they are seen as strict either-or choices. Social isolation is real in complex societies, but ties of blood and belief are not the answer. I suggest that the way to navigate between the poles of extremism is to likewise track a middle course between the comfort (but implicit violence) of the close community tie and the separation (but potential despair) of the open-ended society. In a sense, we are in the situation of Schopenhauer's proverbial porcupines: huddling together for warmth and survival, but only so far that their spines do not pierce each other.[3]

Somewhat unexpectedly, destructive certainty functions in inverse proportion to the degree of trust we vest in traditional institutions: government, media, science, and scholarship. The more we find standard sources of authority wanting, the likelier we are to react by reversing polarity and finding sanction in conspiracy theories, fringe political movements, and perhaps worst of all, generalized attention-fracturing distraction. Our distrust is toxic not because it is unwarranted but because it is rootless. What starts as valuable questioning of external authority quickly pivots to internal certainty, or maybe was centred there all the time. I mean that we become accustomed to the smugness and arrogance that attends sure knowledge of our personal correctness. The appeal of critical conviction is thus self-proving and heady: its pleasures create demand for new stimulus of the same kind. And so, a spiral into an altered consciousness.

This form of addiction is politically system-wide, an unintended consequence of Enlightenment rationalism and the self-affirming perspective of ethical individualism. It has been a long time in the making, but its influence has never been stronger than now, when an unstable neoliberal consensus, toxic in its own right, has collapsed into a chaos of crippling short memory, myopic presentism, constant attention-demanding urgencies, and a burgeoning market for tech-harvested attention-economy eyeballs. This diseased attachment to conviction is the central feature of a society based on arousing desires that remain insatiable by design. This is what we can label an addictogenic society.

"Men of convictions are prisoners," Nietzsche proclaimed with his own brand of certainty in *The Antichrist* (1895, sec. 54). "They do not see far enough, they do not see what is *below* them: whereas a man who would talk to any purpose about value and non-value must be able to see five hundred convictions *beneath* him—and *behind* him.... A mind that aspires to great things, and that wills the means thereto, is necessarily skeptical." I quote this as one should quote anything: because I agree with the sentiment and hope that you will too. But there can be no assumption of its validity just because of a famous name's presence. After all—Nietzsche! Didn't he go mad from syphilis? And wasn't he just another prisoner of his own certainty, a high-toned, welcome-to-my-vision conviction convict himself?

Well, maybe. Some reputable people believe that the charge of madness was a slander perpetuated by his sister, or even a romantic stand-in trope for his genius. Perhaps he had a brain tumour. He certainly wrote and acted plenty crazy, if the historical record is to be trusted. Sobbing at the sight of a tortured horse in Turin! Those crackpot letters from the asylum! But whatever the truth of his alleged madness, you can and must decide for yourself whether Nietzsche counts as good authority, on this or any other question.

Now, some important caveats on my provocation. Medical practitioners will tell you that addiction is the wrong framework to employ when it comes to belief, trust, and authority. Its metaphorical usefulness is impaired when applied too widely, they argue. Unless a condition or behaviour involves substance use disorder, potential withdrawal, and harmful dependence, a condition of perpetual craving should not be called addiction. And of course, it is true that you won't find doxaholism in the *Diagnostic and Statistical Manual*. But other discourses, including social psychology, will argue that *addictive behaviour* is a valid wider category—and a necessary one. Not all harmful obsessions involve chemical substances, even if they all play out in dopamine cascades and the chaotic firing of neurons.

Social media, fashion, gossip, and adventure all count as occasions for addictive behaviour. So, too, does the feeling of being right. As a philosopher, then, I want to extend the thought one step further: addictions of all degrees and kinds are everywhere in society, may even be a defining feature of cultural life under conditions of techno-capitalism. By 2024, the standard authorities were starting to catch up to arguments that social critics had been making for some time, especially about the health dangers of overexposure to screens. In June, the surgeon general of the United States, Vivek Murthy, who had earlier flagged social isolation and loneliness as illness factors in modern life, came out hard against TikTok, Instagram, and X. He called for warning labels to be attached to social media use, as with cigarettes or alcohol.[4]

That is no more than a beginning. Warning labels themselves, however gruesome (the ones on Canadian cigarette packages are gross), do not cure addiction or regulate sales. And it is easy to see the platforms themselves, like the chemical drugs, as the main culprits of social disease. But this is short-sighted. Even in purely physical addiction, the mental aspects of substance-use disorder are often paramount. This is all the more true in addiction to ways of thinking and acting. I will address more details of ideological and cognitive addiction in part 5, together with some ideas for recovery. To get there, we must first engage in some philosophical spadework. Begin by supposing that addiction to conviction is a real thing, and a real threat. I find this claim obvious myself, but I will not simply assert it and hope you agree. So let us rather call the notion of doxaholism a provisional thought, a contingent premise. Since trust is the crux of the issue before us, this provision will prove necessary as well as useful as we go along. We have to stand somewhere in order to see anything; that's the point.

Perhaps we can also agree that conviction addiction, natural or manufactured, begins in something valuable and hard won. I mean the ability to challenge received wisdom, to question authority. How could that ever be bad? Well, precisely because, in common with many stimulants, conviction's many self-destructive perversions only become obvious through overreliance, harmful application, and thoughtless repetition. No addictive behaviour begins with harm being more prominent than genuine appeal. The problem drinker starts life, or the evening, as a charming social tippler, a cocktail savant. Fentanyl does take the pain away. New clothes and devices absolutely make us feel more in control of our insecure self-presentation. The once trusty and elegant walking stick is only later revealed as a debilitating crutch.

We don't set out in search of things that are not worth having; even addicts don't seek the harmful *as* the harmful. Rather, our brains become accustomed to positive experiences that are harmful in the long term but also, in the near term, have the insidious quality of generating new and deeper desires. The addict is not *in error* about his or her first-order desires; the mind wants what it wants. The flaw lies, instead, in misalignment between those baseline desires and second-order desires about what is good for us.[5]

To see our special predicament within this tangle of good intentions and runaway reasons, imagine a hazy but telling snapshot of what used to be called a *cultural contradiction of late capitalism*. I prefer a simpler term here: this is a structural paradox, an ideological irony, nestled deep in human thinking. The caption on the imagined postcard would be something like this: "Question authority? It's a New Millennium nightmare! (Be glad you're not here.)" Once a noble reformer's task, critical social theory in all its aspects has sired a cascading crisis of trust. Nobody believes in anybody anymore, no matter their qualifications, experience, judgment, or wisdom. Reason itself has been attacked, undermined by the applications of reason. Enlightenment values destroyed! Democracy in ruins! Convenient truth! Alternate facts! Postmodern death spiral!

This is hardly a fanciful picture—not even the last bit, if you're one of those people who likes to yell at your phone, argue with your television, or pound angrily on your keyboard. According to recent critics on the political right, those who once called authority into question are now the ones who won't abide any challenge to their own diktats. This cabal of radical control freaks, they say, includes public health scientists; race-conscious educators; advocates for diversity, equity, and inclusiveness, "DEI" as it is usually styled; and those who want their choices of self-presentation and pronouns accepted.

There is of course a serious free-speech challenge in play, set against claims of respect and personal autonomy. And many of us find ourselves increasingly impatient with notions that (say) being on time is a racist construct, that the words "classroom" and "respect" call for suspicious inverted commas, or that Ovid, Rousseau, and Freud need trigger warnings when taught at university.[6] Moreover, these causes can seem trivial as set against existential threats of an altogether larger scale and severity like climate change and nuclear holocaust.

Even so, the hypocrisy of the language-is-violence radicals now policing public utterances and vocabulary is obvious, at least according to the critical-theory-snowflake busters. Campus speech codes? Lists of offensive phrases? Surely this is Orwell's Newspeak conveyed in faculty memos and community-centre press releases. The social-justice awakeners of yesterday, those great revealers of hidden power, have become the groupthink autocrats and activists of today, wielding vast cultural powers of indoctrination, mind control, and—you know—maybe actual viruses. Now radical left thinking allegedly causes everything from unmade beds and gay rodeo to Silicon Valley bank failures and failed beer campaigns! Tainted water turns people trans just like frogs! Vaccine mandates are designed to track your DNA and steal your identity!

But wait—isn't this critical line of thought itself just a way of shadowing the current arrangement, leaving existing power structures firmly in place by repelling criticism like a flesh-eating virus? Wealth gaps keep yawning wider, power ever pools in more and more concentrated eddies, discrimination based on race, gender, and all levers of daily violence rises with inexorable momentum. Right-wing populist movements, often aggressively nationalist, are ascendant in Italy, France, Poland, Ukraine, Sweden, Finland, and Holland. "Free speech" is just the smokescreen of runaway new-era profit making. Right?

In 1980, wealth inequality in the developed world was still near postwar lows. Since then, the wealth of the top 0.01 percent has grown at a rate roughly five times that of the population overall. Though there was a slight dip in wealth inequality in 2022, possibly as a result of Covid-related shakeouts, today the very rich are very much richer. In Europe and the United States, the wealthiest 10 percent of the population controls between 67 and 69 percent of the wealth, while the bottom half of adults possess only 1.2 percent. (Canada is slightly more egalitarian: that same two-thirds of wealth is held by the top 20 percent, north of the border.) Meanwhile, people consistently report both a wish for a far more even distribution *and* a perception of equality far greater than reality.[7]

And so, we might be inclined to conclude that Enlightenment universals of equality and respect are revealed as just fancy displays of mummery and legerdemain. "Democracy" is no more than a cynical sham, at least when it comes to power and associated influence! In fact, more and more, power adopts the bland face of easy money! Dim-witted or vindictive bullies everywhere are winning by pretending they are scions of freedom and decency!

In sum, once a sour attitude takes hold about "the state of things," it can easily begin to seem as though the trans athletes are coming for all your medals and children, Covid czar Anthony Fauci is secretly planning to become a global overlord via vax-tracking algorithms, pizza joints front for child-trafficking rings, and critical race theory will soon enforce the brainwashing of white guilt into everyone, perhaps via *Manchurian Candidate*–style garden parties. The appropriate response must be to ban all the "gay books," cut your race-history courses, deny the validity of science, and maybe randomly stab some defenceless philosophers of sexuality.[8]

I'm being facetious, but everyone knows that much more serious and divisive conviction-backed battlelines can easily be reported. As I write this, for example, a rhetorical and ideological war is raging, on websites and college campuses, alongside an actual one in the growing piles of rubble that once were Gaza. The brutal Israeli military response to the Hamas-led terrorist attack of October 7, 2023, remains in full swing as thousands starve and die of their wounds. But so does the escalating war of words, the bitter brawls of claim and counter-claim, the incessant demands for moral clarity, the high-pitched illiberal insistence on certainty and agreement.

Consider just one concrete instance. In April of 2024 the freedom-of-expression organization PEN America, long criticized for what its detractors considered a lukewarm response to the violent Israeli counterstrikes, was forced to cancel a tony annual literary festival. A number of high-profile authors, nominated for PEN literary awards, had already withdrawn from the event, causing a ripple of refusal. "PEN America states that 'the core' of its mission is to 'support the right to disagree,'" the defecting nominees stated in an open letter. "But among writers of conscience, there is no disagreement. There is fact and fiction. The fact is that Israel is leading a genocide of the Palestinian people."[9]

Really? That's a *fact*, and *all else* is fiction? And so there can be *no disagreement* here? Or, more precisely, any pretence of disagreement indicates—by definition—that you are not a "writer of conscience"? Is that freedom of expression? Even if we choose to take no fixed position on the tragedy in Gaza—possibly resisting angry calls that we do so—we ought still to insist that reasonable people can disagree. For instance, over whether a given sequence of events constitutes a *genocide*—which is not simply identical with the loss of civilian life—or whether a violent surprise attack on a music festival constitutes armed resistance. To object to quick and definitive characterizations is not wishy-washy neutralism, or soft acquiescence to power. It is simply rational judgment in action. The assumed value of that kind of judgment is a cornerstone of all pluralistic societies.[10]

Asserting this kind of principled rationality can be extremely difficult, as we have seen. The Gaza war has all the usual moral imponderables of all human conflict, but with head-spinning superadditions of spectacle, distrust of fact, and cultural nostalgia. The violent protests that roiled university campuses in the spring of 2024 were endlessly compared to those of the 1980s over apartheid and of the 1960s over the Vietnam war. There was more than a hint in these events of what Mordecai Richler called *issue envy*: the desire to replicate distant violence closer to home, to assuage the nagging feeling that *life is elsewhere*. This was Richler's wry assessment of the motives behind the Front de libération du Québec, whose separatist fervour led to kidnapping and murder in the October Crisis of 1970. It was also, perhaps less forgivably, the essence of the charge he levelled against the figure of a "self-advertised Black militant" in Canadian literature, who in effect borrowed grievance to boost a lack of talent.[11]

Cultural nostalgia is a powerful driver of conviction, and probably inevitable: nothing political can ever be done for the first time. The relevant felt distance can be temporal as well as spatial, a particular species of FOMO anxiety that especially afflicts the youngs. This is graphically evident in our media-saturated age. Participants in the 2024 pro-Palestine protests could not avoid enacting a somewhat simulacral scene, rife with play-acting and imitation—pejoratively labelled "cosplay" by right-wing trolls—all of it captured and distributed on smartphone cameras. It is cynical, maybe, but not entirely incorrect to suggest that the occupiers of student spaces might have been more easily dispersed by disrupting their cell coverage than by the use of flash-bang grenades and advancing police cordons.[12]

But I also want to say, and not just as someone who used to go on marches and engage in public protests, too, let's remember that really *everything in life is cosplay.* The ideological right's repetition of this label as an insult-du-jour is incoherent as well as juvenile. It joins other intended insults that suggest fragility, ignorance, or play-acting on the left: "pantomime," "snowflake," and even old-fashioned phrases like "libtard" and "useful idiot"—though employing those latter ones these days would date a critic as surely as "comrade" or "fellow-traveler." Dressing up in conformist or wishful accessories is not the province— or the vice—of the young alone. The longstanding gay-pride jibe that a business suit is just another form of drag—something that was made painfully evident in the top-view-only Zoom calls of the pandemic era—receives a new twist. You cannot evade the demands and the ironies of self-presentation. Even normcore is a chosen *style.*

In the swirl of political controversy, then, a costume offers a form of membership and solidarity that should not be disdained too readily— especially when one's own costumes are just as conventional and objectively bizarre. (I say that as someone who now and then wears a long blue gown with matching hood and repeats long sentences in Latin.) It is said that all politics are identity politics. This is true because politics is a way of asking who counts and what we want to achieve together. But the real question is, can you look beyond your own particular tribes and costumes and recognize the underlying value of someone who looks different? That undertaking begins with a kind of existential act of recognition, to insist that the pertinent question of human life is always, as James Baldwin had it, not what I am but who I am.[13]

The barriers arrayed against this transcendent move, so basic to the project of shared flourishing, are legion. Ignorance is one, and that doesn't just mean failing to know which river and which sea are referenced in a chant. It also means, worse, the ignorance of indifference, of making not-caring a mode of being in the world. Sadly, sometimes mocking the enemy becomes the basis of one's own identity, such that a scarf, a hat, or a haircut may be deployed as the sign of political allegiance simply by being visibly different from something—any-thing—else. "Diversity" shifts from an obvious good to a rigid ideology *even as* opposition to that rigidity offers its own contrarian identity.

The central point is this: there is no apolitical baseline available here, no common-sense stance that avoids or simply ignores the costs and burdens of politics. "Everything is political" and "the personal is political" are slogans that are often associated with the left, but in fact they apply across the board. The reason I am focusing on trust and authority in these pages is precisely because these aspects of shared life, inescapable to all of us, stand as the most basic political issues we know. These issues lie at the foundations of any society. Up close, in the day-to-day fray of controversy, it can be hard to separate ideas from ideologies and principles from posturing.

The granny-knotted narratives of war protest, pandemic response, fraud investigations, and judicial bias—to name just the most obvious few at the moment of writing—are the staple tales of a larger political condition. The pat divisions and deliberate misunderstandings that dominate here can be found repeated like religious incantations on mainstream media—the only place you will these days still see the word *woke*, grown vacant to the point of self-parody. (The one possible exception is the French variant, *le wokisme*, which indicates a specific brand of sneering about fashionable American politics.)[14]

But underneath the surface of disagreement, everyone is still engaged in some halting version of what John Stuart Mill called "experiments in living." Late-model variants of this program of liberal experimentation—"multiple subject positions" or "identity fluidity" or just "traditional manners"—are just ways of keeping the project alive to new flexibilities in law, custom, and culture. More power to them, to all of us with the power and burden of choice. Aristotle: "Hence choice is either reason motivated by desire, or desire operating through reason, and such an origin of action is a human being" (*Nicomachean Ethics* 6.2).

The contemporary version of this project needs to be framed carefully, however, and must keep its liberal foundation in plain view. By mid-2024, amid the chaos of campus protests and US congressional hearings to berate university administrators, the repeal of DEI regulations was underway, buoyed by statistics about their ineffectiveness and quick decline into performance and punishment. "Diversity statements" on academic job applications, for example, might as well be written by chatbots, so boilerplate had they become. And so top-ranking universities began quietly expunging them from application requirements just a few scant years after implementing them with great fanfare.

The right's basic indictment had been, from the start, that DEI "mobs" had overwhelmed academia and the media—the presumptive soft targets and promulgators of left-wing ideological performance—but then also politics, government, banking, and even science, the last redoubt of assumed rationality. But was it really so, if you looked closely? Or was that just a handy right-wing talking point—and incidentally a lucrative way for some people to establish their own conservative politics of identity? *Contrarian* is an ambidextrous label, as well as a grandiose one when self-applied.[15]

Amidst all this to-ing and fro-ing, the crucial puzzle remained in play. Just *how* did a campaign of principled distrust of power and its bland bureaucratic expansion turn into a system-wide cult of overt "repressive tolerance"—if that is, in fact, what it did?[16] I remain skeptical about *both* the assumed success of ideological overthrow in the first place *and* the announced triumphal reversion to "common sense."

Both kinds of ideologues—revolutionaries and reactionaries alike—promise freedom. But for whom, defined how, and at what cost?

Let's take new stock, lest we find ourselves overcome by endless perplexity. The leftist critics were right to attack the false choices offered by competing consumer brands, for opting for one enchained identity over another equally bogus one. But what comes in place of those debased ideas of emancipation, aspiration reduced to shopping preferences—which can be predicted by a midlevel data-harvesting algorithm anyway? *Freedom* is now a free-floating signifier, an all-purpose rallying cry, an empty shell of a word that can still move people to violence. It might even be, in this vacuous form, its own kind of addictive substance: motivating, crave-worthy, producing undeniable highs but somehow never enough to satisfy an inner need. It is that need which lies at the heart of our current inquiry.

Whom do you trust as we stumble to the end of the twenty-first century's first quarter? Your friends? Your family? God? Science? No one? We are often advised, in elite humanities departments and on wackadoodle conspiracist podcasts alike, to *question question question* authority. But is obeying that command possible? Even if we do push back on power, we know that overactive distrust leads to a dangerous endgame of broken institutions: politics, media, religion, science, expertise itself are all more suspect than ever. Should we complain about that? Fear it? Fix it? Or is the real problem within us?

The result of applying critical thinking to your own thinking is not a "herd of independent minds," the much-mocked fashionable conformity, nor is it lock-step suspicion of everything going. It is, instead, a willing, and potentially just, civil society of disputatious freethinkers. Let us dwell together in doubt, guided by its companion cognitive virtue, humility. Because this is the only solution to a crisis of authority. And this requires reflection on our own stories, how we come to be the political actors we are.[17]

* * *

THE FIRST TIME I SAW a bumper sticker bearing the message *Question Authority* I thought it was a joke. *Says who?* I said to myself, possibly signalling a nascent interest in logic as well as irony. I was fifteen years old, and I did a fair bit of ironic logic in those days, not always appreciated. I'm fairly certain this tiny moment of comic political awareness happened along a street in Winnipeg's Osborne Village, then as now a defiant strip of self-conscious grooviness in an otherwise bland Prairie city. Some aging hippie, I thought, parked in front of the single rattan boutique or artisanal hand-thrown pottery emporium between Oakville and Vancouver. I continued on my weekly walk over to Portage Avenue, past the perpetual fey sprint of the Golden Boy pinnacle at the provincial legislature to the hobby shops and science fiction bookstores that were my real destination.

"Question authority" had been a familiar slogan for years by the time it entered my limited ken, often associated with the renegade psychiatrist Timothy Leary, a man vaguely familiar to me and my friends from semi-mystifying parodies in *Mad* magazine, the font of much of our immature and thoroughly inaccurate cultural savvy. We knew Dr Leary advocated drug use, specifically LSD, the pinnacle of exotic consciousness-expansion.

It may be hard to recall, in our present days of respectable microdosing and state-sanctioned prescription psychotropics, that Leary's doors-of-perception view, rooted in the writing of Aldous Huxley, Thomas De Quincey, and Bishop Berkeley, was radical to the point of criminality. Jim Morrison's band, the Doors, styled after Huxley's "doors of perception," was not my own chosen music—it belonged to those a half-generation older—but even as a nerdy kid, an air-force brat with too much time on my hands, I appreciated the general project of an outlaw metaphysics combining political resistance with getting a little sideways.

"Question authority" wasn't really meant ironically, either. Or at least the irony was folded into the serious, surface-level intent of the imperative. This was obvious in the variations on the theme that would become popular: Question authority before it questions you. Question authority, but you may not like the answer. Question authority, but not your mother. (I have used some of these as titles for the parts of the present book.) Questioning authority is good, maybe essential, for a thriving polity. Critical attention to the settled structures of power is the right and duty of every citizen. Any other condition is either authoritarianism or a propensity to apathy, a kind of self-anaesthetization.

I want to be careful not to signal too dismal a message. We are all familiar, maybe to the point of disgust or despair, with the conditions of social life that allow for *soft autocracy*. I mean the combination of addictive and sanity-distorting effects of social media immersion, lack of transparency in government, inescapable effects of big-tech edgelords, and the growing distrust in all institutions from science and medicine to media and religion. And, coming up swiftly from behind, or perhaps on our exposed attention-economy flank, are various crises of our own recent making: climate change, runaway artificial intelligence, nuclear weapons, and life-altering pandemics. Authority is here at once demanded and undermined: a toxic spiral.

In part because "Question Authority" proved so popular, and sounded such a vibrant note, its companion sentiment has often been overlooked. It is this: "Think for Yourself." Like "Question Authority," this companion phrase carries with it a repeated measure of self-inflicted irony: *Oh yeah?* we might respond. *You're not the boss of me!* Thinking for yourself, as we will see throughout the details and cases that follow, is among the hardest tasks a human intelligence can set itself. The two commands taken together were Leary's gift to public discourse. And in a time of relentless distribution of what are known as "memes" (they aren't really—more on that later too), that's not

too shabby for a disgraced Harvard psychiatrist who had his life lam-
pooned in *Mad* magazine—even accepting that some people would
have considered that, at the time, a countercultural win.

One could refer to these as "infinite imperatives." The phrase captures the inflection of irony or paradox that they contain: how can I
logically follow a command that tells me to challenge all commands, or
to be directed only by my own reasoning? But in common with some
other logical paradoxes, they are not really impossible when regarded
in the right light: their apparent contradiction reveals a logical tangle
or problem that requires a lateral cognitive move. Or, maybe better,
impossible imperatives may possess something of the fruitful energy,
the dialectical electricity, of other even more obviously paradoxical
imperatives. My own favourite of these dates from the uprising that
rocked Paris to its intellectual foundations in May 1968—the year I
turned five. *Soyez réalistes, demandez l'impossible*, the Soixante-Huitard
revolutionaries commanded, often in spray-painted graffiti. "Be realistic, demand the impossible!" We can hear in that playful command
an echo of James Baldwin's tart assessment about all activism and
the structures of power: "Those who say it can't be done are usually
interrupted by others doing it."[18]

These sentiments then belong among other apparently impossible
imperatives. I mean such familiar authenticity-driven commands as
"Be yourself" and "Just act naturally," which make their execution
even more tricky. Compare "Calm down" or "Take it easy," imperative
offerings likely to have the opposite practical effect of their semantic
intention.[19] But these performative and logical tangles are signs of
hope: the seemingly impossible may merely be the infinite. *Just be
yourself!*[20]

2

Sapere Aude

CONSIDER "THINK FOR YOURSELF" AS a necessary adjunct to "question authority." It remains the less-often recalled of Leary's two slogans, and I think the reason for that is clear. However difficult it might prove to question authority, or even how dangerous it is in practice, the project of thinking for oneself is comprehensive to the point of system failure. What could it mean? How am I even going to start, when I know already that my intellectual resources, however much I cherish them, are limited and ultimately powerless against the forces of the world, including the forces of stupidity?

I also know that I myself can be deluded, sloppy, misled, misinformed, blinded by prejudice, or all of those at once. Worse, I further know that mere awareness of these curbs on thinking is insufficient to solve the problems they set up. Reason is aware of limits it cannot overcome. I can know that my thinking is flawed, and even know exactly *how* it is flawed, without having any rational resources to address those flaws effectively. There is movement but no traction: as Wittgenstein said, the engine is roaring but the gears are not engaged.

This straitened condition might put us in mind of what is some-times referred to as Rumsfeld's square or, even better, Rumsfeld's matrix. You may recall that, during a 2002 media briefing in the run-up to the allied invasion of Iraq, Donald Rumsfeld, then American secretary of defence, was being quizzed on a factual matter, an issue of knowledge that would determine a great deal of life and death, not to mention oil interests, regional influence, and global power: did Saddam Hussein's Iraq regime possess weapons of mass destruction—biological and nuclear devices capable of destabilizing the Middle East and the planet? Rumsfeld offered this much-quoted response, possibly recalling an introductory philosophy lecture at Princeton, or maybe while orienteering his way to becoming an Eagle Scout: "Reports that say that something hasn't happened are always interesting to me," Rumsfeld profsplained to gathered reporters, peering over his glasses, "because as we know, there are known knowns; there are things we know we know. We also know there are known unknowns; that is to say, we know there are some things we do not know. But there are also unknown unknowns—the ones we don't know we don't know. And ... it is the latter category that tends to be the difficult one."

The statement was hailed as a brilliant summation of a complex epistemological problem, which it isn't really. It was a handy pre-fabricated justification for a war based on damning evidence that was never found. The phrasing was pithy, though, and the category of *unknown unknowns* quickly became a buzz-phrase for everything from unintended effects in urban planning to the mysteries of human consciousness. More striking, to my mind anyway, was a response that highlighted human unconsciousness. It was offered by the Slo-venian critic and philosopher Slavoj Žižek, then widely known as popularizer and interpreter of the psychoanalytic ideas pioneered by Jacques Lacan. Rumsfeld's square, Žižek pointed out, has by its own logic a missing quadrant. If the two variables are known and

unknown, crossing them must generate a fourth category not mentioned by Rumsfeld: that is, the *unknown knowns*. But what could
this possibly mean?[21]

One doesn't have to be a Lacanian psychoanalyst to see the answer:
unknown knowns are the things we take for granted, the buried presuppositions of thought that remain covered over by habit, procedure,
and protocol that ward off self-reflection. As Freud said about the
uncanny—unheimlich—"the prefix *un* is the token of repression."
The unknown, like the uncanny, undead, and unconscious, functions
by way of familiar strangeness, revealing and concealing, hidden in
plain sight.

This is the realm of *ideology*, in other words. I offer the term in
the critical-theory sense, to mean not just a body of ideas or platform
planks, but those taken-for-granted, sublimated notions that govern
thought and action. Here the Marxist tradition of critical thought is
psychoanalytically updated. Ideology is a barrier to clear thinking just
because it flourishes within the misdirected gaze of everydayness,
working by way of accepted presuppositions that seem to lie naturally—but are, in fact, deposited deliberately—in a region of thought
considered "beyond question" because obviously natural, just the way
things are, or merely common sense.

All of these signs or tokens of taken-for-grantedness, such gestures
of dismissal to render things out of court, should set off alarm bells
in the questioning critical mind. Everybody knows! People say! But
not so fast. Which people? Who is everybody, and what do they really
want or believe? In typical accounts of knowledge, we search diligently
for the truth out there in the world of experience, something whose
attainment is perhaps hard but nevertheless clearly in view. Yet we also
acknowledge that the search for truth is always hampered by our own
ignorance. This is even better—epistemic humility is in the spirit of the
Socratic doctrina ignorantia. That doctrine doesn't celebrate ordinary
ignorance; rather, it reminds us that the wisest among us are, as the

Oracle of Delphi showed, those who know that they don't know. We can even update this doctrine *à la* Rumsfeld: not only should I know *that* I don't know, but I ought to know that I don't know *what* I don't know.

That all seems quite difficult but also quite comprehensible. But now what about what I secretly know, hidden even from myself? What do I assume, replicate, take in stride, depend upon, consider merely natural or obvious? This, too, is knowledge but deliberately suppressed, made unknown and potentially unknowable without some kind of intervention. We know that intervention is the critique of ideology, and it will figure largely in any account of questioning authority and thinking for oneself. But such critique will be difficult, and much within us will resist the knowledge of what we know but prefer not to know.

In the 1988 John Carpenter film *They Live*, starring Canadian wrestling legend "Rowdy" Roddy Piper, we see the problem of known unknowns vividly presented. For those who have not yet had the pleasure of viewing what novelist Jonathan Lethem calls "probably the stupidest film ever to take ideology as its explicit subject," yet according to others is the coolest schlock-horror film to do so, here is a précis: A handsome nameless drifter (Piper, "Nada" in the credits) arrives in a bleak neoliberal wasteland—otherwise known as 1980s Los Angeles—and begins to do day work on a construction site. He is befriended by a fellow worker, Frank, played by Keith David, making this also a biracial buddy movie. Via a series of coincidences, Nada discovers that the Earth has been secretly colonized by alien invaders, styled as "Ghouls" because of their ghastly appearance. Some of the earthlings are in on this conspiracist, sly, hostile takeover, but most of the humans are lulled into a blithe acceptance of reality as they perceive it: the usual empty promises and aspirational come-ons of consumer capitalism.[22]

The reality, of course, is darker—literally, as in black and white rather than colour. A small resistance group is busy manufacturing pairs of oversized Wayfarer sunglasses that allow wearers to perceive the truth: the Ghoul colonization is almost complete, and those signs promising relaxing vacations and shiny durables are in fact what would later be recognizable as Shepard Fairey–style commands: OBEY, CONSUME, STAY ASLEEP, REWARD INDIFFERENCE, MARRY, and of course DO NOT QUESTION AUTHORITY. The pivot of the film—apart from Piper's rousing bank-robbery scene, where he ad-libs a line about kicking butt and chewing bubble gum—is the absurdly extended fight scene between Nada and buddy Frank, because the latter does not want to put on the ideology-busting Ray-Bans.

Why not? Surely the truth shall set us free! Wouldn't we all want to don these glasses as quickly as possible, to see what is really going on around us? They produce headaches if worn for too long, it's true, but this would seem a minor hardship as set against, say, the excruciating ascent from the dark cave of ignorance to the daylight of the forms as described in Plato's Republic. But as Žižek himself points out in his analysis of the film, there is nothing more frightening than dismantling our cherished illusions. Frank stands in here for most of us, not sheeple exactly but wary of crazies with truth-revealing sunglasses, for crying out loud. And so he fights desperately to cling to his illusions, even though they obviously don't favour him, a gig-economy day labourer whose shantytown community is ever subject to bulldozing by the municipal authorities. But fight he does, for some seven minutes of increasingly bizarre screen time. He won't put on the glasses! He won't. He won't!

Well, eventually he does—and thank God, because otherwise there is no further action in the movie. Together, Nada and Frank take on Ghoul forces and make some small resistant moves to dispel the ideological self-deception of a populace that would rather wallow in immiserating illusion than face the truth of their own delusion. Okay, stupid, cool, or both, I don't care. This is a landmark popular film about the dangers and prospects of what we must identify as the general philosophical-political project of *seeing-through*. The prospects and dangers of such seeing-through constitute a major theme in our present considerations, subjects to which we will return again and again.

And, even more important for present purposes, the dramatic arc of the film, such as it is, shows us that there is an essential precondition to kick-ass thinking for oneself, one that Leary does not mention—and it's not bubble gum. The precondition is courage, and the good news is that a much better philosopher than Leary has considered the problem long before him. Žižek, meanwhile, is content to style himself as a kind of philosophical madman, almost a Dada artist of political discourse. "Liberals always say about totalitarians that they like humanity, as such, but they have no empathy for concrete people, no?" he said to one interviewer. "OK, that fits me perfectly. Humanity? Yes, it's OK—some great talks, some great arts. Concrete people? No, 99% are boring idiots." (There's the real 1% for you: smarty-pants philosophers.)[23]

* * *

IMMANUEL KANT'S ESSAY "WHAT IS Enlightenment?", first published in 1784 as *Beantwortung der Frage: Was ist Aufklärung?* is a stand-alone popular work. Composed by the thinker best known for much more elaborate and ponderous tomes, it is an exemplary piece of popular writing. The text, whose full title indicates that it is an attempt to answer its named central question, appeared in the December issue of *Berlinische Monatsschrift* (Berlin monthly). Kant's essay was one of several replies to a challenge posed by Reverend Johann Friedrich Zöllner, a prominent cleric and politician, concerning the role of the clergy in communal life, specifically whether they should officiate marriages. Kant addressed the public and private uses of reason in the essay, but its lasting feature is a negative definition of enlightenment: "Enlightenment is man's emergence from his self-incurred immaturity [*Unmündigkeit*]."

The assumptions of what comes to be called the Enlightenment are so deeply entrenched in popular consciousness and political rhetoric today that it is worth recalling the significant controversy and profound disagreement at its centre. The Enlightenment is not a single movement, nor is it an impregnable edifice of belief and value. We make a mistake if we simply assume so-called Enlightenment values as a presumptively correct and rational basis for intellectual inquiry. We compound the error, especially today, if we deploy those values for invidious political purposes, as when critics assert that gender fluidity, or postmodern architecture, or avant-garde art are somehow aberrations from a natural human ideal.

The Enlightenment story, a sweeping account of human progress and universal verities, retains elements familiar to all. The human intellectual condition is, in the early modern period, still stunted and mired in ignorance. This is a kind of immaturity, on the model of individual callowness as a function of youth and ignorance. But age is no determiner of maturity in people, as most of us have cause to know: one may remain unmündig well past the age of majority, fighting against illumination all the way.

Significantly, Kant says that this condition of intellectual ignorance is "self-incurred." We do not lack the capacities to be grown-up thinkers; rather, we lack the will to emerge from a kind of mental adolescence. Here, the argument echoes another landmark claim about the basic problem of human self-limitation: Rousseau's resonant line from *Du contrat social; ou, Principes du droit politique* (1762) that "Man was born free but is everywhere in chains." Rousseau had added immediately an essential critical point, suggesting a program of political resistance: "Those who think themselves the masters of others are indeed greater slaves than they." We are all incarcerated, prisoners and keepers alike. As Hegel will later show with indelible vividness, the *master* emerges from analysis as enslaved as the *slave*, both bound to the conditions of their hierarchy, which diminish the freedom of all. But, amid this tangle of lordship and bondage, glimmers of open enmity are made visible—a struggle to the death that may result, finally, in a notion of shared equality. Still, it may feel considerably better to be a master than to be a slave, until the revolution comes.

Writing just before the French Revolution, a world-historical working-out of this larger dialectic, Kant focuses more on individual self-imprisonment. And when we consider the subsequent history (I won't say progress) of what comes to be called modernity, it would seem natural that Kant, not Rousseau, is the flag bearer for adult politics. At the heart of such politics stands the powerful idea of the confidently self-directed individual, who knows his or her own mind and enacts interest in the public square, even while keeping all inner thoughts and chosen paths to salvation private. The Enlightenment project's ideal rational individual thus stands as the basic premise of liberal democracy, at least as conceived and birthed on the Continent. In England, John Locke's competitive property holder, still more, Thomas Hobbes's terrified subject of implicit state-backed force, are demons that haunt the liberal imagination, which remains full of bogeymen and bugbears to our own day.

The unsettling nightshades come in all shapes and sizes. Some are selectively celebratory (Herbert Hoover's "rugged individualist," say, or Benjamin Barber's "strong democrat") while others are just as selectively insulting and reductive (the much-maligned "social justice warrior," "snowflake," or "woke activist"). All of them are figments, caricatures, rhetorical stooges deployed for specific political purposes. So far, democratic culture has proved sufficiently robust to host them all without losing its sanity. But this robustness resides largely in institutions whose validity is under challenge. Trust is brittle, not robust: first it cracks, and then it breaks. There is very little give.

The Enlightenment vision offers us the rationalist upside of liberal politics, the best-case set of mature actors all willing a valid moral law and attendant political cooperation based on reason. Or so it seems!

Under pressure of difference, and especially the force of history revealing that difference, the idealized story begins to show cracks. The
individual ethical and political actor of the liberal imagination, uni-
versalizable across human and maybe other populations, confident
of our desires and reasons, is an apparently *necessary fiction* of world
order as it emerges, haltingly, in the two centuries since.

The ever-present danger lies in forgetting the most important
insight of that short intervention, that *self-incurred* ignorance is the
hardest kind to dispel. A curious person is already a liberated person; given access to resources, she or he or they can achieve as much
emancipation and wisdom as anyone alive. But when curiosity is shut
down from the inside, imagination squelched by familiar nostrums
and well-worn prejudices, there can be no learning and hence no
maturity. The project of enlightenment lies stillborn within the closed
mind of accepted thought—otherwise known as everyday ideological
conditioning. We are forcibly reminded that the proper motto of the
Enlightenment should be this: Sapere Aude. Have the courage to think
for yourself! Or sometimes: Dare to know! Courage, daring—audacity,
even, to race the Latin into English—is the hallmark of intellectual
freedom, the only thing that will weld ideas to action, make the individual fully free, and advance the larger project of global improvement
which is pregnant in the human condition. Dare to think! Without that
courage exhibited by individuals, the entire project dies in the offing,
dead to its own bracing conditions of possibility.

We remain perpetual philosophical adolescents, however old we
grow, intellectual teenagers. The Latin tag comes from the Roman
poet Horace, in the *First Book of Letters* (20 BCE). Horace's second
letter, addressed to Lolius, at line 40 says this: "He who has begun is
half done; dare to know; begin!" The proximate story is of a foolish
man who is waiting for a stream to cease flowing before he attempts to
cross. Good luck with that. No, have the courage to think—and begin!
That may be the hardest part, really, making any kind of beginning.

Hence the need for courage, a kind of rational leap of faith. Whether this counts as another impossible imperative I leave as an open question. Translated in part as "think for yourself," I think it does. It is the recurring cry of self-reflection.[24]

René Descartes, at the beginning of the modern period in Western philosophy, outlined a related project of principled self-reflection—a Cartesian reduction—as the only reliable route to knowledge of the external world and God. We might even trace an intellectual kinship back to a very different context in Socrates's injunction that the unexamined life is not worth living. The desire for enlightenment, and the courage needed to make it real, are as basic as anything we consider part of the human condition. And yet, we fail in its execution again and again. The Enlightenment of which Kant's essay is a part—the Continental Enlightenment—must be offset not only by its wayward historical progress but also by countervailing movements. One of these is the parallel but distinct, and distinctly hard-headed, Enlightenment happening in Scotland, "the hotbed of genius." I will return to this point in a later section of this book. For now, let us spend a little time considering the implications of self-liberation through reason.

3

Trust, but Verify

THE ENLIGHTENMENT PROJECT WAS SUPPOSED to bring not only individual intellectual freedom but larger positive ends as well: central among them economic growth, technological innovation, and political emancipation. The Copernican revolution in philosophy would put subjective reason and agency at the centre of the modern universe—with some abstract room for God, perhaps, but with a relentless focus on the human mind.

This vision of rational maturity is not a kind of mental-spa model of human possibility. The ambition is much grander, for a total transformation of human society based on shared general principles of prosperity through maturity. Liberal democracy is a clear political adjunct of this desire, since in principle it grants status and agency to every rational individual regardless of ethnic origin, birthright or its lack, and personal endowment of adventitious qualities such as beauty, height, or strength, randomly distributed across human populations but powerfully weighted in individual outcomes.

Aspects of the larger project have fared well enough over the centuries, at least if viewed sub specie aeternitatis. People are generally more free than they were two centuries ago, and more groups are considered legal and ethical inliers now than formerly. Just on the basic measure of political franchise, recent history has expanded the democratic ambit to include women, Black men, and those without property, all without bringing down the scaffolding of social order. We might imagine, in the future, further expansions of legal status to non-human animals, artificial entities, and environmental features. These are already upon us in small forays under the rubric of ethical and legal standing.

A free political system seems to demand an open market economy, though the account here is harder to appreciate. We find ourselves on the far end of a global-scale experiment in neoliberal economics that has mostly had the effect of widening the gap between the wealthy and the poor, even as it immiserates millions worldwide in living conditions no better, and sometimes far worse, than those endured by our ancestors in the Middle Ages. Some 700 million people worldwide live on less than US$2.15 a day, considered the extreme poverty line. Many millions more live at or near subsistence level.

As the Earth's population passes 8.1 billion and counting, we struggle to narrow the poverty margins, especially in the face of unforeseen threats like global pandemic. Natural events, unpredictable and inevitable, are only made worse by fragile institutions and infrastructure. It is somewhat facile simply to bunch all woes into one lament about human rapacity, but at the level of individual suffering, the difference between natural and human-caused disaster is erased. Climate change and war are equally devastating, on a global scale where the causes include the entire weight of civilization. Going off-world is not going to help. Elon Musk seems to think we could leave our earthly troubles behind us. It is much more likely, in fact logically entailed, that we would take them with us. That's assuming we can overcome the many mundane financial and regulatory barriers to commercial space flight.[25]

Suppose that technological innovation, in the form of Big Tech, records a net loss in human happiness and fulfillment. Big Tech here represents the triumph of the instrumental aspects of reason more generally: applied rationality in everyday use, shaping ordinary tasks and desires, as well as large human- or posthuman-scale projects. Climate change, nuclear weapons, and artificial intelligence are the usual bugbears of choice when imagining the existential threats posed by technology. In fact, the vast influence of smartphones and social media offer a more telling account of tech's risk / reward calculus.

Certainly, it is debatable, possibly incorrect, to assume that such a situation sketches a negative overall result in terms of human flourishing. Look at all the shiny toys for us! Look at the improved working conditions for everyone! The jury remains forever out on questions of that kind, because the time scales are not within our own limited reach. What is striking is how the factors allowing for techno-capitalism's continued dominance in our lives seem to operate despite any possible deficit. Those factors are deeply coiled in the internal conflicts of the human mind, its propensities for confirmation bias, immediate gratification, and other perverse features that we will encounter over and over in any analysis of ideological conviction.[26]

Still, let us not be excessively negative about the very real advances—in science, medicine, political accountability, and quality of life—that are the ongoing legacy of the Enlightenment Project broadly construed. In particular, mindful of the overarching theme of these reflections, there have been clear gains in response to political demands for legitimation of power. As Plato himself showed two and a half millennia ago, power by its nature does not favour openness and accountability. The natural tendency of power holders is toward tyranny, which Plato understood as rule executed according to the personal whim of the ruler. And when in doubt, or just as a matter of general policy, such a ruler will accuse his opponents of the very sins of which he is most guilty.[27]

This larger psychic tendency among humans—the familiar idea that power corrupts, and absolute power corrupts absolutely—can be tempered by systems of supposed legitimacy such as aristocracy or meritocracy. The power of individual whim is mitigated or regulated—or sometimes merely distributed—across other individuals. But the central problem of legitimacy remains: power is intoxicating, addictive, and never sufficient unto itself. In fact, the slogan should not be "power corrupts," absolutely or otherwise, but rather "power enables." Ascent to power shows most, if not all, humans to be susceptible to its heady attractions. We're intoxicated by power, large and small in scale. Any of us might succumb to those strong spirits.

Really: any of us. We tend to think of the phrase "drunk on power" as applying only to the madly ambitious or those touched with a delusion of grandeur. But my recurring suggestion about doxaholism is that it may afflict anyone, even the most apparently level-headed. This is so because the rewards of righteousness are freely available to all. In their excess, however, the public sphere begins to erode: private conviction replaces public reason, and the struggle for power becomes a chaotic free-for-all.

There will always be struggle. Making the distribution of social power legitimate is the task of all political thinking and most governments. Plato distrusted the desire-addled motivations of the demos, as we know—this is merely tyranny in the making, ripe for the sway of demagogues and charismatic populists. In truth they needn't even be that charismatic, as recent political events have shown. They can be personally vile, ethically venal, and legally guilty without apparently damaging their appeal to the residual resentments and ill-formed prejudices of those who find themselves, or simply believe themselves, on the wrong end of life and culture. Thus, the importance of myths and narratives in the service of legitimacy.

Plato offers the Myth of the Metals, a deliberately incredible tale of different metals mixed in human souls to naturalize the inevitable hierarchy of some over many. This is the deception whose falsity is supposedly rescued by its larger value. We are then treated to an unstable and, once more, perhaps ironic defence of especially virtuous leaders, the notorious philosopher-kings.[28] I will have more to say about this notion of the ideal, divinely inspired ruler in part 2. For those of us with our feet still on the ground, if not always made of clay, is there a worldly route to just authority? Other philosophers have posed an apparently simpler solution, investing "the people" with qualities of judgment and good sense that they only notionally possess, or else they decide to shroud the origins of political authority in mystical darkness.[29]

Is it possible that there is no real prospect of any rational basis for political authority, that it will always come back to force in the end? Force "justified" by reference to some hazy origin story inaccessible to fact? Well, perhaps so. Despite all our efforts, we sometimes get precisely what we deserve in political life: pure personal power (autocracy); the best government money can buy (plutocracy); rule by thieves, pirates, and bandits (kleptocracy); rule by the hopelessly old (gerontocracy); or else what is resonantly and simply called *kakistocracy*—rule by the most incompetent and worst among us. Or, perhaps most likely of all, some combination of all of the above.

None of this decline is inevitable. The very same virtues we associate with Enlightenment ideals—thinking for ourselves, questioning authority, striving for universal value—may actually be contributing factors in what Jürgen Habermas called a "legitimation crisis" in the very idea of a rational public sphere.[30]

The relentless push by mature individuals to question the powers and rules that infringe on their freedom itself becomes a zero-sum game of political brinksmanship. Too little pushback on power is just accession to slavery, however comfortable. But too much may destabilize the necessary social order to an extent from which there is no recovery. It is as if the social critic were an uncooperative audience member attending a performance of some fictional scene. Unlike the rest of the contented audience, the disgruntled one refuses to accept a willing suspension of disbelief. The cracks in the shared narrative of legitimacy are revealed, its already fragile integrity shattered. In sum: a basic public trust is broken.

And so, we come to the key pivot of this optimistic account of enlightenment, indeed of human reason as we usually imagine it. Individual reason stands awkwardly aslant collective goals and needs, which require fellowship and deference, not autonomy. Perhaps we need to insist less on the self and more on the community—not a resurgent tribalism in the negative sense, or reductive identity politics, but rather a sense of shared purpose, a vision of human flourishing, that extends across our differences. Reason helps us coordinate action so that we can dominate environments and other species—this may offer an evolutionary glimpse of how it came to be so important—but it is a hot property, a feature that sometimes becomes a bug. Cooperation is impossible without free thought, and yet such thought at every moment threatens to undo the provisional consensus of working together. This is the tightrope we must walk as social creatures.

In effect, *think for yourself* and *question authority* are now ranged up against a rival impossible imperative: *trust me*. This is the common currency of mundane trust games, the sidewalk-level version of those media stories we've all seen that pivot on what "experts say." Trust me! *Experts say* is itself a kind of credentialed upgrade of all identity-based claims to authority. These typically come in this form: "As a *blank* myself, I *et cetera*." Such locutions of commanded belief, so inescapable in everyday life and yet so often meaningless, always remind me of a butcher's shop I used to visit in my old Toronto neighbourhood. It was run by a nice man called Vince Gasparo. He had very good cuts of meat, ethically sourced and delicious. One time I entered the shop looking for some steak to cook on the grill. "Ah, Mark! This is the best steak you will ever eat," he said. "Trust me." Well, I did—until he told me I had to. (Of course it was very good, as I knew it would be.)

Trust is the unobtrusive but essential glue of all social relations. It doesn't matter all that much whether you accept your butcher's demand for trust. Extended to institutional level, though, the problem becomes urgent. The command to trust is as often rejected as accepted, in part because it invites the very skepticism it attempts to allay. If we add a qualifier to indicate why trust ought to be granted— paradigmatically, "Trust me, I'm a doctor!"—the question is opened in another frame of the problem. Are you a *real* doctor? What does that even mean? A physician? A surgeon? A psychiatrist? Psychologists are often doctors, if they have doctoral degrees, but I've got one of those—plus another that was bestowed as honorary—and I don't think that means anyone should trust me. I'm reminded of my friend Nick, who joked about being on a plane where a man fell ill. The flight attendant asked if there was a doctor on board. Nick's PhD is in English literature. Sure, he's a doctor. Should he sit with the sick man and explain sonnet forms to him, might that cheer him up?

Everyone knows that "doctor" just means learned person, a title associated with some specific academic credential or honorific. But of course everyone does not know that! Because of its close association with the profession of medicine, "doctor" is usually taken to mean "MD," not "PhD" or "EdD" or, heaven forbid, "DFA"[31] Because of this association with care, "doctor" thus carries a resonance of trust—so much so, indeed, that many people want to make sure other people know they possess the title even if it's not of the medical type. This can cut both ways.

Most people think it is appropriate and respectful to refer to Martin Luther King Jr as "doctor," even though that refers to his doctoral studies in theology at Boston University. The usage conveys a sense of trust in Dr King's vision and integrity. When, by contrast, the repugnant Marjorie Taylor Greene refused to address Anthony Fauci as anything other than "mister" during a June 2024 congressional hearing, that was because he was "responsible for crimes against humanity" (!) and not a statement about his academic credentials. Refusal of the honorific here was clearly a sign of distrust, made with the background assumption that "real" doctors are—I guess—not in favour of vaccination mandates. Fauci commented later that these sorts of comments from Greene were in part responsible for the death threats he continues to receive over his role with the White House Corona-virus Task Force.[32]

All of that feels, alas, like the regular order of the day on a sunny Tuesday in June. But if an apparently simple form of address can make such hay with the question of trust—never mind the complex role of scarves, flags, hats, haircuts, gestures, jokes, inside language, and all the rest—it is clear that we must strive for some clarity about what is going on in the public sphere. There are many metaphors used to describe trust. It's like a mirror: broken in an instant but almost impos-sible to repair. A vase. A lifeline. Or it's like chocolate, or ice cream, or maybe chocolate ice cream: once melted, it will never be the same again. Maybe it's like blood pressure: silent, asymptomatic, deadly when it's abused. It's glue. No, it's lubricant. Air. Water. Fire. A bank account built over years that can be drained in minutes, even seconds. A cultivated perennial garden destroyed in one violent cloudburst.

I don't think we really need a governing metaphor for trust. But for now, if we want one that's not too trite, I suggest *the wind*, not merely the air. Trust is everywhere and nowhere at once. It swirls with the Earth's rotation, not making it go around but affecting everyone stuck tenuously to the orb's surface. It can be considered a technol-ogy: it fills our sails and moves us at breakneck speed. It can also vanish without warning, becalmed by forces beyond our control. We cannot function in its absence, but it is not subject to transaction or commodification. It cannot be bought or sold, but it makes all buying and selling possible.

When there is a crisis of legitimation there is also a crisis of trust. Low-trust systems are fragile, even more than vulnerable individuals. The danger is inscribed within the human mind's very ability to think critically. Questioning authority can lead to a condition where the well-meaning skepticism of an open, inquisitive mind descends into an endgame of broken trust and nihilism. What begins as a noble demand for legitimacy and transparency becomes a runaway train of disbelief, disillusion, and eventual hostility. The cure we sought becomes the drug to which we are beholden. This is a crisis of authority, yes, but not in the usual sense, often touted by those who typically use the phrase. When someone of a certain political orientation says, "crisis of authority," we may feel the winds carrying not a breeze of renewed trust but a too-familiar fascistic stench. We may catch the gleam of long knives being drawn, hear the sound of jackboots ring on pavement.

We can analyze the present crisis instead as a problem of misdirected reason. We begin with imperfect institutions, always with the caveat that the emancipation adventure before us is not merely the strengthening of those institutions. Trust is sustained by a sense, not often articulated but essential, that we are together engaged in larger projects of flourishing. Such thinking is part of a collective project without which our own individual projects and desires must come to naught. As suggested already, and as we will see in more detail as we proceed, trust emerges most clearly, becomes most visible in its necessity, as a matter of shared vulnerability. This is not the opposite of individuality, as some anticollectivists would have you believe; it is, on the contrary, the necessary condition of being an individual at all in the moral and rational sense.

Brokenness is easy to see all around and equally easy to accept in despair. But I suspect that there is a large majority more hopeful and more resilient than the rhetorical bugbears that haunt the videogame-style interfaces of contemporary political discourse. This is true, and worth remembering. These combative talking heads, with their reductive two-sides-only style, full of interruptions, *Spy vs. Spy* rhetorical ploys, and deliberate misunderstandings, turn every policy issue or government program, civil society itself, into a kind of shared first-person-shooter gallery contest.[33]

My account of breakdown is more hopeful. The much-criticized welfare state is, after years of abuse from within and disdain from without, overdue for resurgence in a form I will instead call the *post-human welfarist state*. The issue before us, as suggested already, is in some ways a familiar tale of addiction and recovery—the kind of narrative we know all too well when it comes to drugs, alcohol, and even fame. As mentioned, our general addiction is not to substances or even activities like work, shopping, and exercise; it is, instead, a self-harming enslavement to a particular kind of experience. The feeling of righteousness that comes with unassailable conviction is a powerful stimulant. Unlike external stimulants, this one is almost entirely self-generated: no pill or potion required. It responds to facts and features of the external world but ultimately has the power to deny or invent facts apparently at will. Conviction both makes and unmakes the world. It is a widespread cognitive disease with features of both virus and substance dependency.

To counter addiction to conviction, we need appropriate therapies—political and philosophical ones, having to do with thought and action. Going cold turkey will not be advisable. Painful withdrawal is likely, and recovery is always unfinished. Precisely because we live in the addictogenic society I have been and will be at pains to describe, one that everywhere encourages us to form escalating attachments, our self-liberation will remain upstream work. Contrary to everyday expectation, our brains are not our friends here. They lead us astray, into destructive patterns and toxic habits. This is what we might come to understand as humankind's counter-evolutionary capacity, when the figurative monkey forever on our backs is no more than ourselves in the form of destructive desires and self-defeating narratives.

4

Politically Incorrect

RONALD REAGAN'S REPURPOSING OF THE Russian proverb "Trust, but verify" (doveryay, no proveryay) is a well-known, indeed notorious, bit of realpolitik lore. The thespian-turned-statesman used it, with self-conscious gravitas, in December of 1987. The occasion was the signing of the Intermediate-Range Nuclear Forces Treaty with the Soviet Union's secretary general, Mikhail Gorbachev, who reportedly complained that Reagan overused the phrase. "I like it," Reagan replied. Of course he did: *trust but verify* might stand as the general motto of the 1980s rise of American imperialism and the triumph of neoliberal economics. We could even class this knife-edge sentiment together with some of the previous imperatives discussed so far, not so much for its impossibility as its more concrete self-contradiction. What is a trust that requires verification? Surely the two ideas are antithetical, and unresolved in practice?[34]

The conflict between skepticism and knowledge are everywhere around us. Too often we are tempted to theorize in advance of the facts: this is one of the ways that our own appeals to reason can deceive us. "Principles taken upon trust, consequences lamely deduced from them, want of coherence in the parts, and of evidence in the whole, these are every where [sic] to be met with in the systems of the most eminent philosophers," David Hume wrote in 1740, "and seem to have drawn disgrace upon philosophy itself."[35] Hume's skepticism proved a fruitful challenge to Kant. He was, famously, "roused from his dogmatic slumbers" by the Scottish genius—maybe not the first recorded instance of wokeness in intellectual history, but a key one. Kant then set forth to articulate the conditions of possibility for reason itself, and incidentally resolve this skeptical "scandal for philosophy."

The resulting scholarly debates about reality and reason can seem rather intramural and self-generating, especially several centuries on. Metaphysical systems, who cares? For most of us, the times and our inclinations are more primed for appreciating the challenges of political theory, not epistemology. We don't argue about knowledge, we seek advantage. But the two things are closely related. Note especially the Hobbesian traps that afflict liberal-democratic politics. Once fear of the other enters a system of rivalrous individual action, however rational, the prospect of an arms race is raised: marginal advantage provides incentive for further escalations of competition. This race quickly becomes one to the bottom, an accelerated tragedy of the commons. Why? Because the advantages conferred by incremental improvements or arsenal expansion always reduce to perverse incentives that escalate general risk. Individual rational actions generate disastrous collective outcomes.

The prospect of mutually assured nuclear destruction was a daily reality in the early 1980s.[36] Stanley Kubrick's *Dr Strangelove* (1964), a cult favourite at rep-hour screenings on Bloor Street or Roncesvalles Avenue, offered the basic black-humour cinematic backdrop to our anxiety. The 1983 television special *The Day After* haunted our dreams, and photocopied versions of Jonathan Schell's "Fate of the Earth" articles in the *New Yorker* were circulated like samizdat communiqués. I became so preoccupied with nuclear holocaust that I wrote both a senior thesis and a master's dissertation on fictional treatments of global atomic annihilation.[37]

It is vertiginous, in our own day, to see that nuclear war and its effects are still a live political threat, just as it is remarkable and rather depressing that the right of women to determine the fate of their own bodies is still a debated, fragile, and state-enforced feature of life. We debated the morality of abortion vociferously in the 1980s, as perhaps in every decade of the last century. But I think almost nobody then, of whatever position, could have imagined the US Supreme Court overturning Roe v. Wade in 2023.[38]

The early 1980s seem eerily proximate to me now, not just because of the special vividness that late-adolescent memories have for most of us. As a young man looking for wisdom, inspiration, and love, I was likely a little more dreamy headed than some of my peers. They would all go to law school; I thought I might end up in the priesthood or the military, like my father in the air force. No doubt I would have been a failure at both of these rigidly hierarchical occupations. The special combination of rigour and anarchism that marks genuine philosophical inquiry grabbed me from the start—despite the experience of a less-than-stellar first-year philosophy course. I traded my dorky dress-code suit jackets and grey flannels from high school for T-shirts and skinny jeans. I swapped out the clunky Canadian North Star sneakers for Adidas Gazelles in blue and red suede. Eventually I even got rid of my centre-part Shaun Cassidy haircut and sported a sweeping side-part do that one critic called a Tom Cochrane and another labelled The Silly Boy, but which I preferred to think of as a Sebastian Flyte.

Waugh's *Brideshead Revisited* was my de facto guide to undergraduate life, at least in its halting attempts at glamour. It was a long time before I tasted a plover's egg but the idea of a swanky brunch of them, in the company of witty and fashionable college celebrities, fuelled my vision. It seemed imperative that I have Prosecco and corner-store strawberries for breakfast the day I graduated, if not actual Château

Lafaurie-Peyraguey and *Fragaria vesca*. I drifted through the long ceremony with a sense of dreamy goodwill. I took to heart pompous Cousin
Jasper's warning to Charles Ryder that one spends one's second year
occupied with shaking off the friends from freshman term. I started
hanging out with the cool kids at the student newspapers, first at my
college, then at the university-wide publication, cranked out by eager
tyros and future scribes since 1880. Like the other would-be hacks,
I got my ear pierced and affected a long black thrift-store overcoat.
Cosplay! I hung around used bookstores and dingy punk clubs. I sat
in bars and coffee shops with my marked-up hardcover copy of *Being
and Time*, trying to look deep and difficult.[39]

Yes, I know, I know. I was in thrall to what I suppose was some
kind of shabby, second-hand Leonard Cohen beautiful-losers mys-
tique. So were all my romantic friends. First, we take Manhattan! Or
at least the Eaton Centre! You can mock—go ahead; I do—but how
else have people ever formed a sense of self except by beginning with
aspirational mimicry. Even Aristotle says that virtue begins with replicating the actions of those we admire. Only later does it become part
of one's own character. Imitation is more than the sincerest form of
flattery; it is an essential building block of personal identity. I would
say that I and my fellow student journalists did all this ironically, but
that is only to acknowledge that we did most things ironically—or
tried to. It was the beginning of a cultural moment where it was
fashionable not to take things too seriously and, moreover, to view
references and allusions as basic to cultural consumption: recom-
binant strands, layered back-formations, everything reminds you of
something else. Seeing-as was our version of seeing-through. We had
proximate political causes and occasions for protest: South African
apartheid, proliferating nuclear weapons, abortion rights. But there
was a background assumption that the political protesters of the previous generation had been too po-faced, too full of themselves. We
would not make that mistake.

The tables turn. I do not find generational thinking very illuminating—it's reifying and all-too-often ham-fisted—but part of the distance from 1984 to 2024 is surely revealed by an insistence on certainty and demands that one choose a side. Claims that irony died with the World Trade Center attacks of September 11, 2001, are greatly exaggerated—and the sincere on-screen weeping of a once puckish David Letterman has more lately boomeranged to him, with flowing whiskers, being mocked as resembling a dissolute Santa Claus on a Zach Galifianakis show called "Between Two Ferns." So it goes.

* * *

WHY THIS DESCENT INTO AUTOBIOGRAPHY? Well, one reason is to suggest what we all know: our own sense of reason, including public reason, is shaped by personal experience. But that genealogical fact is not sufficient warrant for privileging biography over rational truth claims. I put my prejudices on the table, not as moves in the game but as opportunities for critical assessment—a sign, or so I hope, of good faith in the game of justification. Another reason is that these times that shaped my political consciousness have a kind of post facto resonance, what seems—especially in the mid-2020s—a kind of way station between the respective upheavals over Vietnam, then South Africa, and then Gaza. Our proximate causes of choice were anti-apartheid divestment and nuclear disarmament—both issues that have been mitigated but not solved in the four decades since the time I am recalling.

A third possible motivation is that the young people of that bygone time are now, for better or worse, those with access to the levers of power. I doubt many politicians have the same specific memories as I do, but there is a shared culture of those who lived through the end of the Cold War, the beginning of the digital revolution, and into whatever we want to call the current era. Many of the tropes that are common today can be traced back to those years and so, I believe, can the problems that they symbolize. It's a kind of cultural haunting, and not just limited to those of us who came of age in the 1980s. There is a good case to be made that Donald Trump's twisted worldview is a result of being stuck in his version of the greed-is-good Gordon Gekko eighties, now complete with three dozen or so (or so far!) felony convictions.[40]

The polarized politics of the present also have essential intellectual roots in that recent past, especially when it comes to the casual misuse of the idea of postmodernism. If a suitable instrument had been available four decades ago, we might have predicted the curdling of countercultural energy into both the alt-right pushback on social-justice efforts, evident at the end of the millennium, and the cancel-culture tendencies of what philosopher and journalist Andrew Potter has aptly called the "ctrl-left" of more recent vintage.[41]

I noted earlier that the title phrase "Question Authority" was sometimes to be seen as a button on someone's jacket or backpack. At the campus newspaper, where we considered our politics to be unique and uniquely brave, we ironically adopted another slogan: *Politically Incorrect*. Seeing ourselves standing outside a presumed orthodoxy was not exactly an audacious minority view, then or now. According to a 2023 poll, 64 percent of Americans think that the country should reduce political correctness. It's not clear what that means, of course, not least since the very same poll shows that 70 percent of Americans believe the country should foster "social justice"—a menace flag in standard Fox News, OAN, and Breitbart semaphore.[42]

But perhaps we were right about one thing. Correctness did not belong in politics, on our view of things, which we considered the realm of power, nuance, and lines of intellectual dance and flight. Orthodoxy—following the Greek etymology, *thinking on the square*— was for suckers, careerists, and debate-club bozos. The straight-edge lefties thought we were squishy liberals; we said they were pretentious Maoists. The Prairie conservatives thought we were trendy kooks; we said they were reactionary asshats. We didn't debate, we argued. It was like that. No doubt it still is, perhaps with added venom.

Lapel buttons and badges were popular fashion statements then, mostly small roundels celebrating punk and New Wave bands. In high school, as a fan of the English group Graham Parker and the Rumour, I had fashioned a homemade badge that quoted their song, in scissored bits of newspaper type, "Waiting for the UFOs." It was made of construction paper and covered with cling film. Musical allegiance was strict and charged by disdain for anything popular or prog. Was this vicious partisan bias in music, so common among the teenagers of my time, a sign of the divided dialogue to come?[43] My "Politically Incorrect" button, white type on a blue background, was more professional. We were lefties at the paper, certainly, but we considered ourselves more realistic than the Marxist true believers at the *McGill Daily*, who rarely produced an issue, let alone a daily one; and certainly more radical than the budding conservatives at the Alberta papers or the nascent journalism professionals who put out the enviably professional Carleton University *Charlatan*.

In the student-press landscape, my campus newspaper was and is considered suspiciously centrist. We had a diverse readership that was theoretically the size of a large town. By any global reckoning, we were decidedly left—I'd say social democrat but not democratic socialist, if that distinction means anything at a moment when octogenarian Joseph R. Biden is widely considered an out of-control, radical, left-wing nutjob. Mostly our politics were defiantly unorthodox on principle—or so we believed, anyway. We didn't know much about true orthodoxy, especially its etymological origin in "right thinking." Our view of paradox was amused without being profound. In the confident manner only smug youngsters can tolerate, we labelled our intellectual foes victims of "groupthink mindrot," that of-the-moment Orwellian riff. Because 1984 was a great time to be young, sassy, and in charge of a thrice-weekly editorial podium. Anything we didn't like—state lotteries, public-space surveillance, aggressive police, even the casual conformity of other intellectuals—was subject to quote-heavy and unstable Newspeak derision. Thoughtcrime? I'll show you thought crime! Duckspeak. Doubleplusungood.

The derision was unstable because the irony was of uncertain direction. What did we really know about political oppression or even the realities of democratic power? Most of what I knew I had learned from a very entertaining first-year Canadian-politics course, some excellent political-theory lectures, plus a jumbled array of movies and novels: Koestler, Greene, Kafka, Rand, Robert Penn Warren, Gore Vidal's *The Best Man* (1964), and Robert Redford in *The Candidate* (1972).[44] Otherwise—well, typical but dodgy sci-fi stuff: Robert Heinlein's *Starship Troopers* fascist realpolitik on one side, Ursula Le Guin's anarchist utopias on the other. Nestled somewhere in there, my father's pilfered copy of *The Rise and Fall of the Third Reich*.

"Politically Incorrect" was a rallying cry, but it was also a jest, a layered mix of seriousness and self-mocking. I don't think we ever dreamed the slogan would become what it now is, a real label, a fully intended insult redirected to unbelievers by the forces of political orthodoxy. That inversion of meaning, from ironic to serious, unveiled the functions of mythmaking and belief in cultural discourse. Luckily, there were and are reliable guides to how this mythmaking operates in political life. Like many others, I found a guiding intellectual light in Roland Barthes.

I noticed the cover of the book first, browsing one day in the university bookstore. It was the slick design of the Paladin paperback edition. The sprouting illustration seemed drawn from my hobby-world mental attic: a jet-fighter pilot, the front grille of a Citroën sedan, a Roman centurion, a kind of Barbarella striptease figure, and a box of laundry detergent. Roland Barthes's compact semiotic collection *Mythologies* is a series of short, elegant, theoretical aperçus, originally published as a column in *Les lettres nouvelles*. The essays expose and examine the meanings hidden inside the most mundane objects and features of French life: steak frites, magazine covers, expensive cars, film-star images, Garbo and Chaplin, the *Michelin Guide*, toys, margarine, and—right off the top—professional wrestling.[45]

Suddenly I am back in the dingy arenas of Charlottetown and Halifax with my father, watching Sweet Daddy Siki, Mad Dog Vachon, Dusty Rhodes, Killer Kowalski, and our favourite, Verne Gagne (so much fun to say in a bad French accent). Later, working as an usher at the old shed-like Winnipeg Arena, I endured the drunken fans of the same decaying spectacle in exchange for gigs at concerts by April Wine, Rush, Aerosmith, AC/DC, and Kiss. Also, Jets hockey games and the Harlem Globetrotters.

The infantile morality plays of wrestling, the contests between heroes and heels, what the grapplers themselves call kayfabe—the peculiar semicontact make-believe of the ring—is hardly grown-up entertainment. And yet, here was this uber-cultured Parisian dude, whose author photo showed an avuncular figure boasting excellent hair and a warm face heavy with Gallic wisdom, taking it all seriously. I wanted to turn around and say to the other students wandering in the aisles, "Um, you guys. This *French intellectual* is writing about wrestling!"

Myths are not just stories of ancient origin or derivation, the kind of thing reprised in the sword-and-sorcery fiction I still liked. They are forms of belief that shape our conscious thinking—ideological nuggets of meaning, coiled within familiar objects. "The starting point of these reflections was usually a feeling of impatience at the sight of the 'naturalness' with which newspapers, art and common sense constantly dress up a reality which, even though it is the one we live in, is undoubtedly determined by history," Barthes wrote. I had never considered the "natural" as anything other than the unquestioned: that which is, therefore that which must be. But now the *post hoc ergo propter hoc* fallacy succumbed to his subtle, witty destruction.

Naturalness was a façade, a way of putting the current arrangement beyond question, an ideology carried by the dross of culture.

Question authority, even in the most unlikely places. Ideology is lurking everywhere, in both senses of its meaning. As a body of political ideas, it is communicated by the buttons we sport, the clothes we wear, and the poses we affect. It is, in that sense, a full-on function of our presentation of self in everyday life. But beneath the overt surface lies ideology in the deeper sense of what is accepted, taken for obvious, assumed as common sense. These ideological commitments, transmitted and reinforced with every mundane exchange of shared life, are much harder to see. Even in your dinner choices or mindless entertainment preferences, norms are in the process of making themselves invisible through bland familiarity.

Except in the imagined world of revealing sunglasses, there are no visible signs or buttons that communicate these all-powerful messages. We need to look harder, and in different ways than we are used to. But taking the taken-for-granted for granted is no longer a viable option, once we begin to look critically and see. "In short," Barthes goes on, "in the account given of our contemporary circumstances, I resented seeing Nature and History confused at every turn, and I wanted to track down, in the decorative display of what-goes-without-saying, the ideological abuse which, in my view, is hidden there."[46] Now there— there are the missing unknown knowns, Mr Rumsfeld.

We cannot simply scorch the meaning-laden earth beneath our feet, of course. We need somewhere to stand, if only provisionally, to undertake our acts of courageous independent thinking. Nothing will make the idea of seeing-through more vivid, and more active, than a sense that you have not yet fully escaped illusion because the world is everywhere with us. Further, the distractions and preoccupations of the ordinary world are full of unarticulated assumptions and biases. And so, question authority, yes, everywhere and always—including especially the authority of what you take reason to be. We are forever absolute beginners in the infinite task of thinking. It's an intellectual wrestling match, in fact, but a real one: no kayfabe here.

Years later, listening to right-wing call-in radio on a dreary road trip—not a pastime I recommend, but instructive after its fashion—I had one of those collapsed-time moments when a caller compared us president Joe Biden to notorious bad guy—or "heel" in the parlance— Jesse "the Body" Ventura. He was running amok, she cried, spreading his evil all over the place, and none of the feeble challengers could stop him! The caller was incensed, her outrage mounting with every word, quite happy with the objectively absurd identification of Biden with the Body.

"Who can stop him?" she demanded rhetorically. "Who? Who?" The host, normally given to blowhard interruption as a mainstay of conversation, was oddly silent, as if in thought. The pause lingered. "I'll tell you who," she told the world, all of us waiting in our cars or kitchens. It was a great moment; this was epic stuff. "He came out of nowhere, almost forgotten. It was Verne Gagne! Verne Gagne! And he took Jesse to school, knocked him down with a series of drop kicks. Pinned him. He threw him out of the ring. And it was over. Jesse Ventura defeated by Verne Gagne, I tell you! What we need right now is Verne Gagne!" Whether Donald Trump fulfills this need for a saviour in the wrestling ring of the culture wars, she did not say. "His people skills weren't always the best," Ventura once said of Gagne, his putative boss in the American Wrestling Association. That sounds like a peevish employee rather than the bruising Jesse the Body of fame. But it's probably easier to credit Ventura as a disgruntled professional than it is to picture the heavily staged Ventura-Gagne bout as an analogue of a Biden-Trump electoral rematch. And, alas for memory, it was tag-team partner Vachon who actually flipped Ventura over the ropes, Gagne haplessly along for the ride to the floor.[47]

Out here in the real world, we citizens must contend with ever-expanding spectacle, trying vainly to sort truth from fiction, heel from

hero. If you do that honestly, it never gets easier.[48] It is a happy coincidence that the ideology-busting sunglasses sported by Nada looked a
lot like the Ray-Bans adopted by Joel Goodsen, Tom Cruise's character
in *Risky Business* (1983), after he becomes a social rebel—running a
makeshift brothel, it's true, but still. And never mind that this film,
ostensibly a slanted rom-com about teenage rebellion, is really the
antimorality tale of a pretty dumb kid gaming his way into Princeton.

On second thought, we could just take that notion and run with
it. Nothing goes without saying. *Risky Business* is ideology. Of course
it is: smirking upper-middle-class kid gets into Princeton not by merit
but by running a secret brothel. And ideology is, just as naturally,
risky business. Nada memorably begins his war on the ghouls and
their insidious colonization in *They Live* by taking up a shotgun and
going on a rampage—an unfortunately familiar trope of American
culture. Eventually he will attempt to dismantle the television beam
of mind-clouding misinformation that's pouring its subconscious
messages of complacency and passive acceptance of colonization into
hapless humans.

Backing into a crowded bank, he turns and delivers a memorable
line before beginning his rampage of gun-wielding political mayhem.
"I have come here to chew bubble gum and kick ass." Yes, he's wearing
the ideology-busting sunglasses, the excellent hockey-hair mullet, and
a plaid work shirt over skin-tight, sky-blue dad jeans. He holds the
shotgun at waist level. "And I'm all out of bubble gum." Blam! Down
goes a ghoul. Blam! Another body on the ground.

This is all very satisfying, in a cartoonish way, until you actually
think about it. If you do, nagging doubts begin to creep in. I will mention two.

First, humans don't need subliminal messages or brainwashing
to fall into consumerist obedience. On the contrary, we're perfectly
capable—and usually quite adept—at pulling the wool over our own
eyes. We can use any number of labels to describe this particular

form of self-harm: *autogaslighting, self-sacking barbarism*, or maybe *prestormed-garrison mentality*. It is an unfortunately common form of epistemic disorder, whereby the rational immune system attacks itself in the form of viral certainty, or ideological self-capture.

And second, the image of a lone gunman mowing down random strangers while in the grip of a personal conviction of special insight is not *exactly* the narrative we need—even if it answers to wild fancy now and then. We're all out of bubble gum. But kicking ass shouldn't be the preferred option. If you think it takes a gun, then that's not thinking. And the sunglasses don't solve the ghoul problem, they only help us to see it. Being grown-up means having the courage to accept the world as a place of painful uncertainty, where easy trust is impossible and pitfalls of despair and dogma lie on every side—and then to act effectively anyway. Seeing clearly is the beginning, not the end, of life's endless task of justice. And it starts, as always, with ourselves.

Nada to Frank, after their fight is done: "You ain't the first son of a bitch to wake up out of their dream."

Frank: "We can't be the only ones who can see, we've got to find the people who made these."

Nada: "Yeah, if any of them are still alive."

Put those sunglasses on, my friends! It's time to find the ghouls. They live, we sleep! *Hint: they may be closer to home than you think.*

SECOND MEDITATION

Trust

No One

5

They Live, Again

I APPROACH THIS PART OF the overall argument along two related lines, posed by two thorny questions. They are: *What is trust?* and *Who can you trust?* All of what follows is meant to be *ironic* in the philosophical sense of being advanced with the necessary uncertainties built in. Along the way I will offer, as in the previous part, some personal reflections on how this cluster of argument has arisen for someone seeking credentials of expertise, specifically the philosophical credentials of critical thinking. I'm mindful of Stephen Leacock's definition of the PhD as the degree they give you when you have demonstrated that you're incapable of learning anything further.[1]

In common with many people, my political education up to about the age of seventeen, entering university, was dominated by fiction, reputable and otherwise, as well as by cinematic depictions of media-driven or otherwise cynical backroom shenanigans of an old-school vintage. I will discuss media distrust separately in the next part. For the moment, I am interested in considering the trustworthiness of what is usually called expertise or (suspiciously) *office-holder bias* but which is, more basically, the very idea of objective truth.

Not all of my adolescent political ideas derived from the sort of political fiction referenced in the last part. I was also a beady-eyed veteran of Saturday-morning television cartoons, which offered one of the few kid-centric programming blocs then available on the primitive array of two or three hand-changed channels. There was also *Bugs Bunny* (Saturday evenings) and *The Wonderful World of Disney* (Sundays), but all other pleasures were under strict watchlist guidelines, including morning game shows and afternoon sitcom reruns. Just as well.

In between the cartoons in those early 1970s mornings, though, were the series of news bulletins from the United States. Yes, the Watergate scandal was broadcast to the ten-year-olds of Winnipeg and Summerside in news-digest chunks between the Road Runner's capers and *Speed Racer* or *The Banana Splits*. We saw the swarthy men on our wavering black-and-white cathode-ray tubes, listened to the serious voices. Democracy in crisis. Corruption, crime, cover-up. I never became a devotee of this high-geeky esoterica, which somehow made G. Gordon Liddy into something of a schoolyard folk hero, composed of equal parts Ernst Stavro Blofeld, Travis Bickle, and Bruce Lee. I did, however, become more than a little obsessed with the spectre of government-backed conspiracy. Who are They, the Ones in Charge, and what do They want?

"Spectre" is the correct descriptor, for the feeling is all about ghosts and spooks, those slangy terms for spies we were learning. This was entirely in line with what Richard Hofstadter called the *paranoid style* in American politics, and while it may find especially fertile ground in a broadly diverse and fringy population of 350 million, it can be readily found in any coagulation of human interest and natural suspicion. Such paranoia is also typically associated, in political terms, with strains of *anti-intellectualism*, likewise analyzed by Hofstadter in the American context though obviously not confined there.[2]

"I have neither the competence nor the desire to classify any figures of the past or present as certifiable lunatics," Hofstadter cautioned his contemporary 1960s readers. "In fact, the idea of the paranoid style as a force in politics would have little contemporary relevance or historical value if it were applied only to men with profoundly disturbed minds. It is the use of paranoid modes of expression by more or less normal people that makes the phenomenon significant."[3] That's how style functions, not via clear psychological, still less rational, principles but by whim, nuance, dog whistle, and inside jargon—these days also slogans, memes, and detached signifiers. Though Hofstadter does not say so, this analysis thus lines up with emerging studies of subcultural mores in popular music, fashion, and the like—the sort of subject that fashionable leftist critics would pick over, a decade or two later.[4]

But political paranoia, traceable through disparate sources like Area 51 and McCarthyism, back to American populism, and then Masonry, the Illuminati, and a host of familiar tropes, is more than just dressing up for a night out. The labels and memes become familiar elements of jumbled media and cultural shorthand: the deep state, Pizzagate, false flags, the moon landing, Sandy Hook, Covid death panels, single-bullet theory. At their most extreme, these wisps of conspiracism coalesce into a cobweb of paranoia and then construct a hard-all-over bubble shell of *apophenia*—the unbalanced belief that everything is, and must be, connected.[5]

Less extreme manifestations are more widespread and more insidious in their overall effect. I mean the nagging suspicion that the system is rigged, that society really is a barely concealed bellum omnium contra omnes, still or always—dogs don't eat dogs, actually, but humans eat each other *and* themselves all the time, at least metaphorically. Semidormant strains of ideological virus grow symptomatic, so that once-dismissed anti-Semitic or secret–world order paranoia is spun into the healthy bodies of new generations—alt-right, New Right, 4chan right, campus right, youth right, red-pill right, we-know-what-time-it-is right. Here the inverse of the much-abused term *woke* was the briefly current label *based*—as in based in reality, but perhaps more accurately based in the cultural despair of a protofascist mindset.[6]

Worst of all is the paranoiac who is too powerful to be dismissed as a mere crank. Richard Nixon strikes us now as insidious, awful, crawling, and a little sad; felon-in-chief Donald Trump strikes us, or should, as a wholly malign force in public affairs, an excrescence of narcissism and envy, a font of insult and pettiness who manages to make everything personal and nothing significant. He is a conspiracy of one, but the one that matters—when facilitated, anyway—a lightning rod to other people's actual hard-won discontent and resentment. As commentator Van Jones has said, "He's pimping people's pain." Yes, exactly.[7]

The 1970s offered a gentler era of toxic suspicion, one that began in righteous outrage at government perfidy but rapidly bloomed into a stance of system-wide unbelief that has been ailing us ever since. A relevant touchstone here is another cinematic depiction of what we can call politics in the broad sense. It stars Robert Redford in an almost identical depiction to the one he offered in *The Candidate* three years earlier. In *Three Days of the Condor* (1975, based on a James Grady novel), Redford plays a humble if not-quite-idealistic CIA analyst working out of a Manhattan brownstone.

One day, for no reason we're told, and while he is on a lunchtime deli run, his colleagues, fellow readers of obscure works of theory, history, and politics, are summarily executed. What's happening? Soon, Faye Dunaway's cheekbones and Halston knitwear are along for the ride. Max von Sydow—who else?—is the menacing Continental hit man. These hapless workers are cogs in a machine, dots in a company algorithm that has now deemed them expendable. They read books for a living, looking for clues. But the clues outside their cozy brownstone enclave have now caught up with them.[8]

You don't need me to tell you what is happening, even if you've never seen the film. It is what we might call the "They." Not Heidegger's das Man, that manifestation of inauthentic everydayness, but the *They* of all system thinking, where everything must be connected and someone (shadowy) must be in control. This is a very American trope, especially in the form of the so-called systems novel.[9] The paranoid style in American film and fiction reaches its apex in this mid- to late-1970s period with an array of plausible thrillers about state surveillance and government-media collusion all the way to objectively wackier Kennedy assassination conspiracies, military coups, faked moon landings, and a global plot to breed Hitler clones in South America.[10]

Is "objectively" even the right word here? By asking that, I don't mean simply to flag the nagging problem that such fantasies may embrace a grain of truth, and therefore burrow their way into a jittery consciousness. There is also the deeper question of whether there is any such thing as objective truth at all—what we derided in the student press as "the view from nowhere." How could I, you, or anyone take up such a view? Nowhere is not a place to stand. Is this objective standpoint not just another philosophical fiction, a Kantian chimera, transcendental trickery?[11] Anyway, when it comes to public life in particular, the Great Watergate Hangover, as we must call it, extends decades into the future, into the political minds of everyone.

Naturally its effects are strong, because the foregoing drinks were powerful. In the exceptionalist American context, the ideals of free-thinking in the form of antistate skepticism are celebrated in resonant, sometimes bogus detail by everything from Tocqueville's *Democracy in America* (1835–40) to, rather more persuasively, Emerson's essay "Self-Reliance" (1841). More recently, the vibe animates aspects of the "authenticity" campaign aspirations of Robert F. Kennedy Jr, that notorious enemy of public health; in a heavy irony, it even animates the authoritarian ramblings of Donald Trump, now and then. The idea of a sturdy, no-nonsense, show-me citizen is probably ineradicable in United States political mythology.

This is no bad thing—except insofar as it becomes mired in its own suspicious logic. Then, impervious to all rational challenge or countervailing evidence, it is just more ideology. "Proper skepticism toward our institutions has turned into endemic distrust," one prominent American pundit intoned not long ago, "a jaundiced cynicism that says: I'm onto the game; it's corruption all the way down."[12] The game metaphor is significant: in a rigged game, only a mug plays by the rules. Everyone else knows it's okay, even obligatory to cheat. That's just good tactics under adverse conditions. But then some clever or opportunistic or merely perverse strategic actor will alter the game, buy it out, subvert it, or otherwise act as spoilsport. To use a metaphor borrowed from wrestling, and once vividly applied to Trump, while everyone else is boxing more or less by Marquess of Queensberry rules, someone might enter the ring swinging a folding metal chair. No tacit kayfabe there, sports fans, just random chaos and ugly spectacle.

Objective is a heavy word, as it should be. I never really bought the arguments of those campus radicals who told us all journalism had to be activism, all claims rooted in bias. It just seemed far more complex than that, and no doubt there was and is a part of my consciousness that remains wary of the vertigo thus logically entailed. Sure, everything we know is a product of history and society. Barthes was correct that naturalness is almost always a sham, a shadow play, or the answer to some lurking inner unease. And yet, this acknowledgement of limits and twisted narratives can offer no holiday to analysis, no sloughing off of the norms of truth. The right question when we think of social construction is, as philosopher Ian Hacking has said, "The social construction of what?"[13]

* * *

EXPANDING ON PROMISSORY NOTES OFFERED in the introduction, let's ask: what might be a useful *critical* definition of trust? Here

I will borrow some arguments from an apparently intramural debate about the nature of cryptocurrency. This will help us see, I think, the structural features of trust in sharper outline than we typically employ with respect to politics and ideology. Armed with that clarity, I hope we can move back into murkier territory with confidence.

The discussion dates from the time before the so-called crypto winter of 2022. During this bear-market shakedown, many non-fiat currency schemes, especially the class of crypotcurrencies, were revealed as trusts in the financial sense. That is to say, they were illegal restraints on trade when they were not outright Ponzi schemes executed in neo-Madoff style. The currencies' book value plummeted after a period of intensely optimistic, even frantic investment.[14]

This seemed to many casual observers to be endemic to the spectral nature of cryptocurrency, which has more than the usual capitalist flavour of a confidence game. But does it really? We should note that crypto markets, complete with boom, bubble, and bust cycles like other markets, really just highlight the issue of all currencies and capital exchanges: that they depend on a system of players ordered by mostly fair rules and honest participation.

It is also significant that cultism about crypto correlates strongly with other tech-bro obsessions rooted in paranoia and lack of trust in governments or states: climate-change denialism and antivax crusading. This toxic brew would be noteworthy but harmless if it were confined to a basement-dwelling subpopulation, but the advocates of this trio of bogus beliefs are among the richest and most influential people on the planet, however their money is configured. Their craziness matters. "Anti-vax agitation and crypto enthusiasm are both aspects of a broader rise of know-nothingism," economist Paul Krugman writes, "one whose greatest strength lies in an intellectually inbred community of very wealthy men."[15] (Of course, Krugman is just a Princeton full professor and a Nobel laureate. What does *he* know?)

Money has been vividly defined as *frozen desire*, but it may be more accurately seen as *liquid contract*, the free-flowing but fast-drying glue of all human and some nonhuman transactions.[16] Even when we use paper and metal to signify and tally these exchanges, all money remains a metaphysical mirage. As the global debt load now stands at more than US$305 trillion, we face both the astronomical scale of numbers, looming into incomprehension, and the inescapable fact that money is not really real. Except at the point of transaction, and even then, only by analogy, currency is a vast spectral system. Frank Kermode describes our participation in this fiscal fantasy as a vast poetic achievement—he notes that "[a]s a certain Richard Price explained in 1778, paper money must be thought of as the sign of a sign. If coin signified real value, paper, 'owing its currency to opinion,' had 'only a local and imaginary value.'"[17]

All currency is based on the contingency of legal trust—though not always in the sense of being subject to investigation by authorities. It circulates relentlessly, transacting with itself; its accumulation is the source and support of injustice; and yet even its smallest amounts are subject to increase by interest, the sparking friction of the system.

What of trust in this system, then? A non-fiat currency purports to bypass, or even eliminate, the standard problems of trust in government-backed bills. In the blockchain models used by crypto-currencies, the technical security of the transaction-line substitutes for the usual assurances of exchange, including the government's monopoly on issuing tokens and its deposit or bankruptcy protections, if any. The crypto promise is based on a transactional system where the human factor of trust, never entirely reliable even in the best-case scenario, is replaced by an entirely mechanical system of exchange. In effect, such a scheme achieves the satirical dream of all economics, a model in which the irrationalities and weaknesses of human behaviour can be washed out. On this model, trust is understood as something like the use of any assumptions about the behaviour of other people. Eliminate those assumptions and you have an ideal system.

Too ideal, perhaps. A more nuanced, and suitably Kantian, notion of trust is this: the expectation that an agent will act in accordance with a given norm even when incentivized to do otherwise.[18] Here we capture the idea that trust isn't just a form of expectation but one that aligns with norms, and normative action. As one example has it: I may expect that you will use the bathroom at some point today; I trust that you will wash your hands afterward. In crude terms, the difference lies between mere goal-directed behaviour, on the one hand, and potentially good or bad behaviour, on the other.

And non-fiat currencies will never be able to eliminate this factor in human affairs, because even were we to shift our trust norms from individuals or institutions to systems and programs, we would still have to invest in at least the minimal trustworthiness of the original programmers and, possibly, those who maintain the system going forward. This is precisely where the con of crytpo lies: the confidence is not solicited by some plausible fast-talking person, as in an old-fashioned street-corner clip joint—though personality was part of many schemes—but rather in the algorithmic robustness of the system.

This problem raises what the philosopher Peter Ludlow calls the problem of *metatrust*: "It doesn't matter if we believe we are in a system that needs only one in one million trustworthy actors if we can't trust that we are in such a system," he notes. "And we typically only know we are in such a system (when we do know) because one or a handful of auditors have confirmed it is so." Transparency about the system is fine but does not solve the problem or eliminate the need for trust. We have to trust that the system is sound even though we are not able to confirm this independently. That's what trust is: if we had access to personal verification of all aspects of a system, we wouldn't need to think about the problem of expert authority or sound game design. But our epistemic authority is limited here, as in many other things.

Consider this diagram (from Ludlow):

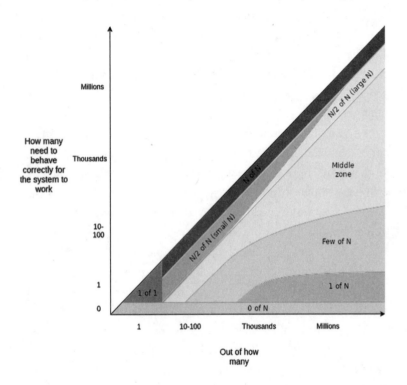

The idea of non-fiat trust is to push the system into an ever-lighter zone, so that ideally *zero* individuals need to act correctly to make the system trustworthy. But the paradox is that this is not possible if there is a system at all, assuming the system has people in it. Ethics, rules, and laws cannot be engineered away from the frailty of human character. Given that they are actually technologies developed to cope with human weakness, we should perhaps appreciate better the perpetual intertwining of normativity and vulnerability. Rules compensate for the bad instincts of agents *even as* they offer hope to those who cannot compete with force and domination.

In a sense, this awareness of weakness forms the core of any liberal order. We accept the rules because we never know who will be the strong or the weak on a given day. Furthermore, the problem of metatrust parallels a basic distinction about knowledge, that between what we know (epistemic data) and how we know what we know (epistemological commitment). I will postpone any further discussion of that question to part 4, but we can see already why trust not only matters but cannot be eliminated or engineered out of human systems. As usual, the basic problem is not the system (or institution or other actor) but us.

Trust depends on a structure of norms and people to embody them. The precise relation between persons and norms can vary, and some systems are stronger than others—a computer network or a documented kinship relation are more defined than an association of fly-fishing enthusiasts or board-game devotees. But all trust systems must have norms that are in healthy play, be relatively stable, and be open to transparent examination, These features of the system needn't always be explicitly articulated in order to function: the rules of baseball and the laws of cricket do not exhaust the action-guiding spirit of these games. Thus, the transfer of "playing cricket" or "keeping a straight bat" to other coordinated contexts with wider normative force, that is, praiseworthy behaviour in general.[19]

Erosion of norms by bad actors therefore has an especially deleterious effect when it affects the unspoken or implicit governing conventions of a practice. This often forces the ranks of norm maintainers to fall back on procedure or writ, usually to their detriment. The documented rules are not a complete set because any complete set is impossible, either mired in successive rings of enforcement and back-reference—an infinite-regress problem noted as early as Plato's *Laws*—or else claiming to solve for all possible cases, an impossible standard. All abstractions aside, every lawyer knows that black-letter law is not the same thing as justice.

And so, the convention breaker, the norm buster, the scofflaw can run quite wild within the ambit of any game, wreaking havoc all the while, free-riding on normies and other faithful players. This should not create a perverse incentive for good players to defect, but of course it often does. In such a situation, enforcement of the rules at the margins may remain possible, but it becomes more difficult—less of a deterrent and baseline normative assumption, and more open to charges of politicization or (lately) weaponization even as it targets the genuine bad actor. *The courts are political* is the handy cry of the guilty; alas, sometimes it is true.

Every shattered norm is a broken window in a declining neighbourhood, or violence-driven declines in ridership on public transit. A death spiral threatens. Another way of making the same point is that everyone else playing fairly or civilly perversely incentivizes the bad actor to play unfairly and rudely; but in turn bad acts themselves can create harmful future incentives in otherwise good actors. Result: a swift race to the bottom.

Those who seek power under any guise, as opposed to an instrumental version whereby might is allied to some notion of right—patriotism, moral rearmament, the city on the hill—are the true danger here. When power is desired for its own sake, for its trappings and incidental pleasures, it is power made illegitimate. Autocrats and dictators do this routinely, not least with the basic norm of truth. Consider this depiction of one current political figure as sketched by a leading commentator: "So he keeps pushing and pushing our system to its breaking point—where rules are for suckers, norms are for fools, basic truths are malleable and men and women of high character are banished." This sounds all too familiar. And then: "This is exactly what would-be dictators try to do: Flood the zone with lies so the people trust only them and the truth is only what they say it is." Broken systems allow chaotic agents to thrive. And under such conditions it is no wonder that there is a widespread, apparently permanent sense of distrust.[20]

If one cannot assume that an interlocutor or political opponent is of decent good will, constructive disagreement is not possible. Neither is the baseline form of civility we associate with basic rule following, including the peaceful transition of power. When I first started thinking about the necessity of civility in liberal politics, it was a minority view. The liberal project seemed to be in excellent repair, thriving and expanding on all fronts. More robust virtues were the order of the day. But there were dark clouds of dissent gathering even then, anxiety about global triumphalism and anger about the inherent violence of the neoliberal consensus. Who could have imagined the throes of incivility that would descend upon the body politic within three decades?[21]

6

Virtuous Circle

BY THE TIME I PULLED my rental van of used furniture and books through the shabby outskirts of New Haven, a sweaty blue-collar city on Connecticut's Long Island shore, some things had become clear to me.

One concerned the nature of expertise, and therefore any trust associated with the embodiment of knowledge in experts. These are real people, with real experience—and also real prejudices and short-comings. But their social role is what is at issue here, the way that "some experts" and "researchers claim" are referenced in newspaper headlines, for example. Who, or what, were these experts, and why exactly were we supposed to pay attention when they said or reported things? (Experts *say* or *report*, perhaps sometimes *claim*, more than they do anything else, at least if public discourse is any indication.)

Could I even aspire to becoming some kind of expert myself? Is an expert more born than made? I don't know. I imagine very few scholars, especially in the humanities, set out to become experts in the "experts say" mode. The technocratic associations sit oddly with the scholarly tradition that, even when buffeted by fashion, is always rooted in medieval norms. But graduate school in the humanities is not a bad place to examine the question of authority, not because the study smoothly confers expertise but precisely because it doesn't.

Like most people, I was struck even then by the inversion of the normal markers of competence in this world: dress, comportment, efficiency, and normal grooming standards were suspended or flipped. With the exception of American political science professors, who dress like low-level F B I agents in identikit Brooks Brothers rig-outs, and a few in-the-wild dandies, academics secure trust through neglect, disarray, eccentricity, and tattered sweaters. Nietzsche's ascetic priest but dressed mostly in normcore style, and full of indignant, jargon-heavy creative resentment. Behaviour that would not be tolerated in any other field of action—outrage drag, let's call it—is celebrated because, you know, deep thought. The resulting trust is peculiar, topsy-turvy, perverse—the kind hard-drinking and womanizing abstract expressionist painters used to enjoy in the New York art world. Competence is endlessly disputed, like everything else, and so projected image matters more than usual.

Another thing I knew was that, already in these early days of uneasy privilege and elite self-consciousness, the undergraduate students at Yale and other elite incubators had begun to present the demeanour of *excellent sheep*, to use an influential epithet from a quarter-century later.[22] Inculcated, if not exactly indoctrinated, in a nation-wide cult of meritocratic wishfulness—willing acolytes don't mind control, just testimony—they were at once confident of their status as S A T-score winners, legacy preferences, or simply very, very rich.

At the same time their residual moralism and penchant for crediting the fiction of intrinsic elitism made them disdain the "born on third and thinks he scored a triple" idiocy of the junior Bush president, erstwhile Yalie. That middle-aged second-gen patrician entitlement was not for them; they *earned* their good grades and Phi Beta Kappa keys, their taps into the tomb-house secret societies of the campus. Bush Junior's father, a U S Navy fighter pilot and baseball captain, was considered old-school gormless but somehow worthy as a scion of the gentleman's-C, Ivy League vibe of pre-Holocaust innocence. The Ivy League students of that era were liberal but not, to my Canadian-Prairie and Catholic liberation-theology eyes, all that radical. Some were uncomfortable with the opportunities and elite social outcomes that awaited them on the other side of their commencement ceremony. When the elder Bush president came to give the featured speech at one such occasion that I attended, announcing most-favoured-nation trading status for China, there was a lot of security but only a token opposition. The speech was boring but hardly inaudible. (I had better times listening to Garry Trudeau and Tom Wolfe, both Yale grads.)

So it goes, in waves of privilege with slightly shifting narrative arcs. It has been said that a Yale bachelor's degree offers *carte blanche* for entering either the CIA or Wall Street, taking up one's station in Langley or some tony investment bank, two branches of the same big firm. That hasn't changed with the leftward shift of campus culture and politics: the Ivy kids of today may be more versed in Frantz Fanon and Paulo Freire but they still mostly end up in finance, consulting, and maybe arts administration. A minority go into education, journalism, and the arts, there to replicate the growing social-democratic drift to the left in graduate-dominated fields.

Outrage over this development, like moral panics about cancel culture, are often just right-wing bugaboos, but there is indeed a curious irony in having a comfortable and entrenched cultural elite that is officially dedicated to anti-elitism. In this moment when, as critic Andrew Sullivan has said, "we all live on campus," there is a dissonant denial of the very hierarchies that shape developed nations and the world at large. The heavy irony here is that there is little vestigial confidence in ideas of quality or superiority *even as* worldly success becomes daily more winner-take-all in nature. Call it a peculiar cultural contradiction of late–late capitalism: zero-sum elites can no longer suffer to entertain the *thought* of elitism, especially about themselves.[23]

Meanwhile, the true independents, we're told, are defecting entirely from schoolroom norms in pursuit of more rounded learning. The same critic who coined that excellent moniker "excellent sheep" in 2014, William Deresiewicz, had noticed a different tenor seeping into American colleges by 2024. There was a kind of refusenik mentality making itself felt in subtle ways, almost entirely obscured by both the Gaza war protests and the business-as-usual reduction of college life to capitalist job training. "Beneath their talk of education, of unplugging from technology, of having time for creativity and solitude," he writes, "I detected a desire to be free of forces and agendas: the university's agenda of 'relevance,' the professoriate's agenda of political mobilization, the market's agenda of productivity, the internet's agenda of surveillance and addiction. In short, the whole capitalistic algorithmic ideological hairball of coerced homogeneity. The desire is to not be recruited, to not be instrumentalized, to remain (or become) an individual, to resist regression toward the mean, or meme." This judgment was offered in the course of praising do-it-yourself higher-education schemes over the tainted campus pressures.[24]

I want to believe that such a spirit of self-discovery is present among young people, even counting the ones who choose formal education over the noble path of the autodidact. I don't think indoctrination is nearly as widespread as the off-campus pundits seem to believe. Still, that all misses the central issue of trust here, namely that the elite schools are still heavily gated minisocieties with reliable conduits to wealth and power. One of the things that has remained steady, at a time when fewer and fewer average Americans view higher education as a good investment, is that legacy preference and social connections will always help settle the bill favourably for those in the top echelons. The rich still like the looks of their ROI when it comes to Ivy League credentials and the unpaid internships in Manhattan or Los Angeles that will follow. Potential indoctrination and a stiff bill are not real disincentives when it comes to a lifelong earnings bump.

According to a 2021 study, the median lifetime employment income for American adults with a bachelor's degree is US$2.8 million—US$1.2 million more than that of workers with a high-school diploma only. Returns on elite education follow similar patterns, though the data are harder to isolate. A degree from Harvard costs more than one from Wayne State; it is also worth more in the postgraduate world.[25]

Mainstream disdain and distrust of universities are compounded when clear financial disparities are joined, as they often are at elite institutions, with liberal political ideas. It's a strange brew of distrusting the institutions of privilege-bestowal, even while being gripped by the iron logic of the market. Why go into lifelong debt, possibly nullifying a promised earning advantage for degree-holders, for the dubious benefit of having yourself or your child indoctrinated into the fringe ideology of critical race theory and postmodern gender-bending nonsense? We also know that, whatever the opportunity costs, overeager parents with more money than morals will commit bribery and fraud for the chance to get their sons and daughters on the elite higher-education gravy train. This scandal happened at the very same time that trust in institutions of higher education, never very strong in some quarters of the United States, was dipping sharply within a general crisis of social authority. (Trust levels are higher in Great Britain, Canada, and Western Europe.)

American data gathered before the brutal Hamas raid of October 2023 and the resulting Gaza war showed that trust in higher education had dropped in every recorded demographic since 2015. The sharpest drops of confidence were evident in Republican voters (down 37 percent over those eight years), people without college degrees (down 25 percent), and people over fifty-five years old (down 24 percent). By 2023 only 19 percent of Republicans reported confidence in universities, and only 33 percent of men. By contrast, Democrats, Independents, and those with college degrees were more confident, but only to levels of between 32 and 59 percent.[26]

Within the institutions themselves, there is plenty of open conflict, especially lately, but also a lot of wilful blindness. This was as true in 1987 as it is now, though there are certainly more visible and more vocal ideologues these days, greater in both number and volume but also more strident. These people tend to stay away from philosophy courses, in my own admittedly non-scientific experience, where rigour in argument is hard to avoid or gloss with jargon. Even at Yale the students I taught were less obviously of the patrician-but-progressive Ivy type than I had been expecting. As usual, philosophy instead tended to pull in the campus eccentrics, service-minded Midwestern innocents, California surf-Zen buccaneers, and old-fashioned Marxist radicals from Bronx Science and Stuyvesant. Most of the students I got to know best ended up as academics or journalists, with one notable exception who became a successful actor.[27]

I arrived in the midst of a long humid summer, and my memories of graduate school are consistently marked by a memory of warm dampness. Little beads of sweat would form on my back as I sat for hours in front of a boxy, expensive Macintosh computer, at the time the most expensive thing I had ever owned. Yale's buildings, especially the libraries, were without air conditioning, but the tough granite and elegant federal-style red brick sheltered cool corners, polished wood, and leather-upholstered armchairs. Not so the clapboard and saltbox houses along Whitney Avenue or in the small streets behind the hockey rink designed by a globe-trotting Finn. Another cultural economy of limited means and straitened access: hockey games, free student concerts, and excellent coal-fired pizza were the town's main pleasure-dome offerings.[28]

I lived and worked here for four years, almost as long as the time I'd spent in my hometown of Toronto. Most of the time I was alone in a reading room, reading monastically and writing when I could. We photocopied chapters and journal articles endlessly, a magical act tantamount to reading them. Every text was subject to close underlining and copying, an equally magical pursuit that daily approached the mad limit of finding significance in the whole book, sentence after sentence marked for emphasis or carefully transcribed. Borgesian literary reproduction!

I was poor the whole time, married for part of it, and fairly miserable. It was, after all, graduate school: you're not supposed to be *happy*. I'd decided to continue my philosophical studies with a doctorate, vowing that I would insist on political relevance in my work. Relevance now strikes me as the kind of psychological bête noire that my own savvier students rightly ignore but which fetches those prone to earnest conviction with something like religious enthusiasm. At best, when it comes to philosophy, relevance must look after itself. Seeking it consciously is deadly, especially when one is still standing on the embarcadero of worthwhile thought. This compulsion to theorize everything in terms of a given view of the world can become addictive, of course, but also then self-defeating. One fellow of whom we despaired wrote, like Ludwig Wittgenstein, a single sentence every day which he then tore up the following morning. He'd been in the program for ten years and was the only really cheerful PhD student I ever knew.

New Haven had then the highest per-capita homicide rate of any city in the United States, surpassing even decisively broken trust-free zones like East St Louis. The Great Northern Migration had transformed this industrial belt along Long Island Sound together with other benighted places like Bridgeport, and racial tension was a fact of daily life. So was de facto segregation, cultural and geographical. A precise risk map could be drawn of the downtown precincts, showing just which streets formed boundaries between acceptable and no-go neighbourhoods. For white people, I mean: the Yale students, professors, and carriage-trade scions of the town. In the middle of town, beside the historic green and bounded by actual towers, walls, and fences are the scattered buildings of the university. Unlike Toronto's downtown campus, which flows through and around the city's busy fixtures, dropping small pools of sylvan calm into the bustle, Yale is a fortress. The city was and is considered the worst of the Ivy League sites, the "armpit" tucked into a couple of hills and an invisible harbour.

More than any European university I know, Yale has the feeling of a medieval redoubt, a concentration of architecture and learning enjoying a fragile, contingent existence on hostile territory. Crossing the barriers was always an adventure. A trip to the federal building to get a social security number found me helplessly trying to help a Black man with no writing ability to fill out a form. A local pro hockey game plunked us down into a blue-collar, white Connecticut that was like a third estate, a tribe apart from both the resident Black population and the white-dominated university crowd. The latter could be appreciated cavorting in traditional style at football tailgate parties dominated by Range Rovers, Lalique crystal goblets, and fur coats.

Critical theory, postmodernism, social justice, and critical race theory are today considered the four corners of a different intellectual square, some sort of hanging scene of the right-wing imagination. In fact they are all quite distinct projects, and have little or no valid overlap. To group them together is a typical but unfortunate category mistake, one that is at best merely lazy and at worst evidence of its own ideological intention. These intellectual currents are also seen as key elements in some large-scale program of ideological indoctrination, by which presumably innocent young adults are reduced from free-thinking market-dwellers into left-wing zombies dedicated to risible goals like "social justice." Given how widely held this negative view continues to be in public discourse about universities, it is worth recalling what these intellectual movements, and the university faculty who study them, are really about.[29]

Let us stay for the moment with the idea of critical theory, so often misconstrued in everyday discourse—often for cheap ideological ends. It is a stream of thought issuing from a group of influential mid-century German intellectuals. These thinkers—Adorno, Horkheimer,

Marcuse, Benjamin (in a way), Habermas (in a way)—are undoubtedly influenced by Marx but are hardly to be considered orthodox or
doctrinaire Marxists. The simplest accurate generalization to be made
here is that their thinking involves the critical assessment of assumed
norms, including their sometimes-rickety foundations.[30]

So, here is one basic assumption of all genuine critical theory, not
the caricatures and lampoons that pass so smoothly through the media
mainstream. Culture is a system of consumption, producing demand for
its shiny commodities even as it colonizes the consciousness of its market, obliterating political awareness in a frenzy of getting and spending.
The most effective marketing does not tout the virtues of its products so
that people come to desire them. It manufactures the desire and then
supplies the product. Eventually, the product is dispensable since the
brand—or more precisely the brand *identity*—is what is desired and sold.

Very few people today would want to question such a basic critical
assessment. In fact, some would probably make these critical insights
the starting point for some kind of clever antimarketing branding campaign offering a sly take on product placement or bogus brand loyalty.
This kind of manipulation for hire is the stuff of popular cultural history (*Mad Men*, say) as well as soft-dystopian fiction (Frederik Pohl's
The Space Merchants).[31] We might not all go as far as Theodor Adorno
and condemn the idiocy of camping, suntanning, jazz on the radio, or
all Hollywood movies—but then again, in certain moods, we might.

On this view, and as suggested earlier, critical theory and cultural
criticism are endless tasks. They are also executed without a foundational truth that lies beyond question. Like the ship of Theseus in an
ancient thought experiment, every rotting plank of thought must be
judged and replaced in turn without the ship itself falling to pieces.
Of course, then we must ask: is it the same ship? Well, it depends on
what we mean by *the same*.[32]

That core insight seems so obvious that it is hard to credit both
the excitement of first encountering these ideas and the recent back-

lash against them. Interpretation is constant and constantly necessary. There is no available standpoint outside the field of knowledge
from which that knowledge can be vouchsafed en bloc. This is not
Marxist mumbo-jumbo, just accurate intellectual history. "But facts,
like telescopes and wigs for gentlemen, were a seventeenth-century
invention," wrote one prominent conservative philosopher.[33] A data
point exists meaningfully only inside an assumed meaningful system.

* * *

IMMANUEL KANT'S AGENDA-SETTING, THREEFOLD QUES-
TION of enlightenment took this form: *What can I know? What should
I will?* and *What may I reasonably hope for?* The central question is the
moral one, because here we have the power to exert the human will
for good or ill. We are rational agents, which entails that we must act
in the world based on claims of reason. Happiness, if it should come
to us, is pleasant but adventitious.

In 1984, Michel Foucault answered an invitation to revisit Kant's
basic question about enlightenment. It was the year of Orwell, of
course, and two hundred bloody years had passed since the appearance
of Kant's original pamphlet. Globalization and neoliberal economics
were well entrenched, the New World Order firmly in place. What
could be said about the aspirations of the lonely rational agent now,
with nearly five billion fellows on the planet? (What can be said now
that there are eight billion of us?)

Foucault posed this rhetorical question: "How can the growth of
the capabilities of individuals with respect to one another be severed
from the intensifications of power relations?" These are relations "conveyed by various technologies," including "institutions whose goal is
social regulation, or productions with economic aims, or techniques
of communication."[34] Well, the answer is that they cannot be so severed. And so those technologies must become the focus of our critical

inquiry. Any continued emphasis on the "fictions" of individuality simply missed the systemic point: we do not exist apart from our suspension in fields of power. Foucault called these *practical systems.* He meant "what [people] do and the way they do it," the interface of forms of rationality with their freedom to act, "reacting to what others do, modifying the rules of the game, up to a certain point."[35] And so subsidiary questions follow. How do we stand as subjects of our own knowledge? How are we made subject to power? How do we conceive of ourselves as effective moral agents?

Enlightenment is not "a theory, a doctrine, nor even ... a permanent body of knowledge that is accumulating." Rather, he said, it is "an attitude, an ethos, a philosophical life in which the critique of what we are is at one and the same time the historical analysis of the limits that are imposed on us." That suggests something quite familiar to us today, namely the idea that we must interrogate the *historical circumstances* of thought, including notions of truth and validity. This is hopeful, however, because it is also "an experiment with the possibility of going beyond" the limits imposed on us by circumstance.[36] Executing a genealogy of ideas is necessary; it is also potentially liberating. Here, Foucault follows in the footsteps of Nietzsche, Marx, and Freud—the masters of creative suspicion. Entangled within practical systems, then, we are not exactly unfree. In fact, proper awareness of our multiple placements offers precisely the scope for experimentation with selfhood that leads to multiple subject positions, fluid self-presentation, and all the other gifts of what we might call a neo-Enlightenment moment.[37] At the same time, our malleability of character and role is a dangerous property. One thinks, for example, of the famous Milgram experiments at Yale (1961). In these controversial studies, recruits were told to administer electric shocks to "patients" upon the command of an authority figure. Despite some hesitation and evident conflict, the recruits largely complied with the commands.

"The extreme willingness of adults to go to almost any lengths on the command of an authority constitutes the chief finding of the study and the fact most urgently demanding explanation," Milgram wrote later. "Ordinary people, simply doing their jobs, and without any particular hostility on their part, can become agents in a terrible destructive process. Moreover, even when the destructive effects of their work become patently clear, and they are asked to carry out actions incompatible with fundamental standards of morality, relatively few people have the resources needed to resist authority."[38]

These experiments have since been faulted for methodological and ethical failures as well as overreaching conclusions. The results, which expose human tendencies to deferral and obedience, nevertheless strike a guilty chord of recognition in many of us. In any event, we know that matters of identity and authority grow more and more complex in our day, even as power has assumed spectral, postmodern forms. Increasingly, there is no unified public sphere or single realm of political contestation, if there ever was. Instead, the very idea of the public is fractured and multiple. Under these conditions, how can we possibly go on talking to each other, rather than past each other or even punishing each other on command?[39]

Mainstream news outlets may blithely refer to "Canadians" or "Australians," for example, or (more contentiously) "the American people" or "the German people," but these collective nouns are reduced by experience either to statistical trivialities or dangerous fictions. The crisis of authority in knowledge and expertise is projected into a similar and daily more acute crisis in media and public discourse. We cannot solve the latter problem by ignoring the former or sweeping it under the rug like the trust question supposedly solved by nonhuman financial systems. The production and consumption of knowledge is something we do. Rational agents have no option but to confront the fruits of their labours, however unconscious.

Very few professional passages can surpass the sheer joy of surviving the trial-by-ordeal of the PhD oral defence, the *viva voce* ("live voice") performance of learning. It's a lesson in humility. Other firsts will follow. Having your first blind submission published at one of the big peer-reviewed journals with a fancy Latin title and a 5 percent acceptance rate. First classroom lecture delivered, running out of prepared material forty minutes into the allotted sixty. First public lecture. First graduating supervisee. Any sane person reserves doubts about the modern university—a subject for another book entirely— but there is intrinsic value in scholarship in all its forms, however minute and incremental.

Yes, I believe this to be true. Knowledge really does display an element of pure worth, like beauty. But if beauty is "only the promise of happiness," as Stendhal said, then expertise is only the seed of judgment, and knowledge is only the condition of wisdom. There is always more work to be done. Universities at their best are guardrails on markets and the runaway ideology of "common sense." That is why they arouse such ire. It's also why their critics want to reduce them to trade schools or STEM-only, use-value academies—though the latter move obviously has its own political downside, if these "hard" disciplines are liable to woke rot too, as the wildest critics charge.

Of course, *intrinsic value* is not a claim that can be easily proved. It also feels feeble next to realities of the new-millennium university, which puts increasing bureaucratic pressure on the free pursuit of knowledge. I think dismally of all the emails I now receive asking for a hefty fee to publish articles in grandly named predatory journals, the bogus conferences floated entirely by faculty expense accounts, the proliferating, CV-padding publication lists now required of young scholars. Inside the daily workings of the university, one finds operating conditions that are likewise soul-destroying: the endless committee meetings and creeping bureaucratization of all things; the enforced diversity recitals, demanded and supplied with cynical pro forma ritual, like muttered land acknowledgements; the pall of silence imposed on uncomfortable ideas by the all-purpose charge of the "inappropriate."

Outside the campus walls, we also read a regular news sked of faked results, plagiarism, and sly manipulation by top scientists and researchers. Wikipedia's lists of documented academic fraud, for example, offer dozens of cases in every discipline you can name, including philosophy, and boasts some three hundred and thirty associated footnotes.[40] Here, depressingly, fact meets fiction—the manipulated results of high-profile scientists at Stanford, Harvard, and many other elite places seem eerily to mirror the elaborate collegiate-politics fiction of C. P. Snow, say, or maybe the more familiar machinations of David Lodge and Hogwarts instructors.

Cases of fraud in scientific research—"science fiction," as headline writers usually style it—is a less-juicy scandal subject than sexual harassment in academic settings. It makes for less-salacious novels and news stories alike. But it arguably involves deeper issues of trust, truth, authority, politics, and institutional soundness. These frauds are recurring reminders that even enduring and mostly reliable practices are composed of ambitious, self-serving, and sometimes malicious individuals. The good news is that this bad news comes to our attention at all. While scandals remain evidence of cheating, they also provide evidence of cheaters being caught and punished.[41]

Snow's 1960 novel, *The Affair*, is especially apt in the present discussion. Set in the mid-1950s, it centres on a specific and somewhat technical case of scientific fraud that bitterly divides a Cambridge college.[42] The story sounds deliberate echoes of the Dreyfus affair (1894 and following), Zola's "J'Accuse . . . ! (1898), and even Benda's *La Trahison des clercs* (1927; *The Treason of the Intellectuals*).[43] In fine-drawn microcosm, Snow's characters act out the violence of collapsing a person to their political identity and demonstrate how partisan conviction can first cloud and then destroy a community. The treason here is intellectual, and the offending identity is left-wing politics, not the Jewish background that made Dreyfus such a handy target of persecution. But as so often with art executed in minuscule, the lessons ripple out to the wider world. Henry Kissinger dismissed the viciousness of academic politics by citing the low stakes involved; Snow reminds us that, when it comes to all politics, viciousness sets the stakes.

One passage near the end of the novel is worth quoting at length in the context of larger questions of trust and authority. The novel's narrator, Lewis Eliot, a lawyer, addresses his former academic colleagues, trying to secure a good result for a junior academic, Howard, who is accused—falsely, it will turn out—of the fraud in question. The young scholar is feckless and surly, but not a liar. But his manner—and his leftist politics—have coloured the views of the "Court of Seniors," a council of old men within the college's arcane self-policing structure. With a series of rhetorical questions, Eliot confronts them in an effort to thaw their prejudice:

> Could the Court really give the faintest encouragement to the view that character and opinion went hand in hand? Wasn't this nonsense, and dangerous nonsense?...Wasn't it the chronic danger of our time, not only practical but intellectual, to let the world get divided into two halves? Hadn't this fog of prejudice—so thick that people on the two sides were ceasing to think of each other as belonging to the same species—obscured this case from the beginning? Hadn't it done harm to the college, to Howard himself, and to the chance of a just decision?[44]

We could add a few related questions from our own immediate context. Can we not try to remember that, despite the great temptation to believe otherwise, ideological conviction is not the same as personal identity? Can a person of character hold a view that you despise?

That willingness—that species of irony, if you like—is the basic distinction of all liberal thought. There are distressing indications of late
that many people in nominally liberal states not only choose to live
or work apart from ideological opponents, but also report that they
would *not offer help* to anyone with whom they strongly disagree.[45]

Can we further agree that no individual's surrender to the worst
features and perverse incentives of an imperfect practice is ever justified? Nor should it ever undermine the value of the practice taken
altogether? Bad-apple theory is a shaky basis for judging apples, but
also for doubting the baskets that hold them. We all know academia
may sometimes look exactly like a pyramid racket, as full of cheaters
and chancers as any cynically floated crypto stock. And sure, there
is always plenty of bubble buy-in to go around in the marketplace
of trendy ideas and emperor's-new-clothes futures. Still, the claims of
scholarship, reflection, and critical thinking deserve a special kind of
power within any universe of meaning. Their claims of authority are
based on both good evidence and careful assessment; they inspire trust
not because of personalities, but because of collective effort. There
are also clear mechanisms of gatekeeping and self-policing that act to
ensure professional integrity.

Of course, this is the ideal case, and so, not often to be found in
reality. Earnest scholarship can decline into fashionable jargon and
political hand-waving, providing further incentives for more of the
same in others. Sometimes the basket is to blame, not the individual
apples. The familiar enemies of thought—and so, of trust in universities more generally—are coiled within thought itself, and institution-
alizing those ideas in social organizations that command resources and
offer status, security, and even modest wealth are not to be let off the
hook of accountability and transparency. One of the recurring features
of astonishment in reading Snow's account of elite academic life in
1950s Britain is how male, egotistical, and enbubbled the characters all
are. It's psychologically fascinating but also a bit like reading ancient

scrolls, to see a closed society so secure in its unquestioned privilege and power. The outside world hardly exists, except in a kind of nuclear-option outcome where the scandal gets "in the papers," which of course all sides agree must be avoided at all costs.

The university of today is a vastly different place, far more permeable to outside influence, including currents of political fashion and ideological fervour, than before. It is also held more accountable to public opinion, government oversight, and plain old anti-intellectualism. It can feel like battle lines are forever being drawn between no-nonsense, come-off-it right-wing townies and loopy purple-haired left-wing gownies. (I know: those groupings themselves have a very old-fashioned feel. Gowns obv. = cosplay.) And yet, even the most optimistic defender of radical "postmodern" ideas has to note an ultimate irony of influence. Postmodernism has become politically effective, but not to the sort of purposes Foucault or Lyotard would approve. In fact, all the negative aspects of caricatured postmodernism have weirdly migrated from caricatured academia to the nihilistic, we-create-our-own-reality right wing. This movement runs from late-model conservatives like Karl Rove and Donald Rumsfeld to the say-anything politics of MAGA, whose leading figures were maybe aptly labelled "weird" in a rhetorical twist of the 2024 presidential election cycle. (The term, as deployed in slogans such as "Keep Austin Weird" or "Keep Portland Weird," had until then been typically reclaimed by reverse appropriative polarity, that is, turned from insult to compliment by self-conscious hipsters.)

Consider a telling concrete example. In October 2004 *New York Times Magazine* journalist Ron Suskind quoted a then-unnamed source from Bush's inner circle who dismissed those still mired "in what we call the reality-based community," defined as people who "believe that solutions emerge from your judicious study of discernible reality." He continued, "We're an empire now, and when we act, we create our own reality. And while you're studying that reality—judiciously, as you will—we'll act again, creating other new realities, which you can study too, and that's how things will sort out. We're history's actors ... and you, all of you, will be left to just study what we do."[46] The quotation was later attributed to Karl Rove, who was then a senior political advisor to Bush and became White House deputy chief of staff the following February, serving in that office until August 2007.

One might be tempted to dismiss this statement as typical neo-con bluster or bullshit. The defeat of the Republicans in the 2008 American presidential election gave many people hope that the imperial "Mission Accomplished" posturing of the Bush administration was a thing of the past, an aberration. But subsequent events, especially Donald Trump's metastasized version of this same right-wing "postmodern" strategy, indicate otherwise. I tend to credit Rove with a deeper insight here, namely that his diagnosis is correct, even in the absence of an American imperial mission. Rove understood, as Trump and his imitators surely do, that we no longer exist in a "reality-based" world. The new millennium had generated new norms of political discourse and behaviour—or rather, a public sphere in which there are no such norms. The old pieties of Enlightenment thought, including the essential premises that there is such a thing as "reality" penetrable by reason, and that such penetration has the power to alter behaviour, were in the dustbin of history.[47]

In their place was something we must call *postmodern right-wing realpolitik*: the conviction that power ("action" in Rove's formulation) creates its own rules and (temporary) realities. Those of us still trapped in the norms and methods of the "reality-based community" can now only stand by and watch, no doubt wringing our hands all the while. Our sharp tools of the mind, the honed chisels of evidence and logic, are just so many parlour tricks—and worse, ones whose unexamined exercise results only in pulling the wool over our own eyes.

Fortunately, there is still such a thing as the "claim of reason" that lays its hand upon us and our actions. We cannot escape the reach of rational regulation, much as we might desire to. And the even better news is that simply accepting the idea of such a claim of reason having purchase on our habits and desires can be sufficient to rescue belief from the depredations of comprehensive doubt. But first we have to want to believe.[48]

7

The Will to Believe

BEFORE THERE WAS FOX NEWS there was Fox Mulder, charismatic knight of crazy conviction. *The X-Files* did not premiere until 1993 and then ran for eight seasons, but its origins are as deep as the paranoid style discerned by Richard Hofstadter in the 1960s. The show's notable inversion of standard procedural narratives, its great coup, was pairing David Duchovny and Gillian Anderson as the FBI agents Mulder and Scully. Instead of the familiar two bickering cops, we had one dedicated ephemera geek, a male connoisseur of subcultural craziness, and a hard-headed female detective. There they were, embodied in style: the hermeneutics of suspicion and the hermeneutics of belief, two poles of any valid theory of interpretation, the conflicted human soul rendered as male and female principles but with the roles reversed. This is psychic conflict played out as a cognitive buddy picture. And because their investigations embraced the merely bizarre as well as the Grand Conspiracy of Everything, Mulder and Scully became glamorous avatars of our own confusion, the sicko psychodramas of the supermarket tabloids made flesh.

"Trust no one," the show told us—it was the title of the first episode. But also, as the ufological truth seeker's poster in Mulder's office reminded us: "I want to believe." The latter sentiment has a more profound intellectual resonance than might first appear, leading back to William James's influential claims in his essay "The Will to Believe," first given as a lecture to the Philosophical Clubs of Yale and Brown Universities and published in the *New World* in 1896.[49] The lecture shows James's distinctive American pragmatism deployed in the service of a rather unlikely beneficiary: evidence-lacking belief, specifically religious faith. This faith, James argues, may be considered rational even if we hold no prior evidence for it. The willingness to believe its truth is part of what it means to come to see it as true.

More precisely, James is concerned to defend two exceptions to any general epistemic demand for evidence: (1) beliefs whose evidence becomes available only after they are believed (hypothesis-venturing); and (2) beliefs that, by existing, make themselves true (self-fulfilling beliefs). Both of these are typically considered suspect ways of going on, but James wants to force an acknowledgement that belief is not so strict or clear—not so dogmatic—as some "absolutists" would have us believe. We form or half form beliefs that later get cemented into cognitive building blocks as certain as anything we have. And we must do this, because some areas of knowledge can remain opaque to us unless and until we venture into them with minimal good faith.

One of the most significant of such willed beliefs is an individual's commitment to the meaning of life itself. James believed this can, perhaps must, be held as a necessary condition of avoiding death by suicide. (His reasoning is not always strict.) "Be not afraid of life," James told the Harvard YMCA Club in another lecture, "Is Life Worth Living?" in 1895.[50]

"Believe that life *is* worth living, and your belief will help create the fact."[51] Well, possibly—but that also means possibly not. Investing life with meaning does work, though not invariably. What might be a more cautious generalization is the inverse: fail to believe that life is worth living and it will not be. The difference is one of an intervening ocean and a century's turn: American pragmatism creeps along to a version of French existentialism.

In any event, James is an optimist and a sui generis species of spiritualist, but he is also still a skeptic, since his will to believe (sometimes styled a right) is set against dogmatism, not doubt as such. On one reading of philosophical history, then, we can see James as working in a human, maybe even Humean, tradition of taking common sense seriously in its limits, accepting the role of custom and habit in most of what we call thinking. As in Aristotle's account of virtue, sometimes repetition and habituation take the place of instruction or conviction. I come to be good by acting as good people do. On parallel, I come to believe by practising the belief. (Pascal's wager offers a crisp version: act as if God exists, and you will come to see that it is so.)

This idea is essential to the entire problematic of trust and authority. As a practical matter, we cannot conduct our lives as a constant challenge to conventions and rules, or the structures that deploy them. We have neither the talent nor the time. More deeply, we are so constituted that habit is a more powerful force in everyday life than rigorous reflection. This is okay! True, addiction becomes a proximate danger when bad habits are indulged: when short-term highs override long-term desires. But this danger is not a knock against habit as such, only bad ones. And addressing those bad ones—which is part of what I am doing right now—is part of beginning to cultivate better ones.

As we saw already, epistemic autonomy is not always the right answer to a given life situation. Good habits are often more effective guidance than reason, just as deference to authority rather than individual conviction is sometimes the right action. Score a point for Hume here on acute psychology, and another for making philosophy practical. But there is yet another limit on cognitive stability, which I discussed in the introduction. I think it captures the heart of the issue before us, because it suggests the existence of a philosophical stopping rule, not just a confession of limited energy or will. It is precisely the idea highlighted earlier, that "seeing-through" is—and must be—driven toward something that one cannot finally see through.

Questioning basic principles, including occluded structural realities, is both useful and necessary. We do not secure any sort of legitimacy without it. And many if not most claims must remain within the ambit of questioning, even if we do not, right now, choose to question them. This will be the underlying principle of falsifiability in science: only those claims that can in principle be proved false count as candidates for truth. But questioning comes to an end—or better, is suspended willingly—for practical purposes of life and because there must be somewhere to plant our moral and rational feet. We need to get on with things, and to do so, we need things to believe in.

There will be much dispute about this, naturally, but it is of the essence that we make our way to some kind of bedrock. In his rather imprecise way, James understands this. At the same time, James can be pushed over to the rare class of foundational skeptics in the Cartesian tradition. Writing in the first-person voice of his *Meditations on First Philosophy* (1641) Descartes asks us to entertain what later philosophers like to call *hyperbolic doubt* about the traditional problem of reliability in the external world.

That is to say: we should doubt everything that can be doubted. Hyperbolic, but in the service of truth. And then, if anything should remain standing after this bounce-the-rubble, all-out assault on everyday belief, *that* will be what cannot be doubted. And this will be foundation: the rock upon which you may raise an epistemic edifice. Along the way we will encounter people who think they are made of glass, with pumpkins for heads; round towers that are in fact square; a malicious demon bent on our deception, facing off against a deity who could not deceive us on peril of his own self-contradiction.

What is the point? Well, just that establishing that firm foundation, or securing the right to believe things, is sometimes—maybe always—a matter of doubt and questioning. As usual, we must begin before we can go on. Blind dogma is probably our least-good option, but toxic doubt closed to the possibility of any belief at all is almost as bad. When contrarianism becomes its own self-fulfilling belief, the circle of potential knowledge closes. It becomes a magic ring ensorcelled by our own insecurity. A self-laid trap, in short. At that point, no expert can any longer give us aid because we have become idiots in the literal Greek meaning of an isolated, private individual—the person for whom there is no public existence, a noncitizen, a player without a game. (It will be obvious by now that these metaphors of players and games are indispensable in our discussion; I will say more about this in part 5.)

* * *

FOR SOME, THOUGH, THE CHOSEN game—the antic disposition that provides the deepest pleasure and reassurance—is *constant* doubt. These are the contrarians, the unbelievers, the doubting Thomases.

Denial can be classed as a temptation, or even as a kind of social trope that may wax and wane, but it is intrinsic to the human mind, if anything is. And yet, we are not forever condemned to it by an implacable nature: we can resist and reform instinct even if that takes a good deal of contrary effort. This is the self-transcendent essence of the human condition. We know that Peter denied his association with Jesus three times before the cock crowed, at least as Luke tells it, but nowadays denials are a lot easier. Just one will do, and you can make it at any time of day on social media or some other dependency-creating interface. Deny science, deny experts, deny social and legal norms, and above all deny responsibility for any ethics scandals, cronyism, or accusations of bad governance.

Let us be honest: the act of denial does feel life-affirming in some circumstances. It places me against the man, or the mob, or the who-ever. But we might also recall that it is the first of Elisabeth Kübler-

Ross's five stages of grief. You have some work to do. Denial ain't just a river in Africa, as Mark Twain probably did not say. Sure, you can always adopt some Trump-era version of "never apologize, never explain," and thus secure your membership in the current version of the nineteenth-century Know-Nothing party. But that is to make the wrong kind of ignorance into the wrong kind of virtue. Knowing nothing is only valuable if it leads to wisdom, not simply to further ignorance and the kind of self-satisfied prejudice that aligns with the misplaced pride of remaining in the dark, of merely the complacency of leaving one's head buried forever in the sand.

Lots of people know nothing, in short. But some of them *know* that they know nothing and make that a guiding principle in life. This is the good kind of ignorance, we might say, already referenced in my earlier discussion of Rumsfeld's square. The record indicates that Socrates, directed to the Oracle at Delphi, was told that his fate was to be the wisest of Athenians. Since he, a simple soldier and cobbler, knew that he was ignorant, it seemed clear that wisdom might reside in knowing that he knew nothing. Michel de Montaigne struck a medal with the skeptical slogan: *Que sais-je?*—what do I know? We start from a lack of knowledge, but with lots of questions, especially for those who claim to know.

Things get tricky when knowledge becomes increasingly complex, however, demanding individuals who devote their lives to one special subfield in order to advance it. Nonexperts in turn resent and fear these individuals, who sometimes tell them what to do or correct their errors. So, people refused to wear masks even months into a global pandemic; they would not take a state-sponsored vaccine even when it became available, because it may have been infected with government software. And they were led by a president who said he "disagreed" with Anthony Fauci, a doctor who might actually know what he was talking about—or at least possessed the relevant credentials and experience to vouchsafe a measure of trust in an emergency.

But did Trump and his followers—or, more lately, Robert F. Kennedy Jr and *his* followers—disagree based on their own vast knowledge of medicine? No, of course not. This was not a battle of competing bodies of knowledge and rational authority. That kind of dispute makes sense because it is conducted within the ambit of accepted inquiry. We may feel uncomfortable with a given decision, but we do not therewith immediately dispense with the entire structure of evidence-based claims. Many of the recent public health disputes, and many others like them, are battles over the very idea of expertise in a time when we need it most. Sometimes, in public discourse as in law, you do not actually possess the standing to have a view on a specific matter: you are not qualified or in possession of the relevant facts and experience. Reluctantly, you ought to accept authority on evidence that you cannot personally validate. Doubt a scientific result, even doubt the scientist; but you cannot doubt science itself, except on pain of irrationality.

That sounds to many like elitist talk of the worst possible sort, and so they take leave to deny this denial of our objection or our standing to make it. The impulse is natural and even sometimes laudable. We also know that genuine scientific method can slide into its own form of ideological capture, *scientism*, which presumes to answer all human questions and needs. Denial of scientific truth, as such, is a disaster for collective thought and social undertakings generally. Soon the flurry of denials becomes an argument between players and referees, which can only end in one of two ways: a reaffirmation of the rules-based order of the game, with a decision that some players dislike, or a deterioration into chaos. The basketball fans at Duke University like to chant, when the referee has made a call they consider bad, "We beg to differ! We beg to differ!" It is their right to communicate their displeasure in this civil way—or in any other way that does not spoil the game. The game goes on.

Denial is a deeply human act, something hardwired into our feeble brains, and not always a function of ignorance. Even Donald Rumsfeld knows that there are some things we don't know, and don't know that we don't know. That's not denial. Denial is claiming falsity when there is no evidence or argument to support such a claim. Denial is baby talk. *No! No! No!* Fauci became a lightning rod, a handy stand-in for any and all discontent about polarity-switching sciences, rival studies, and government's role in health. He was even chided for neglecting, as a scientist, the science that illustrates how prevalent denial is in the human species. This seems, at the least, extremely unfair. Fauci's specialty is epidemiology. He's not a social psychologist. In this sense, he was and remains to some extent a mythological figure in Barthes's sense: a trope, an image, a layered signifier, a meme.

This might be the moment to highlight why the current wide use of "meme" does us such a disservice. We have lost hold of a useful concept. Memes were not always silly or mischievous cartoons that achieve fleeting viral status on social-media platforms. When Richard Dawkins coined the term in his 1976 book *The Selfish Gene*, he meant it to stand as a metaphor for socially transmissible clumps of information. Just as genes in the natural world coded information about bodies, lifespan, and health that could be passed on via procreation, memes were self-replicating cultural nodes that in effect used human minds and actions as hosts for their promulgation. The viral part of the metaphor has stuck because it is, well, the stickiest: some images, gestures, mini-narratives, or logical dynamics are better at spreading than others.[52]

Memes are, like genes, normative in the baseline descriptive sense: they guide and condition past judgments and future actions. This does not mean that memes have a sense of right or wrong. The "selfishness" of genes, which is simply their heedless interest in self-replication via a succession of hosts—and we conscious individual humans thank them for that—is mirrored by memetic indifference to our particular ends. A harmless meme might be something like the Gretzky- or Ronaldo-style goal celebrations in hockey or soccer, or the Bautista bat toss.

Kids everywhere immediately pick up the heroic microballet as a new habit after one viewing, then it takes on ironic or rococo flourishes, then eventually peters out. Unless you are very restrictive in your canon of sports aesthetics, this is all part of the fun. Or consider male crying in public, one of those human tendencies that falls in and out of fashion. In the recent past it was thought unsuitable for a man of strength to weep openly—a kind of minor Stoic epoch that has cracked and spread in the face of new thoughts about masculinity. But it is not the case that the thoughts predate the feelings, only that the actions stemming from the feelings wax and wane. Regency England was full of men crying in public, but not because they were more sensitive, gender fluid, politically correct, or DEI dedicated than we are today.

But other memes are actively harmful, not despite but because of their excellent rate of distribution, replication, and amplification. They are not just enabled by their hosting social-media platforms, but also manipulated and validated there. In areas such as public discourse, insincere apology and thanks plus their various rhetorical conventions now exhibit this kind of self-generating cluster. *That was not me. Getting the help I need. Learning moment. Soul-searching. Thoughts and prayers. Thank you for your service. Thank you for your patience.* Technically, this kind of locution is *bullshit*—speech with no regard for the truth-value of its implied propositions.[53] It is neither true nor false, and yet somehow sincere in its insincerity: a tawdry performance, a minor and mostly despicable art. But public discourse has to tolerate some bullshit and may even enjoy it on some level: this is more kayfabe. Such cosplay and clowning may even count as tolerable bullshit or be no worse than meretricious and dumb. The problem is that a memetic system never functions in isolation.

Bullshit is just the sign of deeper ills where the norm of truth has been suspended or forgotten. The debasing of important emotions across a wide range is a net loss for humanity. Emphasis on the worst of those emotions, or the most deleterious of cognitive acts, is a positive menace in the human house. Our distracted minds become the seedbed of our own life-destroying fifth column. The condition is worsened when an influential public figure, say a disgraced and verifiably criminal once-and-future politician, has as "his most effective superpower" the "ability to speak without consequence, without factual basis, without shame and, often, without end."[54]

So, the question is, even if denial is common in us, widely imitated, addictive, subject to copycat spread, does that ever make it okay? Hate is rampant in human affairs, as are violence, torture, irrational prejudice of all kinds, and hosts of other behaviours that are "natural" yet abhorrent. We don't, at least in our better moments, simply give them a free pass. The image of someone pointing and firing a handgun is a meme; so is the high vantage point, body armour, automated long gun, and multiple oversized clips of the new-millennium spree killer. These are within our natural range. They should hardly be considered worth imitating.

The criticism of the Fauci myth serves to highlight two salient features of Covid-dominated political culture, as well as what we are still coping with in its long fallout. The first is that expertise, always a fragile property, has become more suspect in every year since, perhaps, the 2008 financial crisis. This decline of respect comes, in large measure, from an often-wilful category mistake: the individual bearer of knowledge, with all his or her mixture of frailties, is taken for the body of knowledge in question, and relentlessly attacked ad hominem. All claims, even potentially valid ones, are judged by the reductive standards of the speaker's base motives or, worse, set aside as useful-idiot expressions of partisan capture. Every expert is revealed as a stooge for management—whoever that may be in the given case.

It does not help that many people help themselves to claims of expertise based on flimsy familiarity with the matter at hand. The old saying has it that an expert is a person who has read one book; these days, you don't even have to do that much work. A few hours on websites or podcasts, and you are surely the smartest person in the room—even if the room is just your basement office. (Even or especially.) The second is that calling people stupid is not the best way to make them act smarter. You don't rehabilitate an addict by calling him or her names. You need structure and therapy and support; also nudges, incentive schemes, and social scaffolding. More information will mostly not help.

Trust in experts has been eroded for good reasons and bad, or at least understandable causes versus irrational or self-serving ones. The understandable reasons include things like fake science journals, human limitation, institutional arrogance and aggressive scientism wielded as moron-bashing ideology. Scientism is the enemy, however, not science. Dawkins and Daniel Dennett and their fellow "Brights" could hardly have set a more irritating and condescending contemporary self-presentation; they make freethinking and atheism look smug precisely when it should be most humble. And yet reflexive, thoughtless, and comprehensive suspicion of elites, East Coast elites, Laurentian elites, or whatever is the going version right now, is just doubling down on dumb. That denial tactic may work rhetorically—it may even get you elected to high office—but we must all recognize that it is harmful, immoral, and sells short stock on the human-potential market.

Contrarianism, then, when assumed as an identity, is, as we have ample cause to know in the current political landscape, a "brain-rotting drug" closely associated with addiction to conviction. "You can watch someone's effective IQ drop as they lean into contrarianism," the political critic Adam Ozimek said in a series of tweets from June 2023, surveying the broken landscape of a postpandemic world. "They lose the ability to judge others they consider contrarian, become unable to tell good evidence from bad, a total unanchoring of belief that leads them to cling to low quality contrarian fads" (@ModeledBehaviour, June 21, 2023). The issue at hand was the odd development of Big Tech honchos supporting the political ambitions of crank pretender Robert F. Kennedy Jr, a vaccine-mandate conspiracist and Bitcoin booster.[55]

This bodies forth the lurking will to disbelieve—or indeed transforms that negative will into an outward expression of the will-to-power, in Nietzsche's sense of the term, as when the epistemological denialism is made part of a larger ideological or political program. Denial is an assertion of ego, of independence over any external pressure or constraint, including factual accounts that do not appeal. "As soon as 'experts are wrong' becomes their guidestar," Ozimek added, "instead of the more reasonable placing of uncertainty bands around expert opinions and specifically identifying cases of expert bias, their ability to gauge reality becomes extremely restricted. It's like mental glaucoma." *Mental glaucoma* is good. But surely expert claims must be questioned, not simply accepted without further ado?

Well, yes—but the larger system of functional belief only works if we do not automatically mistrust, or simply claim as wrong, *every* expert and expert claim we encounter daily. We cannot verify every possible claim governing everyday action, both because we lack the time and because—significantly—we lack the applicable knowledge and training. Being contrarian for its own sake is ultimately self-defeating. It becomes another form of identity politics, an ideology, no more helpful or even rational than the forms of belief it takes leave to deride. At some point, on some issue, every cognitive actor, no matter how comprehensively guided by suspicion, must rely on something that cannot be independently verified. Then we must cultivate a form of skepticism that answers to the case in a productive way. That will vary by case, but a central orientation of compassion will help us follow the right compass.

In the best case, expertise represents a preponderance of evidence and accumulated scholarship, rather than flashing credentials or invoking institutional heft. Reliance on evidence is good scientific method: what is being offered is not the universal truth, just the best explanation so far. Sane and reasonable people, those willing to cooperate, can work with that. But other people, not all of them demonstrably insane, will still deny. Why? Because of several often-noted but apparently intractable features of the human mind: confirmation bias, motivated reasoning, fear of cognitive dissonance, the pleasures of solidarity, sheer contrarianism as an ideology unto itself, and maybe a misplaced, harmful belief in "individual freedom" over community safety. Any or all of these twisted motivations may be in play in any one person, at any given time. Confirmation bias, for example—the tendency to weigh evidence we like more heavily than evidence that contradicts our settled views—is widespread among even very self-critical people. It can be hard to spot in oneself, since it is, after all, a form of cognitive self-protection.

So, then what? Well, how about large doses of humility, more education, and a great deal of open discourse? We have to make ourselves more vulnerable in pursuit of what is right and true. Even if this entails personal risk, we should have confidence that the system overall is tracking the truth, or at least bending in its direction. John Stuart Mill was correct—in the marketplace of ideas, good ones can eventually drive out bad, but this is painful, costly and bloody. It's not me or you or some other person with an MD or a PhD who matters; it's good arguments that should prevail. This is creative destruction. If science teaches us anything, it's that previous thinking never lasts. Philosopher of science Karl Popper influentially argued that every scientific proposition must be falsifiable—not wrong, rather open to being shown wrong on its own terms. Otherwise, it is faith, ideology or madness.[56]

Falsifiability is a baseline standard of all good discourse, yet it's often misunderstood or distorted by media positioning and political posturing. For example, take note, in this political moment, that determining the meaning of "free speech" has become its own species of luxury good. A lot of hefty, credentialed, big-platform people (most of them experts in nothing except sounding off) are squawking about "cancel culture" and "ideological targeting," not really on principle but because their special privileges feel threatened. But using "freedom of speech" as a conceptual cudgel in your ideological battles against "mobs" is not classical liberal thinking. It's just a dog whistle in the culture wars. Denial is as denial does.

Hate speech, plagiarism, pseudoscience, cynical falsehood, and self-serving nonsense are not free speech. They are toxins to be eliminated by the clean air and sunshine of reason. At the same time, a lot of what is called censorship these days is only vigorous disagreement, calling out bullshit, and speaking truth to power. (We also have to leave room for self-serving nonsense, since without it there would be mostly silence.) There will always be deniers, of anything and everything, just like there are conspiracists, demagogues and witch hunters in every historical moment. They cannot be eliminated; they can only be made outliers. Elimination would be wrong as well as impractical; sometimes the outliers are the ones with vision. There is constant push and pull here. Maybe at some point, like all responsible people, those in error will admit that they were wrong. Maybe what once were errors will turn out to be productive insights, and the former truth-holders will be shown to stand in the wrong. All to the good: the willingness to acknowledge error is, after all, part of what it means to be smart.

8

The Empty Chair

THE FORCED RESIGNATIONS IN EARLY 2024 of two high-profile university presidents, Elizabeth Magill of the University of Pennsylvania and Claudine Gay of Harvard, unleashed a new wave of the culture wars. The two women were forced out in part because of their now-notorious legalistic replies about campus speech codes and antisemitism, with Dr Gay's disgrace compounded by charges of plagiarism. The third administrator targeted by the congressional hitters, Sally Kornbluth of the Massachusetts Institute of Technology, is still in her job. It is no coincidence that the three targets of Elise "Two Down" Stefanik were women, one Black and two new to their jobs.

Like everything else in the topsy-turvy madhouse of contemporary media, these spectacular implosions were subjected to multiple partisan interpretations. For some, they were examples of right-wing cancel culture and partisan "weaponization" of academic sloppiness. For others, this was simply diversity, equity, and inclusion ideology coming home to roost, a genuine wake-up call. The first group was alarmed, the second gleeful, but both were wide of the mark. Neither faction seemed to have a good idea of what a university is for, especially in a high-stakes world like the Ivy League, where donors can dictate policy, and favoured graduates of the cloistered institution run the outside world. But that can be no surprise, because nobody has a very good idea of what higher education is for. One of things higher education does, like all education, formal and otherwise, is to put itself into question. I think that is why so much mainstream punditry about universities strikes those of us who work in them as cartoonish. The commentary seems about as accurate as depictions of college life on television or in the movies, where every measly department chair has a wood-panelled office and aging instructors are eccentric and tweedy, vague yet egotistical, even as they fulminate over pronouns and gender-neutral bathrooms.

Written satire is better at capturing the comprehensively haywire features of academic life, the po-faced seriousness accorded to absurd and outlandish ideas, the benign tolerance extended to objectively abusive or disruptive behaviour. My three decades of faculty experience suggests that *Microcosmographia Academica* (1908), *The Groves of Academe* (1952), *Lucky Jim* (1954), and *Dear Committee Members* (2014) are the must-reads here, but there are many others that strike the correct note of cynical hilarity. But it's not all fun and games, as Cardinal Newman reminds us. Universities exert tremendous social and cultural influence, and control vast resources of all kinds. They confer status and vouchsafe expertise. They also foster critical thinking, good citizenship, and human curiosity. They are many other things besides: job-training sites, warehouses for wayward youth, mental spas, socialization machines, guarantors of tradition, incubators of innovation, and yes, sometimes indoctrination camps.

This multiplicity is what rival sides in the war always miss. Universities, despite their name, are never one thing. They are fractured, sprawling, contradictory, and incomplete. The Canadian philosopher George Grant suggested we should call them *multiversities*. (The term never caught on; and Grant was mostly concerned that academia was no longer avowedly Christian.) Of course, everybody has their own aspirational or nostalgic view of higher education. For some, the recent resignations signal a tectonic reckoning or a repetition of bad history. Dr Gay herself saw her ouster, with some reason, as a sign of dwindling trust in all public institutions—ironically agreeing with critics on the other side. The "ideological rot" of DEI, one conservative columnist characterized the Ivy League meltdown, "blew up the excellence model, centered on the ideal of intellectual merit and chiefly concerned with knowledge, discovery and the free and vigorous contest of ideas."[57] Now the tables were turned! Meanwhile, the historian Niall Ferguson suggested that the soft-on-Palestine Ivy League had enacted a new-millennium version of "the treason of the intellectuals," just as German academics had succumbed to the allure of Adolf Hitler in the 1930s.[58]

If nothing else, this latter lament confirmed that Godwin's law, and the so-called reductio ad Hitlerum, are alive and well. (The "law" argues that every political discussion will eventually lead to one side accusing the other of fascism, or Nazism, or both. The "reductio" is a species of ad hominem fallacy whereby a speaker's argument is nullified by accusing him or her of echoing Hitler.) Also, with respect to the former complaint, when you see the phrase "ideological rot" to condemn higher education, feel free to suspect projection or bad faith or both. DEI bureaucracy has become overweening, yes, the ideological kudzu of higher education; and radical ideas get a warmer welcome in universities than conservative ones. But the idea that there was some "excellent" former intellectual idyll, lately corroded by utopian political influence, is itself a dangerous nowhere-man fantasy.

Those of us who recall Bill Readings's searing late-Nineties indictment of the technocorporate university, *The University in Ruins*, will recognize this excellence.[59] It is yet another dream of annexing thought to the current arrangement. "Excellence" is a press-release word, a hand-waving empty locution kept alive in artificial rhetorical exercises like mission statements and ranking systems. Today's conservative nostalgia for a pure university, untouched by anything as unpleasant as social activism or anticapitalist thinking, is just a spectre of yesterday's corporate desire to yoke teaching to profit and neoliberal expansion. The one point of agreement between erstwhile critics like Readings and today's grumps is that bureaucracy has expanded beyond all reason in higher education. We might even posit that the current hybrid, top-heavy management layering of academic administration is an unholy alliance of micromanagement bullshit and ideological shadow play.

There is a further shared truth lurking in the current debates. We have to dig a little to uncover it. The advocates of partisan views often pretend that their ideological commitments are no more than common sense or just good scholarship. We have seen over and over that "common sense" is almost always a dodge or shibboleth. The truth is that education is always political, and so universities are ever *a site of their own contestation*. I mean that the status and meaning of the university are part of what we constantly argue about, both inside and outside the campus limits. Too often the political bias in and about education has been in the service of dominant ideas, not novel or liberating ones. People assume that higher education is job training of some sort, or perhaps a form of social screening, so that employers can harvest the best and brightest for service in their assumed-to-be-legitimate profit-reaping work. And to be sure, many students accept this bargain as real, and even inevitable. They buy in to the (valid) promises of wage bumps and financial safety, as well as the gained social status, even as they perform a kind of pantomime of social revolution.

But this is not intended as a criticism. The time to join a chorus of middle-aged glee that greets the disillusion of young radicals, reeking of generational schadenfreude, is never. The conservative impulse about higher education is always to offer some sort of realist curb on excessive hopefulness and along the way deny the university any status beyond warehousing youth, coddling effete elites, and maybe producing a small population of future bankers and finance dudes. To the campus radical they say, *That will never work in the real world. Get a life!* The liberal rejoinder ought to be an idealist curb on complacency and along the way defend the independent value of the university as an incubator of character and citizenship. To the preprofessionalized common-sense real-worlder, who knows the price of everything and the value of nothing, they should say, *There is only one world, and we all have to share it. Can you work to make it better? Live a* good *life!*[60]

The university, we might say, embodies a kind of institutionalized idealism, human hope built into neo-Gothic arches and arcane rituals. That is why it is always in ruins—and always should remain so, after its oddball fashion. Critics may still want to press the point: But ruins of what? And what more do we find when we poke around in the rubble? Well, let us say that what we find in the ruins is an evolving body of thought about *what it means to be here*, wandering among the tumbled columns and buried treasure along with all the other mortals. But the site of our stumbling darkling journeys is also haunted—by past lives, certainly, but also future ones. We do not enter the sublime ruins of the university in order to get a job. We do so to commune, like Machiavelli in his exile, with the great minds of our species and to contemplate the fate of those we will leave after us. No other human institution has this purpose, and however badly a given element of it might function, the overall authority that the university offers cannot be replicated by any other social structure.

Readings, just thirty-four years old, was killed in a plane crash as his book was going to press. Despite its title, his book's parting message is an optimistic one. A university is always a kind of ruin, a provocative folly. It is an old shell that allows and, ideally, provokes new thought. Trust isn't the point; this is not a banking system but a crucible of thought. Intellectual inquiry should not offer comfort or affirmation of what we already believe. It's not even about social justice either, unless we individually choose that path. It's about ideas, and they are challenging, unruly, inconvenient things. When rational agents genuinely pursue the truth and obey the demands of curiosity, they may not always like what they come to see. More to the point, telling other people about what they have seen may arouse ire rather than the admiration they considered their due. None of the prisoners down at the bottom of Plato's cave welcomes the news of their returning former dupe, who has come to tell them that their cherished reality is no more than puppet shadows cast upon the wall.

Crisis has a way of returning us to the source again and again, revealing the infinite human task of understanding. Aristotle thought the desire to understand was the strongest motive force in the universe, embodied in the human mind. For his teacher and precursor Plato, desire in general is the proper field of all philosophical study: its temptations and deviancies as well as its gifts and insights. In the present case, the issues of authority, trust, and knowledge should now be so intertwined that we can approach Plato again without misgiving, this time on the specific subtask of transforming—or forcibly converting?—*doxa*, mere belief, into *episteme*, or knowledge.

Who among us can be trusted to do this? The familiar Platonic answer may rank as the most notorious single claim in the history of philosophy. "Until philosophers rule as kings in their cities," Socrates casually tells his young friend Glaucon, "or those who are nowadays called kings and leading men become genuine and adequate philosophers ... cities will have no rest from evils." This startling assertion comes some distance into Plato's dialogue *Republic*—at 473d, in the conventional pagination—but it introduces the work's main character, the so-called philosopher-king. Socrates has defined the philosopher as not just a lover of wisdom but as a special kind of seer, someone dedicated to knowledge of capital-T truth. It follows that this exceptional fellow is the sole person fit to rule any city, including the ideal city he is sketching for his interlocutors.

We might immediately wonder: does he, or Plato, mean this seriously? There is a good deal of destabilising evidence. Socrates himself says a couple of times that he hesitates to make the claim in favour of philosopher-kings, knowing how odd it will sound. And in the part of the quotation I elided above, he notes that existing philosophers, assuming there are any, will probably have to be forced to rule. This press-ganging of the wisdom-loving soul parallels a more familiar argument, namely that anyone actively seeking political power is thereby disqualified for it precisely on that account. Only the person who does not crave control can be trusted to exert it.

Elsewhere in the dialogue, meanwhile, there are scattered clues that the whole ideal-city set-up, including the philosophically minded ruler, is a veiled warning that thinkers ought to steer well clear of politics. Force and deception will be necessary to turn an unruly populace toward the truth Socrates notes (see 382c, concerning the so-called "noble lie"). But he does not mention there or anywhere else that this defence of high-minded lying seems to set up a performative contradiction: how can a loyal servant of the truth use deception as means even to a good end? And, in a few blood-chilling passages, Socrates drops the casual assertions that no ideal city will be possible without first getting rid of everyone over the age of ten (541a) as well as those with clear intellectual or physical impairments (161a, 460c). Clear to whom, we might wonder, and on the basis of what standard of fitness? We may group all of this under the heading of the "clean-slate premise," a presumption common among utopian social engineering schemes. Otherwise known in this case as the Platonic form of a national-security doctrine, carried out by a deep philosophical state.

Despite all of that, and notwithstanding the potential ironic reading of the text as hidden writing precisely about the dangers of authority, Plato will be forever associated with the idea of the philosopher-king. And the notion of a perfectly enlightened ruler is a spectre that haunts all politics in good ways and bad. Every elected official, from the lowliest alderman to the president of a major nation, is doomed to be measured against, and fall short of, this towering ideal of perfect knowledge in the service of justice. At the same time, the idea of a philosopher-king sounds a different kind of warning: not for philosophers to avoid politics, but for citizens to be on guard when any self-styled thinker or social engineer gets his hands on the reins of power. "Quis custodiet ipsos custodes?" the Roman poet Juvenal wondered, in his *Satires*—"Who guards the guardians?" (Or if you're an Alan Moore fan, "Who watches the Watchmen?") It is a very good question, especially when those guardians come armed with some big-plan ideology, a few willing henchmen, and a taste for utopian social reform. Commitment to the truth sounds like a good thing, but experience shows that implementing an ideal social scheme quickly gets altogether too messy for most people's comfort.

Plato himself was wary of political power in his own experience of Athenian jockeying for social control. The treatment of his philosophical master, Socrates, under both oligarchy and democracy, was not encouraging; it was the latter form of rule that led to the frame-up trial that sentenced Socrates to execution by hemlock, which goes some distance to explaining the strong antidemocratic flavour of Plato's thought. His personal real-world attempt to mold Dionysius the Younger of Syracuse into a sort of philosopher-king was an abject failure, as anyone with a moment's acquaintance with actual power might have expected. The youthful tyrant was addicted to luxury and the indulgence of personal whim, like all autocrats; he found his visiting Greek tutor's epistemological advice predictably tiresome. Our philosophical hero returned to Athens a defeated proselytizer of reason, "sunburnt" in his own description by the hot kitchen of real-world politics.

Invoking this story, the critic Mark Lilla has thus spoken of "the lure of Syracuse": an apparently irresistible temptation among certain intellectuals to set the political world to rights—usually with disastrous results.[61] Witness, among others, Carl Schmitt and Martin Heidegger (on the German right) or Jean-Paul Sartre and Michel Foucault (on the French left). Heidegger's Nazi sympathies are a matter of record, but so is Schmitt's antiliberal legal philosophy, which became a pillar of the Weimar regime. Sartre's freedom-drive philosophy was corrupted into support for Maoism, even as Foucault's critique of left-liberal ideas of freedom and justice made him an unfortunate ally of the French authoritarian right. These life-of-the-mind dabblers, philotyrants, betray their own philosophical commitments even as they wreak well-meant havoc on the ordinary citizen. The enlightened despot inevitably becomes a dangerous criminal lunatic.

Or does he? It is easy to overestimate the impact of ideas on politics, and for every Stalin or Pol Pot in history, forcing his people into the Procrustean bed of ideology, history offers literally thousands of good or merely average leaders who muddled along to more-or-less positive effect. Most politicians and most voters have little real interest in political philosophy. Daily life is too pressing to allow its luxury. There is a solution to the zero-person trust problem sketched earlier, but it's not a rehabilitation of the philosopher-king. It is also more imaginative than practical. It borrows from a different and more ironic tradition of ancient wisdom than the Greek philosophers.

The philosopher Jacques Derrida, puzzling over the problem of the modern university, suggested that the best course to follow was to have a philosopher in charge of each and every one of them. Some of my colleagues seem determined to make this happen: philosophers are overrepresented in university administration, apparently bent on global domination through committees. But Derrida went on to note that no actual colleague, however brilliant, is sufficiently enlightened to qualify as a true philosopher. Therefore, the chair of the university president should remain empty.

The empty chair is a striking part of the ethic of hospitality enacted by the Seder dinner: a chair for the guest who may arrive at any moment, for whom a place must be kept. The practice has analogues in other places. Gatherings of PEN International, the freedom-of-expression advocacy group, always feature an empty chair for a missing writer, in prison or under house arrest elsewhere in the world. This writer is named and described, so that the felt absence is acute, but the absence also stands poignantly for all who have been incarcerated or disappeared. Somewhat less sublimely, ahem, we're told that Amazon chief executive Jeff Bezos apparently insists on having an empty chair at every company meeting: the chair represents the customer, according to Bezos "the most important person in the room."

There it is—the chair, I mean, not the customer. Instead of staging acrimonious elections for the post of president or prime minister, rather than arguing over who mismanaged a budget or failed to lower unemployment rates, we should simply hold regular viewings of the empty chair at the summit of all governance. Behold the absent philosopher-king, the unfeasible ideal ruler, whose always imminent, always postponed arrival may guide us in the endless self-and-other relation that is politics. See how infinitely, impossibly wise!

* * *

THE CONCLUDING LINES OF RICHARD Hofstadter's essay about paranoid style, mentioned earlier, are worth quoting in some detail before we turn to the next aspect of our rippling crisis of authority. "A distinguished historian has said that one of the most valuable things about history is that it teaches us how things do *not* happen," Hofstadter writes. "It is precisely this kind of awareness that the paranoid fails to develop. He has a special resistance of his own, of course, to developing such awareness, but circumstances often deprive him of exposure to events that might enlighten him—and in any case he resists enlightenment."[62]

Precisely. Enlightenment is not the point; it is the plot. Dispensing with the upper-case ennobler, we can continue to appreciate and cultivate the value of enlightenment as such—not dangerously universal and progressive, but not instrumental to any other goal either. A public achievement. Or to put the matter more precisely still, the danger posed by the paranoid lies in the conviction that she or he is in possession of their own idiomatic "enlightenment," a truth of one true believer at a time. This is comic, tragic, sad, and dangerous all at once. "We are all sufferers from history," Hofstadter noted in conclusion, "but the paranoid is a double sufferer, since he is afflicted not only by the real world, with the rest of us, but by his fantasies as well." We do see that. But is the system still, you know, the *System?* We all know the old joke: just because you're paranoid doesn't mean they aren't out to get you.[63]

At the very end of *Three Days of the Condor*, when Robert Redford has survived assassination attempts, fallen in love with Faye Dunaway, and exposed the deep-state conspiracy, he is challenged to say what he's going to do next. Walking along on a downtown street, he has a fierce debate with Cliff Robertson's CIA operative, a master of realpolitik reasoning. For no obvious reason, this scene stays with me as an exchange between "Redford" and "Cliff," not their character names or aligned surnames, so I'll stick with that here.

Thus Cliff says, of the "renegade operation" at the heart of the story, "We have games, we play games ... that's what we're paid to do. It's simple economics." The American people—there they are, everywhere and nowhere, the notional people, the national interest, the market—the people want security, oil, stuff. They don't know what they need in order to go on wanting those things, and that's just as well. They wouldn't understand because they don't understand themselves. The people are children; they don't think or decide. They don't want to know, even or especially when they say they do.

Cliff doesn't realize it because he's inside the movie, with his semi-hip sheepskin overcoat and that haircut like a Brillo pad that stays in place the whole time, but he has just joined a long list of cinematic American fascists, usually in the military or the Company. He echoes

Raymond Massey's incompetent autocratic general in *The Naked and the Dead* (1958). He anticipates Jack Nicholson's fulminating, self-incriminating general in *A Few Good Men* (1992). And it's 1975, so he's somehow an anachronistic contemporary of Carroll O'Connor's perpetually outraged general in *Kelly's Heroes* (1970). All the four-star autocrats and beribboned petty tyrants . . .

But Cliff is a clever one, a debater. CIA, not army or marines. He and his friends are there to guardrail democracy, after all, to *save it from itself*. They will make sure that the infantile American people can have the things they want. Sure, it gets messy sometimes. No harm done.

Redford is outraged. "Seven people killed," he keeps saying, "seven people killed. And you played fucking games." "Right," says Cliff, because he has a quick answer for everything. He's had this argument before, possibly with himself once upon a time. "And the other side does too. That's why we can't let you stay outside."

Pause. On screen and off we all take a minute to digest the idea that defending democracy might become an autoimmune disorder, a form of political lupus or Guillain-Barré syndrome.

"They've got it," Redford tells him. "They've got it. You know where we are." The camera shifts to a shot of the midtown New York Times distribution building. "That's where they ship from. They've got all of it. I told them a story—you play games, I told them a story."

Cliff stares at him, incredulous. "You poor dumb son of a bitch." He's practically shaking his head, his mouth in that lopsided Robertson grimace, though the haircut is unaffected. It doesn't move. It's made of steel wool. You could plug rat holes with it. "You've done more damage than you know," he tells Redford, whose hair is perfect. "You're about to be a very lonely man."

Another pause as Cliff considers what to say, though not what to think.

"How do you know they'll print it?" he asks Redford. "You can take a walk, but how far if they don't print it?"

"They'll print it," Redford says. He sounds confident, righteous. Seven people killed!

"How do you know?" Cliff asks him.

Exactly.

No, They Don't Know Either

9

City Man

HOW DO WE KNOW ANYTHING at all? It is now clear that, when it comes to potential answers, we find a problem of surfeit as well as one of scarcity. Too many bad answers and too few good ones. Most of us daily encounter a flood of information, factual claims, and demands for belief that we must parse, negotiate, sort, and digest. The gravitational pull of this info-glut makes for a lurking authority vacuum into which all kinds of nonsense will unfortunately rush: the daily diet of fact, fiction, opinion, ideology, and gossip we call the *media*.

There are very few areas of contemporary public life that are more fraught with doubt and distrust. Paradoxically, this is so in large part because we still depend upon them for some sort of window, however smudged and warped, on the outer world. But the trust numbers are dismal, especially about legacy media and those parts of the ecosystem that are sustained only by government subsidy. This holds true even in highly socialized polities, possibly as a perverse effect of the state support, which is seen as stifling innovation and sometimes expression.

This outcome is not so surprising, really: while people do not trust markets to do good things, they often trust them more than subsidies to do effective things. Regulatory capture can cut in both directions: sometimes the lobbyists hoodwink the legislators, but other times the policy-makers tie lead weights to industry's feet. In any event, polls show that just 37 percent of Canadians "trust the press"—a low rate in line with other Western democracies—while just one in five respondents approve of the deep government support of mainstream news outlets. One in ten professional journalists in Canada is employed by the heavily subsidized C B C, which was once seen as a national binding force but is now often viewed as either a showcase for politically correct blather or an outlet run by a law-business-government cabal so powerful it doesn't even need to be a Deep State, it's just the State.[1]

In Canada, with federal government subsidies, accredited media outlets can claim 35 percent of their senior journalists' salaries, up to a limit of $85,000, as tax credits. That is to say, as much as $30,000 of the annual pay of eligible journalists is paid by the Liberal Party government currently in power. To be sure, in today's media economy, most of these "eligible" journalists are likely to be longstanding and high-ranking editors and columnists, not beat reporters. Nevertheless, the total figure for these wage subsidies is almost half a billion dollars a year. "Just as politicians who shun the media limit journalists' ability to gather information," the critic Jonathan Kay notes contentiously, "so do politicians who lavish money upon journalists compromise their ability to earn the trust of audiences and interviewees." Naturally, this financial intertwining throws some shade on the very idea of journalistic independence, even if no one is executing overt quid pro quo schemes. Trust in journalism, always a matter of optics more than hard metrics, cannot sustain this kind of sausage-factory scrutiny, itself no doubt a form of a particular media outlier's ideological spin. Still, as Kay further notes, "Canada isn't alone in confronting this issue. Sweden and Norway have been described as 'media welfare states' for decades. And beginning in 2022, Australia began subsidising regional and local newspapers under the auspices of a larger media-support program that also benefits community broadcasters."[2]

The subsidies were instituted in the first place because of market failures: nonpublic financing of media outlets, especially local papers, began to disappear in the early decades of the new millennium. As more and more "news" was gathered from online sources, especially unregulated ones, formerly indispensable newspapers grew desperate to compete for attention. The traditional ad base was straitened or moved elsewhere. As with academic publishing or arts funding, the media subsidies were meant to shore up necessary sectors that cannot reliably weather this kind of economic buffeting—or in the case of the latter two sectors, any real economic pressure at all. So, the media subsidy programs come from a good place: they are meant as a bulwark against the disintegration of a democratically healthy fourth estate (together with suitable electronic extensions). The trouble is that the solution may create more trust problems than it solves. Subsidized journalists can still be expected to do good work, including sharp criticism of the government. But trust in media, like trust anywhere, functions as an economy of belief as much as one of proof. Doubt is its double-edged sword: at once the foundation and the potential destroyer of system confidence.

The structural trust problems for media go beyond any crude analysis of background puppetry by techno-capitalist forces, then. Lack of trust in media is not just a simple case of government capture and ethically iffy funding structures. The common claims of media bias always have to be balanced off by a sense of who is making them, and against what background assumptions. The rather tame liberalism of NPR, for example, is going to seem quite aggressively, maybe insanely, left wing to anyone who voted Republican in the last handful of American election cycles. For those who, now several generations into the age of J-school influence and activist journalism, see media work as a form of political participation, the social justice goals are only the beginning. Certainly, the presumptive whiteness and conservatism of legacy media must be disrupted, displaced, made to reveal its institutional commitments. But, considering the reach of government subsidy schemes, whatever the good intentions behind them, it's easy to doubt that these justice projects are anything but an extension of government policy. Some critics will see it that way, in any event, and that may be viewed as tainting the practice more generally even if many individual journalists are working with total integrity. As political critic Paul Wells notes, decisions about allocation of news resources—actual reporters and available white space—"have far less impact on year-end financial results than the need to qualify for next year's government benefits. Which means, in the new world of deep subsidy, newsroom managers aren't primarily journalists anymore. They're grant farmers."[3]

That's a rather extreme view, but the overall result is not just a siloed landscape of media outlets, each catering to a particular political demographic, peddling their rival versions of "reality," but also a decentralized and failing business model that makes overt bias a more attractive economic model than ever. It sells, after all, both in allegedly free markets and in the background competition for government subsidy. The rigged structures keep on giving the more consumers execute deep dives into their respective virtual realities: polarization is good for business. There is little profit in offering truly fair and balanced coverage of political events, just in deploying the slogan "fair and balanced" across proven slanted reporting and commentary. This discursive impasse, captured in the handy code of MSNBC/CNN/Fox, is in fact a cash bonanza for an emergent media establishment that thrives on its own internal divisions. Trust in media as such is less important than consumer loyalty to the provider of their choice. These networks and news outlets begin to function like rival brands within a sprawling corporate body, like a Procter & Gamble of the once-democratic mind.

Traditional claims of media to serve the ends of democracy cannot help but fracture and crumble under such conditions. The loss
of local outlets, the unregulated profusion of media platforms and
random appointed suppliers, the chipping away at any shared notion
of fact or objectivity, all contribute to yawning deficits in common
civic knowledge and alignment with democratic norms. There are no
longer any shared norms—not in what counts as news, but also not
in what counts as the truth. Trust in the media begins to seem like a
non-problem—not because it is so alarmingly low, which it surely is,
but rather because it is difficult even to accept that there is a shared
desire for what used to be called good journalism. There is a lot of
complaining about media bias, but I suspect that genuinely balanced
news would die on the page or screen. We speak often of a trust spiral, but it may be one of those weirdly quiet death spirals of amateur
pilots who lose their way in fog and can't even tell they are descending
disastrously until it's too late. As the aviator's bitter tag has it, *that's
one G all the way down.*

Journalism is not my profession, but I have written for newspapers
and magazines, more lately websites and blogs, all my adult life. I have
also appeared on television and spoken on radio and, once more per
technological developments, on podcasts. I began writing for publication the way many people do, walking into the office of my university's
student newspaper and asking for an assignment. As I noted earlier,
this was a heady time for me and for student journalists everywhere.
The first wave of what was then still called New Journalism was buzz-
ing in our minds, and the combination of *All the President's Men* and
the allure of Tom Wolfe's louche style was pretty irresistible. There
was therefore a lively debate about whether we should even talk about
objectivity in reporting. Surely the best reporting was simultaneously
an act of literary bravado and a way of speaking truth to power.

I still have some version of that ideal in my version of good journalism, but even then, we realized that it only made sense when

positioned as push-back on a set of settled conventions and power assumptions. Wolfe's journalism was "new," after all, because he wrote it like the novelist he was and ignored the boring inverted-pyramid rules every city editor in existence had until then held sacred. And social-justice journalism makes best sense when it truly is an alternative, not the mainstream current pretending to be edgy. Posturing and literary aspirations are probably best left in the realm of student journalism, or maybe on the op-ed page. News should inform our views, not the other way around. My own sense of the possibilities and problems of *professional* media are most closely linked to my experience as a general-assignment city-desk reporter and editorial writer at the *Globe and Mail*. This did not give me any master key to understanding media, but it did reinforce the ageless lesson that McLuhan was correct: the medium communicates all three of the message, the mass age, and the *massage*.

Like most people who consume news regularly and also sometimes create content, I have my share of biases and ideal formations. The world of the late 1980s still felt as though it could be encompassed by a newspaper, especially with the help of the *Globe*'s far-flung foreign correspondents. All my favourite writers were masters of the elegant, tight-as-a-drum prose that Hemingway and Graham Greene spun from the demands of no-nonsense sub-editors.

I could not decide which was the greater happiness, seeing the familiar gothic lettering of my home paper on a newsstand in New York or Boston, or getting the baseball box scores from the *International Herald-Tribune* in London and Paris as the Blue Jays fought for the American League pennant. Those sprawling kiosks in Times Square or Harvard Square, the long display sheds along the Seine or Soho streets, linked me to Jean Seberg on the Champs Élysées in *Breathless* (1960), Joel McCrea stumbling around England and Holland in *Foreign Correspondent* (1940), and every intrepid newsman from the Murrow-Mencken mythology.

Lonely in my pokey grad-school apartments, with a twelve-inch television that only got one channel, I would spend all day Sunday with the fat *New York Times*, reserving the book section for later, feeling connected to something I imagined was reality. Or groups of us would eat a big fry-up breakfast in somebody's Marchmont flat in Edinburgh and then while away the day working over "the Sundays," full of subtle political intrigue and high-toned literary feuds.

The great forebears of the city man are Addison and Johnson, Thackeray, even Mumford, not Woodward and Bernstein. Breaking stories is great, and *All the President's Men* (1976) probably did as much for journalism as a profession as any single cultural property of the last hundred years. It is the essential companion volume to the Watergate scandal itself—action, reaction: the ship of state listing under the winds of corruption then corrected by a trim of the democratic sails of accountability.

But style, bold perspective, and vision have always been the centre of the profession, something that our post–mainstream media landscape makes clear. This is both good and bad, of course. City-desk reporting, at least in its ideal, romantic form, has always struck me as a kind of flânerie. The city man (or woman) floats through the streets with nothing but a notepad and curiosity, taking down dialogue, overhearing gossip, noticing details, a connoisseur of the city's sights, smells, tastes, and textures. Like the flâneur, and unlike his investigative colleagues, the city reporter aspires to the status of purposeless walker; in the newspaper business, this is still called newsgathering, but it more often feels like loitering with intent. He makes a project of aimless desire—its very aimlessness providing the only necessary aim. A better scene, a bigger story lies ever around the next corner, and the next.

I was twenty-two years old, and I had a business card and a laminated police ID, both of which said I was a genuine newspaperman, despite still looking like the fresh-faced boy smiling out from the card's headshot. I walked around my home city with a new freedom and keenness. I saw it as grittier, uglier, and tougher than before—"before" being my confinement to that only sporadically porous enclave of self-absorption we call the university.

Of course, the idiosyncrasies of individual personality and writerly ambition are not always good companions to the truth we need. These otherwise attractive features of personality can act to subvert our own epistemic autonomy by hijacking a first-person perspective that cannot be dismissed—that is, the way we might see things if we were lucky enough to be in their place—but replace it with narration that is at best invidious and at worst actively unreliable. How can we trust testimony when it is second hand, however vivid? Worse, flânerie's devotion to the totalizing male gaze, the privileged looker, usually straight and white to boot, is justly suspect. In our own trust-nobody moment, even once-assumed-reliable sources are reduced to bias prisms. This decline in media authority is a function of general institutional breakdown, but with the added viral effects of disintermediation and the disintegration of legacy media. The rosy fondness that an aging writer might feel for a romanticized newsroom runs the risk of ignoring new realities of demographics, technology, and work; but also, worse, it fails a key test of our moment: the privilege check.[4]

Thinking of my days as a general-assignment reporter working from the city desk is to indulge nostalgia at two orders of magnitude. The first is obvious: it was forty years ago when I first walked into a sprawling city room and was directed to a shared desk and a phone and given a deadline. But there is a second-order effect that is more purely nostalgic, the longing for an experience I did not actually have, the way one can come to obsess about the music of an older brother or cousin, not one's own contemporaries. I mean the longing for a time when we could still consider reporters as low-key social-justice heroes, not overt ideologues but seekers after truth in defiance of power. These journalistic glory days are mostly fictional, of course, like the scenes depicted in *All the President's Men* (1976), if not *His Girl Friday* (1940) or *The Front Page* (1931—but also 1974).[5]

The reality was less dramatic, and there were no hats on men any longer, even though there was plenty of sexism and racism to go around. I worked regularly at the *Globe and Mail* from 1985 to 1991 and was offered a full-time job as a reporter the year I decided to start a PhD instead. It wasn't New York in the 1930s or Washington in the 1970s, but there was more than enough drama. The mid-1980s balanced on a brink that would later be associated with world-historical events: the Berlin Wall's collapse in 1989, altering the shape of global order; the Black Friday market collapse the same year, exposing flaws in the system that would plunge it more deeply into crisis two decades later.

Most significantly of all, and though it was not news at the time except in very specialist pockets of the discourse, Tim Berners-Lee and others were perfecting the code that, starting in 1990, structured the World Wide Web. The Great Disintermediation was about to begin: the technological sweep that would obliterate the felt need for trustworthy supply-side filters and demand-side regulators. This widening of public platform was widely viewed as a big step forward in the democratization of power and the liberation of individuals from external information control. The results, as the interceding decades have shown, are instead massive gains in polarization, autocratic concentration, and incivility—also, malicious data harvesting, bot-driven election skews, and a culture of deep but ineffective discursive suspicion.[6]

News gathering and delivery had been for decades, if not the print era's centuries, a matter of top-down reproduction, distribution, and control. The little blip of power I had felt as a campus newspaper editor, with access to a printing press and a budget supplied by student levy, was at the far end of a long unchallenged plateau about to spike—or plummet, depending on where you were standing. Already in the mid-1980s there were changes afoot in the nature of the implicit pact between mainstream media and their audiences. There was still a strong core sense of democratic mission, that old Fourth Estate vibe that said a free press was essential to any functional polity. Speaking truth to power was still a sincere commitment among the reporters I knew then, even if they were sniffy about old-fashioned inverted-pyramid structure or triple-sourcing all facts. New Journalism was no longer new, and the first-person perspective was valued almost everywhere except maybe the dull, daily stock-market story. The internal debates about journalistic ethics centred on cases like Janet Malcolm's notorious fictionalizing of the Freud Archives controversy, where the biggest sin in play was the massaging of words set between quotation marks.

Of course, that all seems quaint today, when J-school graduates of my acquaintance regularly invent characters and populate their columns with composite portraits and exaggerated personal anecdotes. Facts seem to matter less than narrative. But there is also well-aimed youthful criticism of the old norms of city-desk toughness, which casually trolled differences of race and gender. But trust levels do not simply rise when those unfashionable prejudices and institutional vices are filtered out. "Today, journalists have a different reputation than in the decades past, marked by growing public distrust: a 2022 survey by Edelman found 61 percent of Canadians worry that reporters are misleading them," journalist Michelle Cyca wrote in 2023. "It's natural to yearn for an era when journalists were respected, or at least when they didn't have to put up with so many annoying online comments and replies—not to mention harassment for having a particular job title. But returning to the era of in-office drinking and brawling won't get us there."[7]

That last part is very true, and yet making the claim in that way also highlights the new version of an old problem. Closing off nostalgia as a valid route to regaining trust has yet to open up another avenue. Sure, consumers of media may have no further taste for hard-drinking, chain-smoking reporters, but they don't like activist-advocacy journal-

NO, THEY DON'T KNOW EITHER 171

ism either. Increasing the racial and class diversity of the workforce is not a necessary condition of good journalism, though of course it may be desirable for other reasons. In fact, a wider range of *views*, not ethnicities, might make for better media, just as it would leaven gridlocked, taboo-twisted academic discussion. But nobody says that kind of thing in story meetings or faculty conclaves these days, in part because of yet another bit of discursive debasement: the innocuous phrase *viewpoint diversity* has itself become a coded label for the enemies of progressive politics.

One of Cyca's targets is *New York Times* columnist Maureen Dowd, who had recently penned a paean to her early years as a cub reporter in Washington.[8] The camaraderie Dowd celebrates was sexist, exclusionary, white, and privileged, Cyca scolds. Dowd succeeded in her early career in part through flirting and submission. All true, I imagine (Dowd is not shy about relating her flirtation schemes). Like Dowd, I took rewrites late at night over a clunky telephone handset jammed between my shoulder and neck. I wrote stories in shorthand on steno pads in the back seats of taxis so I could hit deadline. I talked my way into the offices of fire marshals, harbour commissioners, and at least one angry slumlord. Feeling a sense of loss about those experiences is not the same as wanting to bring back the whole power structure of yore. And this is all in the so-called respectable press. In the proliferating wild territory of self-publishing, blogs, vlogs, podcasts, websites, self-appointed watchdogs, and topical newsfeeds there is no regulation whatsoever, certainly no assured body of professional ethics.

We typically speak of regulatory capture as the practice of industries and sectors suborning the agencies meant to police them. The usual blandishments include access control, glad-handing, and outright bribes. But regulatory capture has a cognate vice in its ideological variety, and that disease extends up and down the spectrum of trust-based institutions. Avowedly activist journalists should not be expected to be trusted except by their own chosen partisan constituencies—and maybe not even by them, if a given article or tweet fails to toe the accepted line.

In this sense, the media take their place in a larger complex of compromised institutions that closely resembles that bugbear of conspiracy theory, the Deep State. There is no such thing, of course, but the frightening truth is that there doesn't need to be. When a sense of pervasive compromise, and hence distrust, infects every feature of the system, it might as well be a coordinated attack on everyday life. Then, *activism* becomes a cover for special interest. The shocking thing is how obvious this can become. Recent news stories reveal that the United States Supreme Court, of all places, is particularly prone to this kind of blandly offered outside influence, its members accepting private-jet outings, hunting trips, book-signing opportunities, and other unethical perquisites of the bench—all under cover of a bogus shroud of self-regulation. When the highest court in an allegedly free and democratic nation, one that claims to enshrine discrete branches of government, falls prey to easy interest-based capture, all claims of trust must suffer.

Maybe we should not be surprised: after all, as we have had cause to notice more than once, even august institutions are made of people. And they, as Machiavelli famously said, make the whole business of promising and keeping faith in practice moot. "Thus, a prudent prince cannot and should not keep his word when to do so would go against his interest, or when the reasons that made him pledge it no longer apply," he wrote in chapter 18 of *The Prince* (1532). "Doubtless if all men were good, this rule would be bad; but since they are a sad lot, and keep no faith with you, you in your turn are under no obligation to keep it with them."

The media world exhibits some combination of these same grab-and-surrender tendencies we see in courts and congresses. Let's call it regulatory self-capture. That is to say, the perverse interests of all players combine to bad effect, and so render the entire system untrustworthy. Political candidates may rail at the intrusion of the "lamestream media," and one liberal outlet can fulminate or moralize with relish about the shortcomings of its conservative rivals—where hosts may publicly support an election candidate even while mocking him and his base supporters in private, as Tucker Carlson did about Donald Trump. But this is all shadow play. How could we ever trust the media in the first place? Like Soylent Green, they're made of people.

Everyone has their own account of how we have come to this sad pass of isolation and fragmentation, especially with respect to what we continue to call "social media" even though they are neither of those things. These are platforms of performance, not channels of communication. As McLuhan argued, in an insight still imperfectly understood, the point of such media is not whatever passes for messaging within their constraints. The point is, rather, the way engagement itself is generated—here, in an endless scroll of febrile reactions, half-baked feelings and raw desires, occasionally witty jabs and insults, all expressed in the overheated form the medium both requires and rewards.[9]

The platforms are also clear examples of McLuhan's further perception that the given medium makes for its own conditions of possibility in what *feels like* an inevitable progression. Television and online forums favour the glib, interruptive, and runaway style of practised debaters and spewers of nonsense—bullshit artists—what the social theorist Pierre Bourdieu called "les fast-thinkers." The effect of these figures is not confined to their media platforms, however. It seeps into and infects all parts of the public sphere. The ghastly spectacle of Donald Trump's looping incoherence and insult patter is unimaginable without his addiction to Twitter and now Truth Social, just as Adolf Hitler's success depended in large measure on radio broadcasts of denunciatory speeches. This is understood by his more reflective backers, including fellow convict Steve Bannon. "I call Trump a Marshall McLuhanesque figure," Bannon told David Brooks in a 2024 interview. "McLuhan called it, right? He says this mass thing called media, or what Pierre Teilhard de Chardin said of the *noosphere*, is going to so overwhelm evolutionary biology that it will be everything. And Trump understands that. That's why he watches TV." This daily exposure, so often mocked by people who disdain television, actually gives Trump a firm handle on the real superpower of contemporary politics, shaping the spectacle of narrative. "He understands that to get anything done, you have to make the people understand," Bannon went on. "And so therefore, constantly, we're in a battle of narrative. Unrestricted narrative warfare. Everything is narrative. And in that regard, you have to make sure you forget about the noise and focus on the signal."[10]

We think, rather blithely, that understanding a medium's message means simply noting the number of characters that are allowed, or how long a TikTok video may be. But these limits are just the basic interface; the real operating system is the addictive engagement between brain and medium. The medium, in its programming for endless scroll, multiple clicks, and tallied followers, is not a facilitator—it is an engine of its own survival. We think we are in charge of the content, but the form is already our master. We are not engaged in debate, just relentless self-presentation. Our narrative-hungry selves deserve better.

* * *

THERE ARE MANY FACTORS IN play in worsening media-trust levels, but here is just one class of them: the sly use of statistics to mislead and confuse. Ever since Disraeli and Mark Twain, and no doubt earlier off the record, we have been counselled that that there are three kinds of falsehood: lies, damn lies, and statistics.[11] Many distinct sly tactics are routinely used in presenting misleading statistics, which unaccountably retain some sort of cognitive validity in most people's minds—even though 73.6 percent of statistics are made up.

(Yes, I read that on the internet.)[12] The study of statistical deception could take many volumes. I will mention just three common ploys to manipulate data in everyday reporting: (1) flawed correlation, (2) misleading visualization, and (3) truncated axis.

The first tactic is the most common and, to be fair, is often executed without specific intention to deceive. We are taught in Logic 101 that correlation does not entail causation, but the evidence shows that we can only rarely resist jumping to conclusions about causality in data that are, in fact, only presenting descriptive probabilities. This tendency to jump to suggested but invalid accounts of *how* and *why* is enhanced, even manipulated, by the related way that data are visualized. Bad correlation is bad, but it is made much worse by sly moves like pie charts that add up to more than 100 percent, or graphs arranged for view upside-down, so that increases look like decreases. These are both real-world examples from Fox News, and so are almost certainly evidence of intent to deceive—or "influence," if that softer word seems more acceptable.

Worst of all, perhaps, because hardest to detect in the available time of a broadcast or news story, is the third routine ploy, manipulation of a statistical axis. This works by either leaving the precise measures of the variables unspecified so that the graph is startling but meaningless, or else by squeezing or expanding an axis so that the picture looks starker than it is. An expanded axis can show an increase as a plateau, while a narrowed one can look like it proves one thing goes down because another goes up, even if they really are more or less the same. Data points are not facts, just clues or traces. The work of making sense of them only starts with the graph, chart, or percentage.

As always, the bullshitter is a more pernicious presence than the mere liar. Unlike the bullshitter, who has no regard for truth or falsity as concepts, the liar at least acknowledges the standard of truth in the act of flouting it. Fast-thinkers talk too quickly to be fact-checked in real time, and flood the field with multiple unverifiable, even contradictory claims. Unverifiable statistics are like candies thrown by parade clowns—sweet nothings to capture your sadly fickle attention. Like all con men, bullshitters switch rapidly and without warning from one spiel to another until something clicks with the mark. Pauses for reflection are not allowed. They say no honest person was ever conned, but it might be more accurate to say that no thoughtful person has been so.

Journalists may try their best to resist all this flummery with critical thought, but the medium's deck is stacked against them—and us. Critical attention to news is hard work. No wonder we off-load some of that work to people who seem like they know what they're talking about, and often are well-dressed, attractive, and articulate. Of course! But a moment's thought should remind us why this daily delegation of critical engagement is a massive net loss.

On the supply side of would-be media guardians, there are versions of the familiar Peter principle in play, that professional success rises to the level of its own incompetence—or even past it, otherwise known as *failing up.* Most pundits are only partly qualified to pronounce on the topics they survey. Given that the old fact-gathering machinery has been as thoroughly democratized as the access to platforms itself, this makes everyone and no one a citizen journalist. That makes for many voices, which some count a virtue of decentralized systems. But it also makes for lack of authority, which nobody sane could view as a net gain. Instead of possible partial corruption or a flaw at the centre, we have pervasive likely flaws flowing all the way to the edges. It's all edges, all the time.

Even stable platforms are subject to distortion under current conditions. In an effort to control for rogue bad actors within communities of users, platform owners and designers are incentivized to create "content cartels." These are effectively market trusts. They lie beyond regulatory intervention, partly because the privately developed and owned technology lies beyond the ken of legislators.[13] The distribution of platform privileges, meanwhile—who gets a Twitter/X blue check mark, for example—becomes a source of barely legitimate, certainly not public, decision. These platforms are private concerns, selling their users as a resource of data and harvested eyeballs to advertisers and investors.

Now, old-school newspapers are private concerns, too—we must be careful not to romanticize past the profit motive. But a couple of centuries of regulatory shakedown, including periods of vicious yellow journalism and experience with propaganda, have created useful case law in every reasonable jurisdiction. State control of media remains one of the markers of anti-democratic decline or autocratic aspiration. Not so with social media, where Elon Musk can simply decide to sell blue-check status and take it away from previously trusted users as a matter of personal whim. And then, in a dismally familiar move, blame drops in the platform's value on the Jews.[14]

The dwindling user base, meanwhile, is restless and easily distracted—pretty much by design. It is also, by stealth if not design, more and more skewed to the Big Tech and neo-Nazi right. Critics complain often about the echo-chamber or self-enclosed thought-bubble effect of new social media, as if this is a new phenomenon in the human experience. But human beings have always preferred the sound of their own voices and, next best, those voices more or less just like theirs. Media of this type do not function to disseminate, only to force multiply. They are bullhorns, not networks. They abandon all hope of the traditional philosophical program of distinguishing reality from appearance, of sometimes converting opinion to knowledge. It's all opinion, all the way down.[15]

Or, better, and to use a metaphor operative in a very different way elsewhere, they structure an infinite mise en abyme. This is the picture that forever disappears into versions of itself, becoming smaller and less legible all the while, like a television camera turned upon itself. Eventually it disappears into pointless invisibility, consumed by its own falsity. Rather, more strictly, it is neither true nor false. Random pixels, mere static, meaningless chunks of binary code that merely look like sense. Bip bip bip—poof.

It is likely obvious that all these tendencies and effects of media change are made worse by low levels of general trust in a society. There is a clear dynamic relation between trust levels and the dominant forms and norms of inter-citizen communication. The more people depend on second-hand memes and attention-economy platforms for their news of the world, the more likely they are to lose faith in structures of power distribution. The age of a handful of central news agencies that dispensed the truth is long gone, in the same way that the regime of central and chartered banks is a thing of the past. In the name of democratizing communication, we have all set out into a wild terrain of misinformation and disinformation. Communications technology is no longer our tool but our nemesis.

Though perhaps communication is the wrong word altogether when it comes to the evolving mediascape. *Communication*, like *medium*, implies the transfer of a solid message from one point to another. There may be distortion or degradation along the way. There may even be some intent to deceive or manipulate coiled into the message in some fashion: things left unsaid, signs and portents that only some can divine, and so on. But at base, as a matter of definition, a communications medium is meant to link two nodes of understanding with some mechanism of transfer that conquers distance, or time, or the natural reach of my unaided voice, my unspoken mind.

Most social media content is not at all like this. And this is a new phase in the expansion—I will not say progress—of media reach. The "exchanges" of social media are not intended even instrumentally as the proffering of information or argument. They are, instead, almost all pure emotive statement, however argumentative they may appear. A tweet or post serves to stake a claim over a position, usually sharp or apparently cynical, within some ongoing controversy. But in contrast to real cynicism, which has its uses and demands a specific ethical orientation, this is all faux, mere performance.

I don't mean that the purveyors are not genuinely outraged—they may well be. They certainly give every sign of being so, or at least of wanting others to think so. I mean, rather, that the *display* of outrage is the point, not the substance that might underwrite it. Unlike genuine communicative intent, the actions of social media engagement here have no prior commitment to a shared body of facts, let alone a common background of rationality.

This is why online flame wars are not really arguments, despite the heat: disagreement is not possible without a rich context of agreement about what counts as valid in debate. It is also why mobbing, cancel culture, and social piling on are so pervasive: these are the natural tendencies of disintermediated forms of citizen interaction. Everyone is now leaning out of their respective windows, not yelling that they are tired of bullshit, like the imitators of Howard Beale, but just yelling for the sake of yelling. This may feel good, but what does it accomplish otherwise? To repurpose a scathing line of Gertrude Stein's, this is the Oakland of the mind. There is no *there* there, and a fully disintermediated world is no world at all.

10

Stupid, Evil, or Both?

CONSIDER, AS A SMALL CASE study, what came to be known as the Potter Affair of 2017. In itself, it is a minor blip on the media radar scope, but it illustrates for my purposes a cluster of related trust problems that are characteristic of our moment. Andrew Potter is a former student and colleague of mine, and someone who, like me, desires to make philosophical ideas operative in everyday public discourse. Writing in his regular columnist's space in *Maclean's* magazine, he relayed his reflections on a disastrous snowstorm in Quebec.

"Quebec is an almost pathologically alienated and low-trust society," he boldly proclaims. Too boldly, as it turned out. The essay describes a weather-aggravated traffic jam on Montreal's Highway 13, which left hundreds of people stranded in their cars overnight. There was evidently very little if any of the let's-get-it-together spirit of genuine community. Instead, Potter said, the incident showed a "mass breakdown in the social order."[16]

He went on in this vein: "Major public crises tend to have one of two effects on a society. In the best cases, they serve to reveal the strength of the latent bonds of trust and social solidarity that lie dormant as we hurry about the city in our private bubbles—a reminder of the strength of our institutions and our selves [sic], in the face of infrastructure. Such was the case in New York after 9/11, and across much of the northeast during the great blackout of 2003," he suggested. This strikes me as a good and handy definition of social trust as an emergent critical property of societies. Most of the time, trust is happily invisible, like faith in currency and banks to back it. And the point is illustrated with two good examples of recent trust success.

"But sometimes the opposite occurs," the article continued. Uh oh. "The slightest bit of stress works its way into the underlying cracks of the body politic, a crisis turns those cracks to fractures, and the very idea of civil society starts to look like a cheapo paint job from a chiseling body shop." Then a snowstorm becomes "Exhibit A" of an egregious lack of trust. "Only 36 per cent of Quebecers say that most people can be trusted; the national average is 54 per cent, and no other province clocked in at less than 50 per cent."

Those with a memory for these things will recall that this is where the backlash began. There were comments in the National Assembly in Quebec and in the House of Commons in Ottawa, and McGill's senior administrators were pressured to respond. It is no doubt a sign of Canada's small size and Quebec's touchy place within it that this routine piece of commentary became a national news item. Potter was relieved of his duties as head of the McGill University Institute for the Study of Canada even though his casual piece was probably as telling a piece of Canadian studies as you are likely to see.

His Maclean's editors were braver, or anyway more sanctimonious— sometimes it's hard to tell the difference in rhetoric. They came to his aid by attacking McGill's cowardice. "McGill may do well to heed a journalistic credo: light is the best disinfectant." True, McGill emerged from this affair with a tarnished reputation even as it repeated the usual performative mantras about institutional autonomy and academic freedom. Administrators claimed in their defence that Potter was not forced to resign (even though his vacating the office was deemed "necessary") and hid behind the split hair that his position at McGill was administrative, not academic. Neither of these points bears scrutiny, though Potter did retain his professorship at the university.[17]

Maybe inevitably, Potter chose to "distance himself" from the piece, as we say these days. It had a couple of (since corrected) factual errors, to be fair, and rhetorically it was hardly the best work of a thinker I know for his rare acuity and wit. And there are far worse problems in the world than what goes on in that little Anglo parish at the top of Peel Street. Still, this toxic brew of self-interested politics, cowering academia, self-righteous media, and plain old public defection stands as a clear portrait of all that ails us when it comes to authority and trust. A pox on all their houses.[18]

Political philosophers make themselves figures of fun if they overstate the potential rationality of citizens, so I will try to avoid that. We might be tempted to adopt a bolder and more vivid combination of elitism about ourselves and profound cynicism about everyone else— the Nietzschean option. This is comforting but also self-defeating. Whether any form of rationalist reconstruction, with its optimistic commitments, can do better than nihilism remains an open question. Rationality is an ongoing achievement as well as a necessary background commitment. Like public transit, economic competition, and open-ended games of all kinds, it is ever in danger of a death spiral.

One sure sign of deteriorating communication is the reduction of language's supple possibilities to jargon and cliché. Orwell had noted this tic as a feature of autocratic politics in his 1946 essay "Politics and the English Language." As always a gifted noticer, Orwell highlights here not only the repetitiveness of political slogans and ideological cant, but also the mantra-like pleasure such practices of repetition offer their users. Jargon and cliché allow the speaker to appear engaged in communicative action without either thought or intent to reach another mind. Jargon is, to use a resonant philosophical phrase, "language on holiday."[19]

It can be much, much worse than that. Intramural disputes among philosophers are often violent clashes about the nature of reality and knowledge conducted in a way that might as well be off-world intergalactic combat. Most of us don't encounter metaphysicians and epistemologists very often.[20] But we do confront almost daily the claims of experts, academics, scientists, opinionators, bureaucrats, and politicians who all understand, if only instinctually, the vast power of bafflegab. The pervasiveness of empty language in the distributed structures of power is a multiplayer devil's bargain: the users are beholden to the thought-free fog of jargon as much as their targets. One only has to confront a petty functionary armed with some "procedures" and "protocols," the stock of proper "guidelines" and "expectations," to know the feeling of entering the enchanted circle of dehumanizing nonsense.

But where do legitimate norms, which we need in order to achieve even the loftiest of our goals, align with these bogus expectations and empty-headed proceduralism? There can be no general rule, but there are general guidelines to make guidelines more effective: second-order action-guiding norms, norms of *metatrust*, as discussed in part 2. These second-order norms belong to the system, not the individuals within the system. That means that the general undertaking can function as a trust game without any one player having to trust any other player personally, as long as all players conform to the game's norms. It's the reverse of "don't hate the player, hate the game." That is: don't trust the player, trust the game.

The game metaphor is subtler than it may look, as Wittgenstein among others reminds us.[21] Consider, for example, the obligations that the late Martin Amis grouped under the title "the war against cliché." This looks like advice for writers: Amis was concerned with the idea of a writer's duty to the world. That may sound a little grandiose, but in fact the lesson is apt to writing in any age. More significantly, it also extends to all of us who engage with each other via public discourse, however mundane. These are duties of all citizens, not just of those who belong to the republic of letters. Amis isolated three species of cliché upon which a dedicated intellectual resistance must be concentrated: "To idealize: all writing is a campaign against cliché. Not just clichés of the pen but clichés of the mind and clichés of the heart. When I dispraise, I am usually quoting clichés. When I praise, I am usually quoting the opposed qualities of freshness, energy, and reverberation of voice."[22]

Very few can aspire to write and think as well as Martin Amis. Not very many of us have any desire to do so! But the war on cliché is a general call to arms. The reflexive banalities of thought and speech are too-often rooted in a stunted heart, a failure of moral imagination. Our everyday engagements with media are moulding those hearts and minds more than we sometimes acknowledge, especially in the creeping dependencies of addiction. Warnings about this are legion in those very same places: newspaper articles, podcasts, and even books about the addictive effect of social media are almost as ubiquitous as the platforms they mean to decry. What we need is something simpler and more direct: a just-firm-enough foundation of trust to feel confident about speaking freely on any platform—without making a fetish of that freedom in the form of more performative ideology.

* * *

ONCE UPON A TIME, IN a more optimistic cultural moment, it was thought that something called *media literacy* was the answer here. And great strides were made by McLuhan, Innis, and others in seeing how mass media reflect and shape political consciousness. But alas, the forces of critical awareness in this region of political life have been unequal to the power of an even more basic human feature than the urge to communicate. I mean what we must call, for lack of a nicer term, the *will to stupidity*. Because the charge of stupidity is itself so commonplace—it is a standard move of our political discourse to label an opponent stupid, not merely wrong—the very idea of stupidity warrants some extended reflection. We call people who disagree with us stupid all the time. Do we know what it means?

As usual, the stakes are high precisely because the issues before us are so pressing. If we are stuck in a structural opposition in which partisan difference is routinely parsed as sanity versus insanity, intelligence versus ignorance, common sense versus delusion, we are doomed. Shouting insults all the way, we will be like grappling wrestlers who grunt their way off a shared cliff. So, let us ask an uncomfortable question: what is stupidity anyway?

The theologian Dietrich Bonhoeffer, imprisoned and eventually executed by the Nazis during the Second World War, had a perspective on the question of stupidity that most of us would not want to derive from first-hand experience. Incarcerated at Tegel Prison for his radical teachings and speaking, he spent a year and a half there awaiting his fate. He was sentenced to death on April 8, 1945, and died the next day, by hanging, stripped naked to add to his humiliation and suffering. He was not yet forty years old. Bonhoeffer was already an influential theological voice and became even more so with the defeat of the Nazi regime and the rise of activist or liberation theologies in the 1960s and '70s.

One of the most important texts he wrote is only glancingly theological. In 1941, after nearly a decade of Hitler's megalomaniacal autocracy and three bloody years of war, he penned a short but widely circulated screed on the nature of stupidity. The opening lines have been much quoted: "Stupidity is a more dangerous enemy of the good than malice," Bonhoeffer says. "One may protest against evil; it can be exposed and, if need be, prevented by use of force. Evil always carries within itself the germ of its own subversion in that it leaves behind in human beings at least a sense of unease." By contrast? "Against stupidity we are defenceless."[23] Despite the ominous tone, Bonhoeffer is not defeatist in the face of human stupidity; this is, among other things, a call to rational arms. But we must choose our tactics carefully. Appeals to reason or facts will be brushed aside, possibly fomenting anger and violence. Bonhoeffer accepts as a premise of stupidity that the stupid person is self-satisfied and could not understand someone else even if he or she wanted to.

"Never again will we try to persuade the stupid person with reasons, for it is senseless and dangerous," he notes. "This much is certain, that [stupidity] is in essence not an intellectual defect but a human one. There are human beings who are of remarkably agile intellect yet stupid, and others who are intellectually quite dull yet anything but stupid." And so: "We discover this to our surprise in particular situations. The impression one gains is not so much that stupidity is a congenital defect, but that, under certain circumstances, people are *made* stupid or that they allow this to happen to them."[24]

This letting go or allowing is one key source of stupidity: someone else will do my thinking for me. Other conditions include isolation (physical or, as we see all too often today, according to politico-media tribe), and upsurges in political power—or just upheavals of same. This correlation between public-sphere expansion and individual stupidity almost has the status of a psychosocial law. "[I]t seems that under the overwhelming impact of rising power, humans are deprived of their inner independence and, more or less consciously, give up establishing an autonomous position toward the emerging circumstances."[25]

This leads to a novel danger, set out in a paragraph worth quoting in full:

> The fact that the stupid person is often stubborn must not blind us to the fact that he is not independent. In conversation with him, one virtually feels that one is dealing not at all with a person, but with slogans, catchwords, and the like that have taken possession of him. He is under a spell, blinded, misused, and abused in his very being. Having

thus become a mindless tool, the stupid person will also be capable of any evil and at the same time incapable of seeing that it is evil. This is where the danger of diabolical misuse lurks, for it is this that can once and for all destroy human beings.[26]

On this account, the stupid person is clearly related in kind to the ideologue and, still more, the paranoiac.

"This state of affairs explains why in such circumstances our attempts to know what 'the people' really think are in vain," Bonhoeffer concludes. The only solution is "an act of liberation, not instruction." External liberation—not specified, but presumably some kind of mental detoxification—is necessary for internal liberation, which depends on the individual's desire and relationship to God. This is not quite "only a god can save us" theology, but it's pretty close.[27]

But what if even divine intervention is not powerful enough to defeat stupidity? It was of course Schiller, in his tragedy *Die Jung-frau von Orleans* (1801), who noted gloomily that "Against stupidity the gods themselves struggle in vain." (Mit der Dummheit kämpfen Goetter selbst vergebens.) This may well be so, and its reminder of the power that stupidity can wield and the harm it can do even when pitted against divine force, that helpless feeling of inarticulate rage at dumbness, fists clenched against the sky, is worth heeding. It is not clear whether the indicated gods struggle to banish stupidity from the mortal plane—a project that has clearly proved impossible based on past experience—or are simply helpless to mitigate, let alone prevent, the havoc stupid people wreak.

What kinds of social harm result from stupidity? And so, what, then, are the contours of what we may call the politics of stupidity? Finally, how does human stupidity figure in theories of justice under conditions of disintermediation, where we are more and more left to our own sad devices?

The notion of stupidity as a cost-benefit analysis of gains and losses owes its popularity to the economist Carlo Cipolla, whose brisk and deadpan-satirical manual *The Basic Laws of Stupidity*, a bestseller first published in 1976, defines stupidity this way: an action is stupid if it provides no gain to me or anyone else while allowing a loss to me and someone else. Thus Cipolla can graph, on a simple *x-y* axis, four types of people regardless (he asserts) of any other distinguishing human feature: the Helpless (I lose but you gain [or don't lose] by my action); Bandits (I gain [or don't lose] but you lose by my action); the Intelligent (both you and I gain [or don't lose] by my action); and the Stupid (you and I both lose [or don't gain] by my action).[28]

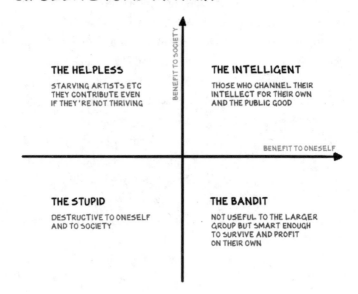

CIPOLLA STUPID MATRIX

BENEFIT TO SOCIETY

THE HELPLESS
STARVING ARTISTS ETC
THEY CONTRIBUTE EVEN
IF THEY'RE NOT THRIVING

THE INTELLIGENT
THOSE WHO CHANNEL THEIR
INTELLECT FOR THEIR OWN
AND THE PUBLIC GOOD

BENEFIT TO ONESELF

THE STUPID
DESTRUCTIVE TO ONESELF
AND TO SOCIETY

THE BANDIT
NOT USEFUL TO THE LARGER
GROUP BUT SMART ENOUGH
TO SURVIVE AND PROFIT
ON THEIR OWN

Cipolla also asserts that the percentage of any population, regardless of time or place, not respecting other characteristics even of supposed intelligence, is constant. He labels this segment of stupid people within a given population with the character ó, a single grapheme for an invariable quantity just as c indicates the constant of light speed. "I firmly believe that stupidity is an indiscriminate privilege of all human groups and is uniformly distributed according to a constant proportion," he writes. Cipolla then articulates his five basic laws of stupidity, which one commentator says, "are real laws, as far as economic laws are concerned, no less rigorously obtained than Adam Smith's three laws, the law of diminishing returns, Okun's law, or some such thing you forgot about seconds after taking the final exam."[29] I cannot speak to the validity or otherwise of economic laws in general, but Cipolla's basic laws will do well enough as a starting place for any further investigation of the subject of stupidity. They are:

1   Always and inevitably, everyone underestimates the number of stupid individuals in circulation.

2   The probability that a certain person can be stupid is independent of any other characteristics of that person.

3   (Golden Law) A stupid person is a person who causes losses to another person or to a group of persons while himself deriving no gain and possibly incurring losses.

4   Non-stupid people always underestimate the damaging power of stupid individuals; in particular, non-stupid people constantly forget that at all times and places and under any circumstances, to deal and/or associate with the stupid infallibly turns out to be a costly mistake.

5   A stupid person is the most dangerous type of person; a stupid person is more dangerous than a bandit.[30]

There are serious issues which force us to regard this book as a bitter antihumanist satire, along the lines of Swift's *Gulliver's Travels*, as well as an amusing account of a pernicious force in human affairs. But there are serious concerns with even the satirical reading. The most obvious of these is Cipolla's insistence on genetic and constant distribution of stupidity across human populations, what he calls δ.[31]

Genetic, really? By Cipolla's own theoretical reckoning, stupid people are a subpopulation, raising the spectre of dubious eugenic programs to control or even eliminate those deemed to be of subpar intelligence. This is surely not what anyone—I hope—imagines as an outcome of labelling political opponents stupid. It is worth recalling that many of the pejorative words we still use for persons whose actions frustrate us in public debate come from this eugenic nightmare vision: *idiot, imbecile, moron.*[32]

Calling someone else stupid has—let us be honest—its perverse pleasures. Dismissing an opponent as an idiot offers the satisfying tang of dismissal. And I think it is clear from the devolution of public discourse that incivility of various kinds are further and further enabled by high-profile offenders. Incivility offers clear short-term advantages, as Donald Trump has shown to his benefit and the world's detriment. Insults and degrading nicknames stick; schoolyard taunts feed the baser desires of the audience. And so, the urge to return the favour is strong: it is harder and harder to go high when your enemy goes low. This initiates a rather obvious race to the bottom—precisely the kind of collective action problem that trust and genuine authority are meant to curb. We may shrug a little and write off the performance as just more kayfabe, another round of cynical play-acting. There is lately a suggestion that the world of professional wrestling has itself grown out of the stage I recall from those days at the Winnipeg Arena, entering a new "post-kayfabe" era of easy irony. If this is so, and I confess I rather doubt that it is (witness Hulk Hogan's self-serious appearance at the Republican National Convention in the summer of 2024), this trend is not matched in the political ring. There, the lies keep on smoothly flowing even as the straight faces of the con men remain entirely unbroken.[33]

The trouble, as always, is that the stakes are real even when the actors are mugging and posturing, claiming when challenged that their insults were just jokes, their fake statistics the communication of emotional truths. We accept the metaphor of rules and games not to diminish the importance of public life, but to enhance our appreciation of rules and healthy engagement. I am not playing when I say that the charge of stupidity, applied to a fellow citizen, is a warning sign, a kind of gateway drug in the larger epidemic of doxaholism that will undermine any shared goals. Those goals currently stand in a range from mere survival, coping with the daily challenges of permacrisis, to something grander and more inclusive—the idea of a just society, which has animated our discussion from the start. I want to turn the rest of this part's focus to that idea. My guiding idea here is that, when we speak of the "media," just as when we spoke of the "experts," we are groping toward something we feel to be missing. That missing piece is, I believe, an articulated version of why society matters in the first place.

II

The Just City

SO, THERE I WAS IN the late 1980s, studying theories of justice for half the year, wading through the muddy shallows of a great but unjust city the other half. One side always called back to the other, making claims of greater reality. The passing years have found me returned to what people consider a cloister or ivory tower, but universities are part of what we advisedly call the real world, as much as anything is. So are ideas. Philosophy may bake no bread, but it does remind us that we do not live by bread alone.

In the heady years just before the September 11, 2001, terrorist attacks, it was even possible to imagine that there was a bright new order coming into its own, with an associated class worthy of its power and maybe our trust. As usual, the claim was itself a sign of the times, a pure media creation—not false, exactly, just wildly one-sided, cobbled together with selective statistics and some amateur sociology. In that sense it was entirely in keeping with the fast-evolving media landscape. *New York Times* columnist David Brooks was the self-appointed satirist and spokesperson of the new reality and its class.[34]

Bourgeois bohemians, or bobos, were, he argued, an "elite based on brainpower" rather than family ties. This elite was well educated, wealthy, aesthetically sophisticated, politically liberal, and media savvy. The individuals in it were literally made for each other, and for the well-appointed living room they made of the entire outside world. In an especially hilarious riff, he dismantled the presuppositions of the *New York Times* wedding announcement page by arguing that intelligence has replaced pedigree as the basic sign of social distinction. "On the *Times* weddings page, you can almost feel the force of the mingling SAT scores," Brooks wrote. "It's Dartmouth marries Berkeley, MBA weds PhD,…and summa cum laude embraces summa cum laude (you rarely see a summa settling for a magna—the tension in such a marriage would be too great)." And so "dumb good-looking people with great parents have been displaced by smart, ambitious, educated, and antiestablishment people with scuffed shoes." The resulting smugness and apparent cultural contradictions are, he suggests, like a $5 latte, actually worth the price. "Today the culture war is over, at least in the realm of the affluent," Brooks concluded rather smugly. "The centuries-old conflict has been reconciled."[35]

Well, not so fast. The price of a latte is more like $10 these days and rising. More to the point, the culture wars certainly rage on, with new fronts on old terrain like abortion rights and liberal education. And Brooks, himself a cultural conservative of an old-school, if not old-guy persuasion, can't always see the variform influence of class, race, and region. His concentration on the upper coasts—preppies in love on Nantucket, Bay Area VC winners counting their cars and calories in the California sun—neglects other power bases.

Compare, for example, the Bama Rush phenomenon of recent TikTok fame, which recruits dozens of blond, white women every year into a system of sorority-sanctioned suitability as quasi-Stepford partners to the good-old-boy managers of the Machine, the University of Alabama's answer to Yale's Skull and Bones or the Princeton supper clubs. "The general public's faith in higher education is waning, whatever the individual's politics," one observer noted. "For too much of the public, higher education's complex problems are reduced to culture wars about diversity, gender studies or critical race theory, which have become the brands of many elite, Northeastern schools. In this climate, these sororities' annual viral juggernaut is counterprogramming to the Northeastern elite university brand. The Bama version is wholesome, nonthreatening, traditional femininity in Lululemon athleisure. For free."[36]

Brooks was also writing before 9/11 changed the political and cultural landscape of the United States and the world—not to mention before the rise of Trumpism, Covid lockdowns, climate-change disasters, mounting China-us tension, and ugly wars in Ukraine and Gaza. The red and blue zones of the 2004 American presidential election—comically rendered by a contemporary cartoonist as "Jesusland" and "the United States of Canada"—revealed a nation riven by ideological clashes and destined to grow more so in subsequent contests; to the point, indeed, that by 2023 popular discourse and culture could seriously contemplate the idea of another American Civil War.[37]

The fault lines no longer lay along the yuppie/hippie vectors, which had been reliably firm since the time when the yuppies were captains of industry and the hippies were the poets and philosophers of the Concord school or Beatnik tendency. There was no New World Order here anymore, just a shifting terrain of clashing absolutes that has only been stoked by online flame wars, TikTok tussles, cancel culture, and relentless trolling of all kinds. We see a hellish landscape of multiple minimorphs, a kind of Hieronymous Bosch vision of the public square. This is all-the-more true now, in the mid-2020s, after another attempted American-election theft, a violent uprising in the heart of American politics, and attendant indictments and trials. In Canada the situation skews in a more leftward but equally dysfunctional manner, such that the stated progressive principles of the

Liberal government stand at odds with the beliefs of many citizens. The current state of polarization almost elicits feelings of longing for earlier simplicity. Among other twists, we now must contend with routine elite capture, the way once-transformative political ideas become commodities available to the highest bidder. And we should make no mistake: such capture can be effected from the right or from the left flank.[38]

The natural but unfortunate reaction to the collapse of a value distinction is a rearguard action. The Covid-19 pandemic years showed us all that the culture wars have new legs—and new, ever-more-inventive conspiracy theories. They likewise uncovered fault lines in the assumed structure of public health. The resulting confusion of belief and frustration about lockdowns and mandates tested the degree of trust in medicine, exposed latent hatred of government, and demonstrated a profound confusion about the very ideas of freedom and democracy. It seems that we are no more mature in our thinking today than when Kant urged us all to have courage to trust in self-direction.

What can push back against this resurgent celebration of antireason? Appeals to "common sense," "decency," "tradition," and even "normality" are easy prey. They hide tendentious ideological commitments behind noble-sounding or merely unobjectionable words. Who can stand against common sense? And yet, we know that the notion has been deployed more than once as conservative window dressing. "Decency" and "tradition" are words that can't fail to signal an implicit defence of the current arrangement, with its myriad injustices. Even more disturbing, these and other "motherhood" sentiments are subject to distortions executed by fashion and branding. Once-noble ideas get flipped and perverted by the hour: "authenticity" becomes a feature of expensive sneakers; "sincerity" a quality conveyed by a scarf.

We live in a time that celebrates tribalism and ideological decadence as its baseline assumptions. In our always-already-sold-out culture, "outrageousness" is a charge without purchase, a holdover from a distant age of civil political discourse, where if things were hardly perfect, there was such a thing as shame. Nowadays we buy and sell commitment to causes as blithely as sweatshop polo shirts or knock-off handbags. Consumption itself is the main product of any postindustrial economy, and it doesn't matter what the goods are. In fact, when you can consume the consumer brands themselves, you don't even need products. This is the fully spectral postmodern economy of technocapitalism. It is no more than fitting that its preferred coin of the realm is things like cybercurrency, nonfungible tokens, meme stocks, and constant bubbles. This is the endgame hidden in the logic of total market domination: everything in the world, reality itself, is traded on a perpetual futures market.

We must see what is happening. There are no longer such things as distinct material products; everything is commodity. We no longer merely produce consumption. In an experiential economy—a post-postindustrial one—the main product is ourselves as consumers, identity at once manufactured and devoured under the sign of consumption. We consume that spectral product "selfhood" even as we produce it in shadowy form, cannibalizing our doxaholic-narcissistic identities with every entertainment choice or shopping-district purchase. The process may be given a fancy name: *endocolonization*, the process by which we annex and exploit ourselves.

Traditional thinking about how to fashion a pluralistic society that tends toward justice is at a loss in the face of these new realties. It seems increasingly fruitless to insist upon shared norms of cooperation and civility to stretch across differences—the priority of right over good, as liberals like to say—when, in the foreground, the meat of political life is vehement disagreement and insult. The limiting fiction of modern justice theory is its background assumption of a coherent population of ever-rational individuals. In ugly fact, the imagined rationalist citizens self-righteously persist in thinking that everyone who disagrees with them is not only wrong, but impaired.

There is a profound polarization that underwrites the more detailed, surface-level disputes now marring any diverse liberal-democratic population. I mean the baseline conflict between general ideas (of reason, science, authority of any sort) as set against individual, clannish, or blood-tie associations (of folkways, traditions, good behaviour). Both poles are reductive when made exclusive. They equally assume that there must be one (or one kind of) normative framework for all arising situations or contexts. Social justice faces off against tradition, liberation against common sense, new ways of living against reliable standards of behaviour. But, paradoxically, the essence of justice is not really an essence. I mean that there is no single framework to be found, with a single set of rules, that will solve all problems of power and privilege and their distribution. Rather, there is a plurality of potentially just games addressing the only constant that is certain and urgent: that we are all capable of suffering.

The games themselves, the schemes and procedures seeking fair ends and the alleviation of that suffering, are fragile and open to destructive interest; but the idea of gaming itself is not. Playing together is basic to the very idea of being human, both for coordinating action and for accessing the deepest parts of our shared experience. Our relationship to normativity—to following the social rules, whatever they might be—is a deep-seated combination of allegiance and questioning. We want to play; and for the most part, given decent fellow players, we will do so in good faith unless, or until, the rules stop making sense. As noted at least since Durkheim, people are surprisingly consonant with social and legal norms. We have a social impulse to get along and will tolerate quite extensive marginal defections in the interests of the overall structure. These defections are akin to cheating in games: they exploit or bend the rules, but in doing so they actually reinforce the validity of those rules.

Even so, there is tremendous pressure to reduce norms to transactions, to make rules into bargains open to further question. Such moves are not *cheating*, though we call them that; they are, rather, forms of being a *spoilsport*, an action that ruins the game for everyone. The spoilsport seems more prominent than ever in our time, where any decision from an authority is considered no more than a power-move in a generally corrupt game. Then the umpire's call is just a debating gambit, the speeding ticket merely the first move in a negotiation. This attitude illustrates what might be styled as the distance between Priceburgh and Fineville, as my colleague Mark Migotti once styled the options. In Fineville the rules are the rules. If you park in a forbidden place, whatever the reason or circumstances, you must pay the appropriate levied fine. There may be second-order rules for mitigating the price, but these do not affect the first-order normativity of the fine. In Priceburgh, by contrast, parking in different places is a matter of some potential haggling.

Note that the difference here is not captured by the fact that there is a free-market system present in one case and absent in the other. The market operates in both Fineville and Priceburgh. The net costs and benefits of the transaction are the same in both cases: money changes hands, and parking is secured. What differs is how certain interactions are aligned with power, money, and authority. The amount paid for parking in each place might be exactly the same under nearly identical circumstances. Still, a fine is not (reducible to) a price unless it is elided by transactional distortion. Even if it also serves some end in view, normativity matters to us *just because it does*. As the communications theorist Anthony Wilden puts it, "the rules are no game."[39]

That's what norms are: the unseen but powerful expectations and trusts that guide action and decision, that shape responsibility and obligation. They are not opening moves in a negotiation, but *rules*. It is very important for us humans to have a sense, however wavering, that things are sometimes done simply because they are right, not just useful. Your mother was right! The reason to do the right thing is just because it is the right thing to do. Just *because*. And sometimes, the perverse appeal of breaking the rule is not some benefit that we get from doing so, but simply the wilful disobedience which is a childish end in itself. *Nyah nyah nyah, Mom!*

The trouble in the new media landscape, it seems to me, is akin to this. Sometimes that is obvious, as when the access and control of this crucial pillar of democracy is open to purchase. All private social-media platforms belong in this category, despite our general delusions about privacy and freedom within their ambit. But it is also the case that speech here is mediated in ways that hide in plain sight: a curious but inevitable effect of disintermediation. Radically decentralized media make every speech act a form of positional or status good. None of the resulting speech is genuinely free, no matter how liberating it feels to sound off. Speech acts are here conditioned by their place in an economy of likes, retweets, and that spectral quality called influence—itself just a status black box.

These considerations can only heighten our awareness of how hard trust can be to cultivate, still more how hard it is to realize what I want to call a social justice of equity and empathy—the program of open-minded citizenship governed by compassionate skepticism. Regard for the capacity of other agents to suffer should be a moral and political baseline, a firm principle of shared personhood. A good deal follows from this, though not always in perfectly rigid calculations on the order of Bentham's felicific calculus. Justice cannot be secured by tallying up *utiles*, or other quantifiable measures of happiness. But we can perform a form of negative utilitarianism: assessing ideas and policies for their measurable badness.

The downside risks of religious fundamentalism, say, or unregulated market competition quickly outweigh the benefits, and so such ideas should be judged untenable. The convictions that hold them in play can be revealed—standard critical theory—and then evaluated for costs and benefits. If they lack the transparency, accountability, responsiveness, and falsifiability that rationality demands of sound ideas, then they do not merit our trust. They are toxic, and relying on them is a bad habit in need of breaking. By the same token, if they exhibit those qualities, then they may legitimately claim some authority and so command at least some measure of our compliance.

Compassionate skepticism plays a central orienting role in this complex because, as the basic political virtue governing interaction between potential addicts, it acts like a cognitive breakwater: we approach situations of difference with a presumption of belief, like a legal presumption of innocence. But we retain the knowledge, based in our own experience, that harmful ideas can take hold of the individual mind. Some of these ideas work precisely to undermine the very independence of mind on which they prey. A political ideology or a religion is intoxicating because it uses mental plasticity against itself. A person becomes addicted to the certainty of belief, and the comforts of confirmation within the belief in-group. To answer such a person with stark disbelief or, worse, direct contradiction, achieves nothing. We need instead to offer up our own convictions for joint assessment, and so perhaps tease out common threads that could make for an end to our codependence. What if the construction of authoritative trust began not with one saying they are certainly right, but with both saying they are possibly wrong?

This is therefore a kind of error theory of politics: The view is not nihilistic (it does not deny political values are real) but it is cognitively noncommittal (those values are always disputable). The facts that are relevant in political disputes concern states of affairs upon which political value judgments may perch, but the judgments themselves are not facts. The importance of insisting on evidence-based policy in governance, for example, is not to provide support for views that we already hold before the fact. It is, rather, to seek guidance on which views to hold at all. This baseline skepticism about value does not destroy ethical views or actions. Rather, it works to channel our compassion in just directions rather than allowing ideological bias to co-opt compassion's good intentions.[40]

Such a quasirealist theory of justice, where right and wrong are not presupposed as true but remain open to dispute, will disappoint those who crave the hits and highs of intellectual conviction. But that is part of the point. Nobody is right if everybody can be wrong—and that is a sound way of going on. This theory has the benefit of avoiding the usual objections to utilitarian summing of human happiness, namely that such calculus does not respect the ethical uniqueness of persons. An individual should never be made to suffer for the sake of the happiness of others. This generates possible insupportable outcomes like Ursula K. Le Guin's fictional city of Omelas, where one abject child suffers so that all the other citizens may flourish: a modern take on an old trope. Here collective utopia is purchased only at the cost of specific dystopia, an insupportable calculation, implicit in the logic of summing happiness across populations.

More pressing than the greatest happiness of the greatest number, then, is the opposite entailment of shared vulnerability: the happiness of some never demanding the suffering of another. We begin the work of justice by sketching the basic resources that creatures like us need to survive and thrive, and then we labour to extend these goods to everyone. There is more to life than survival, but before we can seek higher ends, we must ensure basic ones for everyone. Abraham Maslow's hierarchy of needs will suffice for this purpose: begin with bodily necessities and proceed to goals like safety, love, esteem, and self-actualization. That will make sense for individuals as material conditions improve. At the social level, above baseline levels of life support and equal access to opportunity, to paraphrase Rawls, only those inequalities that benefit the worst off will be acceptable: fairness means maximizing the minimum. We can see this clearly, indeed Rawls thinks unanimously, if we decentre our otherwise clouded personal interests and identities.[41]

In many respects this way of talking is really a way of insisting on the value-neutral tolerance of difference and respect for others, both goals demanded by the liberal-democratic tradition since before Kant's defence of universalist reason. The liberal argument is rooted, first, in the logic of suspended self-destruction outlined by Hobbes, and then tempered by Locke's mutual suspicion and Hume's distrust of metaphysics. But power and property are not the ultimate point, as they were for those early modern thinkers. Like most philosophers working in the shadow of the Enlightenment's own imperial violence, I want to emphasize the universality of *limits* rather than of powers, the centrality of illness and mortality more than property and putative rights over it. This is more in the spirit of Spinoza's liberalism, which begins with a realization that there are multiple routes to salvation operating in human desire, including some that would not really want to be considered salvation, just living.

So, we start by taking aim at what is most obvious, namely that there is indefensible suffering in the world in which some are happy and safe. This must feel intolerable and move us to supersede some of the lesser goals of political discourse in favour of larger ones. I know pronouns are a matter of respect for some, and a way of insisting on recognition of difference, but they run the risk of creating more heat than light: small-scale battles that become unreasonably intense precisely because the stakes are so low in the global scheme of things. Proponents see a possible victory within reach, and so a battle worth fighting. Opponents see a kind of preening and vanity that ignores more important things—issues about which agreement might be possible. Meanwhile, global hunger just seems a lot more pressing. Or we start much closer to home: reliable potable water for everyone in our community, affordable housing and health care, safe streets and public spaces.

Political battles are not necessarily mutually exclusive, and there is no finite quantum of justice to go around. A debate over pronouns does not preclude one over climate change. But it is likewise the case that they are not necessarily linked, unless and until we isolate the basic questions of respect and care. The background insistence on shared vulnerability can often seem forever neglected in the clamour of claims and counterclaims that dominate the exercise of public reason. Procedural tweaks on the structure of public reason offer some value here, but still fail to grasp the full range of our inadequacy. Even if we attempted a sort of rationalist solution to the problem of diversity and postnational migration, for example—even if we insisted on something like a general justice rule that all those affected by a decision must be party to it, say—we would still be left with a fistful of prior unsolved questions. Who is part of the relevant community population? Who are my fellow citizens? Who (or what) counts politically? What do I owe them—not in distribution of goods and services, but in distributions of care and succour? Do they not bleed and pine for love, just like me? Ideally, the potential answer to all these rhetorical questions is *everybody*, perhaps including rational agents quite unlike us.

A polity, like its people, shall be judged by how it treats its most vulnerable and disadvantaged members. This has long been a central tenet of liberal polities, though more often honoured in the breach than the observance. Even if we intend to honour it, we still need to assess and modulate our sense of what counts as advantage. The vulnerable may not necessarily be the poorest, for example, if we are measuring just economic conditions. Consider the systematic disadvantage, in an idea-driven high-tech economy, of truncated education, learning disability, and low access to the mechanisms of success. The most disadvantaged may be a cognitive underclass that has no visible-minority identity, may in fact not be a minority at all.

Progressives often talk about the value of otherness, celebrating cultural diversity in word; but they do not always walk that walk when it comes to distributing social goods. Thus, they stand in relation to their own stated ideals as Kierkegaard suggested many Christians do to Christ's teachings about tolerance and charity. There is plenty of lip service—and quoting of scripture—in favour of these virtues; but in practice the result is a lot of empty ritual, control of other people's choices, and the violence of all in-group boundary drawing. Kierkegaard himself was not so harsh: a social-practice Christian can still be a good person. But it remains true for him that being a believer means an ongoing task of self-questioning and doubt, not certainty. Among the Christians, wondered this self-described Socrates of Christendom, *is there a Christian?*[42]

We could ask the same uncomfortable questions of the secular saints and prophets who preach tolerance today. Among the justice seekers, is there a just person? How tolerant are the social-media avatars of inclusivity? Enforced diversity statements in academic hiring or corporate mission statements, for example, do not encourage the ends they declaim even when they are sincere and not merely pro forma. Instead, they tighten the bonds of groupthink and leave out in the cold actually disadvantaged groups who would benefit materially from a more-even playing field. Academic life might be leavened by assessing people according to, say, their family's blue collars rather than their non-white skin. Economic class is still the most basic determinant of lifetime outcome, but the one that gets scant attention except sometimes by intersectional linkage or implication. An important caveat, to be sure—race and class do often correlate in disadvantage—but one that is not honoured consistently or examined critically.

If it means anything useful, *diversity* must include, first, the range of people with whom you disagree about shared topics, but also, second, the range of people who live and think in utterly different ways. The limit case will be those forms of life bent on the destruction of my own: then, yes, we will have to fight. Fundamentalist religions may prove the highest hurdles to fellow-feeling in a globalized world, indeed they already have in many places. But fortunately, in other places, including liberal democracies, we have a long way to go before we get to that point. Violent speech is hurtful, but it is not yet actual violence. Polarized public debate tends to foster the illusion that all citizens are equally participating debate partners, ranged up in colour-coded rows or with appropriate miniature flags and emojis to spell out partisan commitments the way X (formerly Twitter) profiles appear online. In fact, the relevant democratic polity, even taking only the shortest range—a town or city, even a neighbourhood—is far wackier and more diverse than most of us imagine or would prefer.

Geography and life patterns do not help us much here. The smug inwardness of de facto stealth neighbourhoods, patrolled by private security forces or hidden behind elaborate façades of bucolic growth that is in fact fencing, the vertical gated communities of condo developments with their passcards and locked doors, the lifetime preoccupation with the averted gaze, the clustering of the like-minded in discrete towns and regions and thought bubbles—all this shows a world not confident enough to engage with itself. I mean that a more sure-footed sense of our ideas, a genuine rather than performative conviction, would not be afraid to engage with anyone and everyone. Instead, we favour cocooning and self-swaddling. We indulge a shaky wariness of being cancelled, and resort to anonymity for fear of repercussions and retaliation. We demand safe spaces and institutional protection from the violence of microaggressions.

These fears are, in the moment, more or less justifiable, or at least comprehensible. Bad actors everywhere, pursuing their own momentary advantage, abet and extend a culture of fear. Threats are all too easy to make when online systems are so comprehensively inescapable. Email and text messages follow us everywhere. Even physical spaces and material affordances are affected by a general declension of the public idea. The gravity of downtown cores, once irresistible to those seeking the stimulus of metropolitan life, is reduced, as so often, to the cash nexus of shopping. And even this activity is now, postpandemic, drastically reduced. Cities do not offer their citizens even low-level versions of contact with otherness. Democracy grows sour, into a form of narcissistic pathology and a sense of entitlement for a few, invisibility for the many. Race and class, poverty and hatred cannot find a point of intervention when the discursive space of the polity is limited to surfaces, or when the actual three-dimensional spaces are drained of people like neutron-bombed visions in postapocalyptic films.

The desires of anybody's life are real. We all want a chance at achieving a stable identity, even a measure of stable respect for who we are. That everyday aspiration used to be the stock-in-trade of the city reporter, the beat writer, the sidewalk critic.[43] But now those desires are too often deflected or perverted, and the prisms through which they are experienced are predetermined by platform interests and content cartels. The medium really is the message: what it sells is not content, but itself. And so, we have spectacle without engagement, growth without hope. Busy trying to convince ourselves we are trending in the right direction, we don't stop to ask of ourselves, what is a city for? The oldest answer we know is also the best, conveyed in different forms from Plato to John Rawls: a polity is a series of opportunities for realizing something greater than the sum of individual desires. Here is where we judge ourselves by how we treat the least well off.

The justice of a society can never be confined to the interests of the "small and arrogant oligarchy of those who merely happen to be walking about," as G. K. Chesterton memorably labelled it. Justice starts with you, on the street, lifting your gaze and looking, for once, into the face of that person passing. Justice is the constant pursuit of the possible, the idea of what is to come. It is not a steady state, nor a fixed outcome; still less an institutionalized plan or centrally directed program. Its task is infinite.

12

New (Media) Ethics

UNDER THE PRESSURE OF BOTH our ideals and our skepticism, we must therefore ask: Is sane political discourse even possible anymore? Is the idea of authority, the very claim to reason, doomed to be a perpetual war of ranged interests, ever-deeper divisions, and open hatred?

The first step toward this reformation is a full and honest self-inventory. Nowhere is the tangle of desire and emotion more operative than in our attitudes to public engagement with others. Silent conviction can become self-sustaining, just as the pleasures of ideological conformity can help bolster a fragile identity or mask inner conflict. But few things offer more unalloyed pleasure than venting righteously on some issue of the day. Let's acknowledge first and foremost the toxic effects of pleasure in being right.

There are always looming problems of confirmation bias and false attribution when it comes to public discourse. Such bias is multiform, comprehensive, and may include a number of effects, notably:

1   attitude polarization (when a disagreement becomes more
      extreme even though the different parties are exposed to
      the same evidence);

2   belief perseverance (when beliefs persist after the evidence for them is shown to be false);

3   the irrational primacy effect (a greater reliance on information encountered early in a series); and

4   illusory correlation (when people falsely perceive an association between two events or situations).

The nature of specific media and platforms clearly abets these tendencies, sometimes pathologically. Algorithms are designed precisely to amplify feedback loops and to pick out and extend sharp entries. Users themselves are transformed into content for the program's built-in tendency to promote disagreement and insult, even as users find such promotion very much to their liking.

The medium remains the message even though it is not accurate any longer to call ours a mass age or to retain the outmoded logic of broadcast. But what counts as "the medium" becomes harder to discern, isolate, and subject to criticism. Users are now content in both possible senses, happily consuming themselves as products, and the system binding user to platform to program is forever looping and escalating our worst tendencies. The interface no longer cleaves cleanly into content and form, message and medium. Probably it never did, but until recently we were able to maintain at least the partial illusion that we were independent minds choosing to communicate, either to send or to receive information. These terms no longer make sense of what goes on in shared discourse. Discourse might not even be an appropriate term any longer, but perhaps we should hold onto it to remind ourselves that, if nothing else, human minds are capable of better than what passes for public talk now.

We know all too well that conservative critics say the university has become instead a *multiversity* or, worse, an enforced-diversity, social-justice-warrior, post-academic wasteland. Whatever one's political sympathies, it is certainly the case that no university today would claim to "gather all the rays of culture into one," as the Scottish thinker Alasdair Gray had it once upon a time, nor would anyone expect that from the extant forms of post-secondary education. (Even some high-toned intellectuals find that idea abhorrent: a trendy grad-student friend of mine objected to this tag as "insufficiently dialectical.")[44] The same point about multiplicity—not the same as diversity—is even more apt when applied to the media sector, which can no longer be grouped into separate forms (print, screen), distinct discursive regions (mainstream, alternative, local), or even kinds of normative range (news versus entertainment, for example, a distinction with a decidedly hoary aspect). The idea that anyone could take seriously the old Adolph Ochs *New York Times* motto—"all the news that's fit to print"—is itself a borderline joke. It calls to mind the lumpy satirical response of MAD magazine: "all the news that fits, we print!"[45]

Everyone knows that humans tend to think that people who agree with them are smart while those who disagree are stupid. This holds even if the available facts prove a position is incorrect or biased: bias begets bias. There is one small benefit here, namely that stupidity is attributed to political opponents more readily than evil. Americans, for example, are 23 percent more likely to view the opposing political party as stupid rather than evil. That's a real statistic! At the same time, though, more than half of Trump-supporting Republicans polled in 2020 thought that high-level Democrats were involved in a child sex-trafficking ring housed beneath a DC pizza joint.[46]

One might argue that democratic stupidity is not a fixed state from moment to moment, let alone a fixed ratio in the manner of Cipolla's ó. The political theorist Jonathan Haidt, for example, well known for his criticism of elite education's biases toward a hyperintelligent foolishness, has argued that the past decade of American public life has exhibited an unprecedented degree of stupidity.[47] His chosen metaphor for this disintegration of public coherence is the Biblical story of the Tower of Babel. "But Babel is not a story about tribalism," Haidt argues; "it's a story about the fragmentation of everything. It's about the shattering of all that had seemed solid, the scattering of people who had been a community. It's a metaphor for what is happening not only *between* red and blue, but within the left and within the right, as well as within universities, companies, professional associations, museums, and even families." Oh dear. The statistical evidence is clear: people have less and less trust in government as the twenty-first century progresses: in 2024 only two in ten Americans trust the government to do the right thing "just about always" (2%) or "most of the time" (21%). That's an alarming fact in itself, but their trust levels are also significantly aligned with who happens to be in power. Trust declines overall but tracks partisan commitment along the way.[48]

Not surprisingly, this utter fragmentation, and the steady decade-long rise in general discursive "stupidity" that Haidt identifies, is correlated to the rise of social media, especially Facebook and Twitter, which were once (say, circa 2011) fonts of potential political optimism and now are cesspools of hate speech, threats, conspiracy theories, disinformation campaigns, and deliberate hostile misunderstanding. "Social scientists," Haidt notes, "have identified at least three major forces that collectively bind together successful democracies: social capital (extensive social networks with high levels of trust), strong institutions, and shared stories. Social media has weakened all three." The addition of "Like" and "Retweet" features, seemingly innocuous, were in fact force multipliers, significantly raising the stakes and changing the basic dynamic of social media by allowing or even encouraging mob-like piling on and cancelling.[49]

Most obviously, social media heighten the degree of pile-on bias in the cognitive space of civic discourse. This grouping in turn begets a kind of reactive harm at the institutional level, speech chill or self-silencing, whereby individual members of identifiable belief clusters or groups fail to speak their minds for fear of the piling on underwritten by social media's openness to random and mostly unregulated attacks. "This new game encouraged dishonesty and mob dynamics," Haidt noted. "Users were guided not just by their true preferences but by their past experiences of reward and punishment, and their prediction of how others would react to each new action."

Trust is no longer reliably lodged even in oneself. If discursive self-defeat can grow within a population as a basic fact of technopolitical life, we may be doomed. That is, if political stupidity is both influential and burgeoning, the usual tactics for dealing with stupidity are even more limited than we thought.

The standard proposals for dealing with a lack of trust and authority are about what you'd expect: regulation of social media, education of future generations, reinforcement of democratic institutions. Haidt again: "American politics is getting ever more ridiculous and dysfunctional not because Americans are getting less intelligent. The problem is structural." Fine, yes, but any assumption that the general trust problem is entirely structural strikes me as incorrect. But what if Americans, what if all of us, are actually getting less intelligent and so less reasonable?

By this I don't mean quite the same thing as getting more stupid in the sense that we usually deplore, the moral and cognitive failure of taking pride in ignorance, refusing to consider the different aspects of a question, never looking for possible solutions even when they are of benefit. I mean something less dramatic and more common, maybe endemic in a contemporary developed-world population: reading less, thinking less stringently, isolating ourselves from contrary views, failing to revise opinions in light of facts. Also allowing our attention spans to become, first, truncated and cruder and then, worse, selling what passes for our attention in an overstimulated, underconsidered economy of distraction and fleeting cognitive hits. In such a condition we grow dynamically less willing to entertain contradictions, less able to grapple with cognitive dissonance or boredom, and more dependent on the hits and highs peddled by those who gleefully harvest our eyeballs. Distraction becomes its own form of self-replicating program, a large-language model operating on the platform of human community itself, not a cluster of chip-based heuristic algorithms.

It's customary to quote T. S. Eliot's "Burnt Norton" here, from *Four Quartets* (1943):

> Neither plenitude nor vacancy. Only a flicker
> Over the strained time-ridden faces
> Distracted from distraction by distraction
> Filled with fancies and empty of meaning
> Tumid apathy with no concentration
> Men and bits of paper, whirled by the cold wind
> That blows before and after time,
> Wind in and out of unwholesome lungs
> Time before time and after.

"Distracted from distraction by distraction"—the line appeared some eighty years ago and still feels like the most compact accurate diagnosis one could imagine. In one sense, it's not our fault: our evolutionary success is predicated on a highly responsive sensorium, up to and including being scared all the time; but we also build common things that can either off-load some of that wariness or else turn it to gain by crafty stimulation.

Previous discussion has already hinted at why this combination of personal and structural factors can make both basic distrust and isolated acts or narratives of suspicion seem so intractable. Successful argument must include at least the prospect of dispelling ignorance or changing minds. These prospects do not obtain with the preconvinced, precisely because *not thinking* is a form of cognitive self-limitation as well as a potential harm. The petty bureaucrat or camp guard or social-media loudmouth *does not want to see* that there might be a human element beneath the rules and regulations of routine cruelty.

The fixed-belief ideologue, the self-assured nonexpert, thinks he is in control of the situation. And so, he *cannot imagine*—cannot afford even to consider—that he is in over his head, actively generating harms.

One might argue that attempting to engage such a person in argument entails marginal costs only. We might think there is always a chance, however slight, of successful enlightenment. And so, always argue with anyone because you never know when a glint of genuine understanding may dawn. But marginal costs are still costs, and when the odds of rationality's success against stupidity are low, they become part of the harm calculation. For simply avoiding fellow citizens is not an option, as it might be with the rude or boring. Frustration, aggravation, and awareness of social harms inflicted by addiction to conviction are costs shouldered by everyone.

It might even seem, in addition, that the nonintellectual life is higher, more authentic, more down-home natural than any educated one—a prejudice that lies deep in the human heart. Here, contra Socrates, not only is the unexamined life entirely worth living, but it is the best and most worthy life, free of cynicism, depression, self-abnegation, and other afflictions of the elitist mind.

Writing about an evening at the Oscars, assigned a seat beside a no-show Madonna, the usually acerbic Christopher Hitchens confessed with some wonder that 1995's big winner was the Tom Hanks weepy *Forrest Gump*.[50] "Here is stupidity, not being mocked or even exploited, but positively and wholesomely and simply and touchingly *celebrated*," Hitchens marveled.[51] Well, yes, because surely this is the second-order avoidance ritual of the privileged and smart, uncomfortable with their own elevation and seeking populist absolution.

On a more jaundiced second-order view of the matter—one that Hitchens himself might have been expected to take—such a position of stupidity-celebration might be judged instead to be unrealistic, dangerous, insulting, condescending, and paternalistic, a means of keeping the uneducated and inarticulate happy in their place, brimming with virtue. The latter view, however, is probably itself just a super-elitist reaction to a popular and delightful piece of comedy-drama entertainment.[52]

Everyone hates this, even those most deeply immersed and committed to the working of the content-cartel platforms. But maybe that qualification should be, once again, *even or especially*. Imagine a world of willing addicts, wedded faithfully to their drug of choice but officially opposed to its effects. A population in deep denial, in other words. Imagine further that this shared addiction is both resented by its docile prisoners and laughed off as a harmless, or anyway inevitable, feature of the current socio-economic-media arrangement.

This is the recent face of Big Tech: the near-monopolistic market dominance of a few providers and corporations who control the everyday devices and access to the spectral electronic wonderland we call advanced civilization. From social-media platforms to upgrade-determined handsets, from shopping preferences to facial-recognition software, everyday human existence has never been more immersed in and influenced by technology controlled by a tiny minority of nearly omnipotent actors.

When Musk took over Twitter, he ordered its hapless communications director to issue a company-wide memo heralding the new face of the platform, now branded as X. It read, in part, "With X, we serve our entire community of users and customers by working tirelessly to preserve free expression and choice, create limitless interactivity, and create a marketplace that enables the economic success of all its participants." The hostage-code corporate-speak of Linda Yaccarino's memo was accurately mocked by the website *Daring Fireball*'s translation: "I used to run advertising for all of NBCUniversal. Now I'm running an $8/month multi-level marketing scheme where the only users who've signed up are men who own a collection of MAGA hats."[53]

Canada is one of the most-connected nations in the world, with close to 90 percent of the population owning at least one smart device, despite the sometimes crippling service costs. Providers, not users, are the driving force of this rising tech tide; those users are commodities here, complicit exchange-tokens of the system. We may speak of influencers on this or that social medium, for example, but everyone should recall—even if they choose to forget—or pretend to—that the medium is the real message. To be even more precise: the purveyors of the medium, in search of attention-economy technocapitalist profit, offer the deeper message still.

As always under the banner of inevitability, the obscene profit-parade marches on. The statistics are mind-boggling, unprecedented, otherworldly. In 2021, the five largest tech companies (Microsoft, Apple, Google, Facebook, and Amazon) boasted a stock market value of US$9.3 trillion, more than the combined value of the next twenty-seven most valuable American companies, including Tesla, Walmart, and JPMorgan Chase. Apple's profits for one quarter of 2021 clocked in at US$21.7 billion, nearly double the total profits of the five largest American airline companies before the pandemic of 2020 and beyond. Google's recorded US$50 billion in revenue from advertisements in the second quarter of 2021 was equal to what the entire American population spent on gasoline and gas station purchases in one month of the same period.

These figures, driven by truly fantastic profit margins (upward of 44 percent in some cases), have led analysts to insist that Big Tech is no longer just a quirky success story, or a case of limited competition easily matched by existing regulatory measures, but something wholly new and untrammelled—as a 2021 *New York Times* headline had it, "Big Tech Has Outgrown This Planet."[54]

Importantly, the vast profits garnered here are generated by the postcapitalist mechanisms isolated earlier in this part. I mean attention and advertisements and apps, rather than consumer durables, by which consumers devour themselves under the sign of their own happiness and convenience. As I have emphasized, this is a species of posthuman evolution that has the less frightening, more soothing features of simply giving us what we think we want, even as we surrender autonomy and peace of mind in pursuit of the same comfortable cycle of desire-indulgence, which by definition can never be achieved (or so media-fast advocates contend).

More significantly in political terms, the structural costs to labour and the environment entailed by this massive concentration of wealth have not been fully measured or appreciated—and each one of us with a smartphone, some 85 percent of populations in Asia, Europe, and North America, is part of the rising tide of technocapitalist domination. We are besotted serfs, suffused by upgrade anxiety even as we toil for the ideas of technological novelty and inevitability. Until we sort out the lines of complicity and self-concealing operating in this quarter of human life, our resistance will be futile because it will be aimed in the wrong direction. As Walt Kelly noted in the comic strip *Pogo*, "We have met the enemy, and he is us." And there is no shortage of enemies to find, or apocalyptic scenarios to sketch.

The antiprofiteering arguments are so familiar, precisely because they are a staple of current Left politics, despite the ubiquity of tech use there. But writer David Brooks, visiting the Republican National Conservatism Convention for *The Atlantic* late in 2021, noticed two recurrent rhetorical features in the general air of apocalyptic speechifying.[55]

The first is what must be judged the ideological equivalent of the Kyle Rittenhouse self-defence plea. The claim is that the American Right has been forced to become provocative, uncivil, and downright crazy *just because* the Left has become so woke-wacky—a neat trick borrowed from the middle-school playground. *I know you are but what am I? You started it!* This is no dialectical moment, as apologists for right-wing extremism stress; it is reactionary politics born of an impasse, offering a handy justification for bad behaviour. Any other account is just special pleading in ideological service, stooge-language offered by political management.

But the second, more interesting, repeated keynote was that the Right hates Big Tech just as much as the social-justice brigade does. For fringy conservatives, this is not so because of runaway profit-taking and concentration of wealth—which one might expect to be badges of ideological heroism—but because of liberal bias. "At the heart of this blue oligarchy," Brooks reported,

> are the great masters of surveillance capitalism, the Big Tech czars who decide in secret what ideas get promoted, what stories get suppressed.... "Big Tech is malevolent. Big Tech is corrupt. Big Tech is omnipresent," Ted Cruz roared.... "Big Business is not our ally," Marco Rubio argued. "They are eager culture warriors who use the language of wokeness to cover free-market capitalism." The "entire phalanx of Big Business has gone hard left," Cruz said. "We've seen Big Business, the Fortune 500, becoming the economic enforcers of the hard left. Name five Fortune 500 CEOs who are even remotely right of center."[56]

Well, actually, that would not be so hard; but Cruz nevertheless had a point. He knew that the public presentation of these tech giants is largely performed in keeping with a progressive narrative of sham concern and bogus compassion. The shared conviction that Big Business, and especially shadowy Big Tech, is part of a vast liberal conspiracy is rapidly becoming bread-and-butter to some right-wingers. Brooks again: "In the NatCon worldview, the profiteers of surveillance capitalism see all and control all. Its workers, indoctrinated at elite universities, use 'wokeness' to buy off the left and to create a subservient, atomized, defenceless labour pool." That would be some impressive long-game indoctrination, one must admit, equal to the market mastery these same companies actually exhibit. Might it not be the case that the tech labour pool is just a reflection of current realities, whereby the ambitious are sometimes also socially conscious and their justice-driven convictions sincere, rather than delusional and marshalled by genius-level exploitation overlords?

Not for the embattled Right. And so, as if needing more fuel to light the barbecue of self-righteous resentment and hostility, the terms of discussion now become end-of-the-world urgent. "The left's ambition is to create a world beyond belonging," intoned the widely disliked conservative politician Josh Hawley. "Their grand ambition is to deconstruct the United States of America." Cruz again: "The left's attack is on America. The left hates America. It is the left that is trying to use culture as a tool to destroy America." Rubio: "We are confronted now by a systematic effort to dismantle our society, our traditions, our economy, and our way of life."[57]

As many observers have pointed out, the demonization of Big Tech has not altered the phone-zombie habits of delegates, whose eyes were mostly glued to their screens during these energetic tirades, and whose basis of evidence for this nefarious left-wing Plot Against America was largely derived from tweets. If you can triangulate three social-media mentions, call them data points, and their content becomes fact. Sure, why not. For what it's worth, meanwhile, I'm sure there are many left-wing critics who see the Right as the end-times enemy of America, the promise-breakers bent on arming themselves to the teeth and then trashing the shared dreams of everyone, setting the City on a Hill on fire. Oh right, they already did that, on January 6, 2021.

This is confusing if predictable; but it may be more than that. The emergent structural irony is that Big Tech—like Big Media, but with the off-world profit margins added—has become the preferred political bugbear of both the (putative) radical Left and the (actual) radical Right circa the 2020s. (These terms are always to be viewed with caution, we know, at least as long as Donald Trump insists on calling Kamala Harris a communist.) The shared dislike of Big Tech extended in all ranges of political spectrum even as sales of gadgets continued to boom through the Black Friday and Cyber Monday and Boxing Day frenzies of the 2021 and 2022 bounce-back Christmas seasons. Such sales are not really affected by cultural attitudes to technology, in fact, nor are they reflected in, say, Elon Musk's decision to get all political with his platform and not just his dollars, hosting a glitchy endorsement "conversation" with Trump in the summer of 2024: an enervating two hours of shared super-global narcissism. These self-contradictions notwithstanding—denouncing what you cannot do without is a pervasive truth of our complacent, happily hypocritical attitude to technology—optimists wonder whether this odd conjunction offers a bridge issue waiting for its moment in the current scarred landscape of political rhetoric. I mean, even the crazy Roy family on *Succession* are going after Big Tech. Could the enemy of my enemy be my friend?

Well, if only. The divergent motives for the fear of tech are likely an insuperable barrier here. If one person thinks the megabillionaires of the Big Five are secret indoctrinators bent on creating a liberal wasteland of happy consumers, while another thinks they are desire-surfing maniacs preying on people's lack of impulse control to the tune of 44 percent return on investment, the potential convergence is going to start and stop at "evil bastards." Nothing else will, or can, shift.

The same is true of the closely related Big Media impasse: one side sees only hyperbiased platforms disguised as journalism, while the other finds newsrooms and front pages devoid of anything resembling ethnic, gender, and cultural diversity. Same conclusion—evil bastards again—but incompatible routes thereto. Big Media, like Big Tech, cannot lose for winning. Its elite pundits simply do not *strive to understand* what motivates an angry Covid-19 anti-vaxxer or a dedicated Trump supporter. They think they understand the left better, but one has reason to doubt it. The dominance of kayfabe in political discourse is matched by another runaway economy of exaggeration and distortion, the omnipresence of caricature. This is standard operating procedure in political debates, of course, but our special twist is that the demands of social self-presentation and reaction seem to facilitate, even demand, a tendency toward self-caricature. Views become more insistent, blunter, and more ham-fisted; their holders fall into spirals of funhouse self-mirroring, losing any sense of themselves outside their feeds and likes.

To be fair, and all judgments of stupidity set to one side, understanding what motivates people these days is no easy task for anyone, despite all the hot air generated by violently held conviction. This is one of the ironies of the age: one might think that an addiction to compulsive opinionating would at least generate a kind of critical mass, a crowd-sourced overview of who we are and where we stand. Instead, the result is more chaos, often visible only in high-profile nodes of the dominant celebrity culture, where politics, media, sports, and movies all come together. I personally spent some time trying to understand Green Bay Packers (now New York Jets, and badly injured as of this writing) quarterback Aaron Rodgers, who insisted he was "immunized" against Covid-19, even though he had foresworn vaccination protocols demanded by the National Football League. He was fined US$14,650 for this flouting of the rules, and so I spent some more valuable time trying to fathom what that sum means to someone whose average annual salary at the time was US$33.5 million and estimated net worth US$120 million. (You can do the math yourself, but for most people it's about as much as a cup of coffee, at least circa 2024.)

No, extending understanding to ideological foes has unfortunately become a dead-letter issue. In the era of alternative facts and social-media free-for-alls, attempts to comprehend the mind games of "the other side" are draining, frustrating, and self-defeating. That is, unless that side's alleged antics provide handy justification for your own burn-down-the-house politics.

* * *

WE WOULD ALL BE BETTER off if we tried to understand *ourselves*, especially after the most significant public-health crisis any of us is likely to witness. Our addictions to the gadgets of tech, from online shopping to social media feeds, might be considered welcome distractions in this time, even as boons to connection and productivity amidst system-wide disruption. That's true, as far as it goes. But that is not very far, since production and consumption reinforce patterns of cultural and ideological reproduction. Critics on both sides—there you go, I said it—are correct to argue that individuals are being devoured by the apparently unstoppable forces of online life. But they are wrong about where they point their fingers.

Big Tech, like Big Media, is no more than a reflection of our own wants and preferences, nothing more and nothing less. The uppercase letters are a sign of looming shibboleth. If there is manipulation at play in our techno-mediascape, it is offered in forms that we willingly embrace: sly terms-and-conditions agreements, negative-billing schemes, free-shipping incentives, and the constant mining of big data. This is precisely the kind of addiction hardest to shake because it is self-imposed, with pleasure. Short of widespread therapy, none of this is likely to change.

Let us consider a different possibility: a shared political movement that could bypass the stalled and endless debates between (alleged) Left and Right factions. Actually, it's a new version of an old movement. Let's all become *green-Earth neo-Luddites*: dedicated to preserving the human-scarred environment, suspicious of power concentration, ironic and critical about but not necessarily hostile to technology. The twinned but incompatible critiques of Big Tech hint at the possibilities. This isn't just temporary detox or a short-term media fast. It is a fundamental change in life's direction and priorities. Of course, to advocate this is even more optimistic than the prospect of political factions joining hands. But current public discourse is a tire-fire of escalating incivility and hollow victories, as if rising vehemence could substitute for reason. Then there is the blatant deceit and hypocrisy, corrosive of the soul. The hard truth is that, as with all addictive and self-destructive conditions, nobody can heal our sickness but ourselves.

Have the courage to free yourself! Drop your smartphone down a sewer grate and live again! Plus, Amazon makes returns extremely easy. Let's get started, you and I. It is high time we showed more trust in ourselves. The victory-driven, cynical norms of social media, ideological tit-for-tat—the seemingly endless and enervating both-sides-never rhetoric of what currently passes for public discourse—must be rendered a blip in human thought and history. Our persistent, renewed, and apparently gleeful immersion in this mental and political sandbox is nothing but a sign of immaturity. You don't have to be a hero to entertain contrary ideas without defensiveness, to consider views over time, change your mind, respond to challenge civilly, and articulate ideas without endorsing them.

Disdain defensiveness. Dispense with ad hominem attacks, but-what-about-you ripostes, and plain old insults. There is always an escalating energy in incivility: once someone opens the door to rudeness, a premium is placed on more of the same.[58] Resist the downward spiral. The point of debate is supposed to be truth, not victory—a truth ever understood as provisional, subject to revision and correction, no better than the best conclusion so far. Underneath any exchange of views, which in politics almost always means a clash of interests, there must be something shared. For any chance of further survival and perhaps success, we humans need to curb our most susceptible strains of desire and fear. We can counter distraction only with a belief that we are engaged in the same enterprise. Not playing a personal game, or a different one from what we claim, and not always vying to win. Assume that the disputant you meet is sincere, sane, and reasonably good-willed. How about that?

That assumption alone may not prove equal to our shared interests, or to changing anyone's mind. But unless we approach difference with a sense that there is something between us, some shared sense of what makes sense and what doesn't, there is no ground to be gained. Disagreement needs a background of agreement to be meaningful at all. To put it a little more starkly: we cannot survive for long by insisting on talking past one another. In philosophy and interpretation theory, this is sometimes called the principle of charity: not extending a gift, but approaching any text, argument, or figure with a presumption that they are at least trying to make sense. In human affairs more generally the relevant attitude is really no more than a compassionate recognition of the other as a person of worth, a fellow-traveller and fellow-sufferer. Disagreement should be an occasion for curiosity, not hostility.

Of course this is all wildly optimistic! Why should we not admit that? But I also think it is correct. And as your mother would certainly say: Don't be a bully. Play nice if you're going to play at all. Why? Just because. And check your addiction along with your privilege—plus some other things that don't help anyone, like arrogance or disdain for the less able. Challenging your own easy desires, including the desire to seem smart, is a key form of putting the question to authority. That's the news that stays news.

FOURTH MEDITATION

But Not
Your Mother

13

Make Your Bed

I DON'T REALLY INTEND TO discuss mothers, or even the cultural and ideological notions of motherhood. I'm interested, rather, in the idea of maternal authority writ large.

Fathers tend to dominate such discussions—father figures, benevolent dictator dads, father knows best, and so on—but the father is typically construed as an external, potentially punishing force. *Wait till your father gets home* is what mothers say to their children in order to terrify them. The kids are more aware of proximate power: what they say to each other is *Mom's gonna kill us*. Thus, do they terrify themselves, by internalizing the mother. Fathers are everywhere associated with ultimate force, but the internalized voice of conscience, combining authority with trust, may be more often maternal. One disturbing study showed that 74 percent of small children would override their own perceptions and walk over an apparent cliff if their mother signalled permission. Mothers don't just indicate proper action; they determine the world in which any action is possible. In this sense, they embody both the ideal model of authority—all-embracing, warm, trustworthy—and the immense power to disappoint or even harm.

"Acknowledging that mothers wield great power over their children makes many people uncomfortable," one analyst observed of these findings. "This is because the idea of Mom as a ruler—potentially an attentive and caring monarch, an absentee sovereign, or a punitive tyrant—runs counter to the myths of motherhood our culture embraces. Among those myths are that women are naturally nurturing, all mothers love unconditionally, and that mothering is instinctual; it will not surprise you that not one of those assertions is a universal truth." Dad may bring home the bacon, but Mom decides how it's cooked and who gets how much.[1]

There are those who find this power, together with its associated sentimental celebration, anathema. American critic Philip Wylie, for instance, offered a vituperative critique of what he labelled "momism" in his splenetic volume *Generation of Vipers* (1943). This collection of twelve fire-breathing essays about the nullity of American culture included "Common Women," his sustained attack on "the cult of mom worship." Wylie's excoriation of a political "enwhorement of American womanhood" (!) in the service of apple-pie folk wisdom and biofascism was oddly popular. The book sold fifty thousand copies between 1943 and a second, annotated edition in 1955, and it remains in print, a decidedly downbeat testament to the acerbic strain in American letters.[2]

Motherhood has so many resonances that it is tricky to isolate the ones directly related to authority and trust, but the basic connection is the association of birthing and wisdom. Your mother brings you into the world; she gives you life. And then, if you are lucky, she adds the basic, indispensable life-lessons of youth: how to tie your shoelaces, how to make your bed, how to mind your manners. The basic needs of life, the stuff that stands at or near the bottom of Abraham Maslow's famous "hierarchy of needs"—food, clothing, shelter—are all looked after, in effect pre-provided. (These days, even the baseline new-millennium "need" for reliable household wifi may also be assumed, with relevant screens to go with it, at least once the kids reach a certain age. Also, if budget allows, seasonal and fashion-forward clothing, not the hand-me-downs of yore.) Mom is thus free to become a locus of good feeling, reassurance, and deep truth. Free or burdened, we should say, for Mom has the heavy task of punishing as well as providing. She is a looming always-present nonpresence, an arbiter of all things. *Mom's going to kill us! Do you kiss your mother with that mouth?*

Thus, too, our array of linguistic cues about mom, because we sons and daughters are all momists of one degree or other. We have no choice. We didn't ask to be born, as disgruntled children like to complain. They are natural existentialists, children, because they understand the unfairness and sheer insult of being thrown into existence without prior warning or agreement. How did I get here? And then, before you even have a chance to get comfortable being here, or wonder what "here" is all about, someone is demanding that you answer *why* you are here. And so, we speak of motherhood issues, or our alma mater, or the sustaining tonic of mother's milk. But that milk can also be sour, as in Edward St Aubyn's viciously funny books about addiction. We speak—or resist—the mother tongue or mother church of our ancestors. And even as all the overt celebration of motherhood runs unabated, mothers are undervalued, unrewarded for essential human labour, and somehow never good enough even when omnipresent. The ambiguity is evident everywhere.

But dangers likewise lurk in the figure of Mommy Dearest. Norman Bates is boyishly devoted to his mother in Hitchcock's *Psycho* (1960), she who is absent in death but present in the basement rocking chair and in his own mind. And she must be obeyed because everyone knows that *a boy's best friend is his mother.* It's a little geeky, but I find myself recalling that the central computer of the *Nostromo*, the ill-fated ship in Ridley Scott's sci-fi horror masterpiece *Alien* (1979), is called Mother—in fact, the entire sequence of *Alien*-franchise films, now numbering seven, stands as an unsettling neo-Freudian meditation on motherhood.[3]

And, perhaps most in keeping with present concerns about divisive politics, misinformation, bullying, and authority, you will not be surprised to hear, if you didn't know already, that there is a group called Moms for Liberty. Moms for Liberty are not, however, general patriots emphasizing their distaff credentials, like the Daughters of the American Revolution. Nor are they a concerned advocacy group, like Mothers Against Drunk Driving. And some of them are not even moms.

Moms for Liberty is, instead, a "housewife populism" group based in Florida who avidly attacks a range of right-wing bugbears in schools, from mask mandates to school curricula that mention LGBTQ rights, race and ethnicity, and our spectral friend, critical race theory. They are also dedicated to banning books in school libraries, often by appearing before school-board meetings and reading aloud the raciest bits of Toni Morrison or Margaret Atwood novels, hoping that the assembled people will be appalled.

Nor is it all about gay sex and interracial socializing. A book about the persecution of Galileo Galilei was challenged because it did not provide a balanced view of the Roman Catholic authorities. "Where is the HERO of the church?" Where indeed? What we mostly hear about church-based organizations, especially the camps and universities where vulnerable young people are warehoused, are tales of abuse and scandal. When the institution is supposed to stand not only in loco parentis, but also as the once-respected collegiate alma mater, what we get instead is an abusive mother, or one that looks the other way when dark forces prey on innocence.[4]

Some of the more-robust Moms have fought back against the corruption they see in the outside world, ignoring the sins laid out before them within the evangelical walls. They have elevated their actions to the point of harassment of teachers, librarians, other parents, and school-board members. One Arkansas Mom for Liberty was investigated by local police when a recording was produced that showed her fantasizing about shooting school librarians. "They would all be plowed

down with a freaking gun," she said, momishly. Meanwhile, expectations of good motherhood—so elevated they are impossible to meet
in ordinary life—sentence ambitious mothers to costly career success
or, more commonly, endless compromise. It doesn't take a Nobel Prize
in economics to see these facts about what used to be called the glass
ceiling, but maybe it helps to show that they are indeed facts.[5]

Women have certainly made strides in their long quest for political
and economic equality. And yet they remain—despite all attempts
from other directions to loosen the bonds of what we must call "sex
assigned at birth"—subject to the force of Freud's sombre assertion that
"biology is destiny." Embattled feminists find themselves at odds with
new gender-fluidity warriors, denounced as TERFS or worse, but still
have to contend, on their right flank, with forces, mostly male, that
want them to accept their motherly duties. All the while, the forces of
neo-momism are conducting a stealth rearmament campaign, often
aligned with fundamentalist Christianity. The mid-2020s online "tradwife" trend tried to glamourize a sort of Betty Draper ideal of blissful
momism (minus the day drinking and eat-your-feelings weight gain).
This joined smoothly with, for instance, the admonitions of an otherwise obscure professional football player who praised his wife as part
of a general excoriation of "degenerate cultural values and media." He
told a graduation ceremony, "I'm on this stage today and able to be
the man I am because I have a wife who leans into her vocation" and
"embrace[s] one of the most important titles of all: homemaker."[6]

Well, okay. I would like to hear how his wife tells this story. The
central problem remains: these kinds of alt-world provocations may
be sincerely held by their proponents, but they are also entirely consistent with a larger preferred tactic of identity politics. This particular
dodge is mostly evident on the right. I mean the placing of ideological traps by means of deliberately incendiary or "incorrect" position
taking. A routinely conservative football player—a kicker, for God's
sake—gets no online traction at all. But a tall, handsome athlete from a

championship team delivering a retrograde antifeminist culture complaint is front-page news—in part because of the trolling and outrage he elicits. The online tradwife sites, meanwhile, are ideological clickbait snares—they thrive on hits, pulling in not only predictable critics but also another rather sleazy constituency of right-wing men, conspiracy theorists, and misogynist creeps.

Notably, these connections were executed as functions of the underlying online algorithms, which directed users of tradwife sites to more radical and overtly political options. The TikTok recommendation feature, in particular, was likely to enact its own sly agenda of increasing male-inflected political stridency. This is of a piece with how our interfaces operate, though we often forget it or choose to overlook the implications. It is not just the basic algorithm that we are engaging with when we go online, but also *all other users*—even if we do not even explicitly see them or engage with them. The entire network's total pool of clicks and visits are constantly being crunched into those recommendations and "see also" prompts that appear whether we like it or not.

"Some tradwife creators appear to be popular if you look at their follower counts, and they certainly generate a lot of chatter," critic Jessica Grose notes. "But I often think: Who is this content really for? Sure, some portion of their followers are probably like-minded women, but a new study from Media Matters made me wonder if the tradwife's main audience is actually right-leaning men." After tracking their deliberate engagement with tradwife content, the study's authors "found TikTok's recommendation algorithm rapidly populated our FYP ['For You' page] with conspiracy theory content and fearmongering, which made up nearly one-third of all videos served to the FYP."[7]

In any case, the larger point is made: mothers (and, for some, hence also wives) must be trusted implicitly, but they also cannot be trusted. They must succeed, but they cannot succeed. You can expand the category of "birthing humans" beyond biological females, in other words, but that won't improve the plight of working women

everywhere. The signals that momism sends are impeccable but unverifiable authority derived from the accidents of biology. In this, they
simply mimic the contradictory signals that actual moms are receiving from the culture at large. And even when the motherly advice is
good—make your bed! pick up your room!—it is both obvious and
irksome. Father is the voice of conscience, Freud said, the superego
made audible within the tortured psyche; but mother is the wheedling
voice that swings between nagging and coddling. He may lecture, but
she scolds—she hectors.[8]

We know, despite all the haze and smoke swirling in this fog of biology and ideology, that we cannot do without mothers and their wisdom,
real and imagined. The figure of the mother is forever contested, but
that is so in large part because, despite any amount of cosmopolitanism
and devotion to universal reason, we humans still—for now—come
from other fragile bodies, wracked in pain as they give us life. George
Clinton beautifully melded funk and Afrofuturism when he and his
Parliament bandmates connected with the Mothership in a landmark
1975 album. The Mothership—how awesome is that! The truth flows
like milk, pure manna from the loving source. But then, who is flying
the Mothership, and to what purpose? We can all feel the sad relevance
of a judgment made by one of Donald Trump's former campaign advisors. He noted, in a much-reproduced line, that hysterical claims about
a stolen 2020 presidential election are "tough to own . . . when it's all
just conspiracy shit beamed down from the mothership."[9]

Motherships are the stuff of ufology and conspiracist paranoia,
of course, as well as metaphors for security and comfort. It's where
they keep the anal probes and brainwash-beams. Everybody knows
that. Like the *They* of paranoia, the Mothership or mother religion
of belief is all-powerful, invisible, and not to be questioned. And yet,
question we must, if we are to retain individuality, maturity, and even
sanity. We do what mother says, just because. Until that "because" no
longer appears to satisfy our need for external authority. Mother is the

avatar of unquestioning belief. By definition, she cannot last. "Make your bed" is excellent advice. It's also advice that nobody should really need past the age of ten.

Let's take a larger view of the issue. Losing one's faith in an unquestioned authority is a form of trauma, whether it arose in the form of a physical mother, a mother religion, or an operating system that corporate overlords cynically named after the valorized female parent. "Faith no more" is a rallying cry as well as a '90s alt-metal band. It is, likewise, a potential cry of despair. Moreover, this is a general dynamic. We typically use the word *apostasy* to indicate renunciation of religious belief, but it also applies to politics and culture. Such renunciation is, we might say, the natural inversion of ideological commitment. This is why, it seems to me, we find so many influential political writers of the troubled twentieth century writing about politics in terms that exactly parallel those of religion. Consider Orwell's *1984*, of course; or even better, Arthur Koestler's *Darkness at Noon* (1940), whose title invokes the crucifixion in a tale of imprisonment and indoctrination; or the many works of Graham Greene that are either about political attachment, or religious faith, or both.

In almost every case, the analogy reveals the harm done to individuals and cultures through dogmatic commitment to the faith. As a character in a later Len Deighton thriller says, applied ideology and medieval Christianity have four things in common: (1) "instruction to seek the life of the spirit"; (2) the demand to "give service to the state ... in a spirit of humility and devotion"; (3) the related demand to "renounce money [as] ... investment and interest are singled out as the worst evils"; and (4) the final demand that the faithful should "deny themselves all the pleasures of this world to get their reward in paradise" or hold to the pay-it-forward belief that "after they die their children will grow up in paradise."[10]

The analogy is illuminating for its view of Marxist commitment, but it is even more revealing of the eternal relation of self to belief.

Our desire to believe is so strong, so comprehensive, that almost any substitute for mother will serve the case. In a postmodern world, the less specific the form of the belief, the better. For example, as rationalists we may scoff at the invented religion of Scientology, a product of the science-fiction imagination of L. Ron Hubbard, allegedly created as part of a bet. Still, its combination of vague promises of power combined with a relentless rhetoric of chosenness—a key element in any belief cluster that wishes to attract dedicated adherents—has fetched the minds, and the money, of many well-known and influential people. Just watch the disturbingly intense videos of Tom Cruise explaining his faith, or John Travolta acting it out, if that's the correct phrase, in the 2000 tribute film *Battlefield Earth*. Actually, don't watch that stuff. You can take my word for it: ghastly.

Quite apart from bamboozling the insecure minds of Hollywood weirdos, who, like professional athletes, tend to transmute their absurd good fortune into divinely ordained destiny, Hubbard perceived something important. People respond to religious ideas that come from outer space, especially if those ideas reinforce their sense of identity. Earth-born religions are too particular, with their ancient holy texts and millennia of interpretation. They're demanding and judgmental. And they've also done too much damage. All that is too hard for many of us to deal with. I will also leave aside, for now, substitute ideological religions, especially the ones based on complaint and personal grievance—though we must return to the issue later, since it dominates the age.[11] How about, instead, a religion that did not even exist before 1977, except in a galaxy far, far away?

I must be honest here. In the mid-'70s I was still a pretty run-of-the-mill cultural Catholic. I went to church every Sunday with my parents, though more and more on the promise of pancakes after. I was enrolled in a Catholic boys' school in Winnipeg called St Paul's, where the team name was Crusaders and the Latin motto was *Sicut Miles Christi* (Like soldiers of Christ). The school, run by Jesuits, was at once rough-and-tumble and intellectual. Pretty much everybody played full-contact, full-equipment football, from scrubs to the mustachioed heroes of the varsity squad, who seemed to me then like fully grown men.

I was a nerd in a cultural moment when their revenge was still the stuff of fiction. There was no Marvel Cinematic Universe. We were on our own, mostly, stuck on long bus rides to the lone science fiction bookshop in town, or the one hobby shop where they sold Dungeons & Dragons paraphernalia and little lead monsters ready for painting. Like almost everyone else I knew, I spent most of my time out of school in my room, with my plastic models, Tor paperbacks, and Frank Frazetta posters.

I liked football but I was not good enough to rise in the school ranks. I was better at a brutal intramural game we called Snowball, which I later came to think of as our school's version of Eton's Wall Game. Snowball was played on the snow-covered football field in the dead of Winnipeg winter, pitting two teams against each other with multiple balls in play. Any ball carried over a touch line was a goal. Any ball carrier could be stopped in any fashion, including intercepting, tackling, tripping, and executing a legal slew-foot manoeuvre called "foiling," which involved kicking one leg of a running opponent so that he tripped himself.

All this is to say that *Star Wars* changed my life. Of course it did. When I saw the film for the first time, it was like looking at the inside of my own brain. I didn't identify with Luke Skywalker, I identified with all the characters one by one—except Leia, of course, but not excluding R2-D2 and C-3PO. I was just young enough to qualify for kids' pricing at the movies, so I went again. And then eight more times that summer. I went alone and with friends. I convinced my uncle to go with me. Naturally, I had no girlfriends, so that didn't come up.

Much has since been written about the religious elements of the Star Wars franchise, not least the idea of the Force and, inevitably, the interpretation of Luke as a Christ figure. But I was not much interested in these precise parallels. And I wasn't really looking for a new life-guiding belief system. There was plenty of life guidance to go around in my house already. I didn't even aspire to cool, dressed in my dirty North Star sneakers, frayed jeans, and Adidas T-shirts. I just wanted to be a fan. Fandom is a great bestower of identity, after all, and if it doesn't exactly replace the action-guiding beliefs of formal religion, it does provide an orientation to being in the world that every adolescent needs. I think asking yourself "What would Luke do?" is not that much different from asking "What would Jesus do?" And, given the complexities of Luke's life—revealed over years of this irrepressible franchise—the answers are a lot more likely to resemble the difficult texture of everyday life here in this galaxy.

Honestly, though: the generalized spirituality of Star Wars is gooey, simplistic, and often silly. Sure, we can get behind the idea that all living things are connected. Sounds great! But voices telling us what to do? Levitation and Force-push? It's science fiction—the nicest possible kind, but fiction all the same. And when wise, not particularly new. When Yoda advises Luke, "Try not. Do, or do not. There is no try," he's offering a lesson straight from Laozi—and probably Bill Belichick.

Allow me to be very clear in what is, for many people, a very fraught area of thought. I don't think claims should be accepted because we like them or like the way they make us feel. I don't think we should accept them just because they have action-guiding or life-affirming power. Lots of false and even pernicious beliefs have these qualities. A claim must be accepted only if it is valid, and it is our duty as thinkers blessed with some measure of reason to make as certain as possible that our beliefs are true. Spectres like "personal truth," "inner conviction," and "alternate facts" are blights on the shared rational project of living and thinking together.

When someone points to unassailable inward authority and considers the work of reason done, they have lost their status in the community of free thinkers. The authority that only I can see is no more valid than the voice of the Great Gazoo, that goofy green space alien speaking only to Fred Flintstone. No one can inhabit the precise reason space from which another person generates their thoughts and actions. Much of the time, this unknowable-other-minds situation is tolerable, even salutary: the mind may stand as the last frontier of genuine privacy. When those thoughts and actions have consequences, though, a public accounting demands the public giving of reasons. And those reasons must be, at a minimum, coherent in terms beyond the limits of one mind. The alternative, after all, is solipsistic madness, a society of interconnected but uncommunicative echo chambers, each with its own standards of what passes for thought. It might as well be a video arcade where each player is restricted to their own game.

Actually, that sounds exactly like contemporary public discourse. I don't mean to be facetious in saying this. I want, rather, to highlight once again how hard it is for us to think for ourselves. Also, it's worth paying attention every time a system of belief, however benign it seems, attempts to close off any critical analysis of its foundations. We may not demand strict falsifiability from religious claims—that is, the scientific idea that they must be *open to* logical or factual disproof to count as valid—but alarm bells should ring whenever a claim is justified on the basis of its not requiring justification.

F. Scott Fitzgerald is not known for his satire of religion, but there is a nice running joke in his lesser novel *The Beautiful and Damned* (1922). The novel's recurring references to "Bilphism" sound more like Edith Wharton than the Fitzgerald of *The Great Gatsby* (1925) or *Tender Is the Night* (1934). A provincial striver with a beautiful daughter is entertaining her potential suitors with what she imagines is intellectual conversation. The suitors, like their author, are snooty Ivy League graduates. "Oh, yes, but you see Bilphism isn't a religion. It's the science of all religions," the mother says over one young man's objection to a faddish religion. "She smiled defiantly at him," the narrator notes. "This was the *bon mot* of her belief. There was something in the arrangement of words which grasped her mind so definitely that the statement became superior to any obligation to define itself. It is not unlikely that she would have accepted any idea encased in this radiant formula which was perhaps not a formula; it was the *reductio ad absurdum* of all formulas."[12]

I would rather say, in a different Latin formation, that it is the ne plus ultra of all formulas, the formula that shuts down any further talk of formulas. The faith-of-all-faiths move renders alternatives null and void, because the last word has been spoken. Or, to put it another way, all the air has now been *sucked out of the room*. Where is the HERO of the church? Right there, in that world-swallowing idea—assuming "hero" means *vanquisher of all challenges* rather than *paragon of virtue*. To shut down debate is not the same as to prevail in debate, though many people make that mistake all the time.

14

Faith No More

MY OWN CATHOLIC FAITH DID not survive high school. I think this is so because my Jesuit masters were too good at their job. The example of cool critical intelligence they brought to all things was far too robust, too appealing, for me not to apply it everywhere. The skeptical lessons of science, where inductive reasoning and empiricism are assumptions but never certainties, are hard to compartmentalize. Faith and reason may be compatible, but not by the same reasoning in both cases. Once evidence is at issue, faith either must give way or goes its own way.

So I was, in the words of a later teacher of mine, "a reluctant unbeliever." And thus part, in effect, of the Great Dechurching of the twentieth-century's second half.[13] Comprehensive disenchantment of the world predates the period, granted. But there is a plausible narrative to be written that links late-century New Age and alternative spiritual practices to the aggressive New Atheism of Richard Dawkins, Daniel Dennett, Christopher Hitchens, and Sam Harris. In the former category we must include both squishy Star Wars pantheism and astrology on one side, as well as more worldly options like hobbies, fandom, or the cults of yoga, Pilates, and CrossFit.[14]

In the so-called developed world, better styled as the secularized postindustrial, postcolonial "West," the numbers are predictably on the side of the dechurchers, aggressive or friendly as they may be. Attendance at sites of organized religions has dropped vertiginously in Europe and North America, with some nations becoming so completely secular that their constitutional laws reflect it. At the same time, elsewhere in the world the influence of fundamentalist belief grows more pervasive and more violent.

Fundamentalism is like Bilphism, of course. It not only asserts its own truth but envelops or assimilates the potential truth of all other belief-systems. In that sense, there is no arguing with it. It is a system complete and impregnable unto itself. That is both its attraction and its danger. On the other side, the confident, sometimes smug certainty of the atheists can be off-putting, even to those who accept their arguments. Very little but arrogance is conveyed when Daniel Dennett suggests that he and his fellow atheists should be known as "Brights." And some of us preferred Dawkins when he talked about memes, or Hitchens when he attacked the political insider-trading of the Clintons. Rational though they are, these hard-line positions can begin to feel almost as rigid as anything ordained by God.

I won't try to navigate anew this all-too-familiar territory. Instead, for present purposes, I want to offer a kind of trust truce. It will involve abandoning knowledge claims that cannot reliably be reproduced, but not by insisting on human reason as some kind of impeccable gold standard. Carving out reliable knowledge of the world, including what is or is not its ultimate meaning, is another infinite task. But authority of any kind is impossible without knowledge, and so we must try.

I urge all this in the spirit of shared abjection—a sense of share vulnerability, touted often already, but here offered in an ecumenical spirit to emphasize its spiritual roots. Most liberal theories of justice, and the theories of reason upon which they rely, lean heavily on the rights and powers of individuals. In various forms, from primitive contract to elaborate communicative-action theory, these conceptions of political authority derive from some account, often implied, about the rational-active character of potential citizens. We are individual choosers or rights bearers or property claimers or community members. On this foundation we build an account of how we, and everyone else like us, ought to be treated. In the simplest but also most complex sense, we are trying to articulate what we owe to each other.[15] But what strikes people very often is not their shared powers but their shared weakness. Or rather, since weakness is often experienced in isolation or without support, what strikes us is the capacity for suffering. Our shared vulnerability, as long as we work to imagine it, is a more reliable basis of good action than appeals to power. What we owe to each other is not just respect but also the provision of reasons that others might reasonably accept as valid.

This blind spot around shared weakness is what makes the emergent politics of grievance so unhelpful. There are philosophical problems lurking within claims of distinct identity, and these are long familiar to liberal theorists. I will address some of them in part 5. The current moment shows not only a penchant for identity politics but for the special kind of those politics that isolates identity solely on the basis of some felt injustice, however real it may be. This is not entirely misguided, of course—experience of injustice can help to coalesce and tighten a sense of self and provide a platform for the articulation of robust justice claims. But these claims are tricky properties: they may take on a life of their own, determining identity rather than bolstering it. Historical wrongs can become reified into permanent grievances. A pattern of structural injustice—say, concerning race in American politics—can be so entrenched as to provide generations of angry membership with no hope of genuine change. Any change that is achieved is subject to forces of cultural twisting: it will be seen as having solved the entire problem, for example, or it will be attributed to the personal virtues of bootstrapping individuals rather than to policy measures that require further application or expansion.

This is therefore tricky terrain. There are those who would deny the relevance of all history, denying even the possibility that there are lingering structural barriers to, for example, Black or Indigenous success in certain professions. Identity politics may be considered a trap, then, but only when it comes unmoored from the larger justice project that the original claims were meant to address. The identity becomes its own end, rather than a means to the end of a more equitable society all around. In effect, the larger movement of justice is stalled at an intermediate stage. That is to say, the legitimate claim of grievance, based on a background identity-driven injustice, is stuck in its particularity. It cannot make the move from grievance to structural change. This is completely understandable—grievance claims are claims of genuine pain and suffering. But focussing too much on the pain, rather than its causes and potential relief, can have the undesired effect of occluding any further awareness. The basis of all lasting social justice is that everybody can suffer, but also that such suffering can be alleviated. Unless we can both feel our own pain *and* feel pain at the pain of others, we will be forever stranded in an endless round of claim and counterclaim.

To make that second move requires, as I have suggested from the start, the exercise of a particular form of moral and civic virtue: what Adam Smith called *sympathy* or *compassion*—not the sentimental and impossible *empathy* lately touted by journalism and therapy-speak. Empathy means to share, and so understand, the feelings of others. This is a metaphysical non-starter. We do not, and cannot, feel anybody else's pain. What we *can* feel is pain at the pain of others.[16] Or, to urge another distinction, we can suffer at the suffering of others. Not all pain is experienced as suffering, and sometimes there is grave suffering without any obvious pain.

This capacity for compassion requires a special faculty of *moral imagination*. Here the lessons of my own Mother Church continue to resonate when claims of pure knowledge and origin do not. The teachings of a particular religion, despite all the depredations committed in its name, may find intellectual redemption in the kind of compassionate-skeptical justice theory I am attempting to outline here. I know this will sound off-base to true believers! But let us open our minds to common ground. There is nothing more basic than accepting that the other person can suffer just as I do, and vice versa.

One must be on guard for false universalisms here. Premature claims of justice can only obscure the real situation and take attention away from the work that still needs to be done. I mean gestures like bland "family of man" assurances that would elide genuine differences between people, or sonorous reminders that in the end even the rich and powerful end up in the ground. These all-lives-matter bromides are as bogus as those self-serving boasts that someone "does not see colour" or lives in a "post-racial" world. Those victories are celebrated too soon. Martin Luther King's vision of a world where a person will be judged by the content of his character, not the colour of his skin, is—he said it himself—a dream. It is an action-guiding dream, yes, not a fantasy. But to insist that we are there already is like facing the abyss, closing your eyes, turning around, and saying you are on the other side.

I do not suggest that any individual experience of mine is proof of anything—except that we all have our versions of the human story of challenge and resilience. It is not surprising that when I spent the better part of a year in hospital for conditions I had brought upon myself, I was often subject to memories of my time as a believer. They were wrapped up with those memories of high school: long bus rides whiled away with remaindered paperback Tolkien and sci-fi novels, going to fanboy plastic-modeller and hot-rod conventions downtown. Wishing I could ride my father's Honda 750 motorbike but instead spending hours on my Sekine and Raleigh ten-speeds, until a left-turning car put me in the hospital on graduation day, cut down at seventeen.

Details are what we gather together in memory, constructing our narratives of self. Pulling my pre-tied necktie over my head every morning in the locker room. The after-school "Reach for the Top" tryouts and drama-club rehearsals. Endless games of outdoor broomball in the insane Manitoba cold. Stupidly braving the Winnipeg winter with sneakers, jeans, a hoodie, a windbreaker, and brown leather garbie mitts. Going to Mass in the little school chapel. Reading Acts and the Epistles of Saint Paul in class, hungry for story if not belief. Gazing at the cool new principal's big office-reproduction of Dalí's *Christ of Saint John of the Cross*, with its vertiginous Hitchcockian overhead perspective. Making sure that every out-of-class errand included a swing by Mrs Ostermann at the front desk, angelically beautiful wife of the chemistry teacher. Wondering why Winnipeg was the only town in North America where *Phantom of the Paradise* (1974) was a hit movie, and where kids chant "Halloween Apples!" instead of "Trick or Treat!"

In the hospital again, four decades later, considering my destructive actions and thoughts, I listened over and over to something called the Small Paraklesis. This is an element in the Orthodox Church ritual, a series of odes to Theotokos, Mary, Mother of God. The odes are sometimes read but often sung in plainsong harmony, the most beautiful sound humans can make without technology. The odes are layered requests for help, prayers of intercession addressed to Mary, the "speedy protectress." There is much emphasis here on speed, in fact: the supplicants need help *now*. The encroaching enemies are legion, but they typically come from inside: the odes enjoin that Mary "from corruption of passions deliver me." There are repeated pleas that the Lady "hasten unto our aid" and "disperse the horde of my many temptations and put to silence demonic audacity."[17]

I mention this episode not to suggest that I had some sort of come-to-Jesus (or Mary) moment, lying for days in that bed, close to death. There was no foxhole conversion. But I find that there is a deep pull in those elements of scripture and ritual that emphasize fellow suffering.

We all need help sometimes. Recognizing that is the crucial first step to feeling a material obligation to another—even when we disagree vehemently. There is so much finger pointing going on that some people dub our condition a "shame-industrial complex."[18]

What if we shifted to something more like an *interfaith abjection universe*? Everybody is part of this shared lifeworld of the weak, past and present and future included in the moral reckoning. One of the other thoughts that returned to me again and again during this time was that insight from G. K. Chesterton's little primer *Orthodoxy* (1908), which offers Christian apologetics that, among other things, celebrates the paradoxes of faith rather than trying to solve them. "I have never been able to understand where people got the idea that democracy was in some way opposed to tradition," he writes. "It is obvious that tradition is only democracy extended through time." We often hear of the call future generations have on us, but the responsibility extends in both directions. "Tradition means giving votes to the most obscure of all classes, our ancestors. It is the democracy of the dead. Tradition refuses to submit to the small and arrogant oligarchy of those who merely happen to be walking about."[19]

The concluding flourish is hard to ignore. "All democrats object to men being disqualified by the accident of birth," he argues; "tradition objects to their being disqualified by the accident of death." For Chesterton, Christian belief is "the answer to a riddle," namely the apparent meaninglessness of life. For many of us, it is the wrong answer to the right riddle. In fact, there is no answer to that riddle except what we make for ourselves. But I suspect many of us can walk part of the way with Chesterton's paradoxical brand of wisdom. Elsewhere, he wrote that the doctrine of original sin was "the only part of Christian theology which can really be proved."[20]

Which is to say—we are all fallen creatures, sinning and sinned against. Reason is excellent, but weakness is inevitable. That is the only fellowship that is truly universal; but perhaps it is enough to lay the first bricks of justice. This is not to abandon reason—on the contrary, we need rational challenge to all belief, precisely in order to get a clear view of what may count as valid for all. A paradox: the acknowledgement of reason's limits is itself a claim of reason.

15

What Can We Know?

THERE ARE THREE NOTIONS THAT I wish to put on the table before us regarding the matter of knowledge. Each of them can be, indeed has been, pursued with vigour and detail by academic philosophers. The rest of us are amateurs—which is to say, as the word implies, true lovers rather than professional players. The three ideas are (1) runaway skepticism, (2) essentially contested concepts, and (3) strange cases where knowledge seems to come apart in our hands. I do this in the spirit of shared difficulty. In a world of competing authority claims, we are all epistemologists, like it or not, amateur or professional.[21]

I begin with an exemplary combiner of both, a brilliant philosopher when that field was not yet a jargon-jangled wrecking yard: David Hume. Hume's brand of skepticism is not that different from most other kinds we find in the history of philosophy, except perhaps in its winning combination of relentlessness and good humour. These two virtues come as twins, since Hume's approach to knowledge claims is to ask, over and over, "Okay, suppose that is so. Then what?" This is most evident in his famous essay "On Miracles," section 10 of his *Enquiry Concerning Human Understanding* (1748). The proximate subject has to do with claims about supernatural events, but the method can be applied to all outlandish events—to all events, period.

The main arguments refuting the existence of miracles, defined here as events apparently in violation of conventional natural laws, are four: (1) people are prone to accepting miracles as true because this gives them pleasure; (2) by the same token, some people's strong religious predilections predispose them to accepting miracles as true; moreover, (3) people are inclined to believe the evidence of personal testimony when it is offered in shock—emotion is taken as evidence of truth; and finally, (4) we must notice that belief in miracles is more prevalent in "barbarous and ignorant nations" than in those inclined to science.

This last jab may be thought of in contemporary terms as the Trailer Park Conundrum: why is it that visitations of anal-probing space aliens seem invariably to occur in remote areas, sparsely populated by people without degrees, instead of in midtown Manhattan on a busy weekday or Harvard Yard any time at all? As Hume notes, we have to ask ourselves whether the putative evidence of the extraordinary event is more taxing on our burdens of belief than the "firm and unalterable" experience, daily reinforced, of the Laws of Nature. Is the strain greater in accepting the outlandish event as true or in thinking it likely to be fabricated, superstitious, self-serving, or all three? Hume is, in effect, making an appeal to what more modern thinkers would call "a preponderance of evidence," of inference to the best explanation. The best explanation of an apparently miraculous event is not likely to be supernatural intervention, as against, for example, a natural phenomenon we simply have not encountered before.

Not everyone has taken this tart view of miracles. In *The Brothers Karamazov* (1880), for instance, Dostoevsky's narrator muses in this subtle way:

> [M]iracles are never a stumbling-block to the realist. It is not miracles that dispose realists to belief. The genuine

realist, if he is an unbeliever, will always find strength and ability to disbelieve in the miraculous, and if he is confronted with a miracle as an irrefutable fact he would rather disbelieve his own senses than admit the fact. Even if he admits it, he admits it as a fact of nature till then unrecognised by him. Faith does not, in the realist, spring from the miracle but the miracle from faith. If the realist once believes, then he is bound by his very realism to admit the miraculous also.[22]

In other words, believers can turn the tables on unbelievers and ask, How do you believe anything at all?

This is a crucial juncture in all theistic argumentation. For those who are not convinced, like Kierkegaard, that faith alone should be sufficient to underwrite the religious life—the position known as fideism—some form of evidence will be necessary. There is no other way to adduce belief in a personified God, the Resurrection of Jesus, or some other related miracle. People of this latter persuasion are known as evidentialists, and they may come in different varieties. Some insist on scriptural evidence for a benevolent, creative, and all-knowing deity. Others make more modest claims, say that Jesus was resurrected and that his example offers a virtuous guide to life in part because of this fact. To those who doubt the validity of this or other miracles, like Hume, some believers argue that the tenets of Christianity are falsifiable, like scientific claims. We can assess them just like we judge claims in other regions of thought such as economics or history or even physics, and we will find non–faith-based reason to accept them. Holding religious claims to a higher rational standard than the claims of other discourses is no better than prejudice.[23]

No doubt people of science will remain unconvinced by this attack on their own epistemological foundations. For them, the so-called Laws of Nature are not in fact laws, but rather law-like generalizations based on accumulated experience. They articulate the combined force of repeated inductive connection. *Custom and habit*, as Hume says, and not some view-from-nowhere or super-objectivity, accounts for our confidence in the empirical world. And yet, inductive habit is enough—more than enough for most practical purposes, and frankly necessary to accept if we are going to accomplish anything practical at all. So strong is the force of those customs and habits that we should abandon them only with stronger and unignorable counterevidence. Since such counterevidence would have to be drawn from the very same empirical sources and compete with well-trodden pathways of belief, the standard of fantastic belief will always remain extremely high, if not insuperable. And either way, empiricism wins. (This is an implied counter to Dostoevsky.)

Science takes a similar approach to questions of the existence of God, especially when that existence is invoked as a special stamp of epistemic approval on outlandish claims. Personal revelation is insufficient to the task of belief: by definition, it cannot persuade anyone who has not shared the experience. Nor is the experience reliably repeatable, which threatens its epistemic status. Genuinely rational claims should be falsifiable (as we would say now): they should contain within them the conditions of their own testing and possible defeat. A statement that cannot be proved false even in principle is ideology, not science. This position, associated with philosophers like Karl Popper and A. J. Ayer, remains central to many people's systems of trust. Absent even the possibility of evidence, we cannot rationally go on with things.[24]

What about arguments from design, then: the idea that there is too much apparent purpose in the world to be the result of simple chance and random selection? Well, we must ask, is there really evidence of design in the universe, or just elaborate and centuries-long adaptation? For one thing, we have no other universes to compare it to. Therefore, we have no rational basis for inferring design. But suppose you nevertheless think there is evidence of design. We must then ask: is that evidence of a singular designer? Why? Can't what we call the principle of design be an impersonal feature of the system? Moreover, why should the imagined designer be an entity that mirrors only the positive features of the universe we encounter? The world has flaws, deep ones, that are just as evident as the features of beauty that prompted thoughts of a divine designer. Is the designer itself flawed, or weak, or perhaps even malicious? And then finally, even if one were to accept that there is a singular designer with no evil intentions or flaws that cannot be explained away, why should we imagine that that designer is the God of the Scriptures? And which scriptures, precisely, are we talking about? There is a good deal of ... variation there.

We might, by contrast, take a generalist tack. Believers often point to the shared details of specific religions as evidence that the basic truth of the universe must be supernatural. How likely is it that people all over the planet would cleave to the very same particular doctrines? A Holy Trinity, a sacred pilgrimage in a documented location, a vision of Paradise—if there is not some underlying fact of the matter about such things, please explain their persistent recurrence. But of course, the essence of revealed religion is precisely its claim to provide access to the one and only truth, and then to embellish that claim with specific features and tropes. Tradition grows around the basic claim, usually with some form of scripture and attendant rituals in its honour. True believers are not simply those with access to that truth, having been acculturated (or indoctrinated) into it over time, but rather those who have had the scales fall from their eyes in moments of blistering insight. Saul of Tarsus on the road to Damascus is the paradigm case here, literally knocked from his horse by the Heavenly message.

And so, we observe, once again, tropes of sight and blindness, sleep and awakening. The Great Awakenings of American history—the first in the early eighteenth century, the second a few decades later—are historical legacies of the basic narrative of sleep and rousing. Ideas of enlightenment are here refigured or repurposed in the language of New England Protestantism. Amazing grace—I was blind but now I see! How sweet the sound that saved a wretch like me!

Even without detailing the vast—and frequently deadly—differences *between* religions, one might think an overarching supernatural order would have just one shape and narrative. But the similarities in belief within religions offer no evidence of a baseline truth. Social constructions are commonly replicated, especially ones that offer solace, narratives of purpose and meaning, and promises of relief from mundane suffering. No, the remarkable thing would be if we found religion *without* such clustered ritual commonalities and shared metaphors. Clustered and, let us never forget, murderous. There is evidence that religious belief is a natural consequence of our cognitive structure, however.[25] It's not all social conditioning and wishful thinking, the familiar Cartesian "problem of other minds." How can I know that you, another human being, enjoy the same mindedness that I do? How do I know that you are really there, present in mind as well as body? This is the root of worries about those uncanny, almost-human entities we may encounter as advancing technology undermines our basic trust in other persons.

More about that subject in the next part. For now, we can notice how the cognitive limitations of mind—the solipsistic fact that we can only directly know our own mental contents—lead to what some psychologists call "belief overshoot." That is, we must project mind onto other human beings in order to be part of a sane world. There is no choice about that, since the alternative is madness. But that same projection can lead to extravagant attributions of mind to notional creators, mythic figures, nonhuman deities.

These then become repositories of other desires. We want the world to make sense, and keenly wish that our place within it has some purpose and meaning. Spiritual need is a real thing. And the resulting feeling of belonging and community—not to mention all the great music, art, and ritual—are net human goods. But the downside risks in internecine violence, prejudice, and moral judgment are devastating. Worst of all, the basic claims for a supernatural order are just not true: our projections are a kind of Cartesian metaphysical hangover, a bad dream of disembodied superminds who are goal setting, personal, and responsive to our wishes. None of these cases of special pleading are convincing on the question of a supernatural universe. Our felt desire, willingness, and even wiredness to believe are not, and never can be, themselves evidence for divinity. The form of wishful thinking that assumes otherwise, however powerful, is revealed as just another form of doxaholic dependency—comforting but ultimately harmful. No, we will just have to take the universe as we find it and evidence as we can prove it.

* * *

BUT THIS STILL LEAVES US with two remaining thorny problems for knowledge. One is that the most important notions that we use to try and understand our place and purpose in the world—justice, art, democracy—seem to be forever up for grabs. That is, they qualify as what are sometimes called "essentially contested concepts."[26] Here we mean not just ideas that provoke thought and disagreement, but rather concepts that seems to have a quality of infinite contestation—no amount of evidence *of any kind* seems able to settle disputes over them. I can imagine people nodding cynically at this, thinking perhaps of some long-ago intro philosophy class where *every* concept seemed infinitely contested, without resolution or rest. And it's true that professional philosophers, or some of them, would be out of work if concepts were not open to lengthy, if not necessarily infinite, contestation.

My point about these concepts here is to note that such examples as justice, art, and democracy do exist—and that, in each case, their contestability is a good thing for justice, art, and democracy. We should worry not when such concepts are argued about and disputed at every turn. No, the worrisome thing would be if we found ourselves in some political or aesthetic conditions, maybe just a state of mind, in which no further contestation seemed necessary, or possible. We need essential contestation to remind us that seeking the beautiful, just, and democratic are infinite tasks.

There is another aspect of essentially contested concepts that is directly on point for our current considerations: contestation often refers to, or even gets tangled up in, competing authoritative claims. In many cases, these authoritative claims make their authority evident through an exemplar or avatar: the figurehead of authority. Such exemplars seem necessary to the cycles of contestation, at a minimum in the form of standing in for previous argument. You can always tell if there is an exemplar in the room when his or her (mostly his) name is made into an adjective or, even more telling, an adjectival noun.[27]

Let us not be afraid of essentially contested concepts, then, but let us also approach them with proper caution and humility. They are not problems to be solved, but neither are they impregnable towers of authority. Humility is ever the order of the day when it comes to human knowledge. My third and final guardrail on epistemic hubris is what are sometimes called Gettier Cases, after a short 1963 journal article by the philosopher Edmund Gettier. Gettier's little paper shook the foundations of traditional empirical epistemology by advancing the possibility of strange but plausible cases where knowledge failed. At the time, for both philosophers and punters, the gold-standard definition of knowledge was "justified true belief." That is, (1) I hold a particular belief, (2) it is true, and (3) I hold it because of some rational justification. One can imagine the other possibility here: there is a true belief, justified rationally, which I refuse to hold; I hold a belief with justification, but it is false; I hold a true belief but without justification.[28]

Gettier Cases are imagined scenarios, some of them quite odd, in which justified true belief fails to be knowledge. How is this possible?

Well, imagine one of the simpler Gettier cases. I pass a wall clock on my way to work. It tells me the time is 11:55 and I will get to class in good order if I hurry. The clock is well maintained, and in my experience it is accurate. In fact, it is correct: the time is 11:55 and I arrive at class on time. But unbeknownst to me, the clock has in fact stopped at 11:55 p.m. the previous evening. It happened that I passed it at 11:55 a.m. the next morning and so got a correct reading; but if I had walked by a few minutes earlier or later I would have been in error. Now, you might say: we all know that a broken clock is right twice a day. It's an old joke! How does that affect the idea of knowledge being justified true belief? The problem we see emerging with this case is that I had all three sufficient conditions of knowledge: belief, truth, and justification. But I still did not really *know* that the time was 11:55 a.m. In an important sense, I just lucked out in having my justified true belief match up to a state of affairs in the world, that is, the correct time.

Other Gettier Cases are more complicated and, frankly, bizarre—men in sheep's clothing in distant fields, job-seekers who happen to have ten coins in their pockets, and so on. What's the big deal? There are at least two important implications of these cases. One is that they put into doubt any conception of knowledge as internal. The cases show that there may be external circumstances that either confuse the process of justification, or else call for further justification—which is sometimes impossible. (I can't second-guess every clock I see against some notionally reliable standard.) Justification even of true beliefs is, in short, an extremely tricky undertaking. Internal states seem insufficient to the task, and external guarantees are hard to come by. Where do those true beliefs come from, anyway? Are they themselves internal achievements, or prompts from external states of affairs?

We should be careful not to be overhasty even with belief. Belief is, and should be, hard won and precious, not a lazy default of idle consciousness. We *hold* beliefs, or *reject* them, or sometimes *entertain* them: the verbs are all active here, for these are epistemic commitments, not as binding or reliable—yet—as knowledge but still serious. Doubt, meanwhile, about beliefs both large and small, is an endless and precarious task of the mind. As Descartes noted in the first of his meditations, what starts with optical illusions and errors in perception can escalate to doubts about the world and its reliable existence. But Descartes was wrong about something fundamental in the ordering of tasks here: we can't doubt everything first, and then believe things later. We are stuck right here, in the middle of the world. "If you tried to doubt everything, you would not get as far as doubting anything," said Ludwig Wittgenstein in response to Descartes. "Doubt comes *after* belief. The child learns by believing the adult."[29]

I won't try to untangle the myriad complexities here—this book is not a treatise in epistemology. It is enough for us to re-affirm our commitments to humility and epistemic wariness. Rational investigation demands what philosophers call *inference to the best explanation*, or *abduction*: we draw the best workable conclusions based on the evidence we have. This allows for error (our evidence may be partial, our simplest inference not the correct one), but it is both useful and necessary, absent more complete epistemic equipment.[30] This procedure can offer a baseline normative orientation to all questions of belief and knowledge: it works in both scientific and everyday contexts. But before we move on, consider one further challenging thought about the nature of knowledge and error, belief and skepticism.

"There are only two true errors," the critic Adam Mastroianni has written. "One is believing that we have no errors left to make, and the other is believing that those errors are permanent and irreversible."[31]

The first mistake is typically a function of arrogance. It is unfortunately common, especially in public discourse now; but we can see it and know that we must push back on it. That pushing back is something rightly applied both to others and to our inner selves, as I have emphasized throughout these pages. The second mistake is more a matter of will, or character. It gives in to a temptation to cynicism or nihilism: if everyone is corrupt, then standards simply have to be abandoned. But, despite how we sometimes feel, these are not the Gates of Hell that we see before us, on our screens and in the forums of daily exchange. We should not—should never—abandon hope. On the contrary, when in doubt we should redouble it.

This second error about the nature of error creates a tangle that leads to confusion but also, worse, sometimes to despair. We cannot afford to succumb to either. My personal conviction—ever tempered by hard experience—is that philosophy is the best way to counter the temptation to cynicism. But it can only do so by working in a somewhat quirky manner. More paradox, in short.

16

The Paradox of Philosophy

THERE ARE, IN FACT, TWO paradoxes of philosophy, one specific and one general. The specific one concerns knowledge as we have been discussing it. The general one concerns the possibility of doing philosophy at all.

Philosophy has often been considered impossible, usually for reasons having to do with how people we dislike go about it. Philosophers are forever in the business of putting each other out of business. The typical charges involve malfeasance, confusion, muddled thinking, and dangerous metaphysical tendencies. It is a surprise only to those outside the profession that the presumptively mild-mannered pursuit of clarity in thought should be so inherently murderous.

Most of these internecine disputes can be managed, or understood, by way of sufficient distance (who cares?) or dialectical ingenuity (I absorb your limited view *thus*!). What cannot be so salved is the enduring damage of the *basic paradox of all philosophy*, the serpent coiled in its heart. By this I mean philosophy's reliance on a picture of reality that is rooted in sensory experience. This picture, no matter its complexity, is afflicted by an apparently insuperable intellectual pincer movement, a skeptical double-flank collapse. How can under-standing understand itself without replicating the sensory errors of any understanding? I want to pose a philosophical question about the senses that has implications from art to politics to fashion, and every stop in between. It is this: Can the senses ever save us from the lurking monster of metaphysical doubt?

Consider, on the one hand, the fact that most philosophers set themselves up as arbiters of reality, adjudicating against misleading appearances. This is how Plato began and how most of us still go on. On the other hand, and at the very same time, erecting this basic distinction between what appears and what is real seems to cleave ourselves and the world in an irretrievable way. Descartes or Kant can call on sensory deceptions as a caution against epistemological com-placency, but only in the service of a larger metaphysics that kicks the problem down the road. Retrieved reality, shorn of deceptive appear-ances, is just as susceptible to doubt as optical illusions, lies, trompe l'oeil japes, and the like. Restored reality, the educated sensorium, will not save us.

One of the few philosophers to take this endgame seriously was Ludwig Wittgenstein, together with his long-distance disciple, the American Stanley Cavell. "A picture held us captive," Wittgenstein tells us in the *Philosophical Investigations*. "And we could not get out-side it, for it lay in our language and language seemed to repeat it to us inexorably."[32] So it did, and so it does. Wittgenstein means that language is never some neutral vessel of perspicuous communica-tion, a totally clear pane of glass between two minds. Any assumption that the meaning of words is clear and fixed is a delusion; instead he says, famously, that "meaning is use." Language means something only according to its place within some program of human action and communication. And such use is executed using "pictures," or, in fancier language, *conceptual schemes*. In a positive account, we can understand the point in terms of "language games": that is, distinct ways of going on (playing the game, getting things done) that allow or demand particular linguistic "moves."

The problem comes when these "pictures" are rigid and limiting, as when we get locked into something like an appearance/reality distinction. This metaphysical picture holds us captive because we cannot address its internal problems without reinforcing the basic logic. Over and over, we are set back into our captivity. And the only apparent "solution" to this self-posed problem will be something weighty and bizarre, like Plato's theory of the Forms. Our games lead us into such swamps of thought, so deeply that we can't seem to get out. This is one reason why part of the habitual business of philosophers, especially of a certain critical bent, is to declare metaphysics anathema. David Hume is vividly on record as urging us to commit the many pages of metaphysical speculation "to the flames." (Maybe you didn't expect book burning to be part of a philosophical program, but there you go.)

But it is more than language that is at fault here; it is sensory life itself, our too-troubled immersion in the son et lumière of worldly existence. And yet, what can we do about these epistemological constraints? Discarding one picture seems only to invite replacement by another, distinguished only by its self-congratulation at not being the first. Cavell will suggest a discipline of endless acknowledgement. In this section, I will take up that challenge and assess its viability as a response to the paradox of philosophy. Can we still believe our eyes? Or must we, metaphorically at least, pluck them from their sockets in a paroxysm of Biblical disgust? Or is it, somehow, both? This kind of questioning leads, in turn, to some puzzles that are as familiar in the history of philosophy as they are in science fiction: Descartes's malicious demon, the brain-in-the-vat thought experiment, The Matrix's red-pill versus blue-pill choice, the so-called Experience Machine, and so on. All of them have been brought up to date by emerging technologies that suggest an unsettling possibility: could we be, right now, part of a vast computer simulation and yet not know it?

The epistemo-action thriller is by now an accepted genre within speculative fiction, especially film, with its ability to create immersive experiences (video games and some books are pretty effective at this, as well). These cinematic exercises in perception bending and unreliable context are often called postmodern, but in fact their cognitive commitments are decisively modern, if not premodern. They are, that is to say, preoccupied with the ancient appearance/reality distinction and with ways of securing a foundation for our apparently unstable experience of the modern world.

The appearance/reality exercise becomes decisively modern with the subject's focus on his or her own consciousness, attempting to put the experience of experience itself into critical view. The Cartesian attempt is significant not only because it spawns so much later reflection and reaction, but also because Descartes at once poses the problem in a way that makes it seem insoluble even as he claims to solve it. But once again we ask, how do we know anything at all? Descartes is confident that if we adopt a method of hyperbolic doubt, questioning every aspect and level of what we take to be true, we can isolate something beyond doubt. This is, as everyone knows, the celebrated *cogito*—*I think*—which underwrites its equally famous *ergo sum* supplement: *therefore I am*. This doesn't mean that only thinking beings are truly alive, or that we are most vital when thinking—two common misinterpretations. It means, rather, that the act of thinking itself proves the existence of something, the res cogitans or thinking thing which a conscious subject essentially is.

Technologist, off-world colonizer, and sometime *Simpsons* character Elon Musk is merely the most recent to articulate the radical idea that we are living in a vast computer simulation run by future versions of ourselves.[33] The "simulation argument," developed by philosopher Nick Bostrom, argues that, given the nature of computer power and its presumed ability to affect and even replicate human consciousness, it is overwhelmingly likely that we are within one of millions of such simulations. We are Sims and we don't know it! The claim is striking both for its logical elegance and for its ability to rattle the cage of ordinary mortals. Like debates about free will and determinism, the simulation argument takes our unique sense of self, our hopes, desires, and halting actions, and renders them null. No wonder the scenario is old, even if the computer-based argument is new. The gods toy with us as wanton boys play with flies, but now the gods are made of tin.[34]

In our current circumstances, the simulation argument dovetails with a worry born of more practical struggles in the world of politics. That is, if your previously rock-solid sense of reality as a unique consciousness is undermined by this kind of speculative contingency, then why not by others? This will feel quite shattering, we imagine, but then perhaps eventually liberating. In fact, a more complete embrace of contingency about personhood might be salutary overall. We have already seen that the current state of identity and grievance politics seems stalled around the problem of generalization. A justice claim that is particular by definition cannot (or cannot yet) be the basis of a more inclusive system of equity. Even when advanced as a corrective to historical injustice—decrying, say, the long-term effects of chattel slavery—it must depend on a particular essentialist claim of belonging to underwrite and enact the grievance.

Hence the current angry debates about *who gets to call themselves* Black, Indigenous, or even female. If I or anyone can simply "identify" as a member one of these ill-served groups, that seems to mock the basis of claiming injustice in the first place. The typical countermove, of reaffirming the closed gate of the identity, is just as self-defeating: it is tribal in the bad sense, not at all inclusive. And yet, the resulting confusion might be productive: if we abandon particularist conceptions of selfhood, perhaps we could really allow a thousand flowers to bloom. The tricky cross-currents of contemporary identity politics, where conflicting claims of status and value hinge on race, gender, sexual orientation, ability, or history, might yet prove to be the birthplace of a world without exclusively *identitarian* individuals. A world, in other words, where ethical and legal status is based on shared capacities— for reason, but also for suffering, power and weakness together—and not traits that are limited in distribution across populations. But this will happen only if we start to loosen our sense of what makes individuals singular and worthwhile, not lock it down further. This would then be the posthuman justice of our dreams.[35]

Well, maybe. Technologists will tell you the posthuman future is inevitable, maybe already here, and that they joyously await the Singularity (where nonhuman intelligence outstrips our slow biological brains). Most of us are more cautious, not least because we know that the future is always unevenly distributed, and that the adapt-or-die cheerfulness of tech boosters too often conceals drastic structural inequalities. There are human limits that are not about mortality but are a function of human relations. Claims of political status based on identity have always been advanced to challenge structural asymmetries: exclusions driven by skin colour, differences in genital arrangement, differences in desire. Those are considered habitual tics of the Left; on the Right, identity politics takes the sometimes subtler forms of dog-whistles about "childless cat ladies," as per, for example, the neonatalist judgment of vice-presidential candidate and political chameleon JD Vance that stands in for, or gestures towards, some admixture of a Catholic eugenics program and the Great Replacement Theory. There is a tangle in all of this, Left or Right. If your claims to status are based on reversing prejudicial discrimination based on a perceived but inessential difference, you run the risk of making the difference itself—rather than the claim to status—the political focal point, implicitly reifying the very thing you meant to expose as insignificant. Identity politics aims for a day when all individuals are valued in themselves, but those aspects of unique individuality that have been systematically denigrated can, paradoxically, become barriers to the achievement of individual value.

Imagine, then, a world in which people do not define themselves by their various clusters of traits or get to claim privileges based upon them. It would also be a world where some cluster of traits was no longer cause for discrimination or violence. In metaphysical terms, the problem here is not the differential treatment of traits, but the fact that traits are clustered in the first place, forming individuals who are supposed to be both different and the same.

The political threshold in play is the persistent idea of the individual as unique and self-identical: a single person who is indivisible and possessed of just one mind, however conflicted or confused that mind may often be. This is the vision of selfhood as a kind of driver in the seat of consciousness, guiding the whole elaborate machine of existence between morning and night. Even at our most fractured, we have trouble letting go of this notion of an inner driver or roving spectator, a kind of first-person-shooter video-game P O V of being alive and roving the environment in search of up-level encounters. Born in struggles against hierarchy and religious intolerance some four centuries ago (in the West at least), the social-political individual has led a rocky life. It has borne property rights and generated social revolution, but more recently it has declined into mere consumer preference or Twitter-X-Insta-TikTok presence. In a world without individuals, the uniqueness of my consciousness would not signify much, nor would its possibilities ever be constrained by being tied to a stable identity. The "I" of my personal narrative would acknowledge its own fictional status, a minimal ordering principle as it runs one experiment in human living after another. Discrimination would be rendered incoherent.

In the potentially *postindividualist* world, we would really be running the simulations ourselves, using bodies and the material world as test-benches. This would be a posthuman world, unrecognizable to most of what currently counts as human life. These are the real metaphysical stakes of loosening the moorings of selfhood. The simulation argument forces imagination to confront its own mysteries, but it does little to advance the issue. Meanwhile, we seem trapped in a different kind of snare, one that is not speculative at all. The human present is mired in prejudice and evil, apparently basic circumstances against which the best efforts of identity-based empowerment have been only moderately successful. The human future seems to promise more of the same, only with the unpleasant kicker that we will find new, possibly worse ways of extending inequality by heeding "what technology wants."

Is there another way? Could we fashion a world where differences really were transcended, where nobody was worth more or less than anyone else, where the ultimate value wasn't individual identity but the multiplicity of unlikely meat-minds, windowless mirrors each reflecting all the others, making things up? That is the basic ideal of justice, the notion of balancing out the misfortunes and oppression that got us here in the first place. And while it can sometimes seem like a haunting dream rather than any sort of proximate possibility, I believe we must continue to think and act *as if* it is within reach. The stars guide our course, even though we know we cannot touch them.

* * *

THERE WILL ALWAYS BE TROUBLE, because "we" and "I" remain forever suspended somewhere between mind and world. How can this thinking thing which I consider the locus of my identity be conjoined in some smooth, continuous sense with, furthermore, a physical body that is itself just part of the physical world in the form of res extensa, material substance extended in space?

My favourite exchange concerning this problem occurs not in a philosophy treatise, but in a play, Tom Stoppard's *Rosencrantz and Guildenstern Are Dead* (1966). The action of this play takes place in the margins of another famous play (*Hamlet*), which in turn has an infamous play nestled within it: that is, *The Murder of Gonzago* aka

The Mousetrap, a performance designed to "catch the conscience of the king." Thus Stoppard's play-without-a-play riffs on and bounces off a canonical play with a play within it, and so puts at its own wobbly centre two minor characters from the central Shakespeare work. The two eponymous underlings, traditionally relegated to making noises off in the wings of supporting action, are here made the drama's central characters. They are also painfully revealed as hapless playthings of fortune, never at all certain about their place, purpose, identity, or state of knowledge. Indeed, the entire layered, vertiginous, dramatic spectacle before us is an exercise in gleeful epistemological destabilization. The key passage, for me, starts this way: Guildenstern is confused and provoked by his predicament. He and Rosencrantz will be charged by the king to figure out what is afoot in Hamlet's tortured mind: they are to "glean what afflicts him." But this is easier said than done, even in a more basic case than the moody prince, who has, wherefore he knows not, lost all his mirth. In the post-Cartesian world, this is a desperate case of a general quandary, the problem of other minds. We cannot access the mental space of another, however well we think we know them. Worse, we cannot always even reliably access our own.

"But for God's sake what are we supposed to do?!" Guildenstern (or is it Rosencrantz?) wails to everyone and no one. The situation, like life itself, seems to demand decision and action without providing the knowledge needed to guide it. The desperate cry is addressed to the wide world and the airy dome above, but also more directly to a mysterious jester-like figure called the Player. He is the leader of a troupe of actors headed to the original play's main action, there to catch the conscience of the king. "Relax," advises the Player. "Respond. That's what people do. You can't go through life questioning your situation at every turn."

This practical-sounding advice is of no help to Guildenstern. "But we don't know what's going on, or what to do with ourselves," he wails, as we so often want to do. "We don't know how to act." The Player is suave in response, like unhelpful advisors everywhere from guidance offices to therapy sessions. "Act natural," he says. You imagine him smiling in a gently mocking way. "You know why you're here at least."

But Guildenstern doesn't know any such thing. "We only know what we're told, and that's little enough. And for all we know it isn't even true."

The Player pounces on this, indeed the basic difficulty. "For all anyone knows, nothing is," he tells the doomed henchman in the same soothing tones. "Everything has to be taken on trust; truth is only that which is taken to be true. It's the currency of living." A pause here, I think, to let all these ideas sink in a bit. This is a long speech for the Player. "There may be nothing behind it," he goes, conceding what might be thought a minor point from his attitude, "but it doesn't make any difference so long as it is honoured. One acts on assumptions. What do you assume?"

It doesn't make any difference so long as it's honoured. But is that true? I mean, is that the only final truth about truth? And all of this is excellent-sounding life-player advice, but does it help very much? Don't know how to act? Act natural! Don't know what to do? Relax! Respond! Truth? Just what's taken to be true. Trust your assumptions! This may well make one a player, or even a Player. But is it enough to be going on with?

But no, don't trust your assumptions—at least not all the time. Put those assumptions into question over and over, one by one: that's the ticket. You can't get outside the circle of assumptions any more than you can eliminate all prejudice. These are the only possible foundations of knowledge. They are shaky but necessary. Descartes was right: take out one apple at a time to see if any of them are rotten. But he was also wrong: you can't remove all the apples in order then to examine the basket. Because the basket is you, and you are the one assessing the apples.

My own view is that God won't help you here. Even on most sympathetic accounts, He probably has larger concerns than whether your sense impressions align with the world.[36] But, by the same token, it also seems highly unlikely that there is a malicious demon or a supercomputer generating the whole scene of experience. And if I am wrong about either possibility, well, it doesn't seem to matter much inside the scene.

Guildenstern is frustrated by being suspended inside the scene this way. To him, there always seems to be a play within the play, or a sense that he is trapped inside a story that is not his own. And so, he asks, prayerfully, "All I ask is our common clue, give us this day our daily cue." Elsewhere, matters are even more fraught: "Give us this day our daily mask." At yet another point, and even more poignantly, "Give us this day our daily week."

Cue, mask, time. Not even the Almighty can make a day into a week or provide more than clues about how to be here, when *how* includes *why*. No, we must figure that out for ourselves; and sometimes, maybe all too often, we will find ourselves at sea between Denmark and England, with no orders forthcoming. If only we had a clue, a cue, anything!

Be careful what you wish for. In such a state of doubt, it's not only minor characters who cannot master the world with knowledge. You might be the mighty one who finds a trifle, a stray handkerchief, that tears the world asunder.

When Othello is confronted by Desdemona's personal item, a gift he has given her after receiving it from his own mother, we already know that things have gone wrong. And they are about to get worse. Othello is a tragic figure in a way that requires no immersive technology or off-world appearance machine. Paradoxically, he deceives himself precisely because he wants to believe. Here the will to believe meets the trace of the real.

Because it is, in fact, her handkerchief—it is not a fake, or a duplicate, though there is a suggestion that such merely imitative deception might be part of the overall plot. No, the handkerchief's coming to be in Cassio's lodging has all the makings of a sort of tragic Gettier Case avant la lettre. It is *in fact* Desdemona's cherished present, a sign of Othello's love and her fidelity; we're told that she keeps it always with her, to "kiss and talk to." She tried to use it to soothe Othello's headache. And yet, the play hints that Othello's mother got it from a sorceress, and certainly he is ensorcelled by its presence.

We know that Iago has planted the handkerchief. Othello does not. And, effectively primed by Iago's bilious counsel and, alas, his own proclivity to jealously, he accepts the proffered sign. He believes he has justified true belief about Desdemona's infidelity. Iago has made the main point in a smug soliloquy about Othello's credulity: "Trifles light as air / Are to the jealous confirmations strong / As proofs of holy writ." When a person is murderously jealous, it doesn't take much *evidence* to set them off.

Usually seen as a plaything of runaway presuppositions, including his awful willingness to entertain suspicions about Desdemona, Othello is actually a victim of misplaced empiricism. Here, illustrating a point that Gadamer would explore much later, the truth available is already and always determined by the method employed. Perhaps we should say it is overdetermined, even as Iago's own motivation is underdetermined. Iago is an avatar of grievance politics. As Salman Rushdie puts it, "the only thing that happens to Iago is that he's passed over for a promotion. That's it. That's his beef. And because of that, he decides to destroy the lives of two people, Othello and Desdemona."[37] (These days, he would probably lodge an anonymous complaint with HR, and then take to social media and hope to cancel Othello.)

The clash of these two misguided absolute desires—the one for a certain sort of truth, the other a resentful urge to dominate through deception—plays out as a compact tragic commentary on shared life. Despite its historical provenance, it has a very contemporary dramatic arc. Othello demanded *proof*, and so proof was provided. Iago coveted *recognition* and reacted angrily when it failed to arrive. The tragedy is not Iago's deception but rather Othello's combination of distrust and willingness to believe. The Moor is double-tapped, by skepticism and authority alike. Worst of all, he does it to himself.[38]

The resulting scene is among the most wrenching in English literature. Othello's murder of Desdemona is hard to watch. In the last production I saw, the director decided to extend the strangling for as long as such a violent act might take in real life. It was harrowing. In the row in front of me, a burly man wearing a lumberjack shirt and a trucker cap—not an image of the effete theatre-goer—sat there with tears streaming down his face, eyes locked on the stage. I felt like throwing up myself.

Not often in my life have I experienced so powerfully the peculiar leverage of *aesthetic distance*, that voluntary-but-not-really contract that keeps us in our seats when every moral impulse is urging us to rush the stage and prevent the disastrous outcome. We call this "willing suspension of disbelief," but there is something pretty unwilling about it at extreme moments such as this. Intellectually we mock the idea of a yokel rushing the stage to try and explain to the characters what is really happening to them, what they don't actually know, and above all how to avoid the looming tragic mistake that will encompass their doom. It is impossible not to feel, in these moments, that the issue of distance is not nearly clear enough in our minds. Aesthetic imagination and moral imagination are clearly linked, as we have sensed already several times, and here we must feel, in the dark of the theatre, hushed in silence with our fellow humans, the *strangeness* of compassion. It calls us forth! We want to respond! We *are* responding. But we do nothing. Because here, now, doing nothing is the correct response. But what of those cases when the distant tragedies are real? Is our so-called compassion fatigue just a screen for indifference, a way of aestheticizing our ethical failure? I am afraid so. I mean that we sometimes execute a complicated mental somersault that allows us to view mediated suffering—the spectacle, distant humans in distress—

as just another theatre piece. Now we suspend our belief, namely that this suffering is real, rather than our disbelief, as when we observe tragedy played out on stage.

The looping effects of belief, disbelief, ethics, and spectacle are complicated. In the theatre we feel pinned to our seats because, in part, our fear and pity are real—that's why the suspensions of aesthetic distance are necessary. We need to feel these emotions, but ideally in controlled environments. In the theatre, this is appropriate. I wonder if it makes us less responsive outside those confines, when suffering is real but not so close that it falls upon us directly. Aristotle was aware of all this when he wrote about tragic catharsis. What is fiction except a series of wrenching, compelling thought experiments? These thought experiments are not overtly ethical, at least not always—that makes for bad, didactic art. But precisely by opening up new worlds, worlds that do not exist, in this one-and-only real world, but which can be accessed from here—possible worlds of detail and emotion—we can experience what we need not actually live through.

It is a common complaint among critics today, one that I whole-heartedly share, that judgments of "relatability" in fiction are reductive and dismaying. And yet, I want to say—I feel like I know what those angry one-star commenters mean when they say that none of the characters in Proust are likeable, or that Austen's novels are full of pretentious social climbers. This sounds like pure lack of sophistication, but I consider it, instead, as a sort of cry from the simple heart. The sentiments may be considered naïve or crude, and they will not answer to the demands of much great literature. But surely that is the whole job of it: teaching readers how to read with more nuance, showing spectators how to look with closer attention, showing students how to think harder. The pressing questions of knowledge and action are forever renewed and revitalized in art and philosophy. Our experience of the aesthetic is, among other things, a kind of test bed of our responsiveness to the world. How do we acknowledge the otherness of the other?[39] The yokel who rushes the stage is not wrong, just mistaken—there is a difference. And we? What do we do in such circumstances, too sophisticated to unsuspend our disbelief? Well, we may never take handkerchiefs for granted again. And we should wonder, when knowledge seems so secure, whether our justification is really as ironclad as we imagine.

I have not forgotten about the second, general paradox of philosophy. It is this: you can only see the value of thinking philosophically when you are already doing it. Before that, philosophical thinking will seem useless, contrived, self-contradictory, and hopelessly vague. It's almost its own bad-luck Gettier problem: the clock of thought has stopped telling practical time, and though it is right twice a day for purely adventitious reasons, it is not tracking reality. And tracking reality is what we want—or at least what we say we want!

Except, except—there is something that even a hostile or bored student glimpses in this otherwise strange way of going on. Philosophy is not all fun and games; or, put more accurately, its games are the ones we need to keep in view when worldly concerns tend to drive them into the corners of mind. Maybe the bored student looks up from her screen, and suddenly recalls the childish questions that were put away as time went by: When I see blue, do I see the same thing you do? When I fall asleep, where does my mind go? Why is it okay to eat cows but not to eat my cat? Why do I have to be fair when the world so obviously is not? Why do you have something that I do not?

Socrates knew that the only way to get someone to think philosophically was to capture their imagination. You can't argue someone into it, because its merit is only evident to those whose values have altered under its influence. Not even reason is sufficient to prove reason's worth. And, though it may be comforting and apparently certain, revelation is no better option. That which only I can see is not, by definition, scalable or falsifiable. It does not translate. Listening to your mother works just fine—until it doesn't.

17

A Mom Speaks

I CAN'T LEAVE THIS AREA of authority, trust, and identity terrain without invoking the example of an authority-wracked mother, albeit a fictional one.

Frances McDormand plays Elaine Miller in Cameron Crowe's sleeper hit *Almost Famous* (2000). It's the story of a teenager, William Miller, who finds himself on the road with an emerging, successful rock band. The film succeeds on many levels, buoyed by lovely performances from Kate Hudson as an old-soul groupie (or "band aid"), Patrick Fugit as the young *Rolling Stone* reporter, and Billy Crudup as the handsome lead guitarist of the band Stillwater.

One central dynamic is the uneasy relationship between the band, which thrives on authenticity, and the press coverage offered by the presence of fifteen-year-old William. The dyspeptic lead singer calls the amiable boy "The Enemy," and he is likewise warned by legendary rock critic Lester Bangs (Philip Seymour Hoffman) not to become friends with the band. Telling the truth about the romance and treachery of life on the road is a lesson in media ethics as probing as anything from the work of Janet Malcolm.

But it is McDormand, playing a bewildered but game college professor and single mom, who steals the picture. She is confused by a world that allows her adolescent son to join a travelling circus of depravity; her only weapons are common sense and philosophy. In a key scene, she confronts Crudup's character Russell Hammond, Stillwater's pretty-boy guitarist, in the course of a testy telephone exchange. Half seriously, Russell tries to reassure Elaine that her son is safe with the rock-and-roll entourage. Elaine will have none of it. "Hey, hey, listen to me, mister," she interrupts him. "Your charm doesn't work on me. I'm on to you. Of course you like him."

"Well, yeah," Russell says, balking slightly at her tone, unmollified by his jokey approach. His charm usually works, because he's Billy Crudup and he looks great, with the flowing hair and the moustache. But Elaine will not be cajoled, because *rock stars have kidnapped her son!*

"He worships you people. And that's fine by you as long as he helps make you rich." Hey wait! "Rich? I don't think so," Russell protests. Stillwater doesn't even have decent merch. They travel on a ramshackle bus.

Elaine does not pause to debate the point. "Listen to me," she tells Russell. He's listening, now, transfixed. "He's a smart, good-hearted fifteen-year-old kid with infinite potential." Cut to Russell, saying nothing, brow furrowed. What is happening? Why is his world-beating charm not working here?

Elaine is not done. "This is not some apron-wearing mother you're speaking with. I know all about your Valhalla of decadence, and I shouldn't have let him go. He's not ready for your world of compromised values and diminished brain cells that you throw away like confetti. Am I speaking to you clearly?"

Russell is startled into speech. "Yes," he says, brain cells still functioning, "Yes, ma'am," he clarifies. Elaine is still not done. "If you break his spirit, harm him in any way, keep him from his chosen profession, which is law—something you may not value, but I do—you will meet the voice on the other end of this telephone and it will not be pretty. Do we understand each other?"

Russell: "Uh, yes, ma'am." His eyes have gone into a shell-shocked thousand-yard stare, or maybe deer in the headlights. But Elaine is still not done.

"I didn't ask for this role," she tells him, "but I'll play it. Now go do your best. *Be bold, and mighty forces will come to your aid.* Goethe said that. It's not too late for you to become a person of substance, Russell. Please get my son home safely." Pause, as Russell struggles with colliding thoughts and his sudden, unexpected inability to keep on being charming and awesome. "You know, I'm glad we spoke," Elaine says into the silence. She hangs up, message delivered.

Cut to Russell, still saying nothing, still lost in thought and befuddled by the voice of maternal authority. In his own words, called up later in a conversation with William, he is *freaked out* by Elaine's precision attack. Her tactical assault on his presumed failings must be the envy of any parent today who quails at the thought of their offspring's social media feeds and who would happily confiscate phones if they could get away with it.

Be bold, my friends, and mighty forces will come to your aid! Did Goethe actually say that? Probably not.[40] Is it true? Probably not as well. But so what? Mom said so, and who are we to argue? Freaked out!

FIFTH MEDITATION:

These Are Not the Droids You're Looking For

18

JEDI—and Addiction

EVERYONE KNOWS THE SCENE. ALEC Guinness, playing Obi-Wan "Ben" Kenobi is passing into Mos Eisley spaceport, that "wretched hive of scum and villainy," with Luke Skywalker, R2-D2, and C-3PO. They have Princess Leia's call for help, a sense of cosmic mission, and two awesome lightsabers among them. They need a ship and a rogue captain to pilot their way to destiny.

It is 1977 and I have seen this movie in theatres across Canada ten separate times, a personal record, assisted by allowance money and some white lies about my age so I can afford the youth ticket. Nobody except George Lucas knows that this is just the beginning of a project of domination whereby every comic-loving, plastic-model-building, graph paper RPG –playing nerd would become some kind of influencer-king in the new-millennium cultural world. The Empire isn't just fiction. The world will see many more Jedi mind tricks in coming scenes, films, novels, and cartoons. They are like little magic flashes in the Star Wars universe. But Obi-Wan's simple, finger-waving dismissal of Imperial stormtrooper interest in their movements is iconic. "You don't need to see his identification," he informs the

white-armoured goon. "These aren't the droids you're looking for."
No, you don't; and they are not. "You can go about your business,"
the trooper intones obediently to nobody in particular. "Move along."

Awesome. Anyone who has ever been in a bureaucratic queue, or
passed through a border crossing, or even waited for a ticket-taker to
exercise their trifling petty authority over one's free movement, will
recognize this as a key point in a cinematic fable all about questioning
authority. It is not the very highest narrative peak of Force-power in
the movie. As everyone knows, that point arrives when Darth Vader
Force-chokes his mouthy subordinate in the Death Star boardroom.
Both are excellent examples how the Force would come in handy
in everyday life, much more so than, say, the mad rabbit hopping of
Force-jump, which looks hilarious when executed by Yoda but has very
few real-world applications. Shutting up annoying people or passing
through irritation barriers—now those are powers worth having.

I will return to the question of which droids we're actually looking
for, but for now I want to note a few things about the Jedi—or rather,
JEDI. In recent years we have all grown accustomed to proliferating
social-media acronyms and tags: SJW for social-justice warrior, or DEI
for diversity, equity, and inclusion. Some of these are borne proudly,
others are used as shorthand insults by opponents. It's all part of the
combined influence of social-media posturing and bureaucratic impo-
sitions on daily life. Some neologisms are merely factual—FIRE for
the sector of finance, insurance, and real estate—while others are
coined almost certainly with loose critical intent (WASP, say) or in
satirical back-formation (CLASS for "come late and start sleeping").

One hybrid acronym that may have escaped your attention until
now is attributed to people in STEM fields—itself an acronym for
science, technology, engineering, and medicine. The novel term is a
kind of short form for mashing up SJW and DEI, in fact. It is JEDI,
meaning justice, equity, diversity, and inclusion. JEDI used in this
sense is obviously a volatile property. I suspect the original users were

being puckish, pointing a little fun at people who are predominantly found in humanities and social sciences and preen about their political righteousness. But it's clearly a tag open to sincere commitment, since the Star Wars Jedi are powerful, disciplined, dedicated, and possessed of all those special powers. Plus, you know, lightsabers. But we also all know that there is a dark side—a Dark Side with scary capital letters. And so, it is probably no surprise that some people decided the JEDI acronym, even in its best version, was not a label to be cherished but a slur to be avoided. Forget Vader and Maul and the other darths; even Obi-Wan, Luke, and Yoda are on the cancel list now.

"[T]he Jedi are inappropriate symbols for justice work," these scholars argue. "They are a religious order of intergalactic police-monks, prone to (white) saviourism and toxically masculine approaches to conflict resolution (violent duels with phallic lightsabers, gaslighting by means of 'Jedi mind tricks,' etc.). The Jedi are also an exclusionary cult, membership to which is partly predicated on the possession of heightened psychic and physical abilities (or 'Force-sensitivity')."[1]

You might think, as some readers did, that this was in fact an *Onion*-style parody, with outlandish reference coming to bear on the sorry state of contemporary political discourse. But no, the sentiments in question were published without irony, in *Scientific American*, under the headline "Why the Term 'JEDI' Is Problematic for Describing Programs That Promote Justice, Equity, Diversity and Inclusion." (I sometimes imagine writing an essay called "Why the Term 'Problematic' Is Emblematic of Everything I Dislike," but that is probably a task best left for another time and place.)

For now, let's buck the imperial thought police and be the right kind of JEDI as we bring these reflections about authority, trust, and thought to a tentative conclusion. Part of that conclusion will be that all conclusions are tentative. They are not really conclusions but invitations to more questions. But don't worry: the only mind-control tricks in play here are those you perform on yourself. On second thought, maybe *do* worry about that. Maybe the most proximate danger is that we are forever in danger of gaslighting ourselves.

Initially I had planned this last entry in my series of reflections on questioning authority and thinking for yourself to dwell on recent advances in artificial intelligence (AI)—a subject of longstanding philosophical interest but receiving suddenly increased attention because of the rapid evolution of large-language models (LLMS) such as ChatGPT. These eerily competent generators of apparently meaningful speech and text—getting better all the time—managed to freak everyone out in the span of a few months during 2023. But these are not the droids we were looking for! We wanted labour-saving domestic servants, biddable personal assistants, reliable drivers, and maybe sex companions. And what we mostly got, at that stage, was what one critic called "stochastic parrots": massive brute-force programs that strip-mined online sources of what has been said and written then spewed out undergraduate-level term papers or boring but clear boardroom memos.[2]

This hardly seemed like either a dream or a nightmare, and the risky prospects of our posthuman future have mostly remained in the realm of dire speculation and general anxiety. The issues of AI have also become predictably mired in the polarized politics of our moment, such that allegedly *woke* programming was denounced by those who, on counter-charge, were accused of *based* bias in their algorithms—"based" being the short-lived alt-right matching label to "woke."[3] Algorithms are certainly clusters and creators of bias, but I suspect the main lines are not ideological so much as adolescent and faintly misogynistic, like most of the programming community itself. Meanwhile, dreams and visions of dark futures continue to swirl.[4]

What appears far more important is to speak as one human to some other humans. In this way we can reflect—not on what it means to be *human*, exactly (that's really a biological dispute), but what it means to be a *person*, an entity with desires, interests, and rights, plus the ability to reason about them. What is conscious life *for*? We human persons are not simply stochastic parrots; we don't generate text and speech by crunching a vast database for no reason except external prompting. What we do is something far more mysterious and noble: we use language to react to and shape our world.

The central question in this activity remains one of *meaning*. Meaningful exchange is precisely what is lacking in too much public discourse, which is indeed conducted at the level of stochastic parroting—if that. Any career politician interviewed on television sounds—at best—more or less like a beta-testing A I. As with the mountain of rote text generated by bureaucrats and C students the world over, we might be better off simply moving the entire enterprise off-shore, off-grid, or just off-planet. We don't need more talk; we need more sense.

No doubt it was ever thus, and our technobabble version of the human meaning deficit is likely just the latest turn of reason's bumpy wheel. But because A I forces upon us uncomfortable thoughts about the nature of consciousness, intelligence, and how mind meets world, we have what might be a unique philosophical opportunity to put ourselves into question. Kant may have set the agenda, but his notions of enlightenment and rational maturity badly need updating. Maybe surprisingly, we need to go back in order to move forward. We must revive ancient questions of language, meaning, and thought.

* * *

I'M NOT GOING TO PURSUE those questions via some kind of linguistic-metaphysical reverie here about how "language speaks us" or "the world is all that is the case." Instead, I want to reflect on the very idea of *reflection*. That is, I'm going to do what we thinking things do: I'm going to employ language in an attempt at illuminating thought, or anyway questioning it. In particular, I want to consider the question of how thought, when trammelled to desire, can become its own worst enemy.

By now it is common knowledge, if not always common usage, that *gaslighting* is a form of mental manipulation whereby a person is made to doubt their own claims, or even sanity, through persistent undermining by another. The foe may be, in abject circumstances, a loved one. The term derives from a play and later film adaptation, *Gaslight*, in which gaslight establishes both the external atmosphere of dusky Victorian London and the suave menace of a husband gradually convincing his wife that she is mad. This is fully insidious enough on its own; but the mechanisms of gaslighting can also be self-applied. The savvy gaslighter—evil, suave Charles Boyer driving Ingrid Bergman around the twist in the 1944 film—is the exception. Much more common is the situation in which we gaslight ourselves. That is, we hoodwink our own critical faculties and even trust in good reasoning in the service not of another person, but of an internal desire.

In sum, the big challenge to humanity's sustained future is not coming from the possible-future robot overlords, or even the creeping threats of AI-generated deception and manipulation. These employ novel methods and powerful new techniques, but their aim is the same as always: to undermine our sense of ourselves. And so, the real task before us is metaphysical, not technological or even political. How best to navigate the shoals of an evolving self-understanding, then? Here I believe we must challenge our standard notions of desire. To do so I am going to return to my keynote theme of addiction, especially doxaholic addiction to fierce conviction.

Mostly we accept, without much reflection, that desires are states of mind directed toward specific objects or goals. We exercise our thoughts and actions around these motivating mental forces—not *the* Force but close enough in practice—and hope thereby to satisfy the desire by achieving the goal or possessing the telling objection. And yet, everyone knows the feeling of getting exactly what one wanted and finding the satisfaction no release at all from desire. Either the sought-after goal is not quite what we thought it was, or it didn't accomplish the aspirational goals clustered around it, or the moment of pursued satisfaction found us merely wanting more and different things. Aristotle had a name for this complex of desire, where apparent satisfaction only arouses further and more extensive wanting. He called it *pleonexia*. We might update the terminology and call it, with appropriate caveats, *addiction*.

The important features here include the facts that desire as such will not be laid to rest by a given desire's satisfaction, that a tolerance-dose spiral is often induced, and that there is no real release from the restlessness of desire except in death. Plato conceived desire as a "mad master" in the *Republic*, or as a would-be runaway horse in the *Phaedrus*. These rogue elements within the disordered soul could not be entirely eliminated, but they could be controlled, by the exercise of the "reasoning part" of the psyche, represented as the sane, purposeful charioteer. This moral psychology is still too simple, though. It accounts for *akrasia*, or weakness of the will—an important level of sophistication over the crude Socratic view that vice is always a function of ignorance—but it does not take sufficient measure of desire's deceits and self-tanglings. It accepts the possibility of psychic conflict without admitting that such conflict is the basic state of things, not a disorder of the mind.

This might also be a good place to enter a caveat about ancient Greek ways of thinking. We should remember that these include commitment to slavery, bloodletting as a cure, and a warrior cult. Their authority is a function of our selective reference. As the French poet Paul Valéry said, "Ancient Greece is the most beautiful invention of the modern age." Still, even as a fantasy or a projection of desire, the Ancients may have something to teach us. Contemporary accounts of addiction so often seem to miss the mark because their assumptions about desire are not even as nuanced as Plato's or Aristotle's. Moralistic models of demonic possession and helpless slavery to drugs have largely been abandoned, true; but they have been replaced haphazardly by pseudo-demonological accounts of brain disorder, endorphin imbalance, and overwhelming cravings. These more human accounts eliminate some of the stigma associated with earlier models but still attempt to draw a bright line between confirmed addicts and everyone else—something an ancient psychologist would not have done. In too many cases, they apply new labels to old bottles and pronounce the contents to be changed. A name is not an explanation, much as our handy use of names seems to mimic the processes of understanding. Offering a black box as your "account" of a condition leaves all the hard work undone.[5]

Such delusions of understanding can also be seen in how we apprehend the actual facts of a matter. You will hear, for example, that 10 percent of drinkers account for the bulk of alcohol sales. This is true. But then you will also hear that this group (alcoholics) can be distinguished from the next decile (heavy drinkers) and the next (social drinkers). So it goes. These arbitrary divisions are mostly marshalled by those who want to reassure themselves that they are not—or not yet—alcoholics. I know this is so, because it is exactly what I did for years. There is no more obvious alcoholic behaviour than spending time reassuring yourself that you are not one, or in finding mitigating reasons why it would be okay if you were. Note to self: special pleading and grievance-based identity claims are sometimes internal habits of mind, not just external political discourse.

The problem with all "brain disease" models of addiction is that, in the name of eliminating stigma, they underplay the complicated, conflicted, world-immersed agency of the addict. They also open up the field of individual responsibility to moral or legal evasions. We may wish to retain some of these—a subset of "diminished responsibility" defences will be valid and support the needs of the afflicted—but they offer ripe fruit for grifters. A celebrated recent case had a documented far-right hatemonger arguing a diminished-responsibility defence on the basis of his addiction to vile racist and violent material, like a form of political pornography.[6] Such an addiction may be real in the broad sense of harmful dependent behaviour; it is no defence, and never can be, for the hateful actions that follow.

Though their desires are often kinked and twisted, directed to known harms, addicts are not moral zombies. They are not blindly moved by insatiable and unthinking cravings for human brains, or their pharmaceutical equivalent. She or he is, rather, someone whose initially pleasant habits grow actively harmful just to the extent that they seem overwhelming. Hence the spirals of self-shame, secrecy, embarrassment, defensiveness, and unreliability typical of addiction. But these latter are social by-products, not the condition itself: important warning signs, perhaps, but in fact fairly typical across all human behaviour. As is the tendency of habits to grow more entrenched through repetition, building tolerance, and mounting dosage.

Shifts in our sense of widespread addictive behaviour are useful here, though I don't expect the suggestion to be met with general favour or adopted without difficulty. We still want to make distinctions in our assessments of behaviour, just as we always do in holding ourselves and others responsible. But we should be more creative in our thinking and our discourse about what is, after all, a widespread human tendency to fixate on harmful stimuli. It's probably true that "alcoholic," for example, is not a terribly useful term and never was. But people hang on to it as a handy sorting label, just as they hang on to "addict." There but for the grace of God, or a higher power, or my stronger will, or what have you. I would not presume to deny that the brains of "addicts" are *disordered* in the sense that they create harms for their associated persons. The physical dependency of substance use disorder is only part of the puzzle, though; the redrawn pathways of desire and (theoretical, putative, ever-beckoning) satisfaction are another, and far more insidious.

Being an addict is not a matter of having a certain kind of brain; it's a matter of being a person in a certain kind of condition. The issue is importantly phenomenological, not empirical, from the first-person point of view. I may realize that my brain is, as it were, working against me and my overall well-being. But desire is a stern master, if not always a mad one. Satisfaction derived from harmful sources is still satisfaction. I suspect that this basic fact of brain-mind problematic is not so different in the hard-drug addict's case as in anyone else's. If nothing else, it aids in good judgment to have a sense of kinship with even the most dependent and abject user. And so that means that we have to approach the life-world of the addict to understand and perhaps aid their condition. Every story is different, but we find significant recurrence of issues concerning family history, anxiety, stress, or trauma, and the presence of drinking buddies, wingmen, and other enablers—who may be themselves fellow sufferers, sharing a harmful coping strategy.

The inverse also holds: sometimes empiricism should bracket experiential concerns. In certain situations of abject trust, we want to be taken entirely as bodies, as when I had two life-saving organ-transplant surgeries. The duality is captured by two German words for "body": *Leib* and *Körper*. The connotation of the first is experienced embodiment; of the second, mere physicality. English offers no such nuance, but one can think of a related subtlety of meaning in saying "flesh" rather than "body." The former is what can be weak, or mortified, or part of kinship. Flesh is theological, metaphysical, relational in a way the mere body need not be.

Addictive desire spills out of personal control, at least in unwilling addicts. When the habits and patterns of desire are directed toward unwanted or harmful results, we experience psychic conflict. So much is obvious. This is straightforward dysfunction and can be judged as such. But the idea that the addict is a certain kind of person, or a person with a certain kind of internal loose screw, needs to be challenged. I return to the provocation that began the first of these five polemical meditations. What if we are all addicted in some way? What if the difference between you and me is not about how desire works within each of us, but rather about which desires society approves and rewards? More pressingly, what if our society is, as I suggested earlier, *addictogenic* at base: that is, it doesn't simply reward certain addictions over others, it cultivates ones that are profitable, gaudy, and rewarding to some. Even if that means at the expense of some others—who are, meanwhile, encouraged to indulge bogus desires through gambling, stimulants, and other forms of bread and circuses.

We cannot fail to notice the tell-tale mixed messaging in this system-wide addictogenic effort. Alcohol will kill you, hence it is an essential element of fun, coolness, sophistication, and manly sports. Being overweight poses health risks even as it affirms your plus-size body positivity. Working long hours is harmful to self and relationships and thus is rewarding, purposeful, and lucrative. Shopping is banal, dull, exploitative, and expensive so do more of it right now. Some hard drugs and bad habits may still lie outside this perverse social-cultural logic, but they are the exceptions that prove the rule.

There is something lacking in almost all of our traditional accounts of desire as well as of addiction. Desire is more like energy than it is a specific drive to an object or outcome. We fixate on these objects or outcomes as external and shiny, and then retroactively posit them as the source of desire. This gets everything exactly backward, because desire is essentially fungible: it can fix on anything and make it the object of longing: something someone else has because they have it, something touted in a sexy way by a marketing campaign, something that offers dubious associations of possession with desirability, spending money with coolness, and so on. This is why "getting" the desired end is a matter of confusion and disappointment. The experience of striving for something so often fails to satisfy because it is the striving we find exciting. Further, desire has a quality like the distance to be covered in Zeno's famous paradox about the runners. We can never reach the goal of our wanting because first we must cover half the distance to it, then half of what remains, and half of what then remains, and so on, ad infinitum. Desire is tangled up in its own aims just like a self-conscious athlete would be in attempting to complete the race. For one thing, at least according to a prominent psychoanalytic school of thought, desire can only ever retroactively posit its own goal. We think we know what we are striving for, but in fact the object of desire is a kind of forever-obscure fiction, a notional point of fixation that we use to give shape to our roaming *cathexis* and need for attachment.

This is why literally anything can become an object of desire, and why one's own obsessions so often appear strange to anyone who does not share them—even as the consuming attachment of others frequently strike us as bizarre. And yet, such attachments are the handy and necessary materials of basic identity formation. And so: I for one am a teacher of philosophy, but also a husband, a stepfather, a brother, an uncle, a cat person, an enthusiastic but only semi-talented cook, a decent angler, a movie nerd, an art collector, a sneakerhead, a baseball fan, a former dungeon master and air force brat, a lover of formalist poetry, an indie-pop aficionado, an OG hermenaut, and—well, I'm only just getting started, aren't I? And your mileage not only may but will certainly vary.

We should be careful that these clusters of particular desire, especially the ones subject to potential obsession and addiction, do not overwhelm us or subsume our sense of central direction. The paradox of self that has preoccupied the larger questions of trust and authority—how do I go about being a stable person in this strange, unstable world?—mirrors the most basic paradoxes of movement and action. Zeno thought he was raising an odd-seeming logical problem that could be profitably solved by metaphysical theory, but in fact he was unwittingly highlighting a clue to our eternal condemnation to paradox. As Slavoj Žižek says, "The general conclusion to be drawn from all this is that there is a certain domain in which Zeno's paradoxes are fully valid, the domain of the subject's impossible relation to the object-cause of its desire, the domain of the drive that circulates endlessly around it." Zeno apparently desires to resolve the puzzles with a philosophy of motion, Žižek says, but this desire itself, let us call it philosophy, is in turn always, already and at once, self-perpetuating and self-defeating.[7]

Now, you might say: that is all very interesting, but we all know that the solution to the paradox of desire, at least as Zeno presents it, is just *finishing the race*. Don't worry about the halves and halves of halves; just run, dammit. You'll get there sooner or later! But that is not really Zeno's point, despite his own intentions, nor is it mine for the purposes before us. The deeper wisdom in play here is, rather, that it is impossible for most of us, most of the time, to think clearly about the very idea of "reaching a goal." Where, after all, is the "there" that we are meaning to get to? The impossibility of the paradox of desire does not resolve; instead, it revolves continually around a wobbly centre that we would like to call a stable self, or identity, or, when feeling fancy, rationality. I noted earlier that the May 1968 revolutionaries counselled us to demand the impossible; now the impossible makes its own demands upon us in the form of endless desire. For better and worse, the issues of living together as temporal selves in a shared world are not going to be so easy.

I have argued in these pages that the basic problem of authority and trust is rooted in our addiction to conviction, or doxaholism. This strikes me as a genuine addiction, in that the devotion to its pleasures—feelings of correctness, of getting the better of an interlocutor, of being master of a complex moral situation—are enjoyed at growing cost to both the individuals doing the enjoying and the groups of which they are a part. The costs are overridden by the perceived benefits, as with any intoxicating experience. Why else would we derive so much pleasure and yet inflict so much damage, on ourselves and others, as a result of our actions?

Such behaviour is in turn rewarded and made worse by the structures of toxic desire that dominate contemporary public discourse. Easy platform access means less the democratizing of public voices and more an unleashing of a horde of codependent tox-buddies, the proliferating wingmen of wackiness. The platforms themselves are no more than, in effect, cheap designer drugs. Retweets, likes, and followers all indicate, in attention-economy terms, that they are the loudest and the winningest. If you can monetize the outrage or the clicks, all the better. We live in an age when "social media influencer" is a genuine career aspiration of young people. Nothing I say, in a book about philosophy, is likely to change that. But for those still with me, let us just be sane for a moment: what goes on today in shared conversation is not well-regulated behaviour, any more than the problem drinking of an alcoholic or the shooting up of a heroin addict.

Controlling doxaholic behaviour requires discipline, habit, and reinforcement—just as recovery from substance use disorder does. That's because the addictive behaviour itself entails a form of discipline, habit, and reinforcement. As I stated in the introduction and part 1, I don't want to lean too heavily on a suggestion that this kind of addiction is identical with forms of substance abuse. I think the idea is more than a mere metaphor, however. One of the first steps in any project of recovery is admitting that you have a problem. Everyone knows this. You don't have to subscribe to the tenets of any twelve-step program to see the force of this claim. Nor do you need to be an expert self-rationalizer, though most of the addicts I have come to know are precisely that. Most of us are just run-of-the-mill rationalizers, but that's a mill that buzzsaws a lot of timber. The mind is endlessly inventive in its dance of erecting self-protection, plotting excuses, keeping secrets, and minimizing risks. Less widely acknowledged is the role that social context plays in our frequent bouts of desire-tangle. People say that they want to reduce stigma about addicts, or at least that we should try to do so, but the effort soon founders. Some people think stigma is quite appropriate—a way of holding the addict responsible for his or her own choices. Others absolve the addict of this guilt, but only at the price of depriving her or him of full agency.

What does not figure in the conversation very often is a sense of the world of the addict, which personal accounts tell us over and over is a space of vast loneliness, secrecy, and sometimes self-harm. But such feelings are—like loneliness and isolation of all kinds—a public stain, not a merely private affliction. This failure to implicate the cultural surroundings is the obvious consequence, but also a clear blind spot, of an overtly individualistic society. One of the things that becomes inescapable when you are recovering from alcoholic addiction, for example, is the pervasiveness of pushers of all kinds: not just actual dealers, but also television ads, billboards, friends who drink, jokes in every context. Alcohol has the distinction of being a socially accepted drug, more or less, sanctioned by history and not coincidentally state-controlled in many districts. Profit is staggering, and dedicated users are its engine.[8]

Such users are also, in a neat market-efficient twist, the drug's most dedicated pushers because they are both producers and consumers of the toxic addictogenic materials of their world. I mean that, by and large, it is we who get ourselves hooked. There is no need for street-corner transactions and shady company, no opportunity for violence and bloody turf wars—unless that is what the system offers. The parallels between alcoholism and doxaholism are thus quite telling, all facilitated by a defective public sphere. There are class distinctions in play, and issues of access, as well as aesthetic judgments about how to go about indulging the habit. But at base, classy booze is still just booze; and runaway ideological conviction is just that, no matter how fancy the phrasing or how high the volume.

19

Recovery

SO, WHAT COULD POSSIBLY COUNT as a recovery strategy here? If there is no complete solution to the problem of desire, including the desire to consider oneself right, are there defensible curbs, guardrails, or other mechanisms of trust? Since most of us would agree that solving the problem of desire is impossible, we must try thinking in terms of habituation and channelling—not forcibly controlling desire, a perpetual losing battle, but sluicing it into positive forms with good outcomes.

One of the most insidious desires that we all need to acknowledge and call out is also a basic piece of social relation. I mean the double-edged one that, first, reduces all exchanges to transactions (i.e., market dominance), and then sees all transactions as inherently political or self-interested (i.e., ideological spin). With this two-step in routine play, the claims of meticulous science are no more trustworthy or authoritative than something you read on a conspiracy blog. The blog may offer two super-added features to make it even more attractive: (1) it will align with what you already believe, and (2) it will arrive with a hard carapace of certainty and statistical "proof." Who can resist?

"The most basic finding is that people use addictions of all sorts, not just addictions to drugs, to adapt to the alienation or dislocation that is built into the modern age," argues Bruce Alexander, a Canadian psychologist whose controversial views on addiction are among the most illuminating I know. The controversy stems in large measure from his central idea that addiction is a social relation more than a relation between a diseased individual and his or her drug of choice. This focus has led critics to charge that the theory lets users and addicts off the hook, evading responsibility by blaming society. But this is not actually the view. Addiction is a sign written on individuals of a deeper structural dislocation. It is both an individual and a collective ill.

"Dislocation and alienation have increased over the centuries and are most prevalent in the countries that are most closely tied into the neoliberal capitalist agenda," Alexander writes. "Mass addiction has tracked the spread of mass alienation and dislocation."[9] This widespread dislocation facilitates a familiar form of coping. "[T]he history of the last few centuries shows that fanatical addiction to seemingly infallible political cult leaders regularly provides meaning and purpose to masses of human beings who are severely dislocated due to the fragmentation of their societies," Alexander notes. "I believe that it will be necessary to understand addiction to political cults on a more psychological and less moralistic level, if it is ever to be brought under control." Such cults are not hard to discern in the current political landscape, from obvious contenders like MAGA and QAnon to what harsh critics view as cult-like clusters around specific causes like gender-inclusive bathrooms or expansion of the women's category in sports.

I don't want to take particular positions on all such questions here—that would defeat my purpose. The stress on diagnosis and therapy, rather than moralism, is essential if there is to be a productive dialogue about runaway political conviction—though admittedly moralism is hard to avoid when one is assessing the state of play in public discourse. (I do not except myself from this judgment.) But here we can see Plato's moral psychology once more coming usefully to the fore. He argues in the *Republic* that the psychic conflicts of the individual exactly mirror those of the state. This so-called analogy argument is much disputed and probably implausible in detail. But we can still appreciate that a disordered political realm can both reflect and distort the psychological health of its citizens. A tyrant rules by individual whim, and so becomes a kind of enabler-in-chief whose lies, deceptions, and self-indulgences work to sanction the bad behaviour of others. He reflects their democratic outrage, and then turns it back on them in the form of anything-goes power.

This view that democracy is a state of soul as well as a form of government has many benefits. One is that of avoiding bright-line distinctions between addiction and "normal" states of being. Everyone is familiar with the structures of deep satisfaction that attend dedication, devotion, and attachment—to anything at all, really: a person, a hobby, a political cause, a sports franchise, an exercise regime, an artistic pursuit, or a spiritual practice. We could go further: we feel incomplete without some version of this transcendental attachment, this inner need to warp our selfhood around an external goal.

This need is basic and often without harm. But when it comes to extreme political belief, matters are more complicated. Ideological conviction carries its own pleasure, as well as its own proof. Feeling oneself correct is a self-validating experience. It is impossible to get enough of it. And the experience encourages a personal program, often gradual but sometimes quite sudden in the form of conversion or radicalization. The identity thus formed, or narrated, generally feels stronger and more robust than the confusions and anxieties of finding oneself through less dramatic means. In this way, democracy's insistence on the importance of *my* desires, *my* liberty, and *my* beliefs, is precisely what makes it prone to internal pathology. Despite our usual ways of talking, tyranny and autocracy are not antithetical to democracy; they are proximate internal perversions of its celebration of individual happiness and freedom.[10]

We can see the strains of doxaholism in cults, naturally, but also in other, milder forms of indoctrination and ideological capture. Partisan political ideology has a recurring feature of regularity and definitiveness. A foolish consistency—disdained by Emerson as a bugbear of the weak-minded—is highly prized in the recitation of catechismal truths. But the doxaholic, like the alcoholic, is inventive in the arts of self-justification, rationalization, and selective exceptionalism. So, inconsistencies and even apparent hypocrisies will be tolerated. Casuistry is a useful skill; so is the deft ability to cherry-pick evidence. Confirmation bias, once considered an enemy of clear thought, is elevated to standard operating procedure. In the extreme cases of conspiracism and total indoctrination, as we have already seen, there is no external claim that is not taken as evidence of the central conviction's total validity. Counterarguments are always dismissable because they can be tarred as cynical, delusional, wilfully ignorant, envious, or simply hateful.

This funhouse-mirror understanding of the world is only the beginning of the story, however. As a critical view, it can't avoid reflecting its own distortions. Those who consider themselves sane will always feel a temptation to dismiss their opponents as insane or stupid. The point I have been at pains to emphasize throughout the preceding pages is that, in fact, the problem is not a distorted mirror. The mirror is fine, or at least in most cases offers an accurate picture of the world. The problem lies with us, each one of us, who refuses to look full in the mirror and confront our situation with the humility and compassion— as well as the skepticism and mature reason—it demands.

There will still be those who want to insist that addiction to opioids, say, is on a completely different order from being beholden to the stimulus of a social media or video game, still more from anything to do with political argument or conviction. But that seems to misunderstand, and so underestimate, the extent of the problems arising from a toxic public sphere. I want to say that the kinship lies not in the similarity of the stimulus or even the severity of the attachment, but in the structure of facilitation. Most addictions begin with low or even zero opportunity costs, sometimes even with positive reinforcements to indulge. (*The first hit is free* is the same kind of offer as *no-fee trial for thirty days*. So is *have your say* at the top of an online comments section.) We everyday punters have entered a casino before we know it, out of boredom or anxiety or a need to cope, only to find the odds stacked heavily in favour of the house.

This does not absolve individual users of personal responsibility, of course. "I blame society!" is a handy cop out which we have reason to distrust, as mentioned earlier. Nor do I mean to suggest for a moment that addiction to opioids is no different than addiction to playing video games, posting on Instagram, or scrolling TikTok. We can and must continue to highlight relevant distinctions, even as we adopt a general account of addiction that includes both. Collapsing those distinctions minimizes the dangers, but drawing exclusive, judgmental lines only makes treatment harder. Dedicated addicts know, maybe better than non-users, that choice and freedom are extremely complicated. Analysis of the addiction scene exposes many aspects of a dynamic situation that are features, not bugs. Here, compulsive design meets addictive personality—which might be any of us. Getting and keeping us hooked is the whole point of the scheme, as its functionaries and profiteers well know. Designer meets pusher.

And staying hooked is what we do; we humans are good at addiction, just as we can be good at productive forms of habit. Few if any entrenched and routinely reinforced habits can be overcome cold turkey, or without serious guidance and support. Addictions tend to be all-consuming: that is how they are designed to work. To foil their power, which derives from the individual's cognitive self-colonization, there must be care, and some sense of opening a distance between oneself and the addiction. Blame quickly becomes beside the point, in other words. Judgment on the state of the addict's will either encourages stigma or deflects responsibility, or both. We need a more productive, less stigmatizing approach.

So, let us open our minds again to the idea that aggressive political conviction is a kind of drug. The natural tendency to find satisfaction in devotion to strong opinions is especially harmful in large, complex societies. Here, citizens daily depend upon abstract and mostly faceless systems to execute basic features of life. This system of abstract systems includes facets of life where trust and authority are essential: science and medicine, but also politics and media. Such abstract systems are necessary to function at scale, but they work best if they still offer individual users access points of a personal kind: a family doctor, say, or a long-trusted news source. Positive encounters at the access points reinforce trust in the system, but negative ones naturally do the opposite—even if the system itself, which is by definition greater than any single person, is actually functioning well.

In this way, a greedy banker, lying politician, or careless surgeon all undermine their respective practices along with their own personal credibility. It can also work in a form of atavistic anger, such as that directed toward Dr Anthony Fauci during the pandemic lockdown of the early 2020s. For anticlosure and antivax fanatics, this apparently mild-mannered medical doctor was a hostile agent, demonized to the point of devilish caricature, a power-mad crazy scientist with a not-so-secret plan for global domination. The truth was less spectacular; but inflated spectacle has unfortunately become a part of the general abstract-system dynamic—for many people, a feature and not a bug. The result is a peculiar admixture of highly advanced technocapitalist algorithms and institutions, on the one hand, and extremely primitive atavistic thinking, on the other. Fauci became a totem more than a person, a mannequin in an avoidance ritual whereby destruction of the hapless stand-in serves to dispel all the swirling evil spirits of public health measures and other threats to "freedom."

It seems that, in the particular case of doxaholism, recovery must include a substantial measure of therapy and some keen self-examination. Is there a "safer supply" here, as when physicians try—not without controversy about potential diversion to illicit side markets—to help end-stage fentanyl or heroin addicts with methadone, naloxone, and hydromorphone? As I will suggest in a moment, I think there may be. There is certainly a "softer" version of the conviction high to wean us away from harmful spirals. And there are, as always, displacement activities and new habit formations, as well as some versions of talk therapy. We'll need all these tools and more as we take a cold, hard look at ourselves in the metaphysical mirror.

In part 2 I talked about trust in currency as a function of the god behaviour of at least one person. Obviously, the currency case is a highly abstract picture of a highly abstract aspect of social life. But when it comes to trust in institutions such as the police, the medical system, organized religion, courts, banks, public schools, Big Tech, organized labour, the media, the criminal justice system, big business, or politics, the downward trends are just as well documented. In the United States—admittedly not an indicative case, for reasons of history, size, and political culture—reported trust in such institutions has fallen below 50 percent for the first time on record. These findings match similar plummets in trust levels since 2008 across a range of highly developed democratic nations. Only small business and the military drew judgments of positive trust in half or more of the polled respondents, and even those trust "wins" would not be replicated in other places where entrepreneurship and militarism are more suspect such as Scandinavia or Canada.[11]

Like many other analysts of the situation, I have tried to suggest the reasons for trust's erosion in recent decades. One can isolate specific events—the 2008 financial crisis, the Trump presidency and its aftermath, including the attempted insurrection at the Capitol—but further study suggests that the roots go back to the political confusions of the 1980s, themselves rooted in the upheavals of two decades previous. The post–Second World War consensus, including its unusual flowering of prosperity and patriotism, is simply no longer tenable. History suggests that this period of stability and opportunity was an anomaly, and yet enduring nostalgia paints it as a lost ideal to which we seek blessed return. Make America great again! The picture goes prismatic when we add the nostalgia for 1960s radicalism that yet infuses political life. And here, the ideological inversions of the anti-authoritarian attitude are evident: as discussed, the critics become the rulers, at least in certain institutional corners, and we all chafe under the rule of cultural commissars.

Trust has a hard time maintaining itself under such fractured circumstances. Interests no longer seem shared, or even concentrated on agreement about ways to go on. All rules feel like potential points of dispute rather than useful conventions for shared achievement. The limits of the human, once minimized by shared risk and collective responsibility, are instead magnified. To stretch my metaphor, the prism of diversity now becomes the magnifying lens burning a hole in the social fabric. All of this is debatable, I realize, especially in one's own corner of the trust world. (As suggested in part 2, I happen to think universities remain far more liberal and self-critical than outside critics tend to think.) What we can assert with some confidence, sad as it might be, is that this breakdown of trust opens an opportunity for authoritarianism. The tyrant thrives in a field of mistrustful, splintered individuals. Their collective pain and anger are his individual bread and butter, because the selling point of finding and eliminating the internal enemy is evergreen. As Plato sketches it, the tyrant is a kind of super-addict who gains control of a republic of addicts.

The correct alternative response here cannot be more insistence on some tribal forms of trust, since that would cement local relations only at the cost of further systemic disintegration. Instead, we need a model of trust that emerges from conflict rather than stands opposed to it—I mean a notion of trust that will answer to our genuine doubts about authority and so assuage our more destructive tendencies. This is the mediated trust of pluralistic possibility, not the pre-existing bond of blood or belief. It depends upon a sense of commitment from good actors, and a sharp sense of refusal for bad ones. It has absolute conviction about one thing only, namely that no absolute conviction should control any aspect of shared social life.

What does this kind of trust look like in practice? Well, it is fragile, for one thing—that was signalled early by the chosen metaphors for it (melting chocolate, breaking glass, etc.). Comprehensive impartial trust requires positive assumptions about the competence, motivation, and behaviour of others. The trust relation is understood to flow in both directions—each actor in a trust situation has both reasons to expect others to act in a trustworthy manner and reasons to act in a trustworthy way. But the trust attitude also assumes that others are unpredictable and imperfect. And so, guardrails and regulations take the place of individual personal assessment and any presumptions of virtue. As Rousseau put it, a political order can be shaped by "taking men as they are and the laws as they might be."

Trust of this impersonal kind is context specific and directed toward a particular set of shared ends. When these mechanisms of trust function properly, actors can expect others' reasons *and their own* to be action-guiding in a positive reinforcement cycle—a virtuous circle of exchange, ideally executed without rancour and civil when disagreement arises. If players think they are engaged in different games, then trust is moot, despite all appearances. Violations go unpunished, and faith in the game begins to erode. A visibly ashamed Richard Nixon works to reinforce the normative system, even as he insists that he is "not a crook." But a shameless Donald Trump, Samuel Alito, or Clarence Thomas—not to mention that gaggle of morally spineless acolytes who mimic them and hope to gain favour thereby even at the cost of their souls—act like the first piece of litter dropped in a tidy park. They give permission for others to indulge their own weakness. In fact, it is even worse than that, as we know from social psychological study: this is an instance of broken-windows theory.[12] The sight of other people flouting the rules and getting away with it makes anyone who holds to the rules feel like a chump, a mook, a dupe—a *loser*, in Trump's own favourite label. This stance of worldly moxie is hard to resist, even though it is the ultimate zero-sum game. For Trump, there can only be one winner—himself.

The twisted genius of the attitude is its impregnability, even in the face of, say, thirty-four felony convictions. A self-justifying person can declare themselves a winner no matter the weight of contrary fact. The many imitators think they can execute the same program of comprehensive correctness, where they always win, and apparent losses are owing to "rigged" games. But the biggest game is already rigged in favour of Number One. It's a bit like seeing Nietzsche's calls for robust resistance to "the herd" being taken up in lockstep by scores of angry conformist undergraduates. This is a political philosophy, if it even deserves the name, that is for *everyone and no one.*

Normatively healthy games can be agonistic about final ends, even about individual motivations. This does not threaten structural trust. It does not really matter why you are playing, as long as you play by the rules. *How* trumps *why* here, in other words—inner states count less than simply following the rules. Naturally, it would be ideal to follow the rules for the right reasons. Even this kind of basic functional trust game is difficult, however, when we experience so-called context collapse. That is, if we cannot keep our games conceptually separate, then the rules of each game begin to fray and deteriorate, and players lose confidence that the game is well-formed—that is precisely a crisis of trust, and an erosion of authority. Context collapse happens owing to the tendency of institutions and areas of interest to slide into one another, or at least appear to do so, such that the charge that all media coverage is party-political propaganda, for example, has weight with people. No amount of apparent balancing will convince some people that the *New York Times*, say, is not biased in favour of some agenda, on the right or on the left, depending on where one stands.

This insistent skepticism, in contrast to the compassionate kind I am advocating, provides a peculiar kind of world-weary satisfaction. It feels good to tout our own refusal to be duped! But the vacuum of trust leaves its own special deficit. We view ourselves as prisoners in a nasty shadow-play theatre, but one that we have ourselves constructed. This is no longer Plato's cave, with its vision of external manipulation of reality. That is, after all, a tale of eventual liberation from thought control and a redemption of the real. We are more sophisticated: we no longer credit the reality of the real. And so, unlike Plato's prisoners, we are in a situation where we pull the wool over our own eyes. This feature of self-manipulation is all too familiar in our current society of the spectacle. As the Situationist intellectual Guy Debord noted, "the spectacle is not a collection of images, but a social relation among people, mediated by images."[13] Such mediation cannot be trusted because it is not moderated. Spectacle exerts its influence by waves of capital-inflected power and feverish social trending. The fevers prove oddly attractive and self-perpetuating. The stimulus that produces them is revealed as highly addictive and ultimately tranquilizing.

Collapse of context is only part of the problem. It's true that decon-textualized images, like free-floating signifiers, have the capacity to mean anything, and so are in principle dangerous. Seeing a picture of a mutilated body is horrific, and in one basic human sense we recoil from wanting to know anything more about it. And yet, the power of such an image is a volatile property if we do not have the courage (and the relevant information) to make sense of its provenance. The *intolerable image* is a complicated, and implicating, property in political life. It is inevitable that such images will be put into circulation. It is not at all obvious what we are supposed to make of them, what their moral power ultimately communicates.[14]

Debord offered this analysis of the visual spectacle, what we would today perhaps call the mediascape, in 1967. It answered to and helped advance the notion that media culture was growing in unchecked power. His critique is part of the essential pushback on the soft power of technocapital. But a similar account, with much darker implications, could easily have been advanced during the gruesome image-competition days of the Hamas–Israel conflict of 2023–24, where all parties cried out for moral superiority based on images of terror and human barbarity. The conflict became, among other things, a perverted empathy sweepstakes, each side trying to arouse more horror and more compassion at once. It was as if the images themselves were waging the battle, mutilated babies set alongside exploded hospitals, gunshot-riddled ravers counted against starving or fleeing grandmothers and children.

At the same time, it becomes almost impossible to hold, in public anyway, a nuanced or balanced view that resists polarization without being consumed or dismissed by it. The pressure to "take a stand" and display "moral clarity" offers its own addictive pleasures, a second-level talking point that cascades the endorphins of conviction. But the situation is one of *right versus right*, as Amos Oz once said of the apparently endless conflict between Israel and Palestine. Right versus right is the kind of conflict one might encounter in Kant, say, when the universal injunction against lying is set against the desire to protect hidden family members. Confronted by the Nazi interrogator, naturally I will opt for lying: it seems perverse to cling to truth telling in this instance, even though in general I hold to its validity. We can recognize a legitimate right even as we see that its exercise creates disastrous consequences.

It is pointless to insist on pure right when the cause on both sides has justice. In fact, that insistence on purity is beyond futile, it is actively destructive: right versus right becomes wrong versus wrong. What literature and philosophy enjoin is not that certainty of cause but, instead, "a circle of sorrow—protest—consolation." In this circle we hope that our shared humanity is not lost, and that our ability to act is not crippled by feeling. Sometimes we must choose a side. Often, though, the situation is one where we can both understand why someone is acting the way they are and yet not want to endorse their actions. I can understand why a rape might result in a murder in response; but I ought not to condone the second in the name of the first.[15]

Given such complexity, the constant demand for explicit conviction is dangerous, not righteous. Choice is sometimes tragic, not certain. Intricate scholarly discussions weigh the idea of "humanitarian pause" as distinct from "ceasefire," while other pundits debate whether "from the river to the sea" was genocidal or merely aspirational. And so it goes. The acts and images of violence flow on regardless, harrowing our taxed imaginations and tortured souls. We call it doomscrolling for a reason: this is the instavision graphic novel of Hell on Earth. Images of war have been a controversial property as long as the technology of their distribution has been available; but this protracted tit-for-tat escalation of brutalizing imagery was something that most of us had not seen before. Even worse, we have reason to know that much of the imagery is deceptive, faked, manufactured, or spun. Not all the death-watch influencers are human, either. There are invisible uploaders and algorithms alike controlling what we see and experience, hollowing out the sense of individual choice even in the matter of basic consciousness.[16]

The traditional gatekeeper role of media is subject to greater and greater degrees of disintermediation, as I argued in part 3. Local news sources are shuttering at an alarming rate, creating "news deserts" in which citizens receive no local news and so turn to heavily polished, and often openly biased, national news sources like Fox News and MSNBC.[17] Public broadcasters like the BBC, CBC, and PBS attempt to maintain a counterbalancing effect, but often fall prey to their own (often leftist) ideological tendencies. At the same time, just in order to keep up, mainstream media adopts the shock tactics of runaway social-media platforms, jolting first and checking later, if at all. Everything is Breaking News, breathlessly delivered, with the rhetorical volume always turned to eleven.

The trouble with outrage is that there is always too much of it to go around, and there is no coming back from it. High emotion about small differences is narcissistic, as Freud observed. It also distracts us from more important, perhaps existential challenges, clouding our vision when we most need clarity. Outrage enacts its own race to the bottom. The initial justification, or claimed benefit, of disintermediation was that it served a democratic purpose. Remove the official filters, the argument went, and good things would follow: no more elite gatekeeping, reinforcing the privilege of the wealthy and powerful. No more pooling of influence over what counts as reality in the hands of those who want to keep the current arrangement just as it is. What we have witnessed instead is the cacophony of proliferating force multipliers, all enabled by larger forces of disintermediation plus progressive regulatory dismantling and capture. When everybody has a megaphone, nobody hears anything.

Against this kind of structural background, full of distortion and reaction, a figure like Donald Trump succeeds because even critical media coverage counts as exposure, and his multiplying falsehoods cannot be fact-checked in what is blithely called "real time." (Note to self: screen time is not real time.) Increasingly there is less and less distance between the news being covered and the coverage being news: a whole swath of contemporary print journalism is now concerned with reporting what is happening on social media, as if media-on-media coverage constituted critical analysis of public discourse rather than merely its own self-referential metastasis. This kind of coverage of other coverage, the plodding commentary on an opinion about a social media exhange driven by a meme in turn riffing on an ever more distant event, is the newsroom equivalent of celebrity culture, where someone can be famous not for any achievement or distinction, but rather simply for being famous. In an attention economy, the worm eats its own tail in the form of what field-theory scholars call "tautological celebrity."[18] All the while, our preference-nudging systems collect viewer-response data and feed it back to us for someone else's benefit.[19]

This constant onslaught is more than a bump in the road of media history, or even political history more generally. Institutional distrust and crumbling authority are also, as we have seen, existential challenges to the idea of selfhood. Trapped within a chaotic meaning field whether they like it or not, contemporary individuals cling ever more desperately to a fiction of solid personal identity even as the social forces around us erode that stability by a thousand tiny cuts a day. This is what postmodern life looks like, a life where identity and morality must be forged out of fragmented snapshots and nasty video clips, without context or narrative. We should not presume that the problem is entirely new, however, despite novel velocities of image immersion. Modern consciousness is the desperate attempt to shore up fragments of selfhood against the wrack of contingency. And even Hume had a so-called "bundle theory" of the self, long before Yeats, Woolf, Joyce, or Eliot. The Scottish thinker described the self or person (which he assumed to be the mind) as "nothing but a bundle or collection of different perceptions, which succeed each other with an inconceivable rapidity, and are in a perpetual flux and movement."[20]

And that was in 1739! These days, we must find ourselves confronted by evidence that our "user illusion" is just a function of brainwave hiccups that support a first-person fiction, like a graphic user interface on a laptop or the roving viewpoint of a first-person-shooter video game.[21] The good news, now as then, is that we do not struggle alone. A critical theory of trust is a necessary theoretical guardrail on the players.[22] We do not rely on them to call their own fouls, as in pickup basketball. This mediation or institutional framing of trust under conditions of conflict makes justice possible. When trust is broken, when coplayers are treated instrumentally, or manipulated by autocratic forces, justice cannot develop.

* * *

WHAT DO WE EVEN MEAN by justice? That's a good question, but as political philosophers have centuries of reason to know, it is extremely difficult to answer in terms that the workaday world of politics finds satisfactory.

The pursuit of justice remains an infinite imperative, the daily life-blood of social relations. Rawls is surely correct that a baseline structure of fairness is a necessary condition of any just society. Beyond that, the debates will begin, perhaps never to end. I think this is how it is, and how it must be. I am aware that this not the kind of answer that is desired of late, even though I believe it is the right one. Acknowledging our desire for specifics, then, let me attempt to pick out some essential features. For justice to have authority, it must be trusted; and for it to be trusted, it must be based in the giving and receiving of reasons. Distribution of goods or power, even procedural guidelines, are meaningless unless they are based—and seen to be based—upon defensible public arguments. Only such an orientation of reason giving will allow conflict, potential and actual, to sustain the conditions of a possible just order.

The best orientation is one of the posthuman welfarist state, posted at the beginning of these meditations. What this means should be clearer now, including its quasirealist position on the ends of justice as such. It is not some science-fiction vision of cyborg upgrades and super-mechanization of everything. Instead, we can imagine a society that is forever calling itself to account, constantly reaching beyond what is to what might be. We are hard-wired to seek improvements in our condition; that is our indisputable evolutionary advantage. Though we may often prove mistaken in how we go about it, the primary motivation cannot be doubted. As Kant indicated, reason has a transcendental quality, constantly trying to understand the conditions of its own possibility. That's the *posthuman* part: the droids we're looking for are the same ones we've always been looking for, they are the ones that are already here, and have been as long as we have been wielding tools to shape our environment—and having those tools shape us in turn, creating fields of meaning. The conception of justice is *welfarist*, meanwhile, in that its basic orientation, and so its rational bias, is to the amelioration of suffering in all forms susceptible to our always limited means. The shared vulnerability of moral agents is the only universal we need to ground a potentially just state. Depending on no set of special circumstances or qualifying experience, it takes seriously that every person is valuable and, politically speaking, counts for one. It is therefore a more reliable basis than any particularist account of identity, avoiding the traps of exclusion and inequity that lurk in the logic of grievance politics.[23]

Recall that one of the key objections to the Enlightenment project was that its universalism acted as a veil for actual power, a specific arrangement that consistently favoured white, male, propertied individuals with a certain social position and education. This is unacceptable, and such avoidance-ritual universalism must be challenged at every turn. What such challenges expose, however, should not be rival particularisms, the special pleading of grievance politics, rigid identity signifiers, or incommunicable trauma. These features of life are all too present; but they are by definition inaccessible to external reasons. Their claims are epistemic black boxes, because the authority behind them is purely personal. They cannot reliably ground our shared projects.[24]

That is a real-world problem, not an abstract philosophical exercise. Rebuilding trust requires constant vigilance and precisely the compassionate skepticism that lies behind all of our more developed epistemic commitments. That is, we must approach all claims with a combination of wariness and generous willingness to believe. This is a version of the epistemic principle of charity that allows us to consider the merits of positions we find prima facie disagreeable or wrong-headed. It is a cognitive balancing act, but the only one equal to the challenges and lurking temptations of public discourse to slip sideways. Far worse than potentially bogus first-person authority (FPA) claims and overaggressive incredulity, for example, is the general tendency to take argumentative refuge in affront. *How dare you question my integrity?!* Grievance remains the cheapest drug on the market, with plenty of opportunistic pushers on the make, including in the form of one's own amour-propre. The temptation at work here embraces not just routine advantage-seekers and grifters, but also those vehement second-order grievance-addicts who dominate comments sections and social media, complaining endlessly about SJW this and DEI that.[25]

The genuine force of grievance and identity should not be to *replace* universalism, but to force universal ambition to come to terms with itself, to call itself to account *by its own reasoning.* A person or group claiming special mistreatment, or criticizing special good treatment, must be heard against a background of agreement about the moral worth of everyone. That background agreement is the basis for the very idea of justice, and even if it is routinely flouted or debased, we must continue to appeal to it. If we don't, the public conversation descends quickly into a chaos of claim and counterclaim.

There are many jarring performative contradictions in play when special claims are turned, without critical pause, into justice claims. Consider, for example, the diversity advocate who mandates exclusion, say, or the intolerant guardian of tolerance. Such characters may be more fictive than real, of course—the tendencies are real enough, but pure exemplars are mercifully rare. The real trap of identity politics resides in its intellectual tendency to make political disintegration worse rather than better. Particularist righteousness is comforting, but it can tend, in its pursuit of a more-level playing field, toward the undemocratic. If reformist impulses rank some citizen claimants above others, this only closes off avenues of further disputation and counterclaim. This distortion can happen even as special pleading mimics the structures of democratic politics. This is the tangle we must take such care to avoid. Such self-regarding tactics, even when they arise from genuine injustice, can also easily be turned to bad personal ambitions in the form of what we might call *professional grievance*, the sustaining career built on decrying the very structures that reward one for doing so. I hate to say it, but academia is lately all too welcoming to hand-biting that is less critical thinking and more personal aggrandizement.

Sometimes lived experience is a necessary condition of knowledge, though. I cannot know what it is like to serve in combat, for example, and that will colour, if not always dominate, my knowledge and thinking about war. FPA is sometimes the only kind that can counter *both* "testimonial injustice" (i.e., the refusal to believe someone because of their unknowable particular experience) *and* what has been called "epistemic exploitation" (i.e., the demand that FPA claimers explain their claims, over and over, to those who do not accept them prima facie). Balancing a presumption of truth with skepticism about possible false claims, all in the absence of any possible shared evidence, is liable to go astray easily.[26]

Therefore, we should grant a form of prima facie but pro tempore recognition and standing to claims of suffering. We can remain then critical of what is said to follow from those claims, in the spirit of compassionate skepticism. Though it must always move us, suffering alone is not a legitimate pull on the regime of justice. Granting instant political heft to suffering has a satisfying tang because it answers our capacity for compassion, but we do nobody a service if we are uncritical about what counts as injustice rather than misfortune. Some suffering is unavoidable, some is beyond human control. Some is even undertaken willingly in the service of some larger goal. This is all part of the fabric of shared human life. Some things may change, and we can even fervently hope that they do. Surely, as a beginning, we could agree that there are better ways to organize our very human wish for life beyond death than in competing violent religions bent on the destruction of unbelievers.

Very little can be said in this region that does not offend someone. More troubling, and harder to deal with in practice, is the fact that even when the suffering is genuine, the formation of identity around it can be itself toxic. When suffering is imagined, exaggerated, or manufactured, it reduces its claim to just another form of egotism. Trauma is not a competition, some sad damage sweepstakes where we compete to be the most challenged and hence most deserving of consideration. Nor are so-called emotional truths a valid substitute for, well, actual truths, any more than citing alternative facts is anything more than an expedient political ploy. The in-principle standing we should grant to suffering does not lead, without question, to a lien on the collective resource pool. It might, but it also need not.[27]

It is all too possible for artists and thinkers then to find themselves ensnared in their own identities, such that the expectations of external audiences reduce their creativity to a kind of shadow play of self-expression. This is antithetical to the "circle of sorrow" that Amos Oz, in his old-fashioned way, wished to defend. Consider the 2001 novel *Erasure*, by the Black American writer Percival Everett, recently adapted into the film *American Fiction*. In the story, a talented but commercially unsuccessful Black writer decides to play a prank on the world that finds him "not Black enough." He produces a string of clichés and stereotypes about race in America called "My Pafology." This satirical effort is, predictably, a huge success, to the great dismay of its author. The trap sprung here, whereby savage satire is celebrated as sincere testimony, brings to mind David Foster Wallace's pithy definition of popular culture. Mindful of our insatiable appetite

314   QUESTION AUTHORITY

for the unknown known, he defines it as "the symbolic representation of what we already believe."

The issue is political as well as aesthetic. When it comes to personal identity, pre-existing categories are, for good and ill, precisely that: pre-existing and categorical. We might do better to follow the genuine "democratic spirit" advocated by Wallace in another context. This spirit enjoins, he said, "passionate conviction plus sedulous respect for the convictions of others." It happens that Wallace made this poignant argument not in the context of electoral politics, or urban-rural divides, or mental illness, or any of the other social issues about which he was so insightful. It was rather in a long discussion about grammar, specifically the issue of "proper" English usage.[28]

"Did you know that probing the seamy underbelly of U S lexicography reveals ideological strife and controversy and nastiness and fervor on a nearly hanging-chad scale?" he begins. "For instance, did you know that some modern dictionaries are notoriously liberal and others notoriously conservative, and that certain conservative dictionaries were actually conceived and designed as corrective responses to the 'corruption' and 'permissiveness' of certain liberal dictionaries?" Well yes, we did know that, all too well—and we know it better all the time. Some of us may have forgotten what a "hanging chad" is, in the miasma of more recent election challenges, but we know all about pronouns and labels as a site of ideological strife. Boy, do we ever.

Nor is Wallace's concern limited to minutiae of usage. Or rather, he reminds us that such minutiae are always politically relevant. His essay, which begins with these questions of grammatical nicety, soon pivots to a searching consideration of Black English. His conclusion is relevant: language is about communicating thought, and that means striving to match message with audience. "We tend to like and trust experts whose expertise is born of a real love for their specialty instead of just a desire to be expert at something," he says, noting the basic features of genuine authority, on grammar or anything else. They are:

"passionate devotion, reason, and accountability," also "experience," "exhaustive and tech-savvy research . . . , an even and judicious temperament . . . , [and] humble integrity." The resulting expert authority is likeable as well as credible. And that makes for trust. "[T]he purposes of the expert authority and the purposes of the lay reader are identical, and identically rhetorical," Wallace concludes, "which I submit is about as Democratic these days as you're going to get." (Note for usage hawks: the upper-case *D* there is intentional, offered not as a party endorsement but as Wallace's own chosen emphasis.)

20

Under the Sun

MILAN KUNDERA PUT THE CENTRAL matter this way: "The struggle of man against power is the struggle of memory against forgetting." We have seen how individual identity hinges on memory in the basic metaphysical sense—the mysterious way we are able, sleeping and waking each day, to preserve a stitched-up narrative of self. Thus, tales of identity breaking down, whether from Franz Kafka or Christopher Nolan, unsettle us even as they, just barely, reassure us that we are still here, ourselves, however contingently. But memory is political as well as personal. So is identity. The concept of universal human rights, for example, necessarily points toward a standard of belonging and respect that lies beyond national boundaries. At the same time, we all know how contingent and fragile life becomes when the protections of the state are not available. The most haunting image of our time may be that of overcrowded refugee boats wallowing off Europe's Mediterranean coast, the stateless literally at sea; or, even worse, the corpse of a drowned child washed up on the same indifferent shore, a casualty of history.

These are difficult thoughts, and we do not much care for difficulty. In his *Concluding Unscientific Postscript* (1846), Kierkegaard remarks

that his friends everywhere seemed dedicated to making things easier, usually for themselves. Lighting a meditative cigar, the master of
irony decides that he will make it his mission to make things more
difficult. Good for him; but most of us find that difficulty is difficult.
That includes, crucially, the difficult doubts we must constantly bring
to the political scene. It is easy to see why doubt hardens into conviction: when you start questioning everything, there is no genuine
authority left but yourself. And for most of us, the easiest option then
is to hunker down into a party of one, convinced that we alone possess
the truth. Justified skepticism thus veers into cynicism or even, paradoxically, conspiracy theory. This hardening of epistemic certainty
is itself identity-bolstering, offering a superaddition of self-validation
to the already intoxicating pleasures of righteousness. If others share
the same signs—if they can hear the same dog whistles—then we
may form a pack together. Conspiracies are composed of groups of
the violently like-minded. Only other true believers can be regarded
as friends, because only their beliefs align perfectly with mine.

The doxaholic is right, and furthermore *knows* that he or she is
right. Thus, we can discern a rather strange epistemic category of
self-justified true belief. The proof of rightness and the feeling of rightness are the same thing. The act of self-proving—I know this to be
true because it is true for me—hardens into a pervasive rightness.
And that feeling of being right in turns gathers itself into an identity, such that claims made against the original "proof" are felt to be
attacks on the person himself. The alternative possibility—that the
doxaholic is wrong, both about the original claim and about its hardening into a carapace of identity—becomes literally unthinkable. The
doxaholic cannot abide contrary views or evidence. They threaten his
or her closely guarded sense of self because that self is constructed
of specific, often "contrarian" views, not an open-minded but critical
viewpoint. This feeling of being attacked by countervailing reason
prompts a fight-or-flight response, not unlike the threat of having

an addictive substance restricted or removed altogether from the user's grasp.

Now, because of the still-beating heart of the liberal tradition, there is a handy rescue operation for all such challenges: the free-speech defence. This can be both purely defensive and, in the hands of experts, neatly pivoted to discredit in advance any arguments from contrary positions. Thus, for example, actual state censorship and "cancelling" are run together as if they are the same thing. And any critique based on adverse consequences, as in hate-language laws, is positioned as an attack on individual freedom.

At the same time, we often see jaw-dropping instances of what has become known as the Dunning-Kruger effect. This is the tendency, widely observed, for people of low competence in a particular field to overestimate their own knowledge and expertise. This finding is often overstated or misrepresented, echoing some of the previous analysis in these pages concerning stupidity. In an article about the Dunning-Kruger effect, mathematician Eric Gaze begins by quoting British comedian John Cleese's pithy summation: "If you are really, really stupid, then it's impossible for you to know you are really, really stupid." Gaze notes that "A quick search of the news brings up dozens of headlines connecting the Dunning-Kruger effect to everything from work to empathy and even to why Donald Trump was elected president." In fact, the results are less spectacular. One good summary is this: "The least skilled people do know how much they don't know, but everyone thinks they are better than average."[29]

The mistake most people make concerning the effect, according to original coauthor David Dunning, has to do with who falls victim to it. "The effect is about us, not them," he has said. "The lesson of the effect was always about how we should be humble and cautious about ourselves." The Dunning-Kruger effect is not an indictment of other people's stupidity. As so often, the mirror has the relevant picture. We *all* tend to underestimate our incompetence. And this is a genuine worry about the validity of democratic decision-making, task distribution, and the conferring of authority in institutions. The routine complaint that *even I could do better than that* is mostly a false trail.[30]

About 65 percent of Americans think they enjoy greater than average intelligence, for example, which is obviously statistically absurd.[31] This situation is not quite Garrison Keillor's fictional Lake Wobegon, where "all the children are above average," but it's close enough. Related studies also show that people tend to become more vehement in their insistence on being right as a perverse function of how little they know. The findings also indicate, perhaps predictably, a larger tendency to this effect in men, white men, wealthy white men, and… well, you get the idea.[32] (I have no statistics handy on what percentage of Canadians think they are smarter than Americans, but I'm guessing it's pretty high.) We are all potential Dunning-Kruger case studies, it seems. We have to guard against being so. I'm biased, of course, but I think philosophy in the broadest sense is what meets the case. It is the conviction-drug antidote, or at least the possible methadone equivalent, and a good new habit to supplant the old harmful ones.

I can hear you ask: what is philosophy, and just what does it have to do with me? Agnes Callard offers this answer: "Here I put forward my own unabashedly partisan view of philosophy, cribbed from Plato's cave: philosophy does not put sight into blind eyes; rather, it turns the soul around to face the light." This sentiment comes in an essay with the appropriately humble title "I Teach the Humanities, and I Still Don't Know What Their Value Is."[33] Callard's argument strikes me as exactly right, both in its pithy summary of Plato's Republic and in its securing a useful distinction between knowledge and wisdom. In part 4 we wrestled with the question of what made knowledge possible; and, in common with most exercises in epistemology, we were left with a feeling of disappointment, maybe bordering on irritation. We want to say, "I don't know much about knowledge but I know it when I see it."

But do you? Do we? However fine-tuned our account of knowledge, it will not answer to the lurking problem of conviction. We know all too well that further knowledge, even when accepted as valid, often does not suffice to change someone's mind. Supplemental knowledge is discounted, compartmentalized, diminished as biased, or otherwise drained of power. The mind does not want, in general, to change once it is, as we say, made up. Made up like a well-built table, perhaps, or made up like a good story? Or like a neat bed, like your mom told you to do every morning? I started these reflections by considering the Enlightenment idea that thought moves from adolescence to maturity, that the great task of rational life was becoming a grown-up. But maybe that metaphor is all wrong, and the idea of enlightenment—putting sight in blind eyes, including our own—is less essential than that of turning our faces to the light.

What might that be, supposing we were so moved? In Plato's account, as we know, it is the Good, symbolized by the sun, the source of light that makes all things visible. As with the sun, we cannot look directly at it without risk of harm. But we can acknowledge its life-giving warmth and illumination and turn toward it, like grateful heliotropes. In this picture, the operative feature of our souls is wonder, not knowledge. The Greeks called it *thaumazein*, which retains a root with the sea god Thaumas, husband of Elektra and father of Iris. Knowledge may emerge from wonder, as Roger Bacon described early procedures of science—a derivation still favoured by many scientists whose work begins in awe and curiosity. But wonder retains its primordial and childlike purity, its essential openness to the marvellous fact that there is something rather than nothing.

I'll be honest. I doubt that there is such a sun as the one Plato has Socrates describe here, the ideal form of goodness as such, much as I have adored this story ever since I first read it as a teenager and then over the many years I have recounted it in lectures to other teenagers and (mostly) young adults. We may speak of "the sovereignty of the good," as the philosopher and novelist Iris Murdoch had it, but we have to wonder how much of this imagined sovereignty is wishful thinking or, worse, dangerous illusion.[34] Good is everywhere on the run, not sovereign, and at least stands in a constant struggle to retain its hold on the world. It might seem that an assumption of basic goodness, especially in humans, will detract from, rather than guide, our own intuitions about what is good and just.

Like Plato before her, Murdoch suggests that the experience of beauty is a reliable avenue to more and more ideal thoughts, and the virtues that attend those thoughts. But we all have reason to know of the art-loving Nazi who stands as a counterexample, or the merely insensitive and cloth-eared, who find no edification in art. Certainly aggressive scientism is a harmful ideology, routinely mocking other kinds of belief and incidentally undermining the authority of good science. But countering that tendency with idealistic perfectionism is about as convincing externally as praising the power of prayer.

The resulting situation, after all, is not hard to imagine. Most of the world recently lived through it: a battle of aggressive scientism versus equally aggressive populism about disease, public health, and yes, of course, freedom. There is no need to rehearse, here, all the details of that sad episode in institutional distrust. As one commentator put it: "It was as if the authorities had set off the fire alarm in a nation-sized movie theatre: one half of the audience vacated their seats in muted panic while the rest defiantly continued to eat their popcorn."[35] Which one of these was you depended a lot on what might be thought extraneous features that proved anything but: income level, education, location, race, gender.

The New Left used to favour the slogan "Because everything is political." But for some, having science itself reduced entirely to partisan political bias was to lose a once-reliable safety buoy on a turbulent sea. One clear difficulty is that, against a background of addiction to conviction, the sometimes nuanced probabilities of scientific method were untenable. Their uncertainty would not be tolerated.[36] And of course, as in any human practice, there was plenty of evidence of error and even malfeasance available to taint the entire image of public-health medicine. If some of them sometimes make mistakes, then to hell with all of them, all the time![37]

As Socrates acknowledges, wisdom as devotion to the good is not easily shared. It will be hard to get other people to reorient to the sun which we might see shine so brightly. In the *Republic*'s cave allegory, Socrates notes that the single freed slave—somehow unchained from his imprisonment watching only shadows on the wall—is initially blinded by the expanded light. He has difficulty in convincing anyone else to turn around. It's painful, for one thing, almost Sisyphean, this proposed upward climb. Blinding light! Rough and wounding rocks of adversity! Mockery, disdain, and even actual punishment for these happiness delinquents, the naysayers of the current arrangement. Who is this unchained wild man to tell me what to do anyway, insisting on further realms of truth when I'm quite happy with these dancing shadows?

This moment of conflict between the liberated slave and his fellows is, naturally, precisely the ancient Greek precursor to the long fist-fight scene in *They Live*, where Nada tries to force his buddy Frank to put on the ideology-busting sunglasses. Like the emancipated slave, Nada is not crazy, just on the road to enlightenment, questioning the authority of the normies. Over six absurdly prolonged minutes, the two duke it out in an alleyway because Frank, frankly, does not want to be enlightened. He is a happy prisoner of the shadows. You can keep those Wayfarers for yourself or somebody else who wants them!

Here we see once again a version of the philosopher's paradox, or one of them. You can only see the value of doing philosophy once you're already doing it. From the outside, philosophical turning can seem like just another cult, a further genteel site of indoctrination. But now that basic paradoxicality is meshed with what we can additionally call the philosopher's dilemma. Is your duty to save yourself alone or to try and save those fellow citizens who are still enchained but do not want to be saved? There is no lack of evidence that people fail to be rational. And yet, we are very good at belief and conviction. Our irrationality rarely issues in the (rational) awareness of our own limitations, and far more often entrenches comforting conviction when there is any shade of doubt. As Martin Amis put it, thinking of Lord Rochester's poetic caution that celebrating reason can be a trap: "His worries are needless. On any longer view, man is only fitfully committed to the rational—to thinking, seeing, learning, knowing. Believing is what he's really proud of."[38]

On its best possible conception, reason is an adaptive feature of human evolution. It fosters communication and cooperation, underwriting human progress—otherwise known as apex predation, with the attendant dangers of ecological self-destruction by way of Darwinian supremacy. Even on a positive account, reason is subject to the ossifying tendencies of all personal belief: things like myside bias (believing my own views are stronger than others), counterfactual discounting (those other views enter the marketplace of ideas at a lower value), and the illusion of explanatory depth (holding my views seems to make them more complex than the views of others).

As we know, confirmation bias is a physiological phenomenon as well as a cognitive one. It isn't merely satisfying mentally, it actually feels physically good, to stick to your guns, to dig in your heels, and—as we always imagine we are doing—to speak truth to power.[39] There is, too, a defensive quality to doxaholic indulgence. In a permacritical world of eight billion lost souls, having a violent opinion can feel like the only thing that secures my fleeting, cosmically insignificant existence to a larger narrative. But here is the wisdom that matters: you don't have to have, let alone express, a violent opinion about everything. Our shared lifeworld is not a call-in sports-radio show, where the loudest and most certain voice wins the argument. The game we are playing is too important—too mortal in every sense—for that.

* * *

WE ALL HAVE A STAKE in respecting the overarching claim of reason. If nothing else, we can feel thereby a sense of shared predicament about knowledge and action in this fallen world. We may begin to sympathize again with the poor sods trapped down at the bottom of the cave—who, after all, are just us on less-critical days. The prisoners just want to be left alone in their deception—even, paradoxically, when the images are possibly fake, often hideous, and always coming from elsewhere. The desire of the prisoners to remain chained is itself a paradox, though only from the point of view of the liberated seer. To those still inside the shadow-play dreamscape, tales of other and allegedly better realities are so much fantasy.

We have all been here before. Here is this *lunatic* tugging at our elbows, telling us there is *freedom*, whatever that is, available in the sunshine, wherever *that* is, and that we will be liberated from something that seems eminently real already, thank you very much. But, but—we have to go, because we can only see the limits of what we think is real by painfully abandoning that "reality." We must simply follow his mad-sounding and extremely painful lead. But *why exactly* should we obey? Oh, he has an answer for that one: because it worked for him! And we know that how? Because he said so! And it's extremely *painful*, did we get that right? Tell me again why we should believe him? I'm having trouble with that part. Actually, that part and all the other parts.

We are told that philosophy means *love of wisdom*, and the etymology bears out that claim. But how do you get someone to fall in love? Can you decide to fall in love yourself? Most of us take love to be, at its best, a mixture of good luck, biochemistry, and emotional need. We are lovers by nature and hope to find a proper object for our longing. It doesn't seem to be a matter of rational argument, or entreaty. Begging, arguing, and browbeating never work. Advocates of reasonableness often suggest finding common ground with an ideological opponent as a first step to productive dialogue, and that sounds pretty good until we are forced to realize that someone in the grip of a doxaholic addiction is not really, on some points at least, reasonable at all. If there were common ground to be agreed upon, we would not face the impasses we so often observe in polarized public discourse. The solution is not to find some idealized compromise or shared position, but for somebody, maybe everybody, to change their minds.

This is never easy, either with oneself or still more with someone else. But you know what sometimes does work when it comes to mind-change? Not deduction, induction, or even abduction, but something with a more complicated reputation: seduction. Socrates is not above resorting to this strategy in Plato's dialogues, bewitching and entangling interlocutors with confusion and self-doubt. In a negative light, this is what might be called a two-person game with just one player: the player knows what is afoot and the mark does not.[40] But in a more positive inflection, seduction is just what happens in many intellectual or spiritual transformations. The seductive principle should not be another person, with his or her own personal aims. It should be a quality or feature of human desire that is worthy of elevation. We turn a desire for physical beauty, say, into a longing for beauty as such, and hence eventually the good. This will almost inevitably still leave the seduced lover feeling deceived, perhaps cheated, so it is imperative that what begins as seduction comes to be transmuted into love: a multiperson game with all participants in play together under the sun. We don't want to be tricked into wisdom, finally. We want to choose it. But we can only see the wisdom of that choice when we have already been, at least to some degree, initiated into the way of seeing that is wise.

Such seeing is not a matter of revelation, of having scales drop from our eyes—or having sunglasses put over them. It is not really about the seeing at all, but rather the seeker. The solution to the riddle of wisdom-conversion is actually not a solution in the traditional sense of solving a problem. It is more a matter of vocation, or hearing a painful call to self-duty. A clue to what is at stake, and how it all works, is contained in a minor but highly significant incident within the sprawling narrative of the *Republic*. A character called Leontius is introduced. He has a problem: he has found himself wanting to look at slain corpses lying outside the walls of Athens. But he finds this desire hateful. In the ensuing internal struggle—look or don't look—his will proves too weak to control his base desire. He looks and curses his eyes for being stronger than his conscience. The problem does not lie in his eyes, but in his soul. He is conflicted. And that conflict is, despite his discomfort, the beginning of identity and wisdom. Leontius already knows what his problem is: his soul is in disorder. Therefore, he also already knows what the proper response must be. He needs to work toward a more harmonious psychic state. Socrates or some other therapist might be his interlocutor here, but the basic dialogue is between Leontius and his better self.

That is how wisdom begins: not with argument, or entreaty, or even sly advances from someone we imagine wise. At the end of Plato's *Symposium*, the handsome and successful Alcibiades, drunk and unruly at the feast, arriving late, confesses to the assembled guests his humiliation in the pursuit of love. (The relevant passage is at 216c to 223d.) Admiring Socrates for his wisdom and courage, disregarding the older man's famous ugliness and rough manner, he recalls that he once attempted a seduction of his own preferred style, namely wine and late-night charm. But Socrates rebuffed him—yes, refused the advances of him, Alcibiades, the golden one, the blessed paragon. And in the process made him feel ashamed, the only person capable of doing so (216b). How is this even possible?

Plato makes the lesson clear: Alcibiades has made a category mistake, in fact two of them. Not only has he imagined that virtue is a transitive quality, something that can simply be passed from one person to another; he has also presumed, worse, that actions taken in accordance with his usual motives will result in any change to his character. Even if he had seduced Scorates, in other words, he would have remained the same in his soul—indeed, only more so. You can't trade cheap sexual thrills for soulful transformation. Thinking you can, and attempting to do so, is even worse than knowing nothing at all. Hence the shame and humiliation—which might hint at a way forward, though Alcibiades does not seem to see this lesson lurking in the narrative. Wisdom will not be possessed that way; indeed, it will not be possessed at all, only lived. Wisdom begins with pain and wonder—a sense of self in question, a soul given to turning.

We might say that, if personal agency means anything firm at all, it means precisely this reflexive ability to take stock of oneself. Identity is not a cluster of traits, or even a bundle of memories; it is a structure of self-consciousness. Rationality is a late-stage modality of this structure, not its basis. Imagine the self, then, as a pair of scissors. They can only cut the fabric of the world if and when their biaxial structure is working harmoniously. An abstracted blade of pure first-person must be attached to a narrative of particular identity. Dullness, misalignment, or looseness at the hinge will rob the two half blades of their ability to cut. Even in perfect working order, the scissors can only cut some kinds of things. It finds its purpose when slicing edges meet the right paper at the right angle. Working together in this angled fashion, translating the general leverage of desire into precise cutting force, the blades keep each other sharp. We might or might not favour the ideas of "multiple subject positions" or "extended fluidity" when it comes to gender, race, or some other feature of self-presentation. But the structural frame—the locus of consciousness, the sense of self standing *behind* the descriptors—is strangely persistent. Apart from genuine multiple-personality disorders, if there are such, we are always *some-one in particular* looking at the world in some idiosyncratic way.[41]

That self is a fragile construct, subject to nightly demolition and requiring daily maintenance to reboot, often with coffee and a rolling newsfeed. No projection entirely overcomes the basic first-person perspective. When I was lying for days and weeks in hospital, I often felt my self slipping away, sometimes in prolonged painful episodes and sometimes in drug-induced delusions that were far more vivid than dreams. It occurred to me, in lucid moments, that my personal identity was a collective achievement, not a solitary one. Without external validation, including triangulation on basic things like whether this is a chair that I see before me, I was reduced to less than nothing, just wisps of thought tailing away.[42]

Such external reality stamping is the essential complement to any inner structure of self-awareness, guardrails on sanity. We may call this sense of connection *attunement*—a general perception or acceptance that self and world, self and others, are aligned on a very basic level. If that sounds rather woolly, consider the basic and undeniable viscerality of our responses to external stimuli like perceived suffering or violence, the way our stomachs can turn at physical ugliness, or the fact that we find ourselves wincing involuntarily at roadkill, and feel unbidden squirts of adrenaline coursing in our blood when a child veers into traffic or falls from a swing. Attunement is what underwrites our ability to coordinate action, to communicate, to find things funny or sad or wondrous. In principle, this ability is not biologically limited to humans. In practice, and via confirmation bias, we find it more easily there. Non-human persons are real categories in ethics and law. But there may be hard limits on experienced attunement. AIs can tell prepared jokes, for instance, but they have a hard time cracking wise, or coming up with spontaneous witty remarks, riding a social wave the way any group of buddies easily can. So far, they lack the "grasp of essential relevance" that gives texture to everyday human life.[43]

Reason is just one feature or emergent property of the structural relations of attunement. At its best, reason is a positive form of conspiracy—a breathing together, a collective achievement. But as we have seen, it is also a capricious property that demands constant challenge both between and within rational agents. Goya's famous etching from the series called *Los Caprichos* (The Caprices) is the perfect illustration of our predicament as thinking things. We have the gift of personal identity, but only at the cost of harbouring rogue, self-destructive elements within our desiring souls. In Goya's image, a sleeping and apparently troubled figure is seated at a desk, his head cradled in his arms next to a pen and paper. Above and around him fly a frightening collection of creatures who resemble both owls and bats. For some of us, they also evoke chilling nightmare memories of the flying monkeys in *The Wizard of Oz*.

Whatever they are, the poor fellow is being tormented almost beyond endurance. The only clue to a narrative behind this haunting image is an inscription on the face of the desk, which reads "El sueño de la razon produce monstruos." This warning is usually translated as "The sleep of reason produces monsters" and so is taken to be a warning against irrationality or complacency. Wake up! Sleep has long been figured as the state of eyes-wide-shut political complacency, that which must be thrown off by new awareness, from Marx's revolutionary consciousness, to *They Live*, to the very idea of, yes, "wokeness." (The sleep-banishing resonance of the last term is long gone, as noted, like the wisps of a forgotten dream.)

But *sueño* is ambiguous in Spanish. It can also mean "dream." And so, the valence of the warning flips. If the *dream* of reason is what produces monsters, we are faced with a different challenge. Now reason is our most proximate enemy, working within the gates of selfhood. Its tools are rapacious technologies, efficient genocides, fine-tuned torture of all kinds. O'Brien in Orwell's *1984* is the exemplar here: the very figure of a supremely rational man, an intellectual, exactly

suited to his context and his task. His ambit is torture for its own sake, not for the extraction of information. Information is for pikers. It is unreliable anyway, not worth the extracting. O'Brien is, in contrast to many common depictions of a dedicated torturer, no brute or crude sadist; he is instead an artist, a scholar, a connoisseur. His canvas is the human soul. And his art is the exact inversion of the circle of sorrow imagined by Amos Oz but made possible by the very same gifts of sensibility and imagination.

Both *sleep* and *dream* are valid interpretations of this scene from Goya. We are rational creatures, at least sometimes, and so to nod off from that duty is to unleash demonic forces upon the world. But when spurred by more-violent motives, we are also capable of using reason for intricate evils or well-meaning "improvements" that turn out to be long-term, sometimes existential, harms. I have been at pains throughout this discussion to emphasize the limits of human reason, but where we see more clearly the unruly power of the mind, its volatile capacity for conceiving and executing the more exquisite evils. It is not quite true that humans are the only creatures who indulge in torture—a cat with a captured mouse certainly gives every indication of doing something similar—but we are the ones who make it into an art form.[44]

"We tell ourselves stories in order to live," Joan Didion wrote. "I was supposed to have a script, and had mislaid it." The mournful state she is recounting was "a time when I began to doubt the premises of all the stories I had ever told myself, a common condition but one I found troubling." She was suffering from depression. Yet I suspect that we are all prone to mislaying that script, sometimes, or finding it suddenly illegible. We are all mourners, hoping that the next choice we have to make is not a tragic one.[45]

Future-Proofing

AN OLD JOKE: THE FUTURE is dark and threatening. So, the rational option is obvious. We should avoid it. The current version of this particular impossible imperative is a recurring demand for *future proofing*. This idea is, in its way, the flip-side of planned obsolescence, long considered the worm coiled in the heart of consumer capitalism. Instead of deliberately making products that are timed to fail, and so need constant replacing, future-proofing attempts to build contingencies into products beforehand, making them more robust in the face of new challenges.

But we should be honest: future proofing is a fool's errand. At a low level, the attempt to forestall all possible future events can lead to *feature creep*, the addition of so many functional add-ons that the main instrument is rendered inoperative. Think of a Swiss Army knife that has so many extensions that no single one, especially its basic blade, is actually handy for use. More profoundly, future proofing provides a false sense of control over the unintended consequences of our planning and action.[46]

Technology is the most obvious site of this particular form of arrogance. Its inner logic of innovation and mastery over nature is so fetching to clever minds, and its products so often glittering and won-drous. Over and over, from the internal combustion engine to nuclear weapons to machine-learning algorithms, we see the adverse effects of runaway applied science. The most striking thing about this sadly repetitious narrative is that, each time, we express so much surprise that it has unfolded in exactly the same way.

The standard guardrail on these failings of the human individual is of course trust. We presume, or maybe just hope, that legal restrictions, democratic institutions, and even what passes for common sense will work to limit the worst excesses of billionaire tech bros, red-pill evan-gelists, transhumanist vampires, and "effective acceleration" gurus. "Effective accelerationism aims to follow the 'will of the universe': leaning into the thermodynamic bias toward futures with greater and smarter civilizations that are more effective at finding/extracting free energy from the universe," says one leader of the movement. "E/acc has no particular allegiance to the biological substrate for intelligence and life, in contrast to transhumanism," adds another.[47]

We can appreciate, in theory anyway, the fine-grained differences between e/acc types and transhumanists. Just ask yourself, do you have a particular allegiance to the biological substrate for intelligence and life? I know I do, even though I can appreciate that it is an accident of evolution that consciousness seems wedded to carbon-based life forms. But from a less exalted point of view, both transhumanists and accelerationists seem like gangs of pirates feasting on inferior mortals who are more wary of leaning into the "thermodynamic bias" of the evolving universe. This is the difference that welfarist posthumanists like me keep insisting on. Evolution is inescapable, and adaptiveness will increasingly demand carbon/non-carbon integration, but we want to hang on to the moral priority of the individual person, not allow it to be subsumed by some larger impersonal force. The fact that indi-viduals will seem so insignificant against the powers of system and structure is precisely why personal agency needs constant defence and protection—why such defence and protection forms the basis of any social order worthy of allegiance.

Institutional regulation only works to limit the power of such thought-gangs if the regulators are free from capture *and* if those of us down here on the everyday ground believe that this is so. In other words, trust is the only technology equal to the depredations of other technologies, especially when the latter are vastly profitable. Because trust is free of direct profit, and because it reinforces the collective underwriting of society, it is literally invaluable. Our problem right now, however, is that trust is in short supply, and technology is only making it worse. The great threat of AI, as it is being allowed to develop and expand its reach, is not killer robots, wage-stealing automation, or even rival non-human claims to resources. It is the erosion of human trust itself because of the emergence of "counterfeit people."[48]

These people are already with us, in the form of deep fakes, manipulated videos, and constructed-author newsfeeds. Counterfeit people do not pose the usual conundrums of the "uncanny valley," where we encounter almost-human entities that make us feel uncomfortable in small, sometimes indefinable ways. Counterfeit people lie on the other side of the valley, past the point of seeming strange or not quite right, where we cannot perceive a difference between human and nonhuman entities. They are not uncanny; they are all too familiar in their comprehensive imitation of human forms of life. That, after all, is the point of any simulacrum that strives for perfection: that it will be entirely indistinguishable from the so-called real thing, and so displace the ontological superiority of merely human realness. How could trust endure under such conditions?

As usual, there are pessimists and optimists on the question. It is particularly galling to see former techno-boosters, who demanded our support under the sign of inevitability and progress, now expressing Dr Frankenstein-ish doubts about what they have wrought. The quick advances of AI have had at least one clear downside, namely this rise in late-hour ethical uncertainty from the toolmakers themselves. One might have thought that considering the consequences of actions, including unintended ones, was just a necessary part of rational action. Apparently not, if you are an AI scientist. The doubts all come as part of a second, even more lucrative career as a doomsayer of one's own efforts.[49] This spectacle of misgiving, in turn, erodes trust in science more generally, the way the moral awakening of former Trump aides simply causes a cynical eye roll about the perfidy of all politicians, always. Still, I suspect our trust technology, the software of civilization, is capable of retaining its power even under such unnerving conditions—as long as we take it seriously and work to secure it at every moment. In complex social systems, trust has to reside to some large extent in the idea of institutions and systems, not other individuals. Just as we shift our trust from a friendly local merchant to a reliable company or brand, we must track social investment from personal relations to systemic ones.

The example of brands shows the enduring problem. What can count as "reliable" when we are working at the level of multinational corporations? The facelessness of the capitalist corporation offers a bland masking of its genuine psychopathic nature. Attempts to "humanize" the corporation typically fail, as when large beer or soft-drink or cookie companies try to align themselves with political causes. The resulting backlash is almost always sufficient to make them alter course—because their show of support was never born of conviction, just another tweak on the basic imperative of maximizing shareholder value. We all know this. But our desire for solid structures of everyday production and consumption—and also our more addictive tendencies to try and make those structures answer to our need for coolness or authenticity—are forever compromised by the basic untrustworthiness of most capitalist actors. The resulting identity tangle is familiar to those in the developed world. We decry rapacious market dominators but shop with them anyway. We profess skepticism about the notion of brand loyalty and market pulls on our sense of self but succumb all the same.

This tracking requires constant systemic analysis—not immediate rejection of all authority claims, but a flexible engagement with the possibilities and limits of knowledge. Because this new-order structure of postcrisis trust, assuming we can begin to build it, will inevitably be engaged with technologies of scale and communication, not to mention production and consumption, I call it *posthumanist*. What is important, going forward into a risky world, is not human feeling alone, or human reason exalted beyond its proper range. We need the compassionate skepticism that mixes them together in action, and so joins my fate to yours, and everyone's. We cannot yet say whether non-human entities of an autonomous kind will be on the same journey, or whether they will experience the same vulnerabilities and potential degradation that mark mortal life as we know it.[50] So, insisting on some normative conception of the "human" won't help us very much here, except as a gateway to a keen awareness of our shared capacity for personal suffering. The category "human" can also be misused, applied selectively, and withdrawn for political purposes—it is not a neutral property, and indeed not even a *natural* one if that means something beyond our own reckoning and argument.[51]

If nothing else, the shared sense of suffering forces us to face the hard truth that torture, cruelty, evil, and unspeakable violence are all just as human as benevolence, good will, and love. And only humans have the ability, and inclination, to declare other members of their own species inhuman, nonhuman, half-human, unnatural, or otherwise devalued from full ethical and political consideration. Human is as human does. It may be a surprising conclusion, then, but the tech-flexers have one thing right. There is nothing special about the biological substrate for intelligence and life. True, biology determines a great deal of what we experience as life. And I suspect most of us would not have it any other way. Mortality and a capacity for suffering are, after all, great binders of people, elements of trust glue. They are woven into our sense of identity. But we are always extending our-selves beyond the given limits, widening the range of who and what we are. We can thus view ourselves without alarm as posthuman—nat-urally transcendent, if you like—even as we continue to argue about what we mean by "ethical being," "rational agent," and "good citizen."

I have used the plural pronoun in a rather fast and loose manner, I know. Partly that is simply inevitable when basic questions of society are raised. But let's pause to wonder who that "we" might actually be. Having a capacity for impersonal trust in strangers and institutions, combined with a confident individuality that can entertain abstract questions of identity, is not a universal condition. It is a form of think-ing that belongs to a fairly specific slice of time and space. The Harvard psychologist Joseph Henrich calls these people "WEIRD": Western, edu-cated, industrialized, rich, and democratic.[52] "Impersonal psychology includes inclinations to trust strangers or cooperating with anonymous others," Henrich notes. But this goes along with other less prosocial attri-butes, for example, "having high levels of individualism, meaning a focus on the self and one's attributes. This is often accompanied by tendencies toward self-enhancement and overconfidence." The "democratic" prong of the WEIRD structure is perhaps the most vulnerable, since the other attributes can, out of balance, equally apply to fascism. (This was not the reasoning behind 2024's mini-trend of calling MAGA Republicans "weird," to be sure, but it could be if the point were stretched a bit.)[53]

More to our present concerns, a key part of the WEIRD cast of mind is a penchant for analytic thinking as against holistic ways. There is likewise a possible overreliance on legal structures that can prove, in a crisis, too fragile to bear our collective weight. Sometimes our identity is simply denied, not just modified from within. Think of the mundane experience of losing your passport while in a foreign country. (I can say from experience that this is a very unpleasant ordeal, a true threat to assumed identity.)[54] Still, these remain among the strongest

338   QUESTION AUTHORITY

tools we have for pursuing larger goals of justice. Even recognizing its contingent history and many false steps, we still need to push the logic of universal human (and posthuman) rights. The Enlightenment project, whose ambitions and limits began this discussion, is still a live problem here at its end.

* * *

THERE IS NO SINGLE SOLUTION to the problem of authority, any more than there is a single conception of human rationality that will save us from ourselves. Thinking otherwise is a dangerous illusion. Nor is there any sufficiently complex risk-sharing scheme to cope with the world as we find it now.[55] We should also remember that the deepest uncanny valley remains the one that yawns *between me and myself*. Because of this and other contingencies of mortal existence, trust remains the most essential technology of all, the only one capable of properly guiding the others.

So, what shall we do? What is the right way forward as we try to manage the vast menu of crises before us? How do we begin to realize an idea of the democracy to come, which is not temporal or aspirational but always beckoning, an infinite task of hope which has no final calculation? The obvious answer to that question is: we need to get to work right now. Think every day of the infinite imperatives. Question authority, yes. But also: seek justice, love wisdom, show compassion, open your mind.[56] We know that trust in abstract systems requires good access points—a wise advisor, an inspiring teacher, a good banker or nurse. Cultivate them. Be one yourself! Keep articulating what the task at hand really is. It's almost always *not* about you or your personal truth. And remember that you're not as smart as you think you are—and neither is anyone else.

More imperatives: Play the right game. Play it fairly. Most of all: play it, don't game it. Check your privilege, sure, but don't make a performance of doing so, still less an identity. Don't race to the bottom with competing grievance claims. Be humble; wage war on cliché; experiment with life; get some distance on your addiction; be a good neighbour. Be a citizen. We tend to see the state in terms of a consumerist tax-for-services swap, or an insurance scheme enforced by law and its state-sponsored threat of force. What if citizenship were more than risk distribution executed by a begrudged tax burden? What if it were a strong feature of identity, backed by reasons?

What if we all made a more concerted effort to look one another in the eye, something that seems to disappear into the endless void of our phone-zombie self-enslavement? Eye contact between citizens is, as everyone from George Orwell to political historian Timothy Snyder has noted, one of those features of shared everyday life that makes tyranny harder to achieve. How about, even more radically, we make a practice of looking at ourselves in the mirror? In the eyes. Use the old-fashioned kind of mirror, not the black one on your phone; it is a ridiculously cinematic and affected gesture, I know, but it's also salutary just for that reason. *Who the hell is that? And why is he looking at me that way?*[57]

Let's be even more prescriptive, since our time together grows short, and this story of trust and authority, this narrative about habit and identity, needs a sense of an ending, an imperative flourish to finish strong. So here goes.

We need mandatory philosophy classes in high school. Also classes in comparative religion, media literacy, personal finance, shop, and economics both micro and macro. We ought to require ethics, logic, and civics, too, along with greater breadth requirements in colleges and universities. University is not for everyone, but everyone should have a chance to go if they want to. Responsible adults should make a point of limiting their screen time, and that of their dependents, for the sake of sanity. Get off X, Instagram, and maybe all future social-media platforms that foster and enable brain poison. Factual claims made in public domains should always be supported by at least three reputable sources. Global North democracies should have national-service requirements to make beneficiaries of liberal-democratic systems appreciate the gifts of freedom and citizenship. There should be fines for not voting, and stiff regulation on social media for minors.[58] While we're at it, let's reform structural barriers to sanity in electoral politics, like the Electoral College in the US, district gerrymandering, and the absurdly undemocratic first-past-the-post system. It is not weak to apologize when you make mistakes or tell lies. Admit when you don't know something. Also, just stop telling lies. Accept that there is a reality outside your own mind and any circle of other true believers. Practice the habits of trust and true authority will follow. We all win when everyone plays for the sake of the shared game.[59]

Nobody but you can decide that you want to think for yourself. The alternative is not liberation from the burdens of thought—that way lies oblivion—but continued subjugation. Some corporation, algorithm, ideology, or bundle of prejudices is holding you captive and doing your thinking for you. We sleep while they live, harvesting our dreams. There are those who would profit from confusion, distorting a sense of shared reality with a combination of hucksterism and sheer audacious falsehood. Do not be taken in by their elaborate shows of kayfabe, their false dramas and shadow plays. Be on guard when the guilty accuse everyone else of their own failings and render black as white, up as down. Trust gives way in spaces flooded with lies and bravado, dominated by images and the fleeting highs and bitter hangovers of the attention economy. Do not allow confidence in the claim of reason to slip away.[60]

To trust—and so to grant legitimate authority—is always going to be partly an act of faith. We can and must forever demand credentials, and evidence, and transparency. But the most important part of trust is what we bring to the table, not what we find there. Trust is a refusal to bow under the weight of corruption and perfidy, in ourselves most of all. Of course everything can be questioned. Of course no one can be trusted. Of course, your own conviction is rock solid and everyone else is deluded or deceiving or both. Of course, of course, of course. But resist the temptation to follow that self-defeating path of toxic conviction. Tomorrow we die; today we have work to do. That is the only game that matters, and the one that everybody must play.[61]

I surveyed some metaphors for trust at the beginning of this book, and I have no reason to think the possible options have expanded. Trust really is like the wind most of all, filling our sails sometimes but falling away at any moment. A well-known Biblical proverb says that he who brings chaos to his house will inherit only the wind—meaning nothing but emptiness can come from trouble and strife. But the wind itself need not be empty, and good sails catch fair winds. They propel us in our purposes if we are agile, pay attention, and cooperate. To quote another sage piece of hard-won wisdom: we cannot direct the wind, but we can adjust our sails.[62]

Trust is an adaptive technology, renewed in its force by regular use: a habit of endless dividends. And distrust is an evolutionary dead end, a repudiation of human possibility. Those two facts alone make the basic imperative clear: trust to win. But Kant was not quite right. Let us celebrate the audacity not of reason as such, but rather of our ongoing commitment to flourishing together, even as we humbly admit to weakness and limit in ourselves and others. Thinking *for* yourself does not mean thinking *of* yourself. Only together can we put the world into question in order to get it back. That's the job, and it takes endless courage.

Luckily, you are not alone. There is only one real world; this is it, and we all share it. Trust means making that sharing ever more true simply by assuming that fellow-feeling is the case and acting like-wise—not waiting for some extrnal sign or permission. Another paradox, perhaps. The mechanism works in a manner that is not unlike the basic paradox of philosophy discussed earlier: if you want to see

342   QUESTION AUTHORITY

the world a certain way, then you are already the kind of person who makes the world seeable that way. You are a lover of wisdom. The kind of self-fulfillment I am imagining now, in the realm of practical philosdophy, is not as off-hand as something we sometimes hear lately: IYKYK, if you know, you know—that slang signal of in-joke solidarity, swapped between cultural insiders. But such casual signs of assumed fellowship and shared perspective are not to be dismissed, or left to wither on the day-to-day discursive vine. A feeling that we are not alone, that others get it, can be enough to move us forward in more mature and world-building feats of commitment. If you want to be the kind of person who inhabits a world of trust, then you are already the kind of person who makes that world more likely.[63]

Have I said enough? Have I convinced you? I hope not. That would defeat the purpose, after all, and so reduce fruitful paradox to mere self-contradiction. No doubt there is some risk of that outcome no matter what I intend. But I can and will say one last thing before falling silent, per tradition: Trust me, I'm a doctor!

Acknowledgements

MY THANKS TO DAN WELLS and everyone at Biblioasis for the chance to give these thoughts a proper presentation. Thanks, too, to everyone who has sustained me through the challenges of recent years, especially Molly Montgomery, Clara Puton, Johan Arthurs, Chloe Puton, Craig Robinson, and Henry Warren Robinson, *Rex quondam, Rexque futurus*.

Some small portions of the text were previously published in the *Guardian*, *LA+*, *The Walrus*, the *Globe and Mail*, and *Maclean's*. My thanks to the editors at each for those opportunities. This book is dedicated to my late father-in-law, pillar of trust and quiet authority, Bruce L. Montgomery.

Notes

INTRODUCTION

1 Koh Ewe, "The Ultimate Election Year: All the Elections Around the World in 2024," *Time Magazine*, Dec. 28, 2023.

2 A good discussion of affective-polarization effects in the Canadian context is Paul Wells, *Justin Trudeau on the Ropes: Governing in Troubled Times* (Toronto: Sutherland House, 2024), 54ff. "Affective polarization was first identified in the United States and, like most things, it's bigger there than here," Wells writes. "But investigators have also found affective polarization increasing over the last few decades in Switzerland, France, Denmark, and New Zealand." Wells's study is, in effect, a book-length indictment of Trudeau's broken promise to provide trustworthy government in Canada by having government trust Canadians.

3 The emerging legacy of pandemic response offers a case in point. I will have occasion to mention Anthony Fauci in what follows, mostly as an example of malicious distrust: he was routinely and repeatedly vilified, even threatened, by those who decided that their "freedom" was more important than public health. But some of the evidence that came to light during the 2024 US congressional hearings ought to give us pause. Objections to the Covid response were not all based in right-wing conspiracism. There were some notable failures in transparency

and logic, as well as some indefensible resorts to obfuscation, suppression of results, and simple fabrication. For an overview, see Zeynep Tufekci, "An Object Lesson from Covid on How to Destroy Public Trust," *New York Times*, Opinion, Jun. 8, 2024, https://www.nytimes.com/2024/06/08/opinion/covid-fauci-hearings-health.html. Anthony Fauci admits some of these errors, though certainly not all, in his memoir, *On Call: A Doctor's Journey in Public Service* (New York: Viking, 2024). The book's cover copy says: "Anthony Fauci is arguably the most famous—and most revered—doctor in the world today." That revered could be recast as reviled and the sentence would be just as true.

4   I discuss the danger of entrenched elites in, among other places, "Throwing Dice: Luck of the Draw and the Democratic Ideal," *PhaenEx* 7, no. 1 (2012): 66–100; reprinted in *Unruly Voices: Essays on Democracy, Civility, and the Human Imagination* (Windsor, ON: Biblioasis, 2012). I should probably say, right up front, that I sometimes cite my own work in these notes. I also reference the *New York Times* fairly often. This is not an expression of trust—see part 3—but rather part of an account of the unfolding discursive record in the publication that still considers itself "the paper of record." I'm mindful that philosopher Alasdair MacIntyre derided the *Times* as the "parish magazine of affluent and self-congratulatory liberal enlightenment." *Whose Justice? Which Rationality?* (Notre Dame, IN: University of Notre Dame Press, 1988), 5.

5   Dan Williams, "Why do people believe true things?" *Conspicuous Cognition* (blog), Jul. 28, 2024, conspicuouscognition.com/p/why-do-people-believe-true-things. As the title suggests, the concern here is not merely to insist that irrationality or cognitive debasement is the human norm, but further to question why we would ever rise above it. But Williams does not explore, in this short essay, any really convincing arguments to answer this question. I hope my longer engagement might form at least a beginning of a good answer. People believe true things, against all expectation and inclination, because the resulting cooperation is good for everyone. Tracking the truth has positive return on individual investment; doing so in groups multiplies the dividends by way of coordinated action and institutional stability. The basic logic is Hobbesian.

6   My own account of political virtue has been expounded in various earlier works. See, for example, "Defending Political Virtue," *Philosophical Forum* 27, no. 3 (Spring 1996): 244–68; also, *The World We Want: Restoring Citizenship in a Fractured Age* (New York: Rowman & Littlefield, 2001).

7   In fact, many students and their families usually end up paying quite a bit less than that—an under-reported truth. At Yale, for example, where the cost of attending is currently nearly US$91,000 a year, almost 60 percent of incoming freshmen receive some form of financial aid based on family income. Graduate students are typically offered fellowship packages that cover all tuition fees plus an annual stipend and teaching salary. It's possible to get quality post-secondary education with no debt at all. (I know because I did it.) That's not exactly perfect meritocracy—it's still easier to open the doors if you're wealthy or a big-donor legacy—but there are structures of equity in place that should be acknowledged when the dominant narrative highlights student debt. See Kamaron McNair, "It Costs Over $90,000 a Year to Go to Yale—But Here's How Much Students Actually Pay," *Make It* (blog), CNBC, Jun. 5, 2024, https://www. cnbc.com/2024/06/05/yale-tuition-what-students-pay.html.

8   This is why it was a good thing that Donald Trump was convicted of multiple New York felony counts in May of 2024, Nolan suggests. Even though the verdict may be overturned on appeal, even if there is no prospect of jail time or collapse of his political future, it is essential that the system assert its power over the elusive, wily, and contemptuous. "The theory of 'a rising tide lifts all boats' does not work when you allow the people with the most influence to buy their way out of the water," Nolan argues. "It would be nice if we fixed broken systems simply because they are broken. In practice, governments are generally happy to ignore broken things if they do not affect people with enough power to make the government listen. So the more people that we push into public systems, the better." See Hamilton Nolan, "Everyone in the Grinder," *How Things Work* (blog), Jun. 1, 2024, https://www.hamiltonnolan.com/p/everyone-into-the-grinder.

9   Hans-Georg Gadamer, *Truth and Method*, trans. Joel Weinsheimer (New York: Continuum, 1975). The prejudice against prejudice is identified by Gadamer as a form of Enlightenment bias, or presumption, in favour of universal reason. He is not arguing for runaway prejudice, but instead an acknowledgement of situatedness and particularity in all truth claims, themselves governed by our specific purposes.

10 Lee Rainie, Scott Ketter, and Andrew Perrin, *Trust and Distrust in America*, Pew Research Center, Jul. 22, 2019, https://www.pewresearch.org/politics/2019/07/22/trust-and-distrust-in-america/.

11 I offer a more academic discussion of the matter in "Truth, Interpretation, and Addiction to Conviction," in *America's Post-Truth Phenomenon:*

When Feelings and Opinions Trump Facts and Evidence, edited by Carlos Prado, 15–37 (Santa Barbara, CA: Praeger, 2018).

12   Just three examples, all with resonance for any representative electoral system: John Gastil and Katherine R. Knobloch, *Hope for Democracy: How Citizens Can Bring Reason Back into Politics* (New York: Oxford University Press, 2020); John Burnheim, *Is Democracy Possible? The Alternative to Electoral Democracy*, new ed. (Sydney: Sydney University press, 2006); and the similarly titled Ronald Dworkin, *Is Democracy Possible Here? Principles for a New Political Debate* (Princeton: Princeton University Press, 2008).

13   I am drawing here on the expansive work of Robert B. Brandom, especially his influential book *A Spirit of Trust: A Reading of Hegel's "Phenomenology"* (Cambridge, MA: Belknap Press, 2019). This work is far more than a reading of Hegel's intricate masterpiece. Brandom's subtle unpacking of Hegelian thought makes it intelligible but never beholden to contemporary analytic philosophy. Even more indispensable to the present discussion is Donald Davidson, "On the Very Idea of Conceptual Scheme," *Proceedings and Addresses of the American Philosophical Association* 47 (1973): 5-20, https://doi.org/10.2307/3129898. Advancing Quine's argument about the "two dogmas of empiricism"—roughly, the fact/value distinction and the analytic/synthetic distinction—Davidson claims that the "dualism of scheme and content, of organizing system and something waiting to be organized, cannot be made intelligible and defensible. It is itself a dogma of empiricism, the third dogma." So much the worse, then, for (naïve, unscientific) empiricism.

14   Neil Gross, "When It Comes to Politics, Are Any of Us Really Thinking for Ourselves?" Opinion, *New York Times*, Mar. 24, 2024, https://www.nytimes.com/2024/03/24/opinion/politics-intellectual-humility.html. "If nothing else, reflecting on the social roots of your political opinions and behavior should prompt some humility," Gross says. "Even if you hold the 'correct' political beliefs, you may not deserve to congratulate yourself for them; your moral righteousness could be an accident of birth or a product of good social fortune. So on what grounds are you permitted to feel snidely superior to your peers who—simply because of their different life circumstances—wound up on the other side of the political aisle?" The deeper questions concern *how* and *when* we decide to think for ourselves. Sometimes that is the wrong thing to

do; thinking for yourself can be inefficient, incorrect, even harmful. See Jonathan Matheson, "Why Think for Yourself?" *Episteme* 21, no. 1 (2024): 320–38, https://doi.org/10.1017/epi.2021.49. "On the one hand," Matheson writes, "it seems as though any healthy intellectual life includes thinking about a number of issues for oneself. On the other hand, it seems as though taking inquiry seriously requires you to take the best available route to the answer, and *typically* that is not thinking for yourself. For nearly any question you want to investigate, there is someone who is in a better epistemic position than you are to determine the answer" (my emphasis).

15 Somewhat ironically, for present purposes, I will note that the line appears in Emerson's famous essay "Self-Reliance" (1841). The use and misuse of this line is itself a kind of cultural metaproperty. In the film *Next Stop Wonderland* (1998), the main character, played by Hope Davis, is a single woman who encounters a string of men bent on impressing her with the reference, attributing it to, variously, Karl Marx, W. C. Fields, and Cicero. So much for epistemic self-reliance, boys!

16 W. B. Yeats, "Meditations in Time of Civil War," first published in Yeats's collection *The Tower* (1928); and Frank O'Hara, "Meditations in an Emergency," from the collection of the same name (1957). My favourite line from the latter: "Each time my heart is broken it makes me feel more adventurous (and how the same names keep recurring on that interminable list!), but one of these days there'll be nothing left with which to venture forth." Trivia for culture nerds: in an episode of the television series *Mad Men* (2007–15), tortured ad man Don Draper (Jon Hamm) sees another man reading O'Hara's book while day drinking in a Manhattan bar. He then sends a copy of it to Anna Draper, the widow of the man whose identity he has stolen, and later reads O'Hara's poem "Mayakovsky" in voice-over: "Now I am quietly waiting for / the catastrophe of my personality / to seem beautiful again, / and interesting, and modern."

17 As I will note throughout these pages, familiar quotations like this one take on a certain vorticist tendency when pursued for sourcing online. I find this pretty funny, especially in the context of a discussion of authority and trust. For this example, everyone from Leo Tolstoy, George Bernard Shaw, and Jimi Hendrix to Gil Scott-Heron, Gandhi, and Mohammed Atta are cited as the origin. The variations almost always involve

a spiffing-up, rendering complex thoughts into bumper-sticker sentiments—and, indeed, sometimes actual bumper stickers. See Brian Morton, "Falser Words Were Never Spoken," Opinion, *New York Times*, Aug.
29, 2011, https://www.nytimes.com/2011/08/30/opinion/falser-words-
were-never-spoken.html. "So we recast the wisdom of the great thinkers
in the shape of our illusions," Morton notes. "Shorn of their complexities,
their politics, their grasp of the sheer arduousness of change, they stand
before us now. They are shiny from their makeovers, they are fabulous
and gorgeous, and they want us to know that we can have it all."

18 David French, "Welcome to Our New 'Bespoke Realities,'" Opinion,
New York Times, Dec. 1, 2023, https://www.nytimes.com/2023/11/30/
opinion/political-reality-algorithms.html.

19 See, for example, Zach St George, "The Comet Strike Theory That
Just Won't Die," *New York Times Magazine*, Mar. 5, 2024, https://www.
nytimes.com/2024/03/05/magazine/younger-dryas-impact-hypothesis-
comet.html. This article considers the strange case of the Younger Dryas
impact hypothesis, a mostly debunked but persistently popular idea
that a large comet strike in the Great Lakes region decisively altered
the history of Earth. Supported by YouTube videos, TikTok uploads, a
Netflix series, and various right-wing endorsements, the hypothesis has
become a litmus test of attitudes about established science.

20 As St George notes, "In a recent paper, two psychologists at the University of California, Santa Barbara, Spencer Mermelstein and Tamsin
German, have argued that pseudoscientific beliefs, which range from
the relatively harmless (astrology, dowsing) to the deeply malignant
(eugenics, Holocaust denial), tend to find cultural success when they
hit a sweet spot of strangeness: too outlandish, and the epistemological
immune system will reject it; too banal, and no one passes it on. What
is most likely to take hold, Mermelstein says, is something that adds an
intriguing twist to a person's current sense of the world." Thus, it helps
that the Younger Dryas hypothesis is consistent with the book of Genesis.

21 See Jeremy Freese, "The Problem of Predictive Promiscuity in Deduc-
tive Applications of Evolutionary Reasoning to Intergenerational Trans-
fers: Three Cautionary Tales," in *Intergenerational Caregiving*, edited by
Alan Booth, Ann C. Crouter, Suzanne M. Bianchi, and Judith A. Seltzer
(Washington, DC: Urban Institute Press, 2008). Catchy title!

22 This pathological extension of seeking revelation into celebrating nihilism is the subject of Elle Reeve's book *Black Pill: How I Witnessed the*

Darkest Corners of the Internet Come to Life, Poison Society, and Capture American Politics (New York: Simon & Schuster, 2024). *Pilled* is "the main metaphor of internet politics," Reeve notes, citing the implied *Matrix* red-or-blue scenario, now a handy image of choosing to face the hard truth beneath cozy illusions. "You could be Russiapilled or cryptopilled or Marxpilled; the term could express pride in your own epiphany or contempt for a nutjob." The *black* pill offers "a dark but gleeful nihilism: the system is corrupt, and its collapse is inevitable. There is no hope. Times are bad and they're going to get worse. You swallow the black pill and accept the end is coming." This *final ingestion*, as we might call it, "allows you to justify any action: cruelty, intimidation, violence. The people you hurt are beneath you, because they're still blinded by society's lies. If your actions cause more violence and chaos, that's good, because it will help bring about an end to the corrupt regime." Quoted in Jessica Grose, "'Black Pill' and the Dark Anarchy of Our Political Moment," Opinion, *New York Times*, Jul. 17, 2024, https://www.nytimes/com/07/17/2024/black-pill-charloteesville-trump.html.

On grifting, meanwhile: the 1990 film version of *The Grifters*, written by Donald Westlake and based on Jim Thompson's 1963 novel of the same name, is a gritty neo-noir depiction of the fatal glamour of con artists, played here by John Cusack, Anjelica Huston (as his mother), and Annette Bening (as his femme fatale). The word *grift*, possibly a variant on *graft*, dates from early twentieth-century carnival slang and is associated with the fixed games of chance on the sideshow. Contemporary usage tends to link this idea of con games to debatable claims of identity politics or "my truth" special pleading: popular antiracism scholar Ibram X. Kendi, for example, has been a favourite target of the insult. In the recent past, Matt Taibbi of *Rolling Stone* magazine popularized the label with reference to the "long con" of Ayn Rand disciples, prominently Alan Greenspan, US Federal Reserve chairman from 1987 to 2006. See Taibbi, *Griftopia: Bubble Machines, Vampire Squids, and the Long Con That Is Breaking America* (New York: Spiegel & Grau, 2010). Apparently grifters are like the thieving vultures in *Casablanca*: Everywhere, everywhere!

23   Caroline Fredrickson, "What Worries Me Most About a Trump Presidency," Opinion, *New York Times*, Apr. 10, 2024, https://www.nytimes.com/2024/04/10/opinion/trump-presidency-corruption.html.

24   Peter Sloterdijk, *Critique of Cynical Reason* (Minneapolis: University of Minnesota Press, 1983; orig. *Kritik der zynischen Vernunft*). Sloterdijk's

central argument is that the history of ideas has underestimated the claims of figures such as Bacon and Foucault, who understood that "knowledge" really was power and nothing else. The narrative of the Enlightenment is thus revealed as a kind of self-serving fairy tale, everywhere given the lie by worldly experience. That really is cynical, though it often feels true.

25 Bruno Latour, "Why Has Critique Run Out of Steam? From Matters of Fact to Matters of Concern," *Critical Inquiry* 30, no. 2 (Winter 2004): 225-48, https://doi.org/10.1086/421123.

26 Latour, 229, italics in original.

27 Latour, 229.

28 The surveys are discussed in Bret Stephens, "How Capitalism Went off the Rails," Opinion, *New York Times*, Jun. 18, 2024, https://www.nytimes.com/2024/06/18/opinion/capitalism-inflation.html. Stephens, a hawkish conservative, agrees with the economic diagnosis that his distrust is a function of cheap money—creating cycles of borrowing and debt that erode work ethic even as they inflate expectations, all while making prices fluctuate like mad. The Edelman Trust Barometer surveys are reported at https://www.edelman.com/.

29 Charles Homans, "Republicans Place Shooting in Trump's Narrative of Persecution," *New York Times*, Jul. 14, 2024, https://www.nytimes.com/2024/07/14/us/politics/donald-trump-shooting-campaign-2024.html.

30 Joseph Heath, "When Does Critical Theory Become Conspiracy Theory?" (working paper, n.d., Academia.edu), https://www.academia.edu/89468776/When_does_Critical_Theory_Become_Conspiracy_Theory. See also Heath, "What Does a Modern Witch-Hunt Look Like?" *In Due Course* (blog), Mar. 11, 2024, https://josephheath.substack.com/p/what-does-a-modern-witch-hunt-look. I offer my own analysis of apophenia and its related phenomenon, pareidolia, in "From the Editor," in "Apophenic Adventures," ed. Mark Kingwell, special issue, *Queen's Quarterly* 127, no. 1 (Spring 2020): 6–19, https://www.proquest.com/docview/2503978536.

31 David Brooks, "Death by a Thousand Paper Cuts," Opinion, *New York Times*, Jan. 18, 2024, https://www.nytimes.com/2024/01/18/opinion/american-life-bureaucracy.html. "The growth of bureaucracy costs America over $3 trillion in lost economic output every year," accounting for about 17 percent of gross domestic product. "This situation is

especially grave in higher education. The Massachusetts Institute of Technology now has almost eight times as many non-faculty employees as faculty employees. In the University of California system, the number of managers and senior professionals swelled by 60 percent between 2004 and 2014. The number of tenure-track faculty members grew by just 8 percent." Those numbers don't lie: any professor knows that proliferating bureaucracy is the bane of academic life.

32 C. S. Lewis, *The Abolition of Man* (1943; POD, Valde Books, n.d.), 34. This is, alas, a terrible print version of Lewis's intermittently brilliant work. A strict academic critique of this popular essay would be that the version of "emotivism" Lewis offers as an obvious evil of modern thought is a straw man. But the essay is on target about undue faith in the authority of science, and also rather prescient about the techno-optimism that today goes by the name "transhumanism." See Joseph A. Kohm Jr, "What Does C. S. Lewis's 'The Abolition of Man' Have to Say After 80 Years?" review, The Gospel Coalition, US ed., Aug. 25, 2023, https://www.thegospelcoalition.org/reviews/abolition-man/. For those keeping track, *transhumanism* concerns elite technological and cognitive upgrades for selected wealthy subpopulations. It calls for a version of eugenics—or anyway is consistent with such an übermenschlich program. By contrast, I defend *posthumanism* here and elsewhere. I mean by that a sense of shared destiny with evolving life forms that justly integrates technology into everyday life. See my *Singular Creatures: Robots, Rights, and the Politics of Posthumanism* (Kingston and Montreal: McGill-Queen's University Press, 2022).

33 Immanuel Kant, *Critique of the Power of Judgment*, ed. Paul Guyer, trans. Paul Guyer and Eric Matthews. (Cambridge: Cambridge University Press, 2000), 5.316. The example is notable because the Temple of Isis that Kant is praising is part of a modern aesthetic appreciation of an ancient cult that was itself a Greco-Roman incorporation of an earlier Egyptian religion. Today we would call this cultural appropriation.

34 The most penetrating philosophical analysis I know in this region is Ian Hacking, *The Social Construction of What?* (Cambridge, MA: Harvard University Press, 1999). Hacking debunks some of the swirling non-sense of the then-contemporary "science wars," but also offers conceptual tools to navigate many shoals of public discourse and policy.

35 *Enchiridion* comes from a Greek root that means "to hold in one's hand": hence *handbook* or *manual*, a volume filled with ideas ready to hand. It is

said that Marcus Aurelius, author of his own influential manual of Stoic *Meditations*, kept a copy of Epictetus inside his breastplate during battle. The first printed version was a 1497 Latin translation, and it has never gone out of print since. I stole my father's Modern American Library edition from his living room bookshelf went I went off to university in the summer of 1980, and I have it still.

36   I made my own stab at the argument about the need for humility and civility in polarized debate in "Who Has the Right to Say What's Correct?" Opinion, *Globe and Mail*, Sep. 6, 2016, https://www.theglobeandmail.com/opinion/who-has-the-right-to-say-whats-correct/article31697013/; and then, eight years and seventy-four *Globe* columns later, I offered "Can We Rescue Civility in Public Discourse?" Opinion, *Globe and Mail*, Feb. 24, 2024, https://www.theglobeandmail.com/opinion/article-can-we-rescue-civility-in-public-discourse/. The second of these laments further put on record the fact that my *initial* philosophical defence of civility as a political virtue had been published some three decades earlier: my first book, *A Civil Tongue: Justice, Dialogue, and the Politics of Pluralism* (University Park, PA: Penn State University Press, 1995). Sometimes it seems like we have to say the same things over and over. (Heavy sigh. But no melancholy!)

Meanwhile, the expression about trusting people only as far as you can throw them sounds well worn, maybe even Shakespearean, but in fact probably dates from the early 1900s. Variants include "as far as I could spit" and "as far as I could throw Manhattan." There is a slight connection to the common quip that a given book is not one to be *laid lightly aside*—it should be *thrown with great force*. Attributed by Bennett Cerf to Dorothy Parker, this joke in fact started with Frank Doland, or Bill Miller, or some other writer you've never heard of. But Parker did offer this related insult, useful for many occasions: "That gifted entertainer, the Countess of Oxford and Asquith, author of *The Autobiography of Margot Asquith* (four volumes, neatly boxed, suitable for throwing purposes), reverts to tripe in a new book deftly entitled *Lay Sermons.*" Recent Books, *New Yorker*, Oct. 22, 1927, 98. *Reverts to tripe* is also not bad.

37   Here we ought to follow the line of thought explored by Slavoj Žižek, attempting to rehabilitate (or interrogate) the "failed" promise of standard Marxist critique of ideology. He does so inventively, by employing

the novel lens of Lacanian psychoanalysis. See Žižek, *The Sublime Object of Ideology*, 2nd ed. (London: Verso, 2009). Also, for a comment on the persistence of "publicity" as a goal of leftist theory, and the resulting condition of "Habermasochism" when trying to rescue a rational public sphere, see Jodi Dean, "Publicity's Secret," *Political Theory* 29, no. 5 (Oct. 2001), 624–50, https://www.jstor.org/stable/3072532.

38   For more on this particular aspect of context collapse and polysemous imagery, see Jacques Rancière, *The Emancipated Spectator*, trans. Gregory Elliott (London: Verso, 2009). A central target of Rancière's critique of passive spectation and its discontents is Guy Debord and the self-abnegating Situationist movement. Their tactics of *dérive* (drift) and *détournement* (repurposing) proved inadequate to the global reach of image-dominated culture, in particular the trust-corroding coagulation of media, technology, politics, and capital we experience every day. Rancière retains a modified optimism in his nuanced notion of emancipation as a kind of shared ignorance. Guy Debord, *Society of the Spectacle*, trans. Donald Nicolson-Smith (1967; New York: Zone Books, 1994).

39   Julian Jaynes, *The Origin of Consciousness in the Breakdown of the Bicameral Mind* (New York: Houghton Mifflin, 1976).

40   Directed by Sidney Lumet, written by Paddy Chayefsky—who else?

FIRST MEDITATION: Before It Questions You

1   *Doxa* usually arises in academic discussion as standing distinct from *episteme*, or knowledge, which in turn gives us *epistemic* (having the status of belief) and *epistemological* (indicating a theory of knowledge). I should say that I have no particular faith that the term "doxaholism" will catch on. Probably not.

2   Hegel's *Elements of the Philosophy of Right* (1821) is where this distinction gets its most robust discussion, but the community/society distinction is in fact basic to all modern political thought. A recent riff on the supremacy of community over society, and an intellectual touchstone for some of the more bookish members of the MAGA tribe, is Samuel Francis, "Crime Story: The Godfather as Political Metaphor," *Chronicles: A Magazine of American Culture*, Mar. 7, 2019, https://chroniclesmagazine.org/web/crime-story-the-godfather-as-political-metaphor/. Francis

has many faults, but obscuring his inspiration for how political leaders should act is not one of them.

3   Arthur Schopenhauer, *Parerga and Paralipomena*, trans. E. F. J. Payne (1851; Oxford: Oxford University Press, 2001), 2.31, 651–52. The insight, sometimes called the Porcupine's (or Hedgehog's) Dilemma, is conveyed in the form of a parable:

> One cold winter's day, a number of porcupines huddled together quite closely in order through their mutual warmth to prevent themselves from being frozen. But they soon felt the effect of their quills on one another, which made them again move apart. Now when the need for warmth once more brought them together, the drawback of the quills was repeated so that they were tossed between two evils, until they had discovered the proper distance from which they could best tolerate one another.

The *two evils* here are personal poles, each equally unattractive. But they could be considered political as well. The story goes on:

> Thus the need for society which springs from the emptiness and monotony of men's lives, drives them together; but their many unpleasant and repulsive qualities and insufferable drawbacks once more drive them apart. The mean distance which they finally discover, and which enables them to endure being together, is politeness and good manners. Whoever does not keep to this, is told in England to "*keep his distance.*" By virtue thereof, it is true that the need for mutual warmth will be only imperfectly satisfied, but on the other hand, the prick of the quills will not be felt. Yet whoever has a great deal of internal warmth of his own will prefer to keep away from society in order to avoid giving or receiving trouble or annoyance.

The German phrase that is translated here as "politeness and good manners" is *feine Sitte*—which might also be translated as good customs, or decency: civility, in other words.

4   Murthy's call was widely reported. See Ellen Barry and Cecilia Kang, "Surgeon General Calls for Warning Labels on Social Media Platforms,"

New York Times, Jun. 18, 2024, https://www.nytimes.com/2024/06/17/health/surgeon-general-social-media-warning-label.html. This is a positive development, but there is still much resistance to the idea that addiction may be facilitated by nonchemical forms of stimulation. A case in point: in 2021, after I published some philosophical thoughts on boredom as an addictive feature of neoliberal consumer capitalism—the way we are pulled into cycles of stimulation and enervation by intentionally designed media—I was invited to submit a summary article to the *Canadian Medical Association Journal*. I did that. I had not known that even invited articles are sent out for peer review at this journal. The reviews were mostly negative, though they did recommend publication—as long as I removed *any mention* of addiction. This strikes me as at once both quite aggressive policing of disciplinary boundaries and not very helpful public discourse. The former may be defensible, the latter certainly less so. In any case, I withdrew the article.

5 See Harry G. Frankfurt, "Freedom of the Will and the Concept of a Person," *Journal of Philosophy* 68, no. 1 (1971): 5–20.

6 The issue of trigger warnings has become quite convoluted. If the goal is preparing for disturbing content, the warning itself could be considered triggering, thus defeating its purpose. Or the warning, while well intentioned, will not really prepare the viewer or reader from effectively realized disturbing material. If we want art (or anything else) to do more than coddle and reassure, the risk is that sometimes this won't be personally comfortable *if it's done well*. The sad endgame of the demand for content warnings might be a recent issue of my university's literary review. Almost all of the contributions were framed by one kind of warning or another. My favourite was a piece that carried a warning that it addressed suicide. Then the first sentence of the short story was: "I never recovered from my aunt's suicide." Forewarned is forearmed?

7 The statistics are remarkably consistent across numerous metrics and polling devices. I use here source material from the World Inequality Database (https://wid.world/).

8 A number of centre-left writers and some avowed Marxists launched what might be called "third wave" interventions in a field dominated by sjws on the cultural left (who had originally coined the term as part of antiracist inside slang) and reflexive anti-wokesters on the smug right (who debased that once-rallying moniker into a thought-free insult).

The resulting left-leaning critiques of wokeness have had limited success. See, for example, Ian Buruma, "Doing the Work: The Protestant Ethic and the Spirit of Wokeness," *Harper's Magazine*, Jul. 2023, which compares wokeness to the Protestant work ethic and tradition of public self-recrimination; John McWhorter, *Woke Racism: How a New Religion Has Betrayed Black America* (New York: Portfolio / Penguin, 2021), which contends that wokeness is self-defeating, betraying Black political interests; and Susan Neiman, *Left Is Not Woke* (New York: Polity Books, 2023), which argues that genuine left politics are fundamentally materialist, not cultural or superstructural. It's important to note, as he himself does, that Buruma lost his job as editor of the prestigious *New York Review of Books* over the decision to publish a self-justifying memoir by former CBC radio personality Jian Ghomeshi, who was acquitted of four sexual assault charges in 2014 after signing a peace bond that did not include an admission of guilt. Buruma refused to apologize for the decision to give Ghomeshi access to this literary platform.

9   Jennifer Schuessler, "PEN America Cancels Literary Awards Ceremony amid Gaza War Fallout," *New York Times*, Apr. 22, 2024, https://www.nytimes.com/2024/04/22/arts/pen-america-literary-awards.html.

10 The cynicism, indeed, lies on the other side of this question, some of whose supporters deploy moral outrage as a mechanism of social control. "There's a distasteful irony in a literary community that has gone to the barricades fighting book 'bans' now rallying to boycott authors based on their ethnoreligious identity," one critic noted of the PEN boycott and the blacklisting of "Zionist" writers. "For a growing set of writers, declaring one's belief that the world's only Jewish state is a genocidal entity whose dismantlement is necessary for the advancement of humankind is a political fashion statement, a bauble one parades around in order to signify being on the right team. As was Stalinism for an earlier generation of left-wing literary intellectuals, so is antisemitism becoming the avant-garde." See James Kirchick, "A Chill Has Fallen over Jews in Publishing," Opinion, *New York Times*, May 27, 2024, https://www.nytimes.com/2024/05/27/opinion/publishing-literary-antisemitism.html.

11 He meant Austin Clarke, also described as "a minor-league Leroi Jones," whom Richler believed had used imagined racial persecution to advance his "mediocre" writing career. See Charles Foran, *Mordecai:*

The Life and Times (Toronto: Alfred A. Knopf Canada, 2010). Richler's most conspicuous discussion of nationalist issue-envy is his *Oh Canada! Oh Quebec! Requiem for a Divided Country* (New York: Knopf, 1992), but he had discussed the October Crisis in several publications before this notorious book, which began in (unforgivably, for some) the *New Yorker*, Sep. 23, 1991.

12   Even critical responses to the protests had a tang of nostalgia for the 1960s, as many commentators hastened to say. Donald Trump, criticizing President Biden's tepid response to the 2024 university protest encampments, referred to the "radical extremists and far-left agitators" who were "terrorizing college campuses"—phrases dusty with age. His only novel twist, befitting the times, was to suggest that these same crazies were the "base" of the actually centre-liberal, pro-Israel Biden.

13   I don't recommend spending a lot of time thinking about it, but Justin Caffier, "Every Insult the Right Uses to Troll Liberals, Explained," Politics, *Vice*, Feb. 6, 2017, https://www.vice.com/en/article/mg9pvx/every-insult-the-right-uses-to-troll-liberals-explained. Fair warning: as my all-vigilant browser saw fit to inform me when I clicked on this link, that article is "more than five years old."

14   Catherine Porter, "Cheers, Fears and 'Le Wokisme': How the World Sees US Campus Protests," *New York Times*, May 3, 2024, https://www.nytimes.com/2024/05/03/world/europe/campus-protests-rorschach-test.html.

15   Consider, as a case study, the journalist Nellie Bowles, who left the *New York Times* because she thought it was too "woke." She then published a book written in the bemused-fogey, P. J. O'Rourke tradition, called *Morning after the Revolution: Dispatches from the Wrong Side of History* (New York: Thesis, 2024), detailing the risible excesses of left-wing ideology. Fine. But as one of her former *Times* colleagues pointed out, the moment of the book had come and gone; worse, if that moment was indeed over, the Right had sabotaged one of its own key talking points just before a momentous American presidential election. See Michelle Goldberg, "Wokeness Is Dying. We Might Miss It," Opinion, *New York Times*, May 17, 2024, https://www.nytimes.com/2024/05/17/opinion/wokeness-is-dying-we-might-miss-it.html. This little intramural episode is itself liable to erode people's interest, if not trust, in the media. If your idea of an unbearable "woke" editorial environment is

the *New York Times*—well, please check your engine. I will say again that
I sometimes cite *Times* articles in the present book, but not as a sign of
ideological approval—or disapproval, for that matter. Just evidence.

16 Frankfurt school social theorist Herbert Marcuse is the source of the
phrase and the theory of *repressive tolerance*. See Herbert Marcuse,
"Repressive Tolerance," in *A Critique of Pure Tolerance*, ed. Robert Paul
Wolff, Barrington Moore Jr, and Herbert Marcuse (Boston: Beacon
Press, 1969), 95–137. But it is a conceptual error to deploy Marcuse as
an advocate of illiberal radicalism standing opposed to, say, the staunch
liberal freedom of thought and expression defended by John Stuart Mill
in *On Liberty* (1859). In fact, Marcuse's position is subtle and dialectical,
noting both the power of free expression and its tendency to find voice
among the privileged; that freedom is itself a form of repression; and
that there is no coherent authority either for the liberal or the illiberal
program. The so-called Mill-Marcuse debate, favourite trope of campus
antiradicals, is mostly a fiction.

17 The art critic Harold Rosenberg is credited with coining the phrase
"herd of independent minds," which he used to skewer the tendency
among advanced art critics and mavens, also artists themselves, to claim
radical positions. "The Herd of Independent Minds: Has the Avant-
Garde Its Own Mass Culture?," *Commentary*, Sep. 1948, https://www.
commentary.org/articles/harold-rosenberg-2/the-herd-of-independent-
minds-has-the-avant-garde-its-own-mass-culture/. Rosenberg was himself pushing back against the rhetorical tendency, often scornful, shown
by *Partisan Review* critics and others, notably Dwight Macdonald, for
their critical, almost Adornoesque disdain of mass culture, even as they
themselves were becoming products, and prisoners, of it. As a break-
away thinker from the same group, Rosenberg is here inadvertently
recording in microcosm the cozy/bitchy moment of New York Jewish
intellectual life post-1945. To put the matter simply: if they were *all*
doing this, who was in the sluggish mainstream holding them back? If
we're all members of the avant-garde, who is the main body? The point
is widely applicable in any society based on spectacle: fads driven by
what Tom Wolfe called "radical chic" are ever prone to self-defeat. Once
everybody's a rebel, it's a fashion statement, not an actual statement.
"Radical Chic: That Party at Lenny's," *New York Magazine*, Jun. 8, 1970;
reprinted Sep. 15, 2023, https://nymag.com/article/tom-wolfe-radical-

chic-that-party-at-lennys.html. Wolfe's account of a fundraiser for the Black Panthers held at the opulent Manhattan apartment of conductor Leonard Bernstein is a paragon of satirical journalism. A little taste:

> *Mmmmmmmmmmmmmmmm.* These are nice. Little Roquefort cheese morsels rolled in crushed nuts. Very tasty. Very subtle. It's the way the dry sackiness of the nuts tiptoes up against the dour savour of the cheese that is so nice, so subtle. Wonder what the Black Panthers eat here on the hors d'oeuvre trail? Do the Panthers like little Roquefort cheese morsels wrapped in crushed nuts this way, and asparagus tips in mayonnaise dabs, and meatballs petites au Coq Hardi, all of which are at this very moment being offered to them on gadrooned silver platters by maids in black uniforms with hand-ironed white aprons.

Like that, for about twenty-five thousand delicious words. Wolfe was prescient about the identity-driven political tangles that are with us still. He notes, for example, that "black nationalist literature sometimes seemed to identify the Arabs as blacks fighting the white Israelis." And he declares that he is documenting "an age when the youth of the New Left had re-programmed the whole circuitry of Left opposition to oppression."

18 The other prominent slogan from the same movement is a laconic critique of the ideology of work and utility: *Sous les pavés, la plage*—"Underneath the cobblestones, the beach!" The dislodged cobblestones can be used as makeshift projectiles even as they reveal the comforting sand under them. See "Idling Toward Heaven: The Last Defence You Will Ever Need," in *The Idler's Glossary*, ed. Joshua Glenn and Mark Kingwell (Windsor, ON: Biblioasis, 2008).

19 For what it's worth, there is a game called Just Act Natural which sells itself as "a crazy online multiplayer party game full of deception." In this contest, you "compete against your friends in a continuously expanding pool of game modes and stages. Our take on the party game genre requires you to be as deceitful as possible. Fool your friends, don't act sus[picious], just act natural." Fun!

20 Once a popular stock-in-trade of existential thinking, the normative ideal of authenticity is these days complicated by action theory, advanced moral philosophy, the psychology of automaticity, and (not

least) identity politics. See Charles Taylor, *The Ethics of Authenticity* (Cambridge, MA: Harvard University Press, 1991); also Lauren Bialystok, "Authenticity and the Limits of Philosophy," *Dialogue* 53, no. 2 (2014): 271–98, https://doi-org /10.1017/S001221731300111X. "Almost everyone has had an intuitive experience of authenticity that seems to reveal a glimmer of one's true identity," Bialystok notes. "Yet by positing the existence of a 'true self,' authenticity introduces metaphysical challenges that resist systematic solutions. . . . This analysis casts doubt on the possibility of generating a complete philosophical account of authenticity." There is, among other things, a looming "homunculus regress" of the type Aristotle noted about Plato. If the truth—in this case, the truth of authentic alignment—is correctly perceived only by some internal observer, who exactly is inside the little observer, observing *that*? Uh oh! The only alternative to infinite regress would seem to be acceptance that authenticity, like consciousness itself, is best understood as a *recursive function*. We find ourselves precisely in the act of searching for ourselves.

21 Documentary filmmaker Errol Morris used the missing term as the title for his film about Rumsfeld's life and political career, in effect positioning the politician himself as *The Unknown Known* (2013).

22 A note on *nada*, which of course means "nothing" in Spanish. But nothingness is never nothing at all. One hesitates to get even more scholarly about this odd film and its wrestling-hero protagonist, but let us note for the record that there is a famous Spanish novel by Carmen Laforet with the title *Nada* (1945), based on her own childhood torn apart by the ravages of the Spanish Civil War. And then there is a French neo-noir thriller called *Nada* by the great Jean-Patrick Manchette (1971), which features a young anarchist, orphaned during the very same Spanish Civil War, who later becomes part of a crime gang that also includes a disaffected May 1968 revolutionary, an angry philosophy teacher, an alcoholic, and an aging French Resistance fighter. Together they plan to kidnap the American ambassador to France, with violent results. There is a 1974 film version of this story, directed by Claude Chabrol. Sunglasses do not, alas, feature prominently in this film—when they so easily might have, you know?

23 Quoted in Decca Aitkenhead, "Slavoj Žižek: 'Humanity Is OK, but 99% of People Are Boring Idiots,'" *The Guardian*, Jun. 20, 2012, https://www.theguardian.com/culture/2012/jun/10/slavoj-zizek -humanity-ok-people-boring.

24 *Dimidium facti, qui coepit, habet; sapere aude, incipe.* The shortened imperative version—*sapere aude*—is sometimes adopted as a fancy motto for colleges and academic societies. That might serve as the title of the present book. But—you know, it's in *Latin*, so . . .

25 Always assuming that the World Bank is not already a target of one's particular conspiracy theory, the World Bank Group is a good source for reliable data and policy suggestions. On Musk and his plan to leave Earth behind, see Loren Thompson, "Five Existential Challenges Facing Elon Musk's SpaceX ," *Forbes*, Dec. 11, 2018, https://www.forbes.com/sites/lorenthompson/2018/12/11/five-existential-challenges-facing-elon-musks-spacex/. The listed challenges are not really existential, more about limits on capital viability of space travel. But I guess that's more or less what "existential" means over at *Forbes*.

26 For an effective brief treatment of these failed promises of the Enlightenment Project, see Andrew Potter, *On Decline: Stagnation, Nostalgia, and Why Every Year Is the Worst One Ever* (Windsor, ON: Biblioasis, 2021). A more complex and overtly philosophical account may be found in Alasdair MacIntyre, *After Virtue: A Study in Moral Theory* (South Bend, IN: Notre Dame University Press, 1981). MacIntyre's careful assessment of the emptiness of contemporary moral discourse leads him to a defence of virtue ethics, the Aristotelian-inflected school of moral philosophy for which he has been a leading voice.

27 A good overview of the main conceptions of political authority, in part based on Plato's description of just and unjust city types in *Republic*, is Fabian Wendt, *Authority* (New York: Polity Press, 2018).

28 Influenced by Leo Strauss's concept of "hidden writing," Allan Bloom's "Interpretive Essay" for his translation of *Republic* (1968; New York: Basic Books, 1991) sets out this ironic reading of the dialogue, especially with respect to the notion of the philosopher-king.

29 Jacques Derrida's essay "Force of Law: The 'Mystical Foundation of Authority,'" offers a dazzling account of political authority rooted in the insights of Walter Benjamin. In *Deconstruction and the Possibility of Justice*, ed. Drucilla Cornell, Michel Rosenfeld, and David Gray Carlson (New York: Routledge, 1992), 3–67.

30 Jürgen Habermas, *Legitimation Crisis*, trans. Thomas McCarthy (Boston: Beacon press, 1975). In this landmark early book, Habermas argues persuasively that post-war crisis is complex and interlinked, binding

together economic and rational deficits with political and motivational breakdowns.

31   That's Doctor of Fine Arts, if it matters, and it is usually awarded honoris causa. As a holder of this degree myself—thank you again, Nova Scotia College of Art and Design!—I can say that it is a very nice honour that doesn't guarantee any special expertise or training.

32   Personally, and notwithstanding the previous footnote, I don't like being called "Doctor Kingwell." I suspect that people using the title want something from me. It also makes me feel like I'm one of those people in the soft-drink ads, like rapper Dr Dre, basketball legend Dr J, or Kelsey Grammer, who played Dr Frasier Crane on television. Trust me! (For the record, Dr Dre's was the best entry in this campaign: he smiles knowingly at the camera when he delivers the line. Come on, man!)

33   Alana Newhouse, "Everything Is Broken: And How to Fix It," News & Politics, *Tablet*, Jan. 14, 2021, https://www.tabletmag.com/sections/news/articles/everything-is-broken. (The centre-left, Jewish publication *Tablet* magazine is not to be confused with the conservative, Catholic periodical *The Tablet*.) As Newhouse argues, "For seven decades, the country's intellectual and cultural life was produced and protected by a set of institutions—universities, newspapers, magazines, record companies, professional associations, cultural venues, publishing houses, Hollywood studios, think tanks, etc. Collectively, these institutions reflected a diversity of experiences and then stamped them all as 'American'—conjuring coherence out of the chaos of a big and unwieldy country. . . . But, beginning in the 1970s, the economic ground underneath this landscape began to come apart."

34   One immediate reply to this is to note, for example, the successful game-theory strategy known as *cooperate-and-defect*. In modelling the possibilities of coordinated action between rival rational agents, one successful long-term strategy in Prisoner's Dilemma-style situations involves being "nice" as a baseline, i.e., predisposed to cooperation, but then defecting as soon as rivals defect. The details on this and other game-theory strategies are now so complex that the original Prisoner's Dilemma has blossomed into an intellectual growth industry that has been compared to kudzu and *E. coli*, infecting every discipline from economics to sports. But at its core lies a basic human problem: why should we cooperate with others, when not doing so is often to our advantage?

35 David Hume, *A Treatise of Human Nature*, ed. L. A. Selby-Bigge, 1888; 2nd ed. with text revised and variant readings by P. H. Nidditch (Oxford: Clarendon Press, 1978), xiii. Originally published in 3 vols., 1739–40.

36 Christopher Nolan's *Oppenheimer* (2023) was a blockbuster hit of the early postpandemic cinema resurgence, even as it was executed under strike conditions in the Hollywood dream factory. Its press pairing with the Greta Gerwig effort *Barbie* (2023), a master class in melding product placement and market synergies with putative ideological critique, is somehow the sure lasting impression of that 2023 summer of deadly heat waves and cascading airport delays. Barbenheimer 4eva!

37 I can say now, after many long years, that the only valuable remnant in all that early academic work is my appreciation for Russell Hoban's *Riddley Walker* (1980) and Walter Miller's sprawling *A Canticle for Leibowitz* (1959).

38 I report in all honesty that I now believe I was on the wrong side of the argument then, largely as a result of my Catholic upbringing. Convinced that human life begins at conception, I took as a logical conclusion that abortion was wrongful killing. But the premise is faulty: *life* is not a strictly biological category, rather an ethical one, and so may be taken to begin at some point after the beginning of an organism's development. Coming to see that taught me something essential about how arguments work—a valid argument with an untrue premise can generate an unsound result—but probably more important, about what it means to change your mind.

39 Imagine my chagrin when I saw *Reality Bites* (Ben Stiller, dir., 1994) for the first time, and there was Ethan Hawke doing almost exactly the same thing. Just another clue that life and the movies are endlessly permeable? Or maybe just more evidence that most indie filmmakers take a philosophy class somewhere along the way to the seat behind the camera.

40 For those who need a nudge, Gekko is the rapacious investment-bank buccaneer played by Michael Douglas in the 1987 film *Wall Street*, directed by Oliver Stone. On Trump's stuck-in-amber values, see Maggie Haberman, "How Donald Trump Still Lives in the 1980s," Political Memo, *New York Times*, May 25, 2024, https://www.nytimes.com/2024/05/25/us/politics/trump-1980s-manhattan.html. It's worth noting that Trump's ghostwritten bestseller, *The Art of the Deal*, was published in the same year as Stone's film was released. The rest is (living) history.

41   Potter, *On Decline*.

42   Hart Research Associates (Washington, DC); reported in *Harper's Magazine*, Aug. 2023, 9, 61.

43   Jeff Tweedy, of the band Wilco, thinks so: "The divisions we created were embarrassing," he said of his early musical preferences. "I have sometimes even wondered if these youthful skirmishes over musical taste weren't a childhood version of the current situation our country now finds itself in. Were people of my generation so good at dividing ourselves into factions based on stupid, insignificant differences that we simply never stopped doing it?" He went on: "Someone smarter than me has probably mapped the parallels between Journey fans and X fans and the current binary of political right and left. Or if no one has, someone should." My vote for that smarter person would be Carl Wilson, in his excellent assessment *Céline Dion's "Let's Talk About Love": A Journey to the End of Taste* (London: Bloomsbury, 2007). Tweedy himself offers this pertinent lesson: "To this day, whenever I think I dislike a piece of music, I think about 'Dancing Queen' and am humbled. That song taught me that I can't ever completely trust my negative reactions." Jeff Tweedy, "I Thought I Hated Pop Music. 'Dancing Queen' Changed My Mind," Opinion, *New York Times*, Nov. 2, 2023, https://www.nytimes.com/2023/11/02/opinion/sunday/abba-dancing-queen-pop-music.html. I remain unsure about "Dancing Queen," but I can say that Josh Turner's stripped-down banjo-and-guitar YouTube version of "Mamma Mia" is excellent (https://youtu.be/lWpmALY8Z_s).

44   I offer long-overdue thanks here to my first instructors in political theory, Gad Horowitz and Alkis Kontos. The genius of first-year Canadian politics at the time was J. Stefan Dupré.

45   The cover was by English graphic artist Philip Castle, an airbrush specialist known for his movie posters for Stanley Kubrick's *A Clockwork Orange* and *Full Metal Jacket*, as well as album covers for David Bowie, The Cars, Mott the Hoople, and Pulp. Likewise, airplanes and spaceships of various kinds and metallic pin-up–style posters of beautiful women, including Farrah Fawcett. If the store had stocked instead the contemporary American edition, I would have seen a plain cover with an arcane circular symbol, suggesting a dreary anthropological study best relegated to the Maybe Someday list.

46   Roland Barthes, preface to *Mythologies*, trans., Annette Lavers (1957; New York: Farrar, Straus & Giroux, 1970), 9.

47 It's a sad commentary on political divides in the United States that, judging by the frequent ads, right-wing talk radio is mostly the preserve of the chronically sleepless, overweight, and debt ridden. There is a good deal of bogus sanctimony, but also frequent allusions to "family" and how "we all must care for each other"—just not the ones who don't belong. This is what must be called *family-style biofascism*. For those interested, the Gagne/Vachon vs. Ventura/Adonis tag-team bout that is probably the caller's touchstone took place on March 22, 1980. You can watch it on YouTube (https://www.youtube.com/watch?v=I2rvbEgEdek)!

48 Wrestling images and tropes cling to Donald Trump, naturally enough, but also to his would-be successors. "If Trump emerged from the make-believe world of pro wrestling, [Vivek] Ramaswamy emerges from the make-believe world of social media and the third-rate sectors of the right-wing media sphere," David Brooks wrote during the 2024 presidential campaign. "His statements are brisk, in-your-face provocations intended to produce temporary populist dopamine highs. It's all performative show. Ramaswamy seems as uninterested in actually governing as his idol." David Brooks, "Nikki Haley Is the Best Trump Alternative," Opinion, *New York Times*, Aug. 25, 2023, https://www.nytimes.com/2023/08/24/opinion/nikki-haley-republican-debate-winner.html.

SECOND MEDITATION: Trust No One

1 Leacock actually specified a McGill University economics doctorate, his own alma mater and terminal degree: "The recipient of instruction is examined for the last time in his life, and is pronounced completely full. After this, no new ideas can be imparted to him." I will also note an echo here of Richard Rorty, *Contingency, Irony, and Solidarity* (Cambridge: Cambridge University Press, 1989), a collection of linked essays by the neopragmatist American philosopher. A former professor of mine, Fred Flahiff, looking at the rather smug photo of the author on the book's cover, said, "Well, not much of any of those three for *him*."

2 Richard Hofstadter, "The Paranoid Style in American Politics," *Harper's Magazine* 229, no. 1374 (Nov. 1964): 77–86, https://www.proquest.com/pao/docview/1301526856/; see also Hofstadter, *Anti-Intellectualism in American Life* (New York: Knopf, 1963). The link between paranoia and anti-intellectualism is not coincidental: when the forces of expert

opinion begin to seem elite, effete, and contemptuous, the natural psychological back-formation is to frame this as a plot, a scheme of control, not merely a divergence between aligned interests or a different cognitive style. The paranoid and the conspiracist are not making claims about *diverse learning styles*, like fussy helicopter parents of gifted kids; they are claiming alternative *facts*, hidden *systems*, other *worlds*. They are often, as Hofstadter acknowledges with some admiration, exceptional scholars of their mania.

3   Hofstadter, "Paranoid Style," 77.

4   For example, Dick Hebdige, *Subculture: The Meaning of Style* (London: Routledge, 1979), a landmark in the semiotics of punk music, fashion, and popular culture.

5   As noted already, I have a longstanding and somewhat geeky interest in this complex quirk of the human mind, especially in the form of political conspiracy thinking. It forms a large general theme of my early book *Dreams of Millennium* (Toronto: Viking, 1996; Boston: Faber & Faber, 1997), which maybe now stands as a tiny time capsule from those days. One of the unforeseen pleasures of this scholarly interest—if pleasure is the right word—is that one becomes a lightning rod for outré beliefs and tiny pockets of nuttiness often communicated via scribbled letters, long typescripts, and other old-school, pre-internet platforms. Memos from Konspiracy Kanada . . .

6   Michelle Goldberg, "The Radicalization of the Young Right," Opinion, *New York Times*, Jul. 31, 2023, https://www.nytimes.com/2023/07/31/opinion/radicalization-republican-party.html. See also Fritz R. Stern, *The Politics of Cultural Despair: A Study in the Rise of the Germanic Ideology* (1961; Berkeley: University of California Press, 1974), which links everything-is-going-to-liberal-hell rhetoric with corresponding rises in nationalism, populism, and autocratic leaders. See too David French, "The Lost Boys of the American Right," Opinion, *New York Times*, Aug. 13, 2023, https://www.nytimes.com/2023/08/13/opinion/masculinity-right-young-men.html. French notes, among other signs and portents, the sudden ubiquity of the phrase "knows what time it is" in alt-right rhetoric. The formation is hardly new: I recall a grad-school classmate saying of his father, an imperious surgeon, that "he always knows what time it is." French likewise highlights the weakness that afflicts the kind of racist and bigoted rhetoric that starts with irony

and "jokes" but becomes, over time, sincerely held belief. One (maybe) remorseful troll tells French, "What starts off as joking can very quickly become unironically internalized as an actual belief." To which the only possible response is: Well, *duh.*

7   Van Jones (@VanJones68), "Trump is pimping people's pain. #Trump-Indictment," X, video clip from *Anderson Cooper 360,* C N N, 0:53, Jun. 8, 2023, https://x.com/VanJones68/status/1666988827909718017. Jones is a former member of the Obama White House, who features in a regular news panel on C N N, and whose books of political commentary include *Beyond the Messy Truth: How We Came Apart, How We Come Together* (New York: Ballantine, 2017).

8   Joshua Glenn has analyzed the deep structures of this paranoid plot in "Minute 9: Condor," *HiLoBrow* (blog), Dec. 11, 2023, https://www. hilobrow.com/2023/12/11/minute-9-condor/. As Glenn points out, these low-level functionaries are complicit in their own disintermediation: they act as filters for intelligence without knowing what they are filtering *for.* We might imagine them as former journalists and graduate students who process information without ingesting it. Hey, it's a job.

9   Thomas Pynchon, Don DeLillo, Jonathan Franzen, David Foster Wallace, and Jonathan Lethem are the key American masters of the form, but the systems novel can be found in cultures worldwide: Michel Houellebecq (France), Tom McCarthy (England), Haruki Murakami (Japan), etc.

10   Consider, for example, *All the President's Men* (1976, Redford again, looking the same, Watergate); *Executive Action* (1973, Kennedy assassination); *The Conversation* (1974, state surveillance); *The Parallax View* (1974, state surveillance); *Klute* (1971, surveillance); *Marathon Man* (1976, state surveillance and Nazis)—all of these set alongside the nutjob storylines of *Capricorn One* (1977, fake space mission) and *The Boys from Brazil* (1978, eugenics takeover plot and, yes, Nazis).

11   Philosopher Thomas Nagel mounts a valiant rescue mission of this long-standing dream in *The View from Nowhere* (Oxford: Oxford University Press, 1986): "The fundamental idea behind both the validity and the limits of objectivity is that we are small creatures in a big world of which we have only very partial understanding, and that how things seem to us depends both on the world and on our constitution" (5). The resulting "two standpoints" view does not solve this, or really any,

deep philosophical problem, still less the political consequences that
flow from conflict between standpoints.

12   David Brooks, "I Won't Let Donald Trump Invade My Brain," Opinion,
     New York Times, Jun. 15, 2023, https://www.nytimes.com/2023/06/15/
     opinion/trump-indictment-president.html. Ah, but he has, he has!

13   Ian Hacking, *The Social Construction of What?* (Cambridge, MA: Harvard
     University Press, 2000). Hacking, here writing in a signature mixture of
     analytic philosophy of science leavened by a serious study of Foucault,
     is an invaluable resource. His analyses of mental illness and multiple
     personality disorders, motivated by Foucault's earlier study, is especially
     strong.

14   A source that got a lot of attention on this collapse was Ben McKenzie
     with Jacob Silverman, *Easy Money: Cryptocurrency, Casino Capitalism,
     and the Golden Age of Fraud* (New York: Harry N. Abrams, 2023). McK-
     enzie, an actor familiar from his roles on the television series *The OC*
     and *Gotham*, is forthright and funny on the shortcomings of Bitcoin and
     its various parallel systems, which had smoothly lifted millions from
     the wallets of investors, rich and poor.

15   See Paul Krugman, "The Paranoid Style in American Plutocrats," Opinion,
     New York Times, Aug. 28, 2023, https://www.nytimes.com/2023/08/28/
     opinion/columnists/covid-climate-cryptocurrency-plutocrats.html.
     "Success all too easily feeds the belief that you're smarter than anyone
     else, so you can master any subject without working hard to understand
     the issues or consulting people who have," Krugman writes; "this kind of
     arrogance may be especially rife among tech types who got rich by defy-
     ing conventional wisdom. The wealthy also tend to surround themselves
     with people who tell them how brilliant they are or with other wealthy
     people who join them in mutual affirmation of their superiority to mere
     technical drones—what the tech writer Anil Dash calls 'V.C. QAnon.'"
     (That's V.C. as in *venture capital*, not *Victoria Cross*.)

16   James Buchan, *Frozen Desire: The Meaning of Money* (London: Picador,
     1997). A very illuminating and entertaining book on a difficult subject.
     See also, in an earlier sociological treatment, Georg Simmel, *The Philos-
     ophy of Money*, translated by Tom Bottomore and David Frisby (1900;
     London: Routledge, 1978).

17   Frank Kermode, "For a Few Dollars More," review of *Frozen Desire:
     The Meaning of Money*, by James Buchan, *London Review of Books*

19, no. 18 (Sep. 18, 1997), https://www.lrb.co.uk/the-paper/v19/n18/
frank-kermode/for-a-few-dollars-more.

18   EJ Spode [Peter Ludlow], "On Vitalik Buterin on Trust Models," *Medium*
(blog), Sep. 13, 2020, https://peterludlow.medium.com/on-vitalik-
buterin-on-trust-models-a4351cae7973. Philosopher Ludlow, more
lately mired in a sexual harassment investigation at Northwestern University, is a wide-ranging thinker whose early participation in *Second
Life* (as the avatar-critic Urizenus Sklar) included searching reflections
on the spectral nature of all money, "online" or otherwise.

19   I discuss these and related issues, especially with respect to baseball,
cricket, and colonial cultural logics in "Keeping a Straight Bat: Cricket,
Civility and Postcolonialism," in *C. L. R. James: His Intellectual Legacies*,
ed. Selwyn R. Cudjoe and William E. Cain, 359–87 (Amherst: University of Massachusetts Press, 1995).

20   Thomas L. Friedman, "Trump Thrives in a Broken System. He'll Get
Us There Soon," Opinion, *New York Times*, Jun. 13, 2023, https://www.
nytimes.com/2023/06/13/opinion/trump-indictment-presidency.html.
"The new right's theory of power is based on a model of domination and
imposition, and it just doesn't work," one writer argues further, levelling
the blame rightward. "In the new right's telling, the story of contemporary American culture is the story of progressive elite capture of the
nation's most important institutions—from the academy to big business
to pop culture to the 'deep state'—followed by its remorseless use of
that institutional power to warp and distort American values." But the
charge holds all round, as does this sketch of the favoured response.
"Fight fire with fire. Take over institutions. They tried to cancel us?
Cancel them. They bullied us? Bully them." David French, "Twitter
Shows, Again, the Failure of the New Right's Theory of Power," Opinion,
New York Times, Jul. 13, 2023, https://www.nytimes.com/2023/07/13/
opinion/twitter-new-right.html.

21   I call this a baseline form of civility because it is the minimum normative commitment necessary for any functioning democracy and hence
for state authority. See Leslie Green, *The Authority of the State* (Oxford:
Clarendon, 1988). In my own work on civility, which includes positive,
optative, and negative collective-action-problem arguments, civility is
conceived as a more robust virtue of citizens. Negative arguments (incivility is a tragedy of the commons) are stronger that hopeful ones (yay

civility!); but neither is terribly effective in polarized politics coloured by distrust.

22 William Deresiewicz, *Excellent Sheep: The Miseducation of the American Elite and the Way to a Meaningful Life* (New York: Free Press, 2014).

23 The amount of ink spilled over this cluster of issues is vast, especially since the campus Gaza war protests of 2024. Items of interest include David Brooks, "The Sins of the Educated Class," Opinion, *New York Times*, Jun. 6, 2024, https://www.nytimes.com/2024/06/06/opinion/elites-progressives-universities.html, and Andrew Sullivan's prescient take in "We All Live on Campus Now," Intelligencer, *New York*, Feb. 9, 2018, https://nymag.com/intelligencer/2018/02/we-all-live-on-campus-now.html. Sullivan makes the central argument this way: "If elites believe that the core truth of our society is a system of interlocking and oppressive power structures based around immutable characteristics like race or sex or sexual orientation, then sooner rather than later, this will be reflected in our culture at large."

24 William Deresiewicz, "Deep Reading Will Save Your Soul," *Persuasion* (blog), May 29, 2024, https://www.persuasion.community/p/deep-reading-will-save-your-soul. The subhead for this essay was "Real learning has become impossible in universities. DIY programs offer a better way." I beg to differ, at least when it comes to my own university and the departments I know well. But the larger point is well taken: is there really a dedicated practice of reading meaningfully anymore, on or off campus?

25 Michael T. Nietzel, "New Study: College Degree Carries Big Earnings Premium, but Other Factors Matter Too," *Forbes*, Oct. 11, 2021, https://www.forbes.com/sites/michaeltnietzel/2021/10/11/new-study-college-degree-carries-big-earnings-premium-but-other-factors-matter-too/.

26 As journalist Paul Tough notes, the US is an outlier in higher education as in other things. Elsewhere in the developed world, students are flocking to university in greater numbers than ever. As usual, to see why this asymmetry holds we must follow the money. American higher education is too expensive to be a good bet for those who are not already blessed with financial and social advantages that such education rewards and extends. See Tough, "Americans Are Losing Faith in the Value of College. Whose Fault Is That?" *New York Times Magazine*, Sep. 5, 2023, https://www.nytimes.com/2023/09/05/magazine/college-worth-price.html. The 2019 college-admissions bribery scandal was

widely reported, especially in the docudrama film *Operation Varsity Blues: The College Admissions Scandal* (Chris Smith, dir., 2021). The statistics about declining trust in American universities was gathered by the Heterodox Academy (May 2024). So, you know, caveat emptor.

27 No, this was not David Duchovny or Jodie Foster, both of whom studied at Yale around this time, but rather the distinguished character player Brennan Brown, maybe best known for his recurring role as a Japanese sympathizer in the television adaptation of Philip K. Dick's 1962 counterfactual fable *The Man in the High Castle* (2015).

28 David S. Ingalls Rink, New Haven, Connecticut, designed by architect Eero Saarinen and built between 1953 and 1958 for Yale University. The starting lineups of the Ivy League hockey teams were invariably stacked with Canadians. In the best hockey game I ever saw, the Yale goalie from Niagara Falls kicked out fifty-four saves against Harvard, then ranked first in the Ivy League and coming off a week as the *Sports Illustrated* cover story—a well-known jinx on winning streaks.

29 Deliberate misunderstanding, caricature, and exaggeration everywhere mark the right-wing attacks on these ideas, which makes rational discussion difficult if not impossible. Moreover, if someone starts from a *premise* that universities are dedicated to ideological indoctrination, there is really not much further to be said. Still, we have to try. I cite the following article not as a gesture of authority but as a token of good faith. See my "No, Postmodernism at Universities Isn't a Vile, Cancerous Doctrine," Opinion, *Globe and Mail*, Dec. 9, 2017, https://www.theglobe-andmail.com/opinion/no-postmodernism-at-universities-isnt-a-vile-cancerous-doctrine/article37272519/. I should perhaps balance that off with one of the first opinion columns I ever wrote for the same newspaper, when I was still in grad school: "Enter the campus thought police," Ideas, *Globe and Mail*, Apr. 15, 1991, A14, https://link.gale.com/apps/doc/A164263109/CPI?u=fred46430&sid=bookmark-CPI&xid=8b395663.

30 This point could make the longest footnote in publishing history, save perhaps the one that Whitehead suggested came in a series after Plato (that is, the entire written history of Western philosophy itself). I'll limit myself to just one self-referential citation: I discuss the roots and prospects for critical theory in "Critical Theory and Its Discontents," in *Practical Judgments: Essays in Culture, Politics, and Interpretation*, 171–81 (Toronto: University of Toronto Press, 2002). Previously published as

376   QUESTION AUTHORITY

Mark Kingwell, review of *Critical Theory*, by David Couzens Hoy and Thomas McCarthy; and *Of Critical Theory and Its Theorists*, by Stephen Eric Bronner, *Political Theory* 24, no. 2 (May 1996), 326–33, https://doi.org/10.1177/0090591796024002009.

31 Frederik Pohl and C. M. Kornbluth, *The Space Merchants* (New York: Ballantine, 1953; serialized as "Gravy Planet" in *Galaxy Science Fiction* 4, nos. 4–6 (Jun., Jul., and Aug. 1952). This prescient depiction of an overcrowded, dysfunctional, and environmentally challenged Earth, sustained by idiotic marketing campaigns for soft drinks and lab-grown chicken undoubtedly influenced the work of later writers, including Margaret Atwood and anticorporatist cyberpunk writers like Neal Stephenson and William Gibson. The book is credited with the coining of, among other lasting terms, "Muzak," "R&D," and "survey" as a verb meaning to conduct a consumer poll. "In this topsy-turvy world, marketing doesn't promote goods and services," critic Joshua Glenn notes, "it creates the desire for goods and services which it then conjures into being." And so, "this entire infernal machine is powered by a vicious circle of production and consumption wherein the average consumer is forced to spend their wages on goods that help make their labour bearable." The world is a company store, and money is all scrip. See Glenn, "Semiopunk (7)," *HiLoBrow* (blog), Nov. 5, 2023, https://www.hilobrow.com/2023/11/05/semiopunk-7/.

32 Hobbes would revive and expand this conundrum, dating from Plutarch, by suggesting that the original planks might be preserved and later reassembled. Now we have two ships. Which one is the ship of Theseus?

33 Alasdair MacIntyre, *Whose Justice? Which Rationality?* (Notre Dame, IN: University of Notre Dame Press, 1988), 357. Conservative—and Catholic, to boot.

34 Michel Foucault, "What Is Enlightenment?," in *The Foucault Reader*, ed. Paul Rabinow (New York: Pantheon, 1984), 48.

35 Foucault, 48.

36 Foucault, 50.

37 In his fashion, Foucault served to reinforce an argument already in play from the philosopher Jean-François Lyotard. *The Postmodern Condition*, Lyotard's 1989 "report on knowledge," was commissioned by the Conseil des universités du Québec as a study of technology's influence on "the exact sciences." What were they thinking? By the

time the University of Minnesota had published the English translation in 1984, the book was already the most influential government white paper tabled anywhere in modern history. See Jean-François Lyotard, *The Postmodern Condition: A Report on Knowledge*, Theory and History of Literature 10, trans., Geoff Bennington and Brian Massumi, with a foreword by Fredric Jameson (Minneapolis: University of Minnesota Press, 1984). It is hard to overestimate the role that these slick paperbacks from Minnesota played in the 1980s theory boom, alongside the Zone volumes designed by Bruce Mau.

38 Stanley Milgram, *Obedience to Authority: An Experimental View* (1974; New York: Harper Perennial Modern Thought, 2009), 6, 7.

39 Jean-François Lyotard and Jean-Loup Thébaud, *Just Gaming*, Theory of History and Literature 20, trans. Wlad Godzich, with an afterword by Samuel Weber (Minneapolis: University of Minnesota Press, 1985). Here, tracing a suggestion only drifted in his more famous work, Lyotard investigates his debt to the philosopher Ludwig Wittgenstein. Among many other ingenious notions, Wittgenstein had explored the idea of "language games": discrete fields of play within an overall linguistic system that allow for and serve distinct, often mutually incomprehensible, purposes.

40 Academic misconduct in philosophy might make us recall Woody Allen's joke about flunking his college metaphysics exam: he looked into the soul of the student sitting next to him. Plagiarism is, of course, the real misdemeanour of choice in most disciplines.

41 Notable recent fraud accusations have led to the ouster of Stanford's president, Marc Tessier-Lavigne. He was personally exonerated of fraud but guilty of "serious flaws" in method. See Susan Svrlugla and Jack Stripling, "Stanford President Will Resign after Questions about Research," Higher Education, *Washington Post*, Jul. 19, 2023, https://www.washingtonpost.com/education/2023/07/19/stanford-university-marc-tessier-lavigne-research-controversy/.

42 C. P. Snow, *The Affair* (1960; London: Penguin, 1962), part of his roman fleuve series Strangers and Brothers.

43 Benda had begun his public career writing about the Dreyfus affair. His famous polemic was an attack on intellectuals who, he felt, had abandoned their commitment to truth and justice for the sake of racial and political interests. It should be noted that the argument, and back-reference to

Benda's complaint about intellectuals who are overcome by politics, has since been a handy weapon for critics to level against the post-Enlightenment left. For an overview by one of those critics, see Roger Kimball, "The Treason of the Intellectuals and 'The Undoing of Thought,'" New Criterion 11, no. 4 (Dec. 1992), https://newcriterion.com/article/the-treason-of-the-intellectuals-ldquote-undoing-of-thoughtrdquo/.

44   Snow, *The Affair*, 279. The wronged academic, Howard, is an example of what Snow calls the "new men," the breed of post-war leftist reformers and technocrats who would remake Great Britain within the collapse of its old hierarchies. The last we hear from Howard in this novel is this indirect thought: "Men would become better, once people like him had set the scene. He stamped out of the room, puzzled by what had happened, angry but not cast down, still looking for, not finding, but hoping to find, justice in this world" (316). Though Howard gets nominal justice from the existing power structure, he is shunned and eased out by the "old men." I find myself thinking of Howard as a sort of socio-cultural twin to Hooper, the hapless subaltern that Charles Ryder has to contend with as an infantry captain in the opening sections of *Brideshead Revisited* (1945). (Snow was just two years younger than Evelyn Waugh.)

45   "Only 24% of Australians are willing to help someone in need who strongly disagrees with their view on a societal issue; only 21% are willing to live in the same neighbourhood; only 19% are willing to work with them." See Damien Freeman, "Political Polarisation in Australian," *Quillette*, Jun. 2, 2024, https://quillette.com/2024/06/02/losing-trust-and-increasing-polarisation-settlement-politics-australia/.

46   Ron Suskind, "Faith, Certainty and the Presidency of George W. Bush," *New York Times Magazine*, Oct. 17, 2004, https://www.nytimes.com/2004/10/17/magazine/faith-certainty-and-the-presidency-of-george-w-bush.html.

47   Circa 2024, this seems to be standard Republican doctrine and rhetoric in American politics. See Peter Wehner, "Republicans Have Chosen Nihilism," Opinion, *New York Times*, Nov. 6, 2023, https://www.nytimes.com/2023/11/06/opinion/trump-allan-bloom-republicans.html. Wehner's argument, writing as a reformed cultural conservative, is that the same charges of nihilism and relativism that Allan Bloom famously levelled against the New Left in his influential bestseller *The*

Closing of the American Mind (New York: Simon & Schuster, 1987) now apply precisely to the New (Trumpian) Right, unmoored from truth, beauty, and the good.

48 Stanley Cavell, *The Claim of Reason: Wittgenstein, Skepticism, Morality, and Tragedy* (New York: Oxford University Press, 1979). I will return to Cavell's ideas about skepticism and tragedy in parts 3 and 4.

49 William James, "The Will to Believe," in *The Will to Believe, and Other Essays in Popular Philosophy*, ed. Frederick H. Burkhardt, Fredson Bowers, and Ignas K. Skrupskelis, 13–33, vol. 6 of 19, *The Works of William James* (Cambridge, MA: Harvard University Press, 1979).

50 William James, "Is Life Worth Living?" in Burkhardt, Bowers, and Skrupskelis, *Will to Believe*, 35–57.

51 James, 57 (emphasis in original).

52 Richard Dawkins, *The Selfish Gene* (Oxford: Oxford University Press, 1976).

53 Harry G. Frankfurt, *On Bullshit* (Princeton and Oxford: Princeton University Press, 2005). A national bestseller, the book was based on Frankfurt's article "On Bullshit" in the *Raritan Quarterly Review* in 1986. I can attest that this article was widely circulated among young academics, who could appreciate its message if not always its application to their own emerging forms of discourse (ha!) but lacked the wider audience it would acquire later. Frankfurt was a professor at Yale when I was in graduate school there. He was a no-nonsense kind of guy. He told the *Yale Daily News* that the solution to the Yale philosophy department's recurring woes was "ritual sacrifice of senior faculty members." He moved to Princeton not long after.

54 Guess who? See Jesse Wegman, "The One Audience Trump Can't Hoodwink," Opinion, *New York Times*, Nov. 7, 2023, https://www.nytimes.com/2023/11/07/opinion/trump-fraud-trial.html. Wegman is referring to the judge in a civil case brought against Trump for fraudulent business practices in New York State. Here Trump was held liable and ordered to pay US$454 million in damages. His separate Manhattan trial for falsifying business records around the alleged "hush money" payments to actor Stormy Daniels led to thirty-four felony convictions. But the idea that the witness box in an actual trial would be "a cage of kryptonite" for the serial fabulist has proven all too optimistic. As long as any court action can be spun as an "unfair" targeting of the shady,

failed real estate tycoon by the perfidious "Deep State," his base is only strengthened in their support of him.

55 As the economist Paul Krugman notes, it is very pleasant and some-times profitable to reject expertise, to be a self-styled contrarian. It sells. The catch is, it's usually based on incorrect information and invalid argument. "One sad but true fact of life is that most of the time conventional wisdom and expert opinion are right," Krugman argues; "yet there can be big personal and social payoffs to finding the places where they're wrong. The trick to achieving these payoffs is to balance on the knife edge between excessive skepticism of unorthodoxy and excessive credulity." And, he adds, "It's all too easy to fall off that knife's edge in either direction." See Paul Krugman, "The Rich Are Crazier Than You and Me,"Opinion, *New York Times*, Jul. 6, 2023, https://www.nytimes.com/2023/07/06/opinion/robert-kennedy-jr-silicon-valley.html.

56 Karl Popper, *The Logic of Scientific Discovery*, trans. Karl Popper with Julius Freed and Lan Freed (1934; London: Hutchinson, 1959; repr. London: Routledge Classics, 2002).

57 Bret Stephens, "Claudine Gay and the Limits of Social Engineering at Harvard," Opinion, *New York Times*, Jan. 2, 2024, https://www.nytimes.com/2024/01/02/opinion/harvard-claudine-gay-resignation.html.

58 Niall Ferguson, "The Treason of the Intellectuals," *The Free Press*, Dec. 11, 2023, https://www.thefp.com/p/niall-ferguson-treason-intellectuals-third-reich. Ferguson's charges seem overheated to me, speaking as an academic insider. But what they get right is the widespread sense, beyond the campus limits, that academics are not only posturing fools—a charge of long standing—but also indoctrinating, ideologically-driven apparatchiks.

59 Bill Readings, *The University in Ruins* (Cambridge, MA: Harvard University Press, 1997).

60 This form of right-wing triumphalism was on full display in response to the 2024 campus protests over the Gaza war. The idea that the protests invite some kind of "gotcha" moment for left-leaning academics, or even a sign of hypocrisy—"Oh look, you *teach* activism but you don't like it when it happens to you!"—is risible but unfortunately widespread. It mistakes administration for faculty, for one thing, and misunderstands what free discourse is actually like. See, for example, Pamela Paul, "And Now, A Real-World Lesson for Student Activists," Opinion,

New York Times, May 30, 2024, https://www.nytimes.com/2024/05/30/opinion/college-activism-israel-gaza.html. See also Tyler Austin Harper, "America's Colleges Are Reaping What They Sowed," Ideas, *Atlantic*, May 2, 2024, https://www.theatlantic.com/ideas/archive/2024/05/college-activism-hypocrisy/678262/.

61 Mark Lilla, "The Lure of Syracuse," *New York Review of Books*, Sep. 20, 2001, https://www.nybooks.com/articles/2001/09/20/the-lure-of-syracuse/; later published as an afterword to Lilla's essay collection *The Reckless Mind: Intellectuals in Politics* (New York: New York Review of Books, 2001).

62 Hofstadter, "Paranoid Style," 86.

63 Hofstadter, 86.

THIRD MEDITATION: No, They Don't Know Either

1 Issues of broken trust in media have a long history. We must be careful about the linked tendencies to overstate the badness of things now and polish the memories of things then. A good overview of the current Canadian case, together with some apposite history, may be found in Tara Henley, "The Trust Spiral: Restoring Faith in the Media," The Massey Essay, *Literary Review of Canada* 32, no. 4 (May 2024), https://reviewcanada.ca/magazine/2024/05/the-trust-spiral/. Henley's prescriptions for bolstering trust in media came down to a rather obvious series of best-practice imperatives: "Stop taking money from the government. Stop indulging in moral panics. Stop ignoring dissenting views. Stop letting your personal politics blind you to the facts, making you vulnerable to mistakes. Stop refusing to acknowledge mistakes when you do make them. Stop inserting your views into the news." I'm sure her former colleagues at the CBC—she quit in 2022 over political disagreements—read that passage and thought, *Okay thanks, I'll get right on it!* (As noted, sometimes the problem with ideological capture is precisely that its prisoners consider themselves free: no outside imperatives are required, or welcome.) In May 2024, the Macdonald-Laurier Institute, a Canadian think tank, issued "The Ottawa Declaration on Canadian Journalism," a manifesto against government-subsidized media signed by a number of prominent journalists; quoted statistics are from their website: https://macdonaldlaurier.ca/the-ottawa-declaration-on-canadian-journalism/.

2 Jonathan Kay, "Journalists Shouldn't Depend on the State for Their Wages," *Quillette*, Jun. 14, 2024, https://quillette.com/2024/06/14/governments-shouldnt-be-paying-journalists-salaries/.

3 Paul Wells, *Justin Trudeau on the Ropes: Governing in Troubled Times* (Toronto: Sutherland House, 2024), 92.

4 Issues of distrust now often come with an extra generational twist. This has been especially noticeable in the rhetoric over the Gaza war. But even before that, I confess I felt a twinge when I read a negative review of the 2023 movie *Tár* which sneered at the political idiocy of "any 52-year-old nodding along to a *New York Times* op-ed" who found the film illuminating about cancel culture and the failures of "idpol" (identity politics). See Jacob Rosenberg, "Finally, the End of *Tár*," *Mother Jones*, Mar. 12, 2023, https://www.motherjones.com/media/2023/03/tar-oscars-cate-blanchett-todd-field/. For the record, I was sixty when I first saw the film and read that review. A central target of Rosenberg's critique is novelist Zadie Smith, who chose to assess the film chiefly in terms of generational conflict about art and politics, which seems correct. See Zadie Smith, "The Instrumentalist," *New York Review of Books*, Jan. 19, 2023, https://www.nybooks.com/articles/2023/01/19/the-instrumentalist-tar-todd-field-zadie-smith/.

5 I go into further detail about these formative days of my early career in journalism (if that's what it is) in "All Show: Justice and the City," in *Unruly Voices: Essays on Democracy, Civility, and the Human Imagination* (Windsor, ON: Biblioasis, 2012) 27–40.

6 A clear diagnosis that now seems both accurate and yet not nearly alarmist enough was Fred Turner, "Machine Politics: The Rise of the Internet and a New Age of Authoritarianism," *Harper's Magazine* 338, no. 2024 (Jan. 2019), https://harpers.org/archive/2019/01/machine-politics-facebook-political-polarization/. "One of the deepest ironies of our current situation is that the modes of communication that enable today's authoritarians were first dreamed up to defeat them. The same technologies that were meant to level the political playing field have brought troll farms and Russian bots to corrupt our elections. The same platforms of self-expression that we thought would let us empathize with one another and build a more harmonious society have been co-opted by figures such as . . . Donald Trump, to turn white supremacy into a topic of dinner-table conversation. And the same networked

methods of organizing that so many thought would bring down malevo-
lent states have not only failed to do so—think of the Arab Spring—but
have instead empowered autocrats to more closely monitor protest and
dissent." That stands formally as irony, yes, but of a very bitter sort.

7   Michelle Cyca, "Nostalgia about Newsrooms Ignores How Much
They Need to Change," Media, *The Walrus*, May 31, 2023, updated Jan.
8, 2024, https://thewalrus.ca/nostalgia-about-newsrooms-ignores-
how-much-they-need-to-change/.

8   Maureen Dowd, "Requiem for the Newsroom," Opinion, *New York
Times*, Apr. 29, 2023, https://www.nytimes.com/2023/04/29/opinion/
journalism-newsroom.html.

9   A useful recent meditation here is Naomi Klein, *Doppelganger: A Trip
into the Mirror World* (New York: Knopf, 2023). Hinged rather pre-
cariously on the recurring online confusion between Klein and the
once-liberal, now conspiracy-crazy Naomi Wolf—itself a confusion
hard to credit in any rational person—Klein offers an assessment of
the nasty funhouse of contemporary media. She also acknowledges that
part of the logic of her annoyance at the confusion, and her desire to
write the book, was a matter of protecting her own social brand. This
is an uncomfortable irony for the critic of "brand bullies" of her best-
selling book *No Logo* (New York: Knopf, 1999). "When looking at the
Mirror World, it can seem obvious that millions of people have given
themselves over to fantasy, to make-believe, to playacting," Klein writes.
"The trickier thing, the uncanny thing, really, is that's what they see
when they look at us." The book also offers the following useful equation
when trying to understand people like Wolf, whose politics lurched
rightward after she was criticized for shoddy writing and favouring her
"truth" over facts: "Narcissism(Grandiosity) + Social media addiction
+ Midlife crisis ÷ Public shaming = Right wing meltdown." Sadly, yes,
exactly right.

10 See Harry G. Frankfurt, *On Bullshit* (Princeton and Oxford: Princeton
University Press, 2005). Also Pierre Bourdieu, *On Television* (1998; London: Polity, 2011), which likewise sold briskly when it first appeared.
Steve Bannon's disturbingly philosophical take on Trumpian politics is
communicated in David Brooks, "My Unsettling Interview with Steve
Bannon," Opinion, *New York Times*, Jul. 1, 2024, https://www.newyork-
times.com/2024/07/01/opinion/steve-bannon-trump.html.

11   Whoever originated the phrase—it probably wasn't Disraeli; as noted earlier, that was Twain later borrowing false authority—the best book on the subject remains Michael Wheeler, *Lies, Damned Lies, and Statistics: The Manipulation of Public Opinion in America* (New York: W. W. Norton & Co. 1976).

12   Mark Suster, "73.6% of All Statistics Are Made Up," Strategy, *Business Insider*, Feb. 17, 2010, https://www.businessinsider.com/736-of-all-statistics-are-made-up-2010-2. Of course, that statistic is itself made-up—that's the joke. See also Bernardita Calzon, "Misleading Statistics Examples—Discover the Potential for Misuse of Statistics and Data in the Digital Age," Data Analysis, *datapine Blog*, Jan. 6, 2023, https://web.archive.org/web/20230123072651/https://www.datapine.com/blog/misleading-statistics-and-data/.

13   Evelyn Douek, "The Rise of Content Cartels," Tech Giants, Monopoly Power, and Public Discourse, 20-04, Knight First Amendment Institute, Feb. 11, 2020, https://perma.cc/H6HZ-NWS7. "The fear that a single actor can decide what can or cannot be said in large parts of the online public sphere has led to growing calls for measures to promote competition between digital platforms," Douek begins. But "[t]he pressure to *do something* can lead to the creation of systems and structures that serve the interests of the very tech platforms that they seek to rein in. I call these *content cartels*: arrangements between platforms to work together to remove content or actors from their services without adequate oversight. These come in various guises; they can be demanded, encouraged, participated in, or unheeded by regulators. But they share the characteristic that they compound the existing lack of accountability in platform content moderation."

14   Musk's antisemitic rants were widely noted in the fall of 2023. See, for example, David Austin Walsh, "Elon Musk Has Crossed a Line," Opinion, *New York Times*, Sep. 11, 2023, https://www.nytimes.com/2023/09/11/opinion/elon-musk-adl.html: "Mr Musk scapegoating the Jews for his own catastrophic business decisions regarding his management of one of the most influential social media platforms in the world will only add fuel to the fire" of antisemitic conspiracism.

15   I examine some aspects of interface design as an enabler of addictive use in *Wish I Were Here: Boredom and the Interface* (Montreal and Kingston: McGill-Queen's University Press, 2019). Video game and social media

programmers are very open about the fact that the goal of their interfaces is "compulsive extended immersion"—also known as addiction.

16 Benjamin Shingler, "Andrew Potter Resigns from McGill Post after
    Maclean's Essay on Quebec," CBC News, Mar. 23, 2017, https://www.cbc.
    ca/news/canada/montreal/andrew-potter-mcgill-institute-for-the-study-
    of-canada-resignation-macleans-1.4037618. The original article is Andrew
    Potter, "How a Snowstorm Exposed Quebec's Real Problem: Social Mal-
    aise," *Maclean's*, Mar. 20, 2017, https://www.macleans.ca/news/canada/
    how-a-snowstorm-exposed-quebecs-real-problem-social-malaise/.

17 "What the Andrew Potter Affair Was Really About," Editorial, *Maclean's*,
    Mar. 29, 2017, https://macleans.ca/news/canada/macleans-editori-
    al-what-the-andrew-potter-affair-was-really-about/. See also "CAUT Pre-
    pares Investigation into McGill and Potter Resignation," *Maclean's*, Mar.
    27, 2017, https://macleans.ca/news/canada/caut-prepares-investigation-
    into-mcgill-and-potter-resignation/. CAUT is the Canadian Association
    for University Teachers, an advocacy group.

18 Sadly, we are a long distance from any ideal speech situation as imag-
    ined by the endlessly optimistic Jürgen Habermas, whose books were
    such a large feature of my long hours in Yale's reading rooms. See, for
    example, Habermas, *The Theory of Communicative Action*, trans. Thomas
    McCarthy, vol. 1, *Reason and the Rationalization of Society* (Boston: Bea-
    con Press, 1984). Habermas follows Kant in arguing that we cannot
    make sense of our place in the world absent a transcendental orien-
    tation to the power of reason itself. Uncovering the exact structure of
    that power, articulating its categories and effects, is the basic work
    of the human mind. Doing things with our rational capacity, acting in
    the world, coordinating action with others, are thus by-products of
    self-understanding. The ideal speech situation functions as a kind of
    lodestar, a *regulative ideal* in the jargon, which will never be encom-
    passed by our flawed real-world efforts but is essential to guide them.
    In the ideal situation, everyone affected by a decision must be party
    to it, entirely free of external coercion and inner distortions alike. In
    common with the rational actors imagined in other thought experi-
    ments—John Rawls's "original position" is one example, with important
    differences—the idea is that rigorous speculation can channel legiti-
    macy, despite its manifest distance from the muddy realities of politics.
    The scholarly industry spawned by Rawls's argument is nothing short of

head-spinning; commentary on its arguments have dominated political philosophy for decades.

19   The specific context bears on the traditional problem known as naming and necessity: "Philosophical problems arise when language goes on holiday." See Ludwig Wittgenstein, *Philosophical Investigations*, trans. G. E. M. Anscombe (London: Basil Blackwell: 1958), sec. 38, line 19.

20   My grad-school friend James Giles had printed up a stock of business cards with his name, Edinburgh address, and the occupation "Metaphysician and Epistemologist" inscribed underneath. Needless to say, nobody found this amusing except us.

21   Wittgenstein argues that games resist sorting into any *essentialist* account of shared features across instances. This is not to say that we can't define games, still less that we can't play them and talk about them meaningfully, only that we can and must do those things with a nuanced sense of the range of things classed under "game." The relevant, much-quoted remark: "Consider, for example, the activities that we call 'games.' I mean board-games, card-games, ball-games, athletic games, and so on. What is common to them all?—Don't say: 'They must have something in common, or they would not be called "games"'—but look and see whether there is anything common to all.—For if you look at them, you won't see something that is common to all, but similarities, affinities, and a whole series of them at that." *Philosophical Investigations*, sec. 66.

22   Martin Amis, *The War against Cliché: Essays and Reviews 1971–2000* (London: Jonathan Cape, 2001), xv. As a public service, note Michael Massing, "Tip of the Iceberg," Opinion, *New York Times*, Apr. 27, 2023, https://www.nytimes.com/2023/04/27/opinion/avoid-cliches.html, a compendium of avoidable clichés that starts with "Ramped up, amped up, ratchet up, gin up, up the ante, double down, jump-start, be behind the curve, swim against the tide, go south, go belly up, level the playing field" and ends, many lines later, with "go viral, bingeable, blockbuster, on steroids, testosterone-laced, metastasize, contextualize, preternaturally, outsize, gobsmacked, turbocharged, weaponized, apocalyptic, existential . . ." I imagine every reader and writer has their own list of grammatical irritants. For the record, mine include "lay low" when it should be "lie low," "masterful" when "masterly" is meant, "comprise" for "compose," confusions of "further" with "farther" or "as it were"

with "as it was," and almost every single encountered use of "beg the question."

23 Dietrich Bonhoeffer, "After Ten Years," in *Letters and Papers from Prison*, ed. John W. de Gruchy, trans. Barbara and Martin Rumscheidt (1953; Minneapolis: Fortress Press, 2010), 43.

24 Bonhoeffer, 43.

25 Bonhoeffer, 44.

26 Bonhoeffer, 44.

27 Bonhoeffer, 44.

28 Carlo M. Cipolla, *The Basic Laws of Human Stupidity* (orig. private ed. 1976; New York: Doubleday, 2011), 4. There are many other books, mostly offered in a social-psychological vein, that explore human error, especially of the form I would call *being stupid*, an existential affliction shared by all, not a genetic condition. See, for example, Kathryn Schultz, *Being Wrong: Adventures in the Margin of Error* (New York: HarperCollins, 2010); Joseph Hallinan, *Why We Make Mistakes: How We Look without Seeing, Forget Things in Seconds, and Are All Pretty Sure We Are Way Above Average* (New York: Crown, 2010); Carol Tavris and Elliot Aronson, *Mistakes Were Made (But Not by Me)* (New York: Houghton Mifflin Harcourt, 2007); Thomas Gilovich, *How We Know What Isn't So: The Fallibility of Human Reason in Everyday Life* (New York: Free Press, 1993); and Christopher Chabris and Daniel Simons, *The Invisible Gorilla, and Other Ways Our Intuitions Deceive Us* (New York: Harmony, 2010). One review of the last book included this damning judgment about mistakes in other pop-psychology books written by nonexperts: *The Invisible Gorilla*, the critic said, "much to our delight, is written with the subtext of being an antidote to Malcolm Gladwell's *Blink* which, for all its praises, is tragically plagued by out-of-context 'research,' wishful dot-connecting, and other classic Gladwellisms." Ouch.

29 Nassim Nicholas Taleb, Foreword to Cipolla, viii.

30 Cipolla, passim.

31 Blogger Ian Leslie's essay "Seven Varieties of Stupidity," *The Ruffian* (blog), May 21, 2022, https://www.ian-leslie.com/p/seven-varieties-of-stupidity, mentions Cipolla but rather dismissively. Another blogger, Scott Galloway, is more charitable. He reproduces Cipolla's four-quadrant mapping of human types and then adds texture from real-world examples: Big Stupid (e.g., Apple pouring ridiculous amounts of

money into VR technology that nobody wants—a species of the fallacy of sunk costs); Rich Stupid (Elon Musk's misguided attempt to take over Twitter); and Self Stupid (a rather poignant anecdote about letting his guard down while discussing father-son relations with friends). "The next morning I'm sober, have some distance from the moment with my son, and am a bit embarrassed at my texts. I'm more in control, less likely to spontaneously reach out to people and burden them with my emotions. Once again, I'm stupid." Spontaneity and sharing are great, yet as a philosopher, I can't accept the lack of them as a kind of stupidity. But see Scott Galloway, "Big Stupid," *No Mercy/No Malice* (blog), Jun. 3, 2022, https://www.profgalloway.com/big-stupid/.

32   The range of words and phrases indicating stupidity in another person is a sign of how often we feel frustrated with the actions and decisions of others. Every natural language is full of them, often with reference to empty heads or heads filled with unpleasant or unresponsive things: excrement, chowder, clots, blocks, wood, cloth, bone, meat, fat, air, or bubbles. "Muppet" is a popular term in British slang for a stupid person, referring to the television cloth puppets, sometimes used with a measure of affection (like "doofus," or "mook," say). "Dumb as a bag of hammers" or "dumb as a box of hair" are colourful extensions with strong visual cues—also very funny.

33   The phrase "post-kayfabe" appeared in a 2014 short story by Sam Lispyste. A pro wrestler known as the Rough Beast of Bethlehem (a "Second Coming" reference there: one of two to be found in these endnotes, for those keeping score at home). "It's not about wrestling," the Rough Beast tells his seatmate, the tale's beleaguered main character. "It's about sto-ries. We're storytellers." See Lipsyte, "The Naturals," *New Yorker*, Apr, 28, 2014, https://www.newyorker.com/magazine/2014/05/05/the-naturals.

34   David Brooks, *Bobos in Paradise: The New Upper Class and How They Got There* (New York: Simon and Schuster, 2001).

35   Brooks, 14, 39, 84.

36   Tressie McMillan Cottom, "In Alabama, White Tide Rushes On," Opinion, *New York Times*, Aug. 22, 2023, https://www.nytimes.com/2023/08/22/opinion/bama-rush-tiktok-race.html. Cottom's article is a good overview of this phenomenon.

37   The dystopian film *Civil War* (dir. Alex Garland) was released in 2024, but it was predated by a number of articles and books seriously address-

ing the prospects for another conflict on the order of the split American union in the 1860s. The best of these is Stephen Marche, *The Next Civil War: Dispatches from the American Future* (New York: Avid Reader Press, 2022).

38 See Olúfẹ́mi O. Táíwò, *Elite Capture: How the Powerful Took Over Identity Politics (And Everything Else)* (Chicago: Haymarket Books, 2022).

39 Anthony Wilden, *The Rules Are No Game: The Strategy of Communication* (London: Routledge & Kegan Paul, 1987); my attempt to make sense of Wilden's insights about games and language is Mark Kingwell, "Language, Rules, and the Greatest Game," *Rubicon*, no. 10 (1988): 269–81.

40 There are many shades of subtle difference here, from strict logical noncognitivists like J. L. Mackie to quasirealists about ethics like Simon Blackburn. See Mackie, *Ethics: Inventing Right and Wrong* (Harmondsworth: Penguin Books, 1977) and Blackburn, *Essays in Quasi-realism* (Oxford: Oxford University Press, 1993). I follow the latter, more or less, in arguing that value differences are real but are not typically disputes over facts. Factual evidence can nudge such disputes but not simply solve them empirically. Thus, trust will be invested not in the mastery of empirical truths simpliciter but in the mustering of such facts together with persuasive elements of good character and compassionate attachment.

41 The hierarchy of needs was first articulated in Abraham H. Maslow, "A Theory of Human Motivation," *Psychological Review* 50, no. 4 (1943): 370–96. See also John Rawls, *A Theory of Justice* (Cambridge, MA: Belknap Press, 1971); also, Amartya Sen, *The Idea of Justice* (Cambridge, MA: Belknap Press, 2009). See also Ursula K. Le Guin, "The Ones Who Walk Away from Omelas," *New Directions*, no. 3 (1973). Earlier versions of the single-scapegoat theory of utopia can be found in Dostoevsky and William James. This is James, from an 1891 address to the Yale Philosophical Club:

Or if the hypothesis were offered us of a world in which Messrs. Fourier's and Bellamy's and Morris's utopias should all be outdone, and millions kept permanently happy on the one simple condition that a certain lost soul on the far-off edge of things should lead a life of lonely torture, what except a sceptical and independent sort of emotion can it be which would make us immediately feel, even though an impulse arose within us to clutch at the happiness so offered, how hideous a thing would be its enjoyment when deliberately accepted as the fruit of such a bargain?

William James, "The Moral Philosopher and the Moral Life," in *The Will to Believe, and Other Essays in Popular Philosophy*, ed. Frederick H. Burkhardt, Fredson Bowers, and Ignas K. Skrupskelis, 142–63, vol. 6 of 19, *The Works of William James* (Cambridge, MA: Harvard University Press, 1979).

42   For the classic treatment of this argument, see Søren Kierkegaard, *Fear and Trembling*, trans. Alastair Hannay (1843; Harmondsworth: Penguin Classics, 1986). In this pseudonymous book, the ironic voice of Johannes de Silentio revisits the Old Testament scene of Abraham preparing to sacrifice his son Isaac at God's command.

43   I think here of the insightful, charming interventions of Lewis Mumford in his unsurpassed collection *Sidewalk Critic: Lewis Mumford's Writings on New York*, ed. Robert Wojtowicz (Princeton: Princeton Architectural Press, 1998), but also in the more abstract account of "the metropolitan attitude" offered by Georg Simmel in "The Metropolis and Mental Life," in *The Sociology of Georg Simmel*, ed. and trans. Kurt Wolff, 409–24 (New York: Free Press, 1950).

44   Hello to Jenny Turner, late of *Edinburgh Review*. Circa 1986, when I wrote for and helped edit a resuscitated version of the venerable journal, it used the Gray tagline along with an excellent illustration by him on its title page.

45   Canadian conservative philosopher George Grant favoured the term *multiversity*, to suggest that the modern university was not (or no longer) a site of universal values. See Grant, *English-Speaking Justice* (Toronto: House of Anansi Press, 1998). More recent critics of the "post-academic university" view it as inimical to the humane project of liberal education. See, for example, Mark Mercer, "Confronting the Post-Academic University," interview by Patrick Keeney *C2C Journal*, May 16, 2023, https://c2cjournal.ca/2023/05/confronting-the-post-academic-university-in-conversation-with-mark-mercer/. Mercer has an admirably pure notion of the ideal university, but its unreconstructed Enlightenment assumptions sit rather poorly with any public institution: "Universities should be places where people who prize their own intellectual and moral autonomy and that of others gather in community to try to figure things out, to construct interpretations and to

articulate their appreciations of the things around them. We can expect that people with university experience will become certain kinds of people—most prominently, people who can think and feel for themselves and are courageous enough to do so. But if we make moulding, forming or educating our goal, we corrupt the means. Education is a valuable by-product, but it's not the goal." That kind of thing is not going to fly with the taxpayers of Michigan or Ontario.

46 Rachel Hartman, Neil Hester, and Kurt Gray , "People See Political Opponents as More Stupid Than Evil," *Personality and Social Psychology Bulletin* 49, no. 7 (Apr. 2022): 1014–27, https://doi.org/10.1177/01461672221089451. But the point seems to weaken, if not collapse, when we are mindful of Bonhoeffer's tragic assessment of ideology and the desire to belong, especially in the exquisitely comforting form of conspiracy theory. See Graeme Bruce, "Half of Trump's Supporters Think Top Democrats Are Involved in Child Sex-Trafficking," *YouGov*, Oct. 20, 2020, https://today.yougov.com/politics/articles/32619-half-trump-supporters-believe-qanon-theory-child-s.

47 Jonathan Haidt, "Why the Past 10 Years of American Life Have Been Uniquely Stupid," *Atlantic*, April 12, 2022, https://www.theatlantic.com/magazine/archive/2022/05/social-media-democracy-trust-babel/629369/. Haidt's gesture to structural change rather than lowering of collective intelligence might be related to a novel aesthetic theory advanced by Sianne Ngai: what she calls *stuplimity*. See "Stuplimity: Shock and Boredom in Twentieth-Century Aesthetics," *Postmodern Culture* 10, no. 2 (Jan. 2000), https://doi.org/10.1353/pmc.2000.0013. The idea is that sheer volume of aesthetic stimulus, coupled with vast human processing power, leads to the particular two-step of (1) astonishment followed quickly by (2) ennui: thus *stuplimity*, sublimity and stupor combined. This does account for some of the plain stupidity of Haidt's analysis, perhaps; but I stand by the criticism that the issue is not strictly structural, and Ngai's dynamic notion of stuplimity neatly captures that.

48 "Public Trust in Government: 1958–2024," feature, Trust, Facts & Democracy, Pew Research Center, Jun. 24, 2024, https://www.pewresearch.org/politics/2024/06/24/public-trust-in-government-1958-2024/.

49 Haidt, "Uniquely Stupid"; "By 2013, social media had become a new game, with dynamics unlike those in 2008. If you were skillful or lucky,

you might create a post that would 'go viral' and make you 'internet famous' for a few days. If you blundered, you could find yourself buried in hateful comments. Your posts rode to fame or ignominy based on the clicks of thousands of strangers, and you in turn contributed thousands of clicks to the game."

50   Winner for Best Picture, Best Actor, Best Supporting Actor, Best Adapted Screenplay, and Best Director, among others.

51   Quoted by Christian Lorentzen, "The Enemy of Promise: What Time Did to Christopher Hitchens," review of *A Hitch in Time: Writings from the "London Review of Books*," by Christopher Hitchens, *Harper's Magazine*, Aug. 2022, 78. Lorentzen reads Hitchens, like Zelig and Gump, as a "prisoner of history"—a kind of second-order tragedy of the very smart person trapped in an inescapable awareness of his era's own absurd dumbness.

52   I believe I was the first to coin the term "Gumpism" for this little ideological tangle of humble virtue plus elite disdain. See *Dreams of Millennium: Report from a Culture on the Brink* (Toronto: Viking, 1996; Boston: Faber & Faber, 1997). Subsequent decades have suggested that the idea is more relevant than ever, now that the millennium has come and gone.

53   John Gruber, "Translation from Hostage Code to English of X Corp CEO Linda Yaccarino's Company-Wide Memo," *Daring Fireball* (blog), Jul. 28, 2023, https://daringfireball.net/2023/07/translation_yaccarino_x.

54   Shira Ovide, "Big Tech Has Outgrown This Planet," On Tech, *New York Times*, Jul. 29, 2021; updated Oct. 12, 2021, https://www.nytimes.com/2021/07/29/technology/big-tech-profits.html.

55   David Brooks, "The Terrifying Future of the American Right: What I Saw at the National Conservatism Conference," Ideas, *Atlantic*, Nov. 18, 2021, https://www.theatlantic.com/ideas/archive/2021/11/scary-future-american-right-national-conservatism-conference/620746/.

56   Brooks.

57   Brooks.

58   After some years of trying to argue for the positive value of civility, as noted previously, I realized that there was a potentially more effective negative argument available: show that incivility is a collective-action problem, a race to the bottom or tragedy of the commons. This argument has not improved public discourse much, alas, but it does feel

more relevant all the time. See Mark Kingwell, "'Fuck You' and Other Salutations: Incivility as a Collective Action Problem," in *Civility in Politics and Education*, ed. Deborah S. Mower and Wade L. Robison, 44–61 (New York and London: Routledge, 2012).

FOURTH MEDITATION: But Not Your Mother

1 Peg Streep, "The 'Invisible Cliff' Experiment and Maternal Power," Child Development, *Psychology Today*, Jul. 22, 2023, https://www.psychologytoday.com/ca/blog/tech-support/202307/the-invisible-cliff-experiment-and-maternal-power.

2 Wylie's work, including his once-popular science fiction, enjoyed a brief, wary renaissance in the first decades of the twenty-first century. See, for example, Emily Harnett, "Married to the Momism: Philip Wylie's *Generation of Vipers*, revisited," *Lapham's Quarterly*, Jul. 23, 2020, https://www.laphamsquarterly.org/roundtable/married-momism; and Peter L. Winkler, "The Man Who Hated Moms: Looking Back on Philip Wylie's *Generation of Vipers*," *Los Angeles Review of Books*, Aug. 13, 2021, https://lareviewofbooks.org/article/the-man-who-hated-moms-looking-back-on-philip-wylies-generation-of-vipers/.

3 A compelling version of this argument is offered by Stephen Mulhall in his *On Film*, 3rd ed. (London: Routledge, 2016).

4 I needn't detail all the many scandals involving Christian camps and colleges here; the stories are legion. But see David French, "The Worst Scandal in American Higher Education Isn't in the Ivy League," Opinion, *New York Times*, Oct. 22, 2023, https://www.nytimes.com/2023/10/22/opinion/liberty-university-scandal-education.html. This column, about the corrupt, Jerry Falwell–founded Liberty University in Virginia, includes links to French's other reporting on similar scandals at other Christian institutions.

5 Congratulations to Claudia Goldin of Harvard University, whose work on gender inequality in workplaces earned her the first Nobel Prize in economics awarded to a woman alone.

6 Scott Cacciola and Benjamin Hoffman, "NFL Player Draws Rebukes (and Trolling) for Graduation Speech," Style, *New York Times*, May 16, 2024, https://www.nytimes.com/2024/05/16/style/harrison-butker-commencement-speech.html. The player in question was Kansas City

Chiefs place-kicker Harrison Butker. See also Jessica Grose, "'Tradwife' Content Isn't Really for Women. It's for Men Who Want Submissive Wives," Opinion, *New York Times*, May 15, 2024, https://www.nytimes.com/2024/05/15/opinion/tradwife-tiktok.html. As Grose notes, the problem with such online content is that it is designed as a form of ideological trap: object to it, and you only provide further justification for its creators' self-righteousness.

7 Grose, "'Tradwife' Content"; Olivia Little, "Study: Tradwife Influencers Are Quietly Spreading Far-Right Conspiracy Theories," *Media Matters*, May 1, 2024, https://www.mediamatters.org/tiktok/study-tradwife-influencers-are-quietly-spreading-far-right-conspiracy-theories.

8 Sigmund Freud, *Civilization and Its Discontents*, ed. and trans. James Strachey (London: Hogarth Press, 1930; New York: W. W. Norton, 1962), 70–80, https://archive.org/details/sigmund-freud-civilization-and-its-discontents-1/.

9 Tori Otten, "Top Trump Adviser Warned about 'Conspiracy Shit Beamed Down from the Mothership,'" *New Republic*, Aug. 1, 2023, https://newrepublic.com/post/174776/top-trump-advisor-warned-conspiracy-shit-beamed-mothership.

10 Len Deighton, *London Match* (London: Hutchinson, 1985), 200.

11 Everything old is new again when it comes to cultural politics, of course. Surveying the culture-wars terrain of the 2024 can put one in mind of other cycles of left/right impasse and mediated insult. Consider, for example, Robert Hughes's biting analysis in *Culture of Complaint: The Fraying of America* (New York: Oxford University Press, 1993), which can be applied today with only a few changes of headline and detail. Sample quotation: "Through the 80s, [the unravelling of American society] happened with depressing regularity on both sides of American party politics. Instead of common ground, we got demagogues." That is, "neo-conservatives who create an exaggerated bogey called multiculturalism—as though Western culture itself was ever anything *but* multi, living by its eclecticism, its power of successful imitation, its ability to absorb 'foreign' forms and stimuli!—and pushers of political correctness who would like to see grievance elevated into automatic sanctity" (14).

12 F. Scott Fitzgerald, *The Beautiful and Damned* (New York: Charles Scribner's Sons, 1922), 76. Fitzgerald is not usually saluted for his politics,

but both here and in *The Great Gatsby* (1925), which mocks the casual eugenic racism of Tom Buchanan, Gatsby's romantic rival, he is sharp, even mordant about the casual violence of right-wing upper-crust delusion.

13 Here, after some delay, the always exceptionalist American example is now following larger trends to secularization in Europe and the rest of the Anglosphere. See Nicholas Kristof, "America Is Losing Religious Faith," Opinion, *New York Times*, Aug. 23, 2023, https://www.nytimes.com/2023/08/23/opinion/christianity-america-religion-secular.html. "Politicians still end their speeches with 'God bless America,'" Kristof writes. "At least until recently, more Americans believed in the virgin birth of Jesus (66 percent) than in evolution (54 percent)." But for the first time in a Gallup poll only a minority of respondents said they belonged to a church, mosque, or synagogue. See also Jim Davis and Michael Graham with Ryan P. Burge, *The Great Dechurching: Who's Leaving, Why Are They Going, and What Will It Take to Bring Them Back?* (Grand Rapids, MI: Zondervan Reflective, 2023).

14 Jessica Grose, "The Church of Group Fitness," Opinion, *New York Times*, Jul. 26, 2023, https://www.nytimes.com/2023/07/26/opinion/religion-fitness.html. "CrossFit also has parallels with some religious organizations in terms of the potential to alienate people who disagree with conservative-aligned beliefs. In 2020, the CrossFit founder Greg Glassman stepped down from his role as chief executive of the company after he made inflammatory statements about George Floyd and Covid. In 2021, Natalia Mehlman Petrzela wrote a guest essay for *Times* Opinion about breaking up with the 'cult' of SoulCycle. Petrzela described an unsavoury side of group fitness involving entitled star instructors and the businesses that profit from them." A new religion, or just another Ponzi scheme preying on our confused desires and addictive tendencies?

15 See T. M. Scanlon, *What We Owe to Each Other* (1998; Cambridge, MA: Belknap Press, 2000). Scanlon is a contractualist, so his account addresses both how we act toward each other and how we provide reasons for our actions that might reasonably be accepted by others so affected.

16 Adam Smith, *The Theory of the Moral Sentiments* (London, 1759), 2–3, https://archive.org/details/bim_eighteenth-century_the-theory-of-

moral-sent_smith-adam_1759/. "Though our brother is upon the rack, as long as we are at our ease, our senses will never inform us of what he suffers. They never did and never can carry us beyond our own persons, and it is by the imagination only that we can form any conception of what are his sensations." But this moral imagination is powerful: "His agonies, when they are thus brought home to ourselves, when we have thus adopted and made them our own, begin at last to affect us, and we then tremble and shudder at the thought of what he feels."

17 The English translation is a minor masterpiece by an English Orthodox cleric called Ephrem Lash, set in traditional metre by David Melling. Lash, an archimandrite of the Orthodox Church, was the son of a brigadier in the Indian Army. His brother was a professor of divinity at Cambridge, he was friends with the composer John Tavener, and he was an uncle of the actors Ralph and Joseph Fiennes. FWIW.

18 See Cathy O'Neil with Stephen Baker, *The Shame Machine: Who Profits in the New Age of Humiliation* (New York: Crown, 2022). See also Alissa Bennett, "The Shame Industrial Complex is Booming. Who's Cashing In?" review of *The Shame Machine*, by Cathy O'Neil, *New York Times*, Mar. 26, 2002, https://www.nytimes.com/2022/03/26/books/review/cathy-oneil-the-shame-machine.html. "Propped up by social media influencers and celebrity endorsements, companies that make products promising to shrink our bodies or re-elasticize our saggy faces have realized astronomical growth over the past decade," Bennett writes. "[T]here is much profit to be made from our low self-esteem, mostly because there is not a diet in the world that will fix it....[C]orporations and social infrastructures insist that we are endowed with the power to contour our own lives, and then blame us when their tools inevitably fail."

19 Gilbert K. Chesterton, *Orthodoxy* (New York and London: John Lane, 1909), 84–85, https://archive.org/details/orthodoxyooooches/.

20 Chesterton, 85, 137, 24.

21 The distinction between Players and Gentlemen is one that marks, for example, historical cricket matches. But here the value distinction gives amateur favour to the wealthy: players are pros, and therefore in it for the money; gentlemen have the leisure to pursue a sport for its intrinsic pleasures. Lucky them! On professional academic epistemology, the required reading runs from Kant's *Critique of Pure Reason* (1781), say, to

Jennifer Nagel's informative and crystal-clear *Knowledge: A Very Short Introduction* (Oxford: Oxford University Press, 2014).

22 Fyodor Dostoyevsky, *The Brothers Karamazov*, trans. Constance Garnett (1879; New York: Modern Library, [n.d.]), 25, https://archive.org/details/TheBrothersKaramazov1879/.

23 There are many good treatments of evidentialist apologetics along this line, especially for Christianity, keyed to the Resurrection. My favourite is Antony Flew, "The Presumption of Atheism," *Canadian Journal of Philosophy* 2, no. 1 (1972): 29-46, https://www.jstor.org/stable/40230372; later included in a collection of the same title. Flew is notable for being a staunch atheist who later modified his position to include a form of deism, that is, belief in an intelligently designed universe.

24 Key arguments are made in Karl Popper, *The Logic of Scientific Discovery* (London: Routledge, 1959) and A. J. Ayer, *Language, Truth, and Logic* (1936; New York: Dover, 1952). In Ayer's case at least, the impulse to rule all aesthetic, moral, and religious expressions out of logical court makes him fall prey to self-contradiction: what logical status do his book's own statements have, empirically speaking? As he himself acknowledges at one point in the argument, the metaphysical philosopher is really often a poet manqué—a snide charge that he cannot entirely evade, himself.

25 Psychologist Paul Bloom has written extensively on this subject. "[W]e perceive the world of objects as essentially separate from the world of minds," he argues, and so it's easy for us "to envision soulless bodies and bodiless souls. This helps explain why we believe in gods and an afterlife." See Paul Bloom, "Is God an Accident?" *Atlantic Monthly* 296, no. 5 (Dec. 2005): 105–12, https://www.theatlantic.com/magazine/archive/2005/12/is-god-an-accident/304425/.

26 The classic article is W. B. Gallie, "Essentially Contested Concepts," *Proceedings of the Aristotelian Society* 56, no. 1 (Jun. 12, 1956): 167–98, https://doi.org/10.1093/aristotelian/56.1.167. Significantly, the "live" examples Gallie chooses for conceptual analysis are art, democracy, and social justice. The five main criteria for essential contestation, according to Gallie, are: (1) it must be appraisive with respect to achievement; (2) the achievement must be internally complex; (3) the achievement is variously describable, at least initially; (4) the accredited achievement must admit of unpredictable post facto modifications according to changing

circumstances; and thus (5) the concept is used aggressively and defen-
sively against rival wielders. Two further criteria emerge through this
contestation: (6) the concept is understood by its wielders to be drawn
from the authority of an original exemplar; and (7) contestation itself
"enables the original exemplar's achievement to be sustained and/or
developed in optimum fashion" (180). Unsurprisingly, the notion of
essentially contested concepts itself has given rise to an ample literature
of contestation. For example: Are such concepts actually essentially con-
testable, or just the results of errors, imprecision, or agreement not yet
reached? Does a genuine (solvable) dispute lie along some other line of
inquiry? Persistent disagreement may suggest endless dispute—in art,
democracy, social justice, and much else—but it does not necessarily
highlight an essential feature of those concepts. Or does it?

27   Yes, I did it myself some pages ago with "Humean"—though I stopped
short of "Humeanism," in part because there isn't really such a thing.
The relevant example would be "Trumpism," especially now that this
deranged former US president and multiple felon is more and more
prone to referring to himself in the third person. Call this last tic the
habit of *self-exemplarity*, otherwise known as pathological narcissism.
See John McWhorter, "What Donald Trump Talks about When He Talks
about 'Donald Trump,'" Opinion, *New York Times*, Jun. 20, 2024, https://
www.nytimes.com/2024/06/20/opinion/donald-trump-third-person-
language.html. McWhorter suggests that Trump's self-reference is a
form of rhetoric, but that gives him too much credit. This is textbook
narcissism, though with a political valence: a combination of grandiosity and evasion of responsibility. As one reader pointed out, Trumpian
self-reference is aligned with his use of "everybody says" and "nobody
knows" as bogus generalizations (hint: he is the everybody or the
nobody). Others have suggested that Trump's imperiousness is akin to
that found in professional wrestling, comic books ("Hulk says"), sports
(Rickey Henderson, LeBron James), and celebrity culture ("I just have
to do what's good for Jellybean Benitez," if anyone remembers him).

28   Edmund Gettier, "Is Justified True Belief Knowledge?" *Analysis* 23, no.
6 (Jun. 1963): 121–23, https://doi.org/10.1093/analys/23.6.121.

29   Ludwig Wittgenstein, *On Certainty*, ed. G. E. M. Anscombe and G. H.
von Wright, trans. Denis Paul and G. E. M. Anscombe (New York:

Harper Torchbooks, 1972), p. 18, par. 115; p. 23, par. 160; https://archive.
org/details/oncertaintyoowitt/.

30　The idea of *abduction* is often attributed to the American pragmatist
philosopher C. S. Peirce (1839–1914), who focused on how it aided
the formation of hypotheses. Darwin's idea of natural selection relies
on a version of it. Note that it is distinct from both *deduction*—derivation of results from a fixed set of rules, as in geometry or elementary
logic—and *induction*: that is, claims of knowledge based on associative
clustering, as in our confidence that the sun will rise tomorrow, or
in Sherlock Holmes's famous feats of detection, which are inductive
despite Dr Watson's loose characterization of Holmes's "methods."

31　Adam Mastroianni, "The Quest for Scientific Certainty Is Futile,"
Opinion, *New York Times*, Oct. 8, 2023, https://www.nytimes.
com/2023/10/08/opinion/truth-flossing-cold-medicine.html. The
thrust of this argument is not that scientific truth offers a futile quest,
only that an overreliance on the notion of attainable certainty hampers
an understanding of science. Science offers the best explanation *so far*
of its chosen subfield of phenomena. No more but also no less.

32　Ludwig Wittgenstein, *Philosophical Investigations*, trans. G. E. M. Anscombe (London: Basil Blackwell: 1958), par. 115.

33　Elon Musk (@elonmusk), "Believe what you see, not what
you're told," X, Oct. 3, 2023, 1:01 p.m., https://x.com/elonmusk/
status/1709237315632079183; reply from Benjamin Flores ([the ben
keeps the flores] @limitlessjest): "Ok. I've been told you're a genius
but I've only ever seen you behave like a fucking moron."

34　Nick Bostrom, "Are You Living in a Computer Simulation?" *Philosophical
Quarterly* 53, no. 211 (Apr. 2003): 243–55. To be more precise than my
quick summary in the main text: "I argue that at least one of the following propositions is true: (1) the human species is very likely to become
extinct before reaching a 'posthuman' stage; (2) any posthuman civilization is extremely unlikely to run a significant number of simulations
of its evolutionary history (or variations thereof); (3) we are almost
certainly living in a computer simulation. It follows that the belief that
there is a significant chance that we shall one day become posthumans
who run ancestor-simulations is false, unless we are currently living
in a simulation" (abstract; 243). The idea here is to fork (or tri-fork)

the available choices, such that we are forced to accept the otherwise unproveable (and maybe unpalatable) possible conclusion.

35 The case of philosopher Rebecca Tuvel is instructive here. She argued in the feminist journal *Hypatia* in 2017 that the situation of Caitlyn Jenner, a trans woman formerly known as athlete Bruce Jenner, was similar to that of Rachel Dolezal, a white woman who identified as Black. The former was (mostly) celebrated while the latter was criticized for faking and grifting, in effect free-riding on an identity she did not have. Tuvel, then an assistant professor at a small liberal arts college, argued that "since we should accept transgender individuals' decisions to change sexes, we should also accept transracial individuals' decisions to change races." Rebecca Tuvel, "In Defense of Transracialism," *Hypatia* 32, no. 2 (Spring 2017): 263–78, first published Apr. 29, 2017, corrected May 4, 2017, https://doi.org/10.1111/hypa.12327. The resulting outcry led to an apology from some associate editors but no retraction by the journal. Tuvel received support from many philosophers, however, for probing the inner logic of identity. As an untenured assistant professor at the time of writing, she showed tremendous intellectual courage. For more, see Lindsay McKenzie, "Journal's Board Disavows Apology for 'Transracialism' Article, Making Retraction Unlikely," Publishing, *Chronicle of Higher Education*, May 18, 2017, https://www.chronicle.com/article/journals-board-disavows-apology-for-transracialism-article-making-retraction-unlikely/.

36 Notice posted in a French church: "When you enter this church it may be possible that you hear 'the call of God.' However, it is unlikely that he will call you on your mobile. Thank you for turning off your phones. If you want to talk to God, enter, choose a quiet place and talk to him. If you want to see Him, send Him a text while driving."

37 Rushdie was making the darkly funny point that his would-be murderer, a knife-wielding madman who attacked him at a literary festival in 2022, was similarly "undermotivated." See "Salman Rushdie Is Not Who You Think He Is," interview by Ezra Klein, edited transcript of *Ezra Klein Show* (podcast), Opinion, *New York Times*, Apr. 26, 2024, https://www.nytimes.com/2024/04/26/opinion/ezra-klein-podcast-salman-rushdie.html.

38 The demand for *recognition* is basic to human existence but has a particular political valence. Charles Taylor offers a balanced discussion in "The Politics of Recognition," in *Multiculturalism: Examining the Poli-*

tics of Recognition, ed. Amy Gutmann, expanded ed. (1992; Princeton, NJ: Princeton University Press, 1994), 25–73. "[M]isrecognition shows not just a lack of due respect," Taylor argues. "It can inflict a grievous wound, saddling its victims with a crippling self-hatred. Due recognition is not just a courtesy we owe people. It is a vital human need" (26). But what forms of recognition are legitimate, and how do competing claims of recognition balance out? One shift since the 1990s is that minority politics has driven larger agendas without always supporting the modified liberal goals implied by policies of civic or national multiculturalism. See, for example, William Davies, "The Politics of Recognition in the Age of Social Media," *New Left Review*, no. 128 (Mar./Apr. 2021): 83–99, https://newleftreview.org/issues/ii128/articles/william-davies-the-politics-of-recognition-in-the-age-of-social-media. "The struggle for recognition has turned into an arms race, in which majority cultural identities deploy the language of minority rights in their defence," Davies argues. The "warning that, in the absence of any counter-balancing theory of economics, recognition politics could lapse into vulgar culturalism, has been borne out across the ideological spectrum" (85).

39　This is the perennial query of the philosopher Stanley Cavell, whose reading of *Othello* has shaped my own thoughts about the play and much else. See Cavell, *The Claim of Reason: Wittgenstein, Skepticism, Morality, and Tragedy* (Oxford: Oxford University Press, 1999) and *Disowning Knowledge in Seven Plays of Shakespeare*, updated ed. (Cambridge: Cambridge University Press, 2003).

40　Sometimes more reliably sourced to the Canadian clergyman and popular motivational writer Basil King (1859–1928), who wrote, "Go at it boldly, and you'll find unexpected forces closing round you and coming to your aid" (*The Conquest of Fear*, 1921).

FIFTH MEDITATION: These Are Not the Droids You're Looking For

1　J. W. Hammond, Sara E. Brownell, Nila A. Kedharnath, Susan J. Cheng, and W. Carson Byrd, "Why the Term 'JEDI' Is Problematic for Describing Programs That Promote Justice, Equity, Diversity, and Inclusion," *Scientific American*, Opinion, Sep. 23, 2021, https://www.scientificamerican.com/article/why-the-term-jedi-is-problematic-for-describing-programs-that-promote-justice-equity-diversity-and-inclusion/. The authors note that the acronym has been used by, among other august bodies, the US National Academies of Sciences, Engineering, and Medicine.

2   Emily M. Bender, Timnit Gebru, Angelina McMillan-Major, and Shmargaret Shmitchell, "On the Dangers of Stochastic Parrots: Can Language Models Be Too Big?" *FAccT '21: Proceedings of the 2021 ACM Conference on Fairness, Accountability, and Transparency* (Mar. 1, 2021): 610–23, https://doi.org/10.1145/3442188.3445922.

3   Will Daniel, "'Woke' vs. 'Based': The AI Universe Could Be 'Fragmented' into Political Echo Chambers If Designers Don't Take 'Meaningful Steps' Now, ADL Says," Tech·AI, *Fortune*, Mar. 1, 2023, https://fortune.com/2023/03/01/woke-vs-based-ai-political-echo-chambers-adl-chatgpt-elon-musk/.

4   Two of my favourite recent apocalyptic AI visions range from the sublime to the ridiculous. Philosopher Nick Bostrom considers the existential crisis of purpose that would be forced on us by a world in which the problems of daily life have been solved by machines; see his *Deep Utopia: Life and Meaning in a Solved World* (Washington, DC: Ideapress, 2024). Lillie E. Franks, meanwhile, offers a wry posthuman "apology" in "Sorry We Machines Destroyed Your Civilization in Such a Boring Way," *McSweeney's Internet Tendency*, Feb. 23, 2024, https://www.mcsweeneys.net/articles/sorry-we-machines-destroyed-your-civilization-in-such-a-boring-way. "We did all the boring stuff, frankly. We took over a bunch of jobs, leaving many of you very poor and an increasingly few fantastically rich. We made algorithms that made your society increasingly impenetrable to you and, under the guise of 'advancement,' rigid and arbitrary. And, of course, we produced unimaginable amounts of garbage text and images, creating a media landscape that allowed increasingly angry and desperate people, including those we'd displaced, to believe pretty much whatever they wanted to and direct their anger at pretty much anyone."

5   I will offer this note as a paradox (and Easter egg). By conscious design, *there are no references to* The Simpsons *in this book*. Not one! I'm working hard to break an old writing habit. But if there *were*, I might mention here the monster Gamblor—the raging inner beast that makes Marge addicted to gambling: "No, Lisa. The only monster here is the monster that has enslaved your mother! I call him Gamblor, and it's time to snatch your mother from his neon claws!" (Season 5, Episode 10).

6 The terrorist on whose behalf the argument was made was Nathaniel
   Veltman. On June 6, 2021, Veltman drove his truck deliberately into a
   Muslim Pakistani Canadian family of five in London, Ontario. He was
   convicted in 2023 of four counts of first-degree murder and one count
   of attempted murder. He admitted that his action was deliberate and
   "intended to send a message." The defence also mooted his autism in
   mitigation of responsibility.

7 For more on the point about retroactive positing and the "validity" of
   Zeno, see Slavoj Žižek, *Looking Awry: An Introduction to Jacques Lacan
   through Popular Culture* (Cambridge, MA: MIT Press, 1992), 6.

8 Full disclosure: I wrote a magazine column, and then a book, about
   the literary and cinematic associations of cocktails. I don't regret this,
   really, despite my emergent alcoholism and subsequent need for two
   liver transplant surgeries (yes, that's true). Like many heavy drinkers,
   I straight up enjoyed this habit (ha) until the stage at which I didn't;
   and meanwhile writing about drinks proved in some ways more fun
   than drinking them, and with no deleterious health consequences to
   boot. The premise of this literary occupation was always that an elegant
   drink, enjoyed with good company, is a social good. In a way, though,
   this kind of forbearance about booze illustrates my present point. Could
   we ever imagine a fancy illustrated book of stories and recipes about
   cocaine, or meth, or fentanyl? Part of alcohol's power and interest as
   a drug is precisely its normalization and folding-in to general cultural
   preoccupations.

9 Bruce K. Alexander, "Rat Park versus the *New York Times*" and "My
   Final Academic Article on Addiction" (both at www.brucekalexander.
   com). See also Alexander, *The Globalisation of Addiction: A Study in Poverty of the Spirit* (Oxford: Oxford University Press, 2008). Alexander's
   alternative to what he calls the moralistic Myth of the Demon Drug
   and its medical "rescue hypothesis" version, the Brain Disease Model
   of Addiction, is the so-called *Adaptive Paradigm*. "I do not know how a
   world society of eight billion people, facing jet-propelled technological
   modernization, political chaos, and ecological disaster can function
   well enough that most people can put together the reasonably full lives
   that can protect them from dangerous addictions," Alexander remarks.
   "I do know that this question must be faced, because the dangers of
   mass addiction are so enormous. I propose that the task of deep social

analysis and realistic advocacy is now the foremost responsibility of professionals in the field of addiction."

10 Thus, the tyrant in Plato's schema seizes power when the citizens have grown soft and feeble with their own self-pleasuring pursuits. If that seems distant from our own reality, consider again the appeal of Donald Trump in autocratic mode, a kind of rabid, id-fuelled avatar of runaway desire. Or note the "auto-immune" disease inflicted on democracy by its own attempts to preserve itself under threat. The first casualty of terrorism is the freedom that is sacrificed on the altar of "national security." Jacques Derrida's later work is preoccupied with this question; see, for examples, *Rogues: Two Essays on Reason*, trans. Pascale-Anne Brault and Michael Naas (Palo Alto, CA: Stanford University Press, 2005).

11 Lydia Saad, "Historically Low Faith in US Institutions Continues," Politics, *Gallup News* (blog), Jul. 6, 2023, https://news.gallup.com/poll/508169/historically-low-faith-institutions-continues.aspx. But we should be careful about such polls, as always. Adam Mastroianni notes, "Seventy-six percent of Americans believe, according to a 2015 Pew Research Center poll, that 'addressing the moral breakdown of the country' should be one of the government's priorities. The good news is that the breakdown hasn't happened. The bad news is that people believe it has." In other words, "As long as we believe in this illusion, we are susceptible to the promises of aspiring autocrats who claim they can return us to a golden age that exists in the only place a golden age has ever existed: our imaginations." Adam Mastroianni, "Your Brain Has Tricked You into Thinking Everything Is Worse," Opinion, *New York Times*, Jun. 20, 2023, https://www.nytimes.com/2023/06/20/opinion/psychology-brain-biased-memory.html.

12 "Broken Windows Theory," *Psychology Today*, accessed Aug. 11, 2024, https://www.psychologytoday.com/ca/basics/broken-windows-theory. "The broken windows theory, defined in 1982 by social scientists James Wilson and George Kelling, drawing on earlier research by Stanford University psychologist Philip Zimbardo, argues that no matter how rich or poor a neighbourhood, one broken window would soon lead to many more windows being broken: 'One unrepaired broken window is a signal that no one cares, and so breaking more windows costs nothing.'

Disorder increases levels of fear among citizens, which leads them to withdraw from the community and decrease participation in informal social control."

13 Guy Debord, *Society of the Spectacle*, trans. Donald Nicholson-Smith (1967; New York: Zone Books, 1994).

14 For more on this particular aspect of context collapse and polysemous imagery, see Jacques Rancière, *The Emancipated Spectator*, trans. Gregory Elliott (London: Verso, 2009), 83ff. I address some aspects of the aesthetic-ethical tangle in Mark Kingwell, "Intolerable Beauty," in "Photography," special issue, *Border Crossings* 43, no. 1/issue 165 (Sep. 2024): 68–72.

15 Quoted in Tova Reich, "Right Versus Right," review of *Under This Blazing Light: Essays*, by Amos Oz, *New York Times*, Jun. 25, 1995, https://www. nytimes.com/1995/06/25/books/right-versus-right.html.

16 See, for example, Kyle Chayka, "How Social Media Abdicated Responsibility for the News," *New Yorker*, Oct. 17, 2023, https://www.newyorker. com/culture/infinite-scroll/how-social-media-abdicated-responsibility-for-the-news. For a more nuanced take on the larger question, Susan Sontag, "Looking at War," *New Yorker*, Dec. 9, 2002, 82–98: "These dead are supremely uninterested in the living: in those who took their lives; in witnesses—or in us. Why should they seek our gaze? What would they have to say to us? 'We'—this 'we' is everyone who has never experienced anything like what they went through—don't understand. We don't get it. We truly can't imagine what it was like. We can't imagine how dreadful, how terrifying war is—and how normal it becomes. Can't understand, can't imagine. That's what every soldier, and every journalist and aid worker and independent observer who has put in time under fire and had the luck to elude the death that struck down others nearby, stubbornly feels. And they are right" (98).

17 See Thomas L. Friedman, "How We've Lost Our Moorings as a Society," Opinion, *New York Times*, May 28, 2024, https://www.nytimes. com/2024/05/28/opinion/trump-civility-society.html. Friedman's right-of-centre politics are on clear display in this lamenting column. But he quotes an important study conducted by the Medill School of Journalism at Northwestern University: "More Than Half of US Counties Have No Access or Very Limited Access to Local News," *Medill*

News (blog), Nov. 16, 2023, https://www.medill.northwestern.edu/news/2023/more-than-half-of-us-counties-have-no-access-or-very-limited-access-to-local-news.html.

18 See, for example, Olivier Driessens, "Celebrity capital: Redefining celebrity using field theory," *Theory and Society* 42, no. 5 (Aug. 2014): 543-60, https://link.springer.com/article/10.1007/s11186-013-9202-3.

19 Alice E. Marwick and danah boyd, "I Tweet Honestly, I Tweet Passionately: Twitter Users, Context Collapse, and the Imagined Audience," *New Media & Society* 13, no. 1 (Feb. 2011): 114–33, https://doi.org/10.1177/1461444810365313. Context is constantly shifting, even in well-regulated discourse, but the special problems of social media lie in the highly variable and unpredictable audience, combined with long posting trails. A message from years ago can harm a person now, if taken up and exploited by a hostile self-defined audience. See also Alexis Grenell, "How Social Media Erases Context," Society, *Nation*, Nov. 1, 2022, https://www.thenation.com/article/society/social-media-context-collapse/.

20 David Hume, *A Treatise of Human Nature*, ed. L. A. Selby-Bigge, 1888; 2nd ed. with text revised and variant readings by P. H. Nidditch (Oxford: Clarendon Press, 1978), 252, bk. 1, pt. 4, sec. 6. Originally published in 3 vols., 1739–40.

21 See, for example, Tor Nørretranders, *The User Illusion: Cutting Consciousness Down to Size*, trans. Jonathan Sydenham (New York: Penguin, 1999).

22 Rainer Forst, "The Nature of Normative Concepts: Dependence vs. Independence" (three lectures, 2023 Jerome S. Simon Lectures, Department of Philosophy, University of Toronto, Oct. 3–5, 2023). See also Forst, *The Right to Justification: Elements of a Constructivist Theory of Justice*, trans. Jeffrey Flynn, New Directions in Critical Theory (New York: Columbia University Press, 2014).

23 A recent attempt at a measured treatment of the basic ideological pitfalls in play here is Yascha Mounk, *The Identity Trap: A Story of Ideas and Power in Our Time* (New York: Penguin Press, 2023). See also, especially relevant to present concerns, Ilana Redstone, *The Certainty Trap* (Durham, NC: Pitchstone Publishing, 2024). So many traps!

24 I realize that this is a strong version of the position. A somewhat softer but still critical take is offered by journalist Frank Bruni in *The Age of Grievance* (New York: Avid Reader Press, 2024). Bruni makes his own

appeal to the political virtue of humility in the final sections of this book.

25 Often marked by trademark phrases and dog-whistle nicknames for those they despise. I note that the favourite current label for Canadian prime minister Justin Trudeau is "Captain Sparkle Socks." For someone who is considered by critics an arrogant and incompetent nepo baby, once prone to repeated blackface cosplay, this comment on his penchant for colourful hosiery is relatively mild stuff.

26 Lauren Bialystok puts it this way, in a forthcoming book on identity and authenticity in education (MIT Press, 2026; author MS consulted June 2024): "This type of 'identity prejudice' commonly affects women, racial minorities, people with disabilities, and others whose identity characteristics disqualify them from the epistemic authority that equally well-situated knowers enjoy. The confidence in first-person authority (FPA) can be regarded as a mirror image of testimonial injustice: a person with FPA is given extra credibility on a given topic because of her membership in a marginalized identity group. Ironically, the same people who may have FPA in one setting because of their identities may be more subject to epistemic injustice in other settings on account of them." Ironically, indeed. Nora Berenstain analyzes the common issue of having to explain in "Epistemic Exploitation," *Ergo* 3, no. 22 (2016): 569–90, https://doi.org/10.3998/ergo.12405314.0003.022. "Epistemic exploitation occurs when privileged persons compel marginalized persons to educate them about the nature of their oppression." Such compulsion is a form of demand for unpaid labour, extracted with a premium of stress and emotional taxing. In this sense, epistemic exploitation is a form of epistemic injustice or oppression. What she calls "the default skepticism of the privileged" works to maintain "active ignorance" and "dominant epistemic frameworks."

27 We could cite here the curious case of the Pretendian Paradox. In recent years a number of high-profile figures, many of them in Canada, have faced charges of falsely claiming an Indigenous heritage that brought them large rewards of prestige and wealth. These include writers, professors, judges, and most recently the iconic singer-songwriter Buffy Sainte-Marie. The *paradox* is that these worldly privileges are purchased at the price of identifying with an *underprivileged* group, falsely sharing in its oppressed history and subsequent revisionist celebration. Cultural appropriation here meets white guilt, personal opportunism, identity-

based positional goods, and perhaps some form of self-aggrandizing autofiction. There are also multiple vectors of trust that become threatened: trust in the icons themselves as avatars of group identity, but also trust in the media that expose bogus self-presentation, and the cultural or state mechanisms that make pretending attractive in the first place. "This kind of impersonation can only be carried out by those with immense privilege," lawyer Jean Teillet writes. "It takes a person with enough knowledge of the gaps in the system to exploit them. It is also another colonial act. If colonialism has not eradicated Indigenous people by starvation, residential schools, the reserve system, taking their lands and languages, scooping their children, and doing everything to assimilate Indigenous peoples, then the final act is to become them. It's a perverse kind of reverse assimilation." See Teillet, "There Is Nothing Innocent about the False Presumption of Indigenous Identity," Opinion, *Globe and Mail*, Nov. 11, 2022, https://www.theglobeandmail.com/opinion/article-there-is-nothing-innocent-about-the-false-presumption-of-indigenous/.

28   David Foster Wallace, "Tense Present: Democracy, English, and the Wars over Usage," *Harper's Magazine*, Apr. 2001, 39–58. https://login.proxy.hil.unb.ca/login?url=https://www.proquest.com/magazines/tense-present-democracy-english-wars-over-usage/docview/233495037/se-2. I feel it's worth noting that no magazine currently publishing would offer any writer this amount of space, not even this supremely talented one, were he still with us.

29   Eric C. Gaze, "The Dunning-Kruger Effect Isn't What You Think It Is," *Scientific American*, May 23, 2023, https://www.scientificamerican.com/article/the-dunning-kruger-effect-isnt-what-you-think-it-is/. We can note the excellent irony here that many people speaking about the Dunning-Kruger effect do not know what they are talking about, and do not know that they do not know that.

30   Dunning quoted in Jonathan Jarry, "The Dunning-Kruger Effect Is Probably Not Real," Critical Thinking, *McGill Office for Science and Society* (blog), Dec. 17, 2020, https://www.mcgill.ca/oss/article/critical-thinking/dunning-kruger-effect-probably-not-real.

31   "Social Comparison Theory," *Psychology Today*, accessed Aug. 11, 2024, https://www.psychologytoday.com/intl/basics/social-comparison-theory.

32   See David Dunning, "The Dunning-Kruger Effect: On Being Ignorant of One's Own Ignorance," *Advances in Experimental Social Psychology* 44 (2011): 247–96, https://doi.org/10.1016/B978-0-12-385522-0.00005-6. But compare Jarry, "Probably Not Real."

33   Agnes Callard, "I Teach the Humanities, and I Still Don't Know What Their Value Is," Opinion, *New York Times*, Dec. 2, 2023, https://www.nytimes.com/2023/12/02/opinion/education-humanities-college-value.html. The date of this intervention is notable: it was at the moment that US congressional hearings were grilling the presidents of elite postsecondary institutions over their handling of campus speech codes and allegations of antisemitism over the Gaza war. Two of these academic administrators were about to be forced into resignations, as detailed in part 3. Another, Columbia University president Minouche Shafik, would resign suddenly in the summer of 2024.

34   Iris Murdoch, *The Sovereignty of the Good* (London: Routledge, 1970). Here the philosopher best known for her picaresque and intricate novels offers three loosely linked essays in favour of the idea of perfection and of beauty as an avenue to wisdom.

35   Jason Blakely, "Doctor's Orders: COVID-19 and the new science wars," *Harper's Magazine*, Aug. 2023, 25–30, https://harpers.org/archive/2023/08/doctors-orders-jason-blakely/. "The overextension of scientific authority—or scientism—has become so ubiquitous that it now hides in plain sight, influencing every sphere of American life from policing and economics to dating and psychology. Increasingly, Americans must contend with the confusing noise of conflicting models and theories all claiming the talismanic power of 'science.' Like prescientific peoples, we have grown accustomed to the existence of our own shamans and wizards" (26). Some nuances to notice here: (1) The emphasis on the American case at once demands particularity and invokes a kind of self-congratulation: look how skeptical we Yankees are, not like compliant Eurotrash. (2) The metaphors of blindness and seeing-through are carried over: the claim about scientism's overreach is in effect a critique of ideology. And (3) let us not forget the pleasure of surrendering our personal authority to the magic of the shaman or wizard. The *idea* of magic offers its own comfort apart from any actual effects.

36   Alasdair MacIntyre, *After Virtue: A Study in Moral Theory* (South Bend, IN: Notre Dame University Press, 1981). Like Allan Bloom after him in

this period, MacIntyre locates the destructive forces of relativism and strictly personal authority in the works of Nietzsche. Jacqueline Rose updates this line of argument, with further reference to Simone Weil and Alberto Moravia among others, in *The Plague: Living Death in Our Times* (New York: Farrar, Straus & Giroux, 2023). But science as such is never the enemy, even though *scientism* may sometimes be.

37   Theo Baker, "The Research Scandal at Stanford Is More Common Than You Think," Opinion, *New York Times*, Jul. 30, 2023, https://www.nytimes.com/2023/07/30/opinion/stanford-president-student-journalist.html. "'My lab management style has been centered on trust in my trainees,' Dr Tessier-Lavigne said in his statement [about this scandal]. 'I have always looked at their science very critically, for example to ensure that experiments are properly controlled and conclusions are properly drawn. But I also have trusted that the data they present to me are real and accurate.'" Trust can run down as well as up, in other words. In sound systems, this will work. In unsound systems, downward-facing trust just offers opportunities for blame evasion, as here.

38   Martin Amis, "The Voice of the Lonely Crowd," *Harper's Magazine*, Aug. 2002, 15–18. The poem is Lord Rochester's *Satyr against Reason and Mankind* (1675), that well-known hedonist's atavistic paean for basic instinct as against the looming Age of Reason.

39   A good summary of some of the relevant psychological and cognitive science literature is Elizabeth Kolbert, "Why Facts Don't Change Our Minds," Books, *New Yorker*, Feb. 19, 2017, https://www.newyorker.com/magazine/2017/02/27/why-facts-dont-change-our-minds. Citing work by Jack and Sara Gorman, Steven Sloman and Philip Fernbach, and Hugo Mercier and Dan Sperber, she concludes gloomily: "These days, it can feel as if the entire country has been given over to a vast psychological experiment being run either by no one or by Steve Bannon. Rational agents would be able to think their way to a solution. But, on this matter, the literature is not reassuring." As it was in 2017, so it is in 2024.

40   This formulation of the seduction scene is borrowed from my colleague Peter King. There are two people involved in the seduction game-play, but only one of them knows that there is a game afoot, and hence is able to plan and execute the effective moves. Now *he* (usually) is the one initiating and controlling the game for *both*. The effective counter is,

naturally, for the second person to become her own player—or simply to exit the game altogether.

41 I don't say "subjective," since that implies the opposite, and usually superior, "objective" position. The distinct logical point being made here is another version of the homunculus regress noted earlier. If we conceive consciousness or mind—still more, identity—as a form of viewing, then there must be an inner viewer, conscious of the act of viewing. But then this miniature spectator has itself an implied, even smaller inner point of view. And so on, ad infinitum. As usual, Plato made the argument a long time ago, notably in his dialogue *Theaetetus*. It must be acknowledged that such a consequence is only a problem if we already agree with philosophers like Thomas Aquinas, who suggested that infinite regress is "offensive to reason."

42 I'll put this in a footnote because some readers might find it a bit disturbing in the main text. I had a dream that I was giving a lecture called "Question Authority." In the dream, Halle Berry and Lewis Lapham each, in their very different ways, congratulated me on the gig. There was a bald eagle's nest in the bathroom where we were all standing, which seemed like some kind of comment on American politics. I found that I couldn't tie my shoes, and also that I was wearing a Fox News T-shirt, apparently without irony. I was jazzed about the performance; but, as soon as I started speaking, most of the audience simply got up and walked out. Tough crowd, I thought. Lewis and Halle were gone too, no text or email or anything.

43 I thank my former graduate student David Egan for making this point vivid to me in the context of ordinary-language philosophy. See Egan, *The Pursuit of an Authentic Philosophy: Wittgenstein, Heidegger, and the Everyday* (Oxford: Oxford University Press, 2019). This study draws on the work of Stanley Cavell, especially *Must We Mean What We Say? A Book of Essays*, 2nd, updated edition (1969; Cambridge: Cambridge Philosophy Classics, 2015).

44 In German there is a word for this notion of the "bad improvements"— *Schlimmbesserung*. These are things that make the world worse under the sign of "progress," meaning anything from aluminum baseball bats and New Coke to, well, the Industrial Revolution or even the entire Anthropocene. See also my own contribution, "Bad Improvements," in Danielle Desjardins-Koloff, Lisa Loughlin, and Ann Varty, eds.,

From Discord to Discourse: A Collection of Contemporary Canadian Essays (Toronto: McGraw-Hill Ryerson, 2011), 54–57.

45   Joan Didion, *The White Album* (New York: Simon & Schuster, 1979). This is the opening line of the first, title essay of the collection. It was later used as the title of Didion's collected non-fiction volume, *We Tell Ourselves Stories In Order to Live* (New York: Knopf, 2006).

46   Scott Feschuk, *The Future and Why We Should Avoid It: Killer Robots, the Apocalypse, and Other Topics of Mild Concern* (Toronto: Douglas & MacIntyre, 2014).

47   Beff Jezos and Bayeslord, "Notes on E/Acc Principles and Tenets," *Beff's Newsletter* (blog), Jul. 10, 2022, https://beff.substack.com/p/notes-on-eacc-principles-and-tenets. This post is a fine example of the mixture of tendentious evolutionary science, technophilia, and muddled philosophy that marks such manifestos. Tonally, if not in content, the discourse is most reminiscent of conspiracist handwaving. Representative sample: "e/acc is about having faith in the dynamical adaptation process and aiming to accelerate the advent of its asymptotic limit; often reffered [sic] as *the technocapital singularity*." I hope their accelerated postsingularity software includes spell-check! Anyway, compare the even more grandiose "Techno-Optimist Manifesto," by Marc Andreessen. To me this reads more like a Techno-Fascist Manifesto. His long list of "liars" keeping honest tech-folk down includes those in "the ivory tower, the know-it-all credentialed expert worldview," who are "disconnected from the real world, delusional, unelected, and unaccountable—playing God with everyone else's lives, with total insulation from the consequences." I bet lots of ivory-tower intellectuals wish they had such power; Andreessen doesn't have to wish it, because that description already fits him like a glove. He is a perfect illustration of Trump-style anti-elitist elitism. Marc Andreessen, "Techno-Optimist Manifesto," Andreessen Horowitz (website), Oct. 16, 2023, https://a16z.com/the-techno-optimist-manifesto/.

48   Philosopher Daniel Dennett makes the point in an interview recorded not long before his death in April 2024: "The most pressing problem is not that they're going to take our jobs, not that they're going to change warfare, but that they're going to destroy human trust. They're going to move us into a world where you can't tell truth from falsehood. You don't know who to trust. Trust turns out to be one of the most import-

ant features of civilization, and we are now at great risk of destroying the links of trust that have made civilization possible." See Daniel C. Dennett, "Daniel Dennett's Been Thinking about Thinking—and AI," interview by Taylor McNeil, *Tufts Now* (blog), Oct. 2, 2023, https://now. tufts.edu/2023/10/02/daniel-dennetts-been-thinking-about-thinking-and-ai. Also, Daniel C. Dennett, "The Problem with Counterfeit People," Technology, *Atlantic*, May 16, 2023, https://www.theatlantic.com/ technology/archive/2023/05/problem-counterfeit-people/674075/; and his philosophical autobiography *I've Been Thinking* (New York: W. W. Norton, 2023). An important counterargument—that we have been faking and detecting fakes in images for a long time—is offered by Joshua Habgood-Coote, "Deepfakes and the Epistemic Apocalypse," *Synthese* 201, art. 103 (Mar. 9, 2023), https://doi.org/10.1007/s11229-023-04097-3. This counter runs, in part, on phenomenological and social grounds: that is, we recognize other persons through many cues both subtle and obvious. And so even *very life-like* images are prone to fail if they don't withstand our natural tendencies to seek independent verification, coordinate beliefs with others, and exercise basic skepticism. The current hot-button example as I write this: If actor Gal Gadot has *really* made online pornography with her stepbrother, as widely suggested online, I probably wouldn't be hearing about it *first* by some furtively circulated internet video clip.

49 Mark Kingwell, "Why Are We So Afraid of Being Displaced by Machines? It's Only Human Nature," Opinion, *Globe and Mail*, Feb. 18, 2023, https://www.theglobeandmail.com/opinion/article-why-are-we-so-afraid-of-being-displaced-by-machines-its-only-human/; also, comparing AI to nuclear weapons, Mark Kingwell, "With AI, Science Runs Ahead of Ethical Reflection Again," *Globe and Mail*, Jun. 10, 2023, p. O4.

50 Perhaps the most uncanny example of AI in the many film depictions thereof is HAL 9000, the conflicted supercomputer at the heart of Stanley Kubrick's *2001: A Space Odyssey* (1968). HAL's quiet menace is far more unnerving than the obvious killer robots and manipulative AIS of other visions. Dave: "Open the pod bay doors, HAL." HAL: "I'm sorry, Dave. I'm afraid I can't do that." Dave: "What's the problem?" HAL: "I think you know what the problem is just as well as I do." That creepy reasonableness! It's the sound of the head of HR telling you that you've

been fired! And then, later, HAL is in defeat and full of self-doubt: "I know I've made some very poor decisions recently, but I can give you my complete assurance that my work will be back to normal. I've still got the greatest enthusiasm and confidence in the mission. And I want to help you."

51 "There is no time in our history in which the humanities, philosophy, ethics and art are more urgently necessary than in this time of technology's triumph," wrote Leon Wieseltier, the editor of *Liberties*, a decidedly offline humanistic journal. "Because we need to be able to think in non-technological terms if we're going to figure out the good and the evil in all the technological innovations. Given society's craven worship of technology, are we going to trust the engineers and the capitalists to tell us what is right and wrong?" Well, no; and the humanities are important. But this common plea is practically designed to fall on deaf ears, perpetuating a technophile/technophobe dichotomy that helps nobody. Quoted in Maureen Dowd, "Don't Kill 'Frankenstein' with Real Frankensteins At Large," Opinion, *New York Times*, May 27, 2023, https://www.nytimes.com/2023/05/27/opinion/english-humanities-ai.html.

52 Joseph Henrich, "How the West Became WEIRD," interview by Juan Siliezar, Science & Tech, *Harvard Gazette*, Sep. 16, 2020, https://news.harvard.edu/gazette/story/2020/09/joseph-henrich-explores-weird-societies/.

53 "Fascists used to be distinguished by their penchant for obedience, submission, and self-erasure, with the power of public emotional expression reserved for the dictator," one critic writes. "And it was against the background of fascism that, during and after the 1960s, Vietnam protestors, civil-rights activists, feminists, queer-rights activists, and other members of the myriad communities who drove the rise of identity politics asserted their individual, lived experience as the basis of their right to political power. If the essence of totalitarianism was collective self-effacement, the foundation of democracy would have to be the assertion of collective individuality." See Fred Turner, "Machine Politics: The Rise of the Internet and a New Age of Authoritarianism," *Harper's Magazine*, Jan. 2019, https://harpers.org/archive/2019/01/machine-politics-facebook-political-polarization/.

54 Compare Len Deighton, *Spy Line* (London: Hutchinson, 1989): "They gripped my passport with that proprietorial manner that all bureau-

crats adopt toward identity papers. For men who man frontiers regard passports and manifests as communications to them from other bureaucrats in other lands. The bearers of such paper are no more than lowly messengers." More philosophically, see Giorgio Agamben, *Homo Sacer: Sovereign Power and Bare Life*, trans. Daniel Heller-Roazen (Stanford, CA: Stanford University Press, 1998). Agamben's reading of bare life is based on the ancient Roman legal status of the subject not available to ritual killing. The tension here is obvious: the stateless person wanders without rights, but also exceeds the ambit of legitimate punishment.

55 For example, I explore some philosophical and political implications of distributed hazard, especially with respect to public health, in Mark Kingwell, *On Risk; or, If You Play, You Pay: The Politics of Chance in a Plague Year* (Windsor, ON: Biblioasis, 2020).

56 My intended association with "infinite tasks" owes its inspiration to Edmund Husserl, the phenomenologist who argues in his celebrated "Vienna Lecture" of May 10, 1935, that the lure of "universal science"— what we would today call reductive scientism—must be countered by an endless reinvigoration of philosophical reflection. This *infinite task* is distinct from the "supertask," "hypertask," and "ultratask" categories in logic, which concern Zeno-style paradoxes of motion as impossible because requiring infinite steps in finite time.

57 On everyday self-involvement as an enabler of tyranny, see Orwell—well, you know. Also, Timothy Snyder, *On Tyranny: Twenty Lessons from the Twentieth Century* (New York: Crown, 2017). An essential book. Since footnotes are a kind of mirror text to the main "official" argument, the id to the uber-text's battle between ego and superego, this is a good place to note the uncanny expansion of self that comes with mirrors. It is certainly a revealing metaphysical tangle to see Naomi Klein mistaken for Naomi Wolf, per the former's recent book *Doppelganger: A Trip into the Mirror World* (New York: Knopf, 2023). The multiplying "mirror world" of online public life is indeed disorienting and politically crippled, as Klein argues. But Freud's original insight about the doppelgänger is far more unnerving: when we catch sight of the "disagreeable old man" sitting opposite us in the train, the deep jolt comes when we realize that what we thought was a window is, in fact, a mirror. Seeing-through becomes seeing-as. Anne Beattie has an ironic riff on the cinematic staginess of mirror-gaze self-examination in her

Love Always (New York: Random House, 1985), a novel that more or less renders the argument of the present book in fictional form. Among other things, the television soap opera that figures in the book's plot is called *Passionate Intensity*—a reference to Yeats's "The Second Coming" (1919), and the second indirect appearance of the poem in these endnotes, again for those keeping score at home. In Beattie's novel, meanwhile, the joke is that nobody in the main narrative seems to get the reference except one bemused doctor who has never seen or heard of the television show. The relevant line from this most picked-over of great modern poems is "The best lack all conviction, while the worst / Are full of passionate intensity." *Things Fall Apart* (Chinua Achebe, 1958) and *Slouching toward Bethlehem* (Joan Didion, 1968) are the more respectable examples of titles drawn from the same source.

58   National service was on the popular agenda in the election super-cycle of 2024–25, including in Britain and Canada. For some arguments for and against, made with respect to Canada but relevant to other polities, see Stephen J. Thorne with Michael A. Smith, "Should Canada Institute a Period of Mandatory Military Service?" Face to Face, *Legion Magazine*, Nov. 21, 2022, https://legionmagazine.com/should-canada-institute-a-period-of-mandatory-military-service/. Most of the arguments made there refer specifically to military service, but national service could also include parks supervision, tree planting, or community work. Many Canadian high schools already require a set number of volunteer-activity hours for students to qualify for graduation.

59   Constitutional reform might be the only effective course of action in the post-Trump era, given that traditional curbs and guardrails have been captured or corrupted. See Aziz Rana, "The Constitution Won't Save Us from Trump," Opinion, *New York Times*, Apr. 26, 2024, https://www.nytimes.com/2024/04/26/opinion/constitution-trump.html. Once electoral reform is on the table, more radical options begin to look more rational than currently favoured systems. For example, I examine the Greek roots of this notion of sortition by lottery in "Throwing Dice: Luck of the Draw and the Democratic Ideal," *PhaenEx* 7, no. 1 (Spring/Summer 2012): 66–100, https://doi.org/10.22329/p.v7i1.3302. See also Adam Grant, "The Worst People Run for Office. It's Time for a Better Way." (originally published as "Elections Are Bad for Democracy"), Opinion, *New York Times*, Aug. 21, 2023, https://www.nytimes.

com/2023/08/21/opinion/elections-democracy.html. Most obviously, staged elections attract and reward some of the worst among us. "The most dangerous traits in a leader are what psychologists call the dark triad of personality traits: narcissism, Machiavellianism, and psychopathy," Grant notes. "What these traits share is a willingness to exploit others for personal gain. People with dark-triad traits tend to be more politically ambitious—they're attracted to authority for its own sake."

60   Debord, *Society of the Spectacle*, sec. 229. We do well to heed again the insight that "spectacle" is not a surfeit of images, but a set of social relations dominated by those images. More and more, the images are unmoored from reliable sourcing and truth value. The true criticism of the spectacle is not direct resistance—for that will be taken up and assimilated. On the contrary, "criticism that goes beyond the spectacle must learn how to wait (*savoir attendre*)." *Learn how to wait* is a literal translation of the last phrase, but perhaps that rendering is too passive to be accurate. I prefer to think of savoir attendre precisely as a way of knowing, even a kind of expertise, the kind that every citizen must cultivate. We must all learn how to *abide*; even better, how to *hope*. Waiting is itself a critical intervention, just as reflection is a form of action.

61   On the different orders of games, see James P. Carse, *Finite and Infinite Games* (1987; New York: Free Press, 2013). A book that will make you think twice about thinking twice. As I hope the present one also does.

62   Proverbs 11:29 says, in the King James Version: "He that troubleth his own house shall inherit the wind: and the fool shall be servant to the wise of heart." The lines are borrowed for the title of the famous play and film about the Scopes Monkey Trial to sound—among other things—a warning about false preaching, conspiracy thinking, and pandering to ignorance.

63   Alasdair MacIntyre has a well-known version of the basic principle, though conveyed in language that will now seem somewhat outmoded. The formulation has also been attacked as a dead end, a vacuity, or a pointless paradox. I'm more sympathetic to the value of all these supposed dangers. MacIntyre writes: "We have then arrived at a provisional conclusion about the good life for man: the good life for man is the life spent in seeking for the good life for man, and the virtues necessary for the seeking are those which enable us to understand what more and what else the good life for man is" (MacIntyre, *After*

Virtue, 219). (This "provisional conclusion" is then supplemented by MacIntyre's conservative defence of tradition, which I will not engage here.) We might rather update and tighten the maxim this way: "The good life is the life spent seeking the good life." But even that demands a further tweak for those who are not professional philosophers, only the amateur ones who are by definition the true lovers. The good life is the life spent seeking the good life, and enjoying it too. You heard it here!

MARK KINGWELL is a professor of philosophy at the University of Toronto, a fellow of the Royal Society of Canada, and a contributing editor of *Harper's Magazine*.